Sino-American Détente and Its Policy Implications

edited by
Gene T. Hsiao

Published in cooperation with
the Asian Studies Program of
Southern Illinois University
at Edwardsville

The Praeger Special Studies program—
utilizing the most modern and efficient book
production techniques and a selective
worldwide distribution network—makes
available to the academic, government, and
business communities significant, timely
research in U.S. and international economic, social, and political development.

Sino-American Détente and Its Policy Implications

Praeger Publishers New York Washington London

Library of Congress Cataloging in Publication Data

Hsiao, Gene T
    Sino-American détente and its policy implications.

    (Praeger special studies in international politics
and government)
    "Published in cooperation with Southern Illinois
University at Edwardsville."
    1. United States—Foreign relations—China—
Addresses, essays, lectures.   2. China—Foreign
relations—United States—Addresses, essays,
lectures.   I. Title.
E183.8.C5H728   327.73'051   73-13346

PRAEGER PUBLISHERS
111 Fourth Avenue, New York, N.Y. 10003, U.S.A.
5, Cromwell Place, London SW7 2JL, England

Published in the United States of America in 1974
by Praeger Publishers, Inc.

Second printing, 1975

ACKNOWLEDGMENTS

This volume grew out of a conference that was held at Holiday Inn, St. George's, Bermuda, on June 9-10, 1973, under the sponsorship of the Asian Studies Program of Southern Illinois University at Edwardsville. Thanks are due to the university for its administrative and financial support of the conference, to all participants of the symposium for their contributions, to my colleagues for their moral encouragement of my undertakings, and to Ms. Anita Gonzalez for her secretarial assistance.

I was responsible for organizing the symposium and this volume: the opinions and statements expressed in the individual essays are those of each author.

G. T. H.
Southern Illinois University
Edwardsville, Illinois 62025
October 25, 1973

CONTENTS

PART II. THE SPECIFIC RELATIONS

LIST OF CONTRIBUTORS

William J. Barnds, senior fellow of the Council on Foreign Relations, Inc.

A. Doak Barnett, senior fellow of the Brookings Institution.

Robert W. Barnett, director of the Washington Center of the Asia Society.

Jerome A. Cohen, professor of law and director of East Asian legal studies, Harvard University; chairman of the China Committee of the East-West Trade Council.

William R. Feeney, assistant professor of government, Southern Illinois University at Edwardsville.

George Ginsburgs, professor of political science, Graduate Faculty of the New School for Social Science, and professor of law, School of Law, Rutgers University, at Camden.

Gene T. Hsiao, professor of government and director of Asian studies, Southern Illinois University at Edwardsville.

Akira Iriye, professor of history, University of Chicago.

Stanley Karnow, associate editor of the New Republic.

Kenneth P. Landon, professor of Southeast Asian studies, American University.

Chong-Sik Lee, professor of political science, University of Pennsylvania.

John G. Stoessinger, professor of political science, Hunter College, City University of New York.

Stephen Uhalley, Jr., professor and chairman of history, University of Hawaii.

Dick Wilson, lecturer, writer, and former editor of the Far Eastern Economic Review.

Michael Witunski, chairman, St. Louis Council on World Affairs.

LIST OF ABBREVIATIONS

AEC	Atomic Energy Commission
CCAS	Committee of Concerned Asian Scholars
CCPIT	China Council for the Promotion of International Trade
DPRK	Democratic People's Republic of Korea
ECAFE	UN Economic Commission for Asia and the Far East
ECOSOC	UN Economic and Social Council
EWTPC	East-West Trade Policy Commission
FAO	UN Food and Agricultural Organization
FDA	Food and Drug Administration
IBRD	International Bank for Reconstruction and Development
ICAO	International Civil Aviation Organization
IDA	International Development Agency
IFC	International Finance Commission
ILO	International Labour Organization
IMCO	Inter-Governmental Maritime Consultative Organization
IMF	International Monetary Fund
JCP	Japan Communist Party
LDP	Liberal Democratic Party (Japan)
MFN	Most Favored Nation
NATO	North Atlantic Treaty Organization
PRC	People's Republic of China
ROK	Republic of Korea

UN	United Nations
UNCTAD	UN Commission on Trade and Development
UNDP	UN Development Program
UNESCO	UN Educational, Scientific, and Cultural Organization
UNIDO	UN International Development Organization
WHO	World Health Organization
WMO	World Monetary Organization

Gene T. Hsiao

"The nation which indulges toward another
an habitual hatred or an habitual fondness
is in some degree a slave."

George Washington

Richard Milhous Nixon, the 37th President of the United States
of America, arrived in Peking on the 240th anniversary of George
Washington's birthday and, in his first reciprocal toast to Premier
Chou En-lai, told the Chinese:

We have at times in the past been enemies. We have
great differences today. What brings us together is that
we have common interests which transcend those differences. As we discuss our differences, neither of us will
compromise our principles. But while we cannot close
the gulf between us, we can try to bridge it so that we
may be able to talk across it. (See Appendix B.) (Emphasis added.)

Then, to the great surprise of the entire world the President quoted
six lines from Chairman Mao Tse-tung's poem "Man Chiang Hung":

So many deeds cry out to be done,
And always urgently;
The world rolls on,
Time passes.
Ten thousand years are too long,
Seize the day, seize the hour!

Implicit in the timing of the President's visit and his toast was
the message that in world politics there are "no eternal enemies, no
eternal friends, only eternal interests"—an axiom of Lord Palmerston
that underlies Washington's "farewell" advice.

Although Chairman Mao has made no such remarks, his theory
of contradictions calls for a distinction between the principal and
secondary aspects of every contradiction in the universe and permits,
under given circumstances, transformation of the principal contradiction into the secondary, the antagonistic contradiction into the non-
antagonistic, enemies into friends, and vice versa.[1]

The coincidence of this logic with Mr. Nixon's Washingtonian approach to international problems resulted in the subsidence of ideological differences between the two countries and made the summit meeting in Peking possible. More important, however, is the question: What are the common interests of China and the United States that have brought them together?

President Nixon's quotation from Chairman Mao provided the clue: "Man Chiang Hung" was composed in January 1963 with reference to the growing Sino-Soviet dispute. In that poem Chairman Mao contemptuously depicted the Soviets as "Ants on the locust tree assume a great nation swagger, And mayflies lightly plot to topple a giant tree [China]." Then he exclaimed: "Away with all pests! Our force is irresistible." (See Appendix C.)

Given the political nature of that poem, Mr. Nixon's subtle performance in Peking was in effect a personal notice to the Chinese that before the Sino-Soviet dispute developed into a full-scale war, it was high time for China and the United States to end the 22 years of confrontation and enter into serious negotiations for the building of "a world structure of peace and justice." The Chinese got the message and vowed to work "unswervingly" for the easing of international tension and the normalization of relations between the two countries. (See Appendixes A and E.)

Almost exactly a year after the President's visit and barely a day after the 23rd anniversary of the now inoperative Sino-Soviet treaty of friendship, alliance, and mutual assistance, Dr. Henry A. Kissinger made his fifth trip to Peking, on February 15, 1973.* As a result China and the United States exchanged "liaison offices," with Ambassadors Huang Chen and David K. E. Bruce serving as mission chiefs for their respective countries. (See Appendix H.) "Except the strictly formal diplomatic aspects of the relationship,"[2] these offices enjoy official status and handle all matters that are normally conducted by embassies. Thus, for the first time in nearly a quarter of a century, the two countries reached a rapprochement just short of formal diplomatic recognition.

By the yardstick of history, this remarkable development in Sino-American relations is undoubtedly one of the most momentous events in the 20th century. Its impact on the course of history will be felt for many years to come.

Using the joint communiqué of February 28, 1972 (better known as the "Shanghai communiqué") as a general guide, this symposium

---

*Dr. Kissinger cruised through Hong Kong waters on February 14, presumably to avoid the implications of his arrival in Peking on the anniversary.

examines various implications of the détente in the context of international politics. It consists of two parts. The first part, comprising seven essays, deals with the broad policy problems of the United States in the Asia-Pacific region, its bilateral issues with China, and China's performance in the United Nations. The second, also comprising seven essays, analyzes the impact of the détente on third countries and Taiwan. The epilogue sums up the oral proceedings of the symposium in Bermuda.

Analyzing the détente from a historical perspective of the American role in the Asia-Pacific region since the 1930s, Professor Akira Iriye observes that the détente implies official recognition of the limits of American power as well as the existence of a quadrilateral situation in which all four powers (China, Japan, the Soviet Union, and the United States) are expected to work together as equal partners for peace, order, and stability. However, in view of the failure of the Yalta system, which was built upon a triangular power relationship among Great Britain, the Soviet Union, and the United States for the purpose of maintaining peace in the region, he cautions that power considerations alone will not be sufficient to consolidate a new order because the constituent elements of the "Pacific quadrilateral" are not equal in strength. Moreover, he points out that "a structure of international relations based upon balance-of-power considerations without economic, cultural, and ideological underpinnings would remain unstable, as the history of the Yalta system clearly demonstrates." Consequently, he urges the nations concerned to work out an ideological and intellectual basis for the new balance of power and to develop a sense of interdependence so that all peoples of the region "would contribute to the definition of a new internationalism, through which alone the Asian-Pacific balance of power could be transformed into an Asian-Pacific community of nations."

Professor A. Doak Barnett concentrates his discussion on the strategic balance in East Asia. Through his penetrating analysis he concludes that the overall impact of the Nixon-Chou summit meeting "was to accelerate processes of change that had been underway since the 1960s, highlight the need for all nations to adjust to the emerging pattern of four-power relations and create a new atmosphere of fluidity, détente, accommodation and . . . uncertainty." While the new balance of power is basically stable, at least for the foreseeable future, the occurrence of any one of the following events will surely upset the equilibrium: a Sino-Soviet rapprochement, a large-scale Sino-Soviet military conflict, the breakdown of the United States-Japan security alliance, Chinese military intervention in Southeast Asia, a sudden withdrawal of the United States forces in Asia, or a renewed armed conflict in Korea or Indochina. Thus, Barnett suggests that in order to maintain stability in the four-power relationship, it is crucial for the United States to keep its present security arrangements with Japan, accept or encourage a limited détente between China and the Soviet Union, adopt an evenhanded policy toward both of them, and prevent any one of the four powers from intervening militarily in local conflicts.

Trade is a source of international conflict, but it is also an important means of promoting friendly relations. In this respect Professor Jerome A. Cohen offers a stimulating analysis. Since the Nixon-Chou summit, Sino-American trade has developed at a rather unexpected pace. Its total volume for 1973 may reach $700 million—a figure far exceeding economists' predictions. However, he points out that while the overall prospect for the trade is bright, there are many urgent problems that require immediate resolution. They include the shortage of American institutional resources necessary for the promotion of trade, the delay in settlement of certain pending alien assets claims in both countries, the need for the conclusion of an official trade agreement, the necessity of helping to improve the marketing of Chinese products in the United States, and the desirability of creating certain devices, such as "production sharing", to provide China with some kind of credits or loans without undermining her policy of self-reliance. In particular, Professor Cohen warns Congress to be cautious about the pending legislation that would restrict the grant of most-favored-nation treatment to the so-called "nonmarket-economy countries." Although this proposed legislation, known as the Jackson-Vanik amendment, has its origin in the Soviet government's restriction of the emigration of its Jewish nationals, in Professor Cohen's opinion, adoption of the amendment "would deal a devastating blow to the gradually developing, vitally important Sino-American reconciliation" in general and create a wide range of adverse consequences for the Sino-American trade in particular.

The role of the American news media in world politics is perhaps nowhere more conspicuous than in the recent development of Sino-American relations. Veteran journalist Stanley Karnow, who was a member of the press corps that accompanied the Presidential party to Peking and has recently published a book on China, provides an interesting discussion on the topic. He points out that in the course of developing their new relationship, both China and the United States have consciously used the media as a vehicle to promote their respective causes. It started with ping-pong diplomacy and climaxed in the Nixon-Chou summit meeting when the President acknowledged: "At this very moment, through the wonder of telecommunications, more people are seeing and hearing what we say than on any other such occasion in the whole history of the world."

Mr. Karnow notes that throughout the period and afterward the American media have been undergoing a transformation from one extreme to another. He attributes the root cause of this swing in American news coverage of China to a number of factors, including the traditional "love-and-hate syndrome" of the American public attitude toward the Chinese, the lack of China specialists on the media staff, and, to some degree, government management of news coverage for sensitive political reasons. He believes that "there is a long way to go . . . before we are told by the media that China is neither as bad as its critics have claimed nor as good as its sympathizers assert."

Related to the question of journalism is that of scholarly exchange. On the basis of his personal experience in China, Professor Stephen Uhalley, Jr., suggests that there are as many problems as opportunities in this field. The problems, as he sees them, are occasioned primarily by the fundamental differences in the two countries' political systems, ways of life, and societal objectives. "Adjustments in global realpolitik alignments do not necessarily reflect value transformation." On the Chinese side there is an obvious fear of "the bourgeois influence" that may find its way into China through visiting American scholars. On the American side there remains the question of being "too ethnocentric" in evaluating the Chinese society as a whole. In spite of all this, however, Professor Uhalley does see ample opportunities in promoting scholarly intercourse with China if some of the conventional assumptions and modes of analysis are replaced by "a new disposition to learn," in terms of new attitudes and purposes as well as new techniques and methodologies. He mentions "the cooperative group approach," which has been rather successfully experimented with by a delegation of the Committee of Concerned Asian Scholars to China, as a possible substitute for some of the old methods. At the same time he urges American scholars "to eschew the unrealistic panegyrics of the ideologue and avoid the equally unrealistic and distorting views of the cynic. Only genuine efforts to achieve the balanced view will produce worthwhile learning."

The entry of the People's Republic of China (PRC) into the United Nations (UN) was an important milestone in the development of Sino-American reconciliation. Beyond that, the entry itself has had profound worldwide political implications. In his authoritative analysis Professor John G. Stoessinger notes that the entry "served as a catalyst that both reflected and accelerated a systematic change in the international order." According to him China's performance in the Security Council, particularly on the Indo-Pakistani war issue, reflected the fact that the gulf between China and the Soviet Union is far wider than that between China and the United States. In the General Assembly the PRC insisted on its right to continue nuclear tests, thus losing much of the support it has gained from the Third World nations on questions of colonialism and the like. In the Secretariat the PRC has acquiesced in the election of Kurt Waldheim as Secretary-General and displayed considerable sensitivity to the fate of a large number of Chinese employees hired before the PRC's participation in the organization. On balance, Professor Stoessinger notes, "China has managed to fit into the structure of the United Nations without excessive turbulence." "On several issues China's impact has been negative, but on many more the effect has been constructive."

Dealing essentially with the same subject, Professor William R. Feeney analyzes the PRC's goal in the United Nations on the basis of its performance and voting record. Supported by detailed statistics and documentary evidence, he brilliantly sums up this goal as being threefold: achievement of national reunification, enhancement of national security, and exercise of Third World leadership. In the first respect the PRC has successfully removed Taiwan representation from all United Nations agencies but the World Bank Group and has persuaded the Secretariat to drop all references to Taiwan in the organization's publications. In the second the PRC has pursued a course of action that is more consistent with its national interests than with its cosmopolitan ideology. Its voting record on the Indo-Pakistani war, disarmament, and the Vietnam conflict substantiates this point. In the third the PRC has appealed to the Afro-Asian and Latin American nations through the exploitation of such issues as colonialism, the sea and the seabed, and economic development. Thus, Professor Feeney observes that "like all other member states, the PRC has sought to make use of the United Nations as a forum for articulating its foreign policy views and as one vehicle for implementing its objectives." On balance, he concludes, the PRC "has done remarkably well, considering its brief tenure in the UN, with most of its gains coming at the expense of the superpowers."

Soviet reaction to the Sino-American détente is a matter of supreme importance in view of the fact that it was achieved primarily because of the inherent danger of the Sino-Soviet dispute to peace. On this subject Professor George Ginsburgs offers a provocative study. According to his analysis, the Soviet approach to the détente has been characterized by a "duality": On the one hand, Moscow cannot impugn the propriety of the détente per se because of its own insistence on the legitimacy of Soviet contacts with the United States; on the other hand, since its rift with the PRC, Moscow has always entertained the fear of a Sino-American "collusion" against Soviet interests. Out of this dilemma the Soviet Union adopted a variety of opposite tactics to deal with the situation, ranging from outright condemnation of the détente to conciliatory gestures to both Peking and Washington. In addition, the Kremlin also stepped up its worldwide diplomatic maneuvers to counter the détente. These included Moscow's increased support for India, its quick rapprochement with West Germany, its at-

tempt to enter into a closer relationship with Japan, its invitation of
a North Korean delegation to the Kremlin during President Nixon's
stay in Peking, and its call for a "collective security" system in Asia
as a counterproposal to President Nixon's "Guam Doctrine." These
efforts, however, yielded only limited dividends to the Soviet Union.
In Professor Ginsburgs' evaluation the key concern in Moscow's policy
calculation remains the betterment of its ties with Washington while
continuously casting the PRC as the chief villain in international politics. This, he notes, is the logical outcome of a deliberate policy
decision to avoid any adverse effect on Soviet interests that may result from the détente.

My own essay discusses the impact of the détente on Sino-Japanese
relations and the implications of Japan's rapprochement with China.
For two decades, whether Japan should recognize the PRC as the
sole legitimate government of China was the single most controversial
and explosive issue in Japanese foreign policy. A succession of Japanese administrations were unable to solve the problem, partly because
of their deference to Washington's China policy and partly because
of Japan's self-interest in Taiwan for both economic and political
reasons. The Sino-American détente finally provided the Japanese
government with an irresistible impetus to normalize relations with
China. In the delicate process of negotiations for the normalization,
both sides made significant concessions, including the relinquishment
of war indemnities by the Chinese and the severance of formal diplomatic ties with Taiwan by the Japanese. However, Japan remains
noncommittal on Taiwan's legal status. In point of fact, it has exchanged a quasi legation with Taiwan along with the establishment of
a powerful Dietmen's organization to promote their mutual interests.
Both trade and tourism with Taiwan also have reached a new record
high. As a result difficulties have arisen in their negotiations for
governmental agreements on aviation and other subjects. However,
due to China's internal political stabilization and her desire to accelerate industrialization, an official trade agreement is likely to be
concluded in the near future. In multilateral relations Japan's proposed economic cooperation with Moscow has aroused Peking's
apprehension and for this reason Japan has sought U.S. participation
in the development of Siberian resources. The complexity of this
relationship is further compounded by Japan's intention to reduce its
dependence on the United States through cooperation with China and
the Soviet Union. Consequently, the Sino-Japanese rapprochement,
like the Asian-Pacific quadrilateral, is a relationship of ambivalence.

The impact of the détente on the Korean peninsula is also profound. Professor Chong-Sik Lee reviews the development of events
in Korea following the announcement of President Nixon's planned
visit to China and analyzes the problems of negotiations between the

two Korean governments as well as the prospects of future negotiations. According to Professor Lee, the Pyongyang-Seoul negotiations for reunification of Korea were unmistakably promoted by the Sino-American détente. Thus far, however, no measurable progress has been made for both internal and external reasons. Internally, Seoul favors the achievement of reunification by stages, beginning with the solution of certain "humanitarian" problems and then proceeding to "nonpolitical" and political talks. North Korea, on the other hand, maintains that "tension could be eased and trust built only if the state of military confrontation was removed, and this could be attained only if the United States forces were withdrawn from South Korea. . . ." Externally, the greater powers are incapable of exercising sufficient pressure to overcome the inherent difficulties in the negotiations. Underlying these difficulties are the respective geopolitical settings of the two Koreas and their political alliances and aims. In spite of all this, however, the negotiations are likely to continue because neither side can ignore the international environment. Moreover, continuation of the negotiations will further benefit North Korea in terms of both its international status and its trade relations with Japan. For South Korea the Sino-American détente has been a loss. Nevertheless, domestic and foreign pressures compel Seoul to maintain a dialogue with Pyongyang. As Professor Lee sees it, some limited economic and cultural exchanges may occur in the near future, though reunification is still a long way off.

If the Sino-Soviet dispute is a prime factor in the Sino-American détente, then the Indochina war has certainly served as another catalyst in the détente. Professor Kenneth P. Landon examines this catalytic role of Indochina in the context of international power politics. He points out that before the détente Hanoi had relied on two essential elements for its success: the unity and determination of its people and the "competitive support" of China and the Soviet Union. The détente, in his view, is "a massive stroke" that has deprived North Vietnam of large Sino-Soviet support, with the result that the United States has been able to end a proxy war against China and the Soviet Union. Ironically, however, the continued involvement of the United States in the Indochina affair is not because this nation has continued national security interests in that "parochial" situation but because of the new power configurations in that area resulting from the détente. According to Professor Landon, China favors a "Balkanized" Indochina (a divided Vietnam, a weak Laos, and a somewhat neutralized Cambodia); and in order to attain this goal, Peking needs Washington's support. The Soviet Union, on the other hand, is for a unified Vietnam in control of both Laos and Cambodia so as to encompass China and undermine American influence. Japan is seeking a piece of the action in the reconstruction of Indochina, but both China and the Soviet Union consider Tokyo an "imponderable factor of known economic substance but unknown political weight." Thus, the parochial politics of the Indochina parties are still intermingled with big-power politics. The problem for the United States, after having achieved a rather successful disengagement on the battlefield, is to determine what else needs to be done other than supporting China's desire to keep the area Balkanized.[3]

It is common knowledge that the Sino-American détente came about with considerable assistance from Pakistan amid great turmoil in the Indian subcontinent that involved China, the United States, and the Soviet Union. Thus, to what extent the détente has influenced the realpolitik and the balance of power in that region is a question of great interest to the present symposium. Dr. William J. Barnds provides a highly informative study in terms of the development of Chinese and American relations with the subcontinent and the impact of the détente on the complex regional power relationships, which since 1971 have been characterized by the Indo-Soviet alliance, on the one hand, and a limited Sino-American partnership in support of Pakistan, on the other. According to his analysis the United States has traditionally considered the affairs of South Asia subordinate to the larger issues of global politics. Therefore, the Nixon Administration's close relationship with Pakistan was not particularly directed against India but was motivated by its concern for more important affairs, such as the détente with China. Likewise, China's support of Pakistan was mainly due to its territorial dispute with India and the latter's cooperation with the Soviet Union. The convergence of these interests formed the basis of the limited Sino-American partnership in South Asia, and the Sino-American détente had the effect of prompting the Indo-Soviet treaty of August 1971, which, as a quasi-military alliance, in turn enhanced New Delhi's position in its dispute with Pakistan. However, Dr. Barnds points out that these relationships are basically unstable and susceptible to change.

Within the Nixon-Kissinger version of a pentagonal world, Western Europe has an important part. Veteran writer Dick Wilson analyzes the NATO allies' reactions to the Sino-American détente and its possible effects on Western Europe. According to Mr. Wilson, the détente has generally been welcomed by the allies, for it is consistent with their long-cherished wish. Thus far, all NATO members except the United States and Portugal have recognized the People's Republic of China. Many political leaders believe that as a result of the détente China will be useful to Western Europe at least in two areas. First, a China free from the strains of confronting the United States can serve as a more powerful counterweight to the Soviet Union whose potential threat to Western Europe, after all, is the very justification for NATO's existence. Second, the Sino-Japanese rapprochement resulting from the détente may induce Japan to direct her economic potential toward Asia rather than toward Continental Europe, which is still very suspicious of Japan. However, certain NATO countries have feared that if the effect of the détente develops into a strong anti-Soviet move, it will sabotage their patiently constructed détente with the Soviet Union. This is particularly true of West Germany, which views its ostpolitik as more important than a détente with China. As far as Peking is concerned, a friendly Western Europe can be useful to China in balancing her relations with both the Soviet Union and the United States. For this reason Peking has opposed troop reductions in Western Europe, for this would allow the Soviet Union to station more troops along the Chinese border. Peking has also opposed American or Soviet "hegemony" in the Mediterranean area. Mr. Wilson concludes by quoting an Italian analyst's remark: "It is in Europe's interest to reinforce China. And it is not fortuitous that China is the only major world power to desire, without reservations, that Europe should become more powerful."

In China's policy the problem of Taiwan has two aspects: The presence of the American forces in the Taiwan area is an external matter that requires direct negotiation with the United States; the reunification of Taiwan with the mainland is an internal affair that brooks no outside interference. The Shanghai communiqué represented an ambiguous compromise on the whole problem. Peking and Washington agreed to settle international disputes by peaceful means. This seems to have eliminated the possibility of a direct military confrontation between the two countries. In addition, the United States agreed not to "challenge" the Chinese position that "there is but one China and that Taiwan is a part of China." It also promised to "progressively reduce its forces and military installations on Taiwan as the tension in the area diminishes." But China did not openly renounce its right to settle the Taiwan problem by military means, nor did the United States show its intention to terminate the 1954 mutual defense treaty with Taiwan. Thus, as Professor A. Doak Barnett points out in his essay, the Taiwan issue is "shelved, not solved". Then what kind of future does Taiwan hold? And how can this problem be solved?

The former Deputy Assistant Secretary of State for East Asia and Pacific Affairs, Robert W. Barnett, has invented an "economic" solution for the problem. In his opinion, the vocabulary previously used in discussing a future for the Chinese on both sides of the Taiwan Strait, such as "two Chinas" and "one China and one Taiwan," is already obsolete. What is needed today is to establish an economic interdependence between the mainland and Taiwan, with the latter enjoying "a special 'provincial status' within one China—a status that would envisage a perhaps prolonged period during which Peking would allow Taiwan considerable economic, cultural, and administra-

tive separateness." The basis of his rationale is that since Peking
is short of foreign exchange reserves to expand its economy but at
the same time is unwilling to depend on foreign credits and investments because of fear of undermining its policy of self-reliance and
the egalitarianism of its system, it may be acceptable to the mainland that Taiwan play that "export-oriented, foreign investment accommodating role" for the whole of China. As far as Taiwan is concerned, Mr. Barnett notes, failure to reach some kind of accommodation with the mainland will probably result in Peking's economic
retaliation by forcing its foreign trading partners to make an absolute
choice between the mainland and Taiwan. Should that happen, he points
out, "Taiwan's economy [will] confront dangerous uncertainties and
difficulties for which durable solution might become impossible without Peking's acquiescence or support."

In the epilogue, Mr. Michael Witunski considers the PRC's entry
into the United Nations the beginning of a new era in international
politics. Then he reviews briefly the development of Sino-American
relations with some emphasis on President Nixon's new China policy
and the Japanese factor in the détente. Finally, he raises several
questions about the "Asian Dilemma" that he feels "staggers the
imagination of man."

As I was finishing this introduction, China released Premier
Chou En-lai's political report to the Tenth National Congress of the
Chinese Communist Party. (See Appendix I). Since this is an official
document of the first importance in China's own assessment of the
domestic and world situations, my introduction would not be complete
without a brief note on the international aspect of the report.

Premier Chou is reputed for his masterful skill in the delicate
art of balancing. His report shows the mastery at his best. He bitterly denounced the design on Chinese territory by the present Soviet
leadership as well as its intention to subvert China from within. Yet
he did not foreclose the possibility of normalizing interstate relations
with the Soviet Union through peaceful negotiations. In defense of
China's détente with the United States, he invoked V. I. Lenin's Treaty
of Brest-Litovsk (March 3, 1918) with Germany as a historical justification for compromise with "imperialist countries" under given
circumstances and distinguished this type of compromise from Soviet
"collusion and compromise" with the United States.[4] In support of
China's long standing policy for an independent Europe, he emphasized
"the U.S.-Soviet contention for hegemony" as the cause of world in-
tranquility and marked out Europe as the key strategic point of their
contention. To prevent a full détente between Western Europe and
the Soviet Union, he warned that at present the Soviets are "making a
feint to the east while attacking in the west." He challenged the Soviet
Union to return the four northern islands to Japan while remaining

silent on the latter's continued military alliance with the United States. In regard to the Third World, he maintained the usual optimism that "Countries want independence, nations want liberation, and the people want revolution—this has become an irresistible historical trend."

On the whole, then, the Premier's report is a carefully balanced policy statement designed to serve China's best interests on the basis of her present national strength and her existing relations with individual countries and regions. The Soviet Union remains the principal antagonistic contradiction in China's policy calculation, whereas the United States represents the second most important adversary in the international arena. Anxious to see a full rapprochement between China and the United States, some observers regarded the report as an indication of deterioration in the newly developed Sino-American relations, without recognizing the existence of enormous differences in their national strengths and interests. Moreover, the report is a "State of World Affairs" message written in Marxist terminology for both domestic and foreign consumption. Consequently, it would be unrealistic to expect the charming Premier to replay "America the Beautiful," which greeted President Nixon at the Great Hall of the People on February 21, 1972.

NOTES

1. See Mao Tse-tung, "On Contradiction", in Selected Works, vol. 1 (Peking: Foreign Languages Press, 1967), p. 311; "On the Correct Handling of Contradictions Among the People," any ed. For an interpretation, see Franz Schurmann, Ideology and Organization in Communist China (Berkeley: University of California Press, 1968), p. 17.

2. See "Transcript of Kissinger's News Conference in Washington on His Asian Tour," New York Times, Feb. 23, 1973, p. 14.

3. For a detailed discussion of U.S. policy toward Indochina and the involvement of other powers in the conflict, see Gene T. Hsiao, ed., The Role of External Powers in the Indochina Crisis (Edwardsville, Ill.: Southern Illinois University Publications, 1973).

4. For a discussion of the treaty's background, see George F. Kennan, Russia and the West Under Lenin and Stalin (Boston and Toronto: Little, Brown and Company, 1960), pp. 37-42.

1

THE UNITED STATES AS
AN ASIAN-PACIFIC POWER
Akira Iriye

"The whole trouble with Japan and her intransigence," wrote Henry L. Stimson during the Manchurian crisis, was "based upon her belief that we do not wish to remain a Far Eastern power."[1] According to Stimson, the foundation of America's Asian policy derived from the assumption that the United States was and must remain a Far Eastern power. Such an assertion was fantastic in the early 1930s—a time when the United States was promising independence to the Filipinos, it had no substantial naval base west of Pearl Harbor, and its economic interests in the whole of Asia were infinitesimal in comparison with those in Europe and the Western Hemisphere. And yet Stimsonian thinking persisted throughout the decade and provided the ideology of confrontation with Japan, eventuating in the Pacific War.

Today, 40 years after the Manchurian crisis, the United States is once again at a crossroad, in the process of redefining its role in the Asia-Pacific region. There has been "a profound transformation" in Sino-American relations, Secretary of State William P. Rogers has written in his introduction to United States Foreign Policy 1972—a transformation that "will lead to an improving international climate throughout Asia." But this, he says, will not mean an American withdrawal from Asia; on the contrary, the United States must "remain strong and active" in order to prevent a new war in the region.[2]

From Stimson to Rogers the rhetoric of Asian-Pacific power has underlain America's approaches to the area. There, in those 40 years, the United States has fought three wars; and for all practical purposes it has been involved in one kind of war or another continuously since 1941. To the extent that American foreign policy is ushering in a new era, its dimensions and characteristics can be comprehended only if one examines this history. Such a perspective will serve to place the Sino-American détente in the larger context of the development

3

of the United States as an Asian-Pacific power. Neither the United States nor the People's Republic of China, declared the Shanghai communiqué of February 28, 1972, "should seek hegemony in the Asia-Pacific region and each is opposed to the efforts by any other country or group of countries to establish such hegemony." Since China had never sought such hegemony, the passage implied recognition by the United States that its position and role in the area were to be restricted. How far should the retrenchment go? What are to be the extent and limits of American power in the Asia-Pacific region? The Sino-American détente has opened up a host of intriguing questions. This essay attempts to provide a historical framework for examining them by considering the 40-year history of United States involvement in Asian-Pacific affairs.

THE U.S. ROLE 1930-45

It is well to recall that contrary to Stimson's perception, the United States did not behave like an Asian-Pacific power during most of the 1930s. It failed to take any effective measures to counter Japanese moves in Manchuria and China; it lacked military resources or determination to come to the aid of China; and it so mismanaged diplomatic relations with Britain and the Soviet Union that the three potential allies against Japan, far from standing together to maintain the status quo, became more and more embittered toward one another. In the meantime America's economic interests in China dwindled, and there was less and less to protect in the region. The Japanese military ceased to worry about American retaliation, and its civilian counterpart began to discount the United States as a serious factor in Asian international relations.

And yet Stimson was right in one sense: to be an Asian power was as much an act of faith as a matter of actual military strength and economic interests. What it lacked in visible material ingredients, the United States made up with an image of itself as a great power in Asia and the Pacific. The roots of this image go back to the 19th century, and they need not detain us here. What is noteworthy is that after the turn of the 20th century such a self-image came to contain certain assumptions about China and about Sino-American relations. As early as 1900, the year of the Boxer uprising, some Americans began expressing an idea that was to remain with them throughout the succeeding decades: "Our interests in China are identical with the interests of the Chinese themselves"; "If China maintains her independence through our support, the United States in another decade will have greater material and moral influence than all other nations combined"; "it would be in the best interests of the United States and China

4

if a united, progressive, independent, and popular government existed in China."[3]

The American leaders of the 1930s were heirs to this tradition; they inherited an image of Sino-American relations that was an integral part of their perception of the United States as an Asian power. The United States, as Stimson said, had "a foothold in the minds of the Chinese people which is pregnant with possibilities for good, provided we do not forfeit it."[4] In other words, the United States was to play its role in Asian politics as a friend, probably the friend, of China. To fail to oppose Japanese aggression in China, therefore, was to renounce America's right as an Asian power. Although the United States was not prepared militarily to go to war with Japan over China, it continued the policy of nonrecognition of Japanese conquests in order not to forfeit China's goodwill.

Such thinking exacerbated Japanese-American relations, but it alone would not have brought about the Pacific War. The war came about because the United States chose to remain an Asian-Pacific power in the physical as well as the ideological sense. Before 1940 American power in the region was primarily ideological, without involving a military presence, so that the gap between its pretensions and actuality was widening in the face of Japan's determined push to organize a new order in Asia. The turning point came during 1940-41, when a series of decisions were made to retain and strengthen the American position in the Southwest Pacific. These decisions were ultimately a response to development elsewhere in the world, a response that Dean Acheson called "therapeutic." According to "therapeutic" as against "prophylactic" thinking, he said, the United States must actively involve itself in global politics in order to prevent the further undermining of the world balance of power. This meant that the United States should cooperate with Great Britain against the Axis nations in all parts of the world. Since Great Britain was already engaged in a fierce struggle for survival in Europe and the Middle East, it fell to America to maintain the status quo in the Western Hemisphere and the Pacific Ocean.

Such globalism reinforced the existing ideology of Sino-American relations and brought about the initial phase of America's military entry into the Asia-Pacific region. If a key date were to be chosen for this transformation, it may well be July 26, 1941, when the War Department established a new Far Eastern Command under General Douglas MacArthur. Upon learning of his appointment, MacArthur issued a press statement, saying: "This action of the American government . . . can only mean that it intends to maintain, at any cost and effort, its full rights in the Far East. It is quite evident that its determination is immutable and that its will is indomitable."[5] From this time until December, shipments of aircraft to the Philippines were speeded up, converting the islands, as it was hoped, almost overnight from a defenseless archipelago into a formidable headquarters of American power in the Pacific. Toward the end of November, the Far Eastern Command was instructed to cooperate with the British and Dutch forces in defense of the Malay barrier in the event of war with Japan. Plans were made to dispatch 21,000 troops for the Philippines by December 8, just in time, it was hoped, for the commencement of hostilities. As for the continent of Asia, the American and British governments agreed on December 6 that they "will regard it as a hostile act if the Japanese invade Thailand, Malaya, Burma, or the East Indies." President Franklin D. Roosevelt insisted that if Japanese transports were seen crossing the Gulf of Siam, the British forces "should obviously attack them."[6]

The Japanese attack at Pearl Harbor has tended to obscure the fact that the contest between Japan and the United States was over the future of the Southwest Pacific and Southeast Asia. Obviously there would not have been such a contest if the United States had yielded to Japan's new order with its pan-Asian orientation, aimed at eliminating the Western colonial empires from the region. The United States opposed this attack on the status quo and, in the process, extended its own influence beyond the limits of its traditional Asian empire. But the contest was more than a military struggle for power. It pitted one ideology against another: Japan's pan-Asianism versus the Anglo-American principles that were embodied in the Atlantic Charter. One was a particularistic doctrine, asserting that Asians would set up their own rules of the game, whereas the other was an explicit enunciation of such presumably universal principles as self-determination and economic interdependence. The United States, as a champion of these ideals, would oppose Japanese ambitions with both military might and an internationalist ideology.

It is significant that one of the first decisions the United States made after Pearl Harbor was not to give up the Southwest Pacific. The several ships en route to the Philippines were ordered not to turn back but to proceed to Brisbane. A new United States Army command was created in Australia, and an American base was established at Port Darwin. Of the 132,000 army troops that embarked from the continental United States for overseas assignments between December 1941 and March 1942, as many as 90,000 were bound for the Pacific Ocean, of whom 57,000 went to Australia.[7] This was by far the most sizable bulk of United States reinforcements anywhere in the world at that time. As if to underscore America's leading role in the Pacific theater of the war, the United States and Great Britain agreed to place strategy in the entire area under American control. Britain, which was assigned responsibility over the Middle East and the Indian Ocean, was willing to share command with the United States in Southeast Asia.

It is evident that in a little over a year after 1940 the United States had drastically transformed its position and role in the Asia-Pacific region. It was replacing Britain as the major opponent of Japan's southern expansionism. The future of the area hinged on the outcome of the Japanese-American war.

Once the decision to commit United States forces in opposition to the Japanese thrust was made, it was a forgone conclusion that American would emerge, in the event of victory, as a formidable power in the Asia-Pacific region. The only question was how far it would extend its power and influence. Once the Japanese-imposed order crumbled, there would be profound chaos and instability in the whole of East Asia and the Western Pacific; and the shape of the postwar order depended to a large extent on what the United States proposed to do.

By the winter of 1944-45 American officials concerned with the question had a fairly clear notion of what the United States proposed to do. In retrospect this was an extremely crucial period for America's future in Asia and in the Pacific, and it may be considered a distinctive stage in the deepening involvement of the United States in the area. Decisions made and ideas expressed at that juncture confirmed that America would not retreat to the pre-1940 position but would build upon the post-1941 developments and vigorously assert its power and influence in postwar Asian-Pacific affairs.

THE YALTA CONFERENCE AND ITS RESULTS

To consider the rough outlines that were then emerging, it would be convenient to talk of the "Yalta system" after the Yalta Conference of February 1945. Not all the key decisions were reached at the conference, nor were all the agreements to remain long in force. It is also true that only a fraction of the talks made and negotiations conducted by the Big Three concerned the Far East. Nevertheless, the Yalta Conference marked a transition to the postwar period at which the leaders of the United States, the Soviet Union, and Great Britain discussed their future collaboration as much as their joint strategy for the remainder of the war. In American-Asian relations in particular, it marked an occasion when President Roosevelt and his advisers expressed, explicitly or implicitly, what they had in mind regarding the role of the United States in Asia and the Pacific in the postwar period.

The timing of the Yalta Conference is of importance. By then the United States had successfully recaptured most of the islands Japan had seized after 1941, and American forces had also occupied some of the Pacific islands Japan had held as mandates after 1919. In

Europe, Germany was on the verge of collapse, and it could be expected that the Soviet Union would be able to shift its troops to the Far East. Both the United States and Great Britain anticipated and hoped for Soviet entry into the Pacific War so that Russian forces could immobilize Japanese troops in China. Moreover, the winter of 1944-45 was also the time when the domestic situation in China was growing daily more critical—itself a fundamental reason why Soviet assistance seemed needed to defeat the Japanese army.

The Yalta system reflected these circumstances, and the Big Three came to a rough understanding of their respective prospective positions in the postwar Asia-Pacific region. Generally speaking, the United States was to emerge as the predominant power in the Pacific Ocean, Britain to retain its position in Southeast Asia, and the Soviet Union to extend its control to Northeast Asia. There was no apparent conflict in such an arrangement, since the three spheres of influence did not seem to overlap. Implications of the Yalta agreements for the postwar history of the United States in the region are obviously of fundamental importance.

"Military withdrawal from Asia," C. L. Sulzberger wrote in February 1972, referring to the détente with China and the winding down of the war in Vietnam, "causes the United States to fall back strategically upon its huge Pacific empire about which most Americans are almost wholly unaware."[8] But Sulzberger himself seems unaware that this Pacific empire was consciously and eagerly acquired by the United States at the end of the Pacific War. His view that "Washington 'accepted' the trust territory from the U.N. after World War II" obscures the fact that by early 1945 President Roosevelt and his military advisers had made up their minds to keep the Pacific islands after the war. As the Chiefs of Staff told their British counterpart, "they feel that they acted weakly both in 1898 and 1919, in not securing the Japanese islands for America, and they are determined not to fail again. . . . They . . . have been seeking round for some kind of arrangement which in their opinion will give them the highest degree of sovereignty and control over the islands that can be got short of annexation."[9] The formula devised was the trusteeship system, agreed to at Yalta, which gave the United States undisputed control over the islands.

"If the Americans want to take Japanese islands which they have conquered," wrote Winston Churchill at the end of 1944, "let them do so with our blessing and any form of words that may be agreeable to them."[10] This summed up the British position on the question, as did a memorandum written by the Chief of Staff committee in London that there "should be no limitation on the right of the USA to fortify the islands. [In] view of the close cooperation which they assume will exist between the USA and ourselves in the Pacific, they do not consider that any specific rights need be reserved to us in peace."[11]

8

The British on their part insisted that they be allowed to retain their prewar position in the colonial areas of Southeast Asia. "Hands off the British Empire," declared Churchill, "is our maxim and it must not be weakened or smirched to please sob-stuff merchants at home or foreigners of any hue."[12] To which Foreign Secretary Anthony Eden replied, in January 1945, "There is not the slightest question of liquidating the British Empire. On the contrary, we are anxious to persuade the Americans not to go in for half-baked international regime in any ex-enemy colonies they may take over, not to advocate them for others, but to accept colonial responsibilities on the same terms as ourselves."[13] In British thinking, the United States would be accepting such responsibilities for the defense of the Pacific Ocean after the war, while Britain undertook to safeguard the status quo in the colonial empires of the European nations. Because of their declining power France, Belgium, the Netherlands, and others would be unable to reestablish their position vigorously. It was incumbent upon Great Britain, therefore, to act as their spokesman. It would not only oppose the establishment of trusteeships in the colonial areas but also would insist on placing Thailand, the one independent country in Southeast Asia, under British control so that it would never again collaborate with an alien power against the British Empire.

The United States took no position on Thailand at this time, but it basically accepted the British viewpoint on Southeast Asia; the Yalta agreement on trusteeships excluded the existing colonies of the allied powers from their application. President Roosevelt, it is true, had occasionally talked of self-determination for the colonial peoples, and the State Department had drafted numerous memorandums to give effect to such an idea. Within a month after Pearl Harbor, for instance, Maxwell Hamilton of the Office of Far Eastern Affairs suggested that the British government accord dominion status to India and Burma, and the Dutch government, to the East Indies. In the wartime alliance, he said, "British and Dutch problems are to some extent our problems, and vice versa."[14] President Roosevelt was particularly interested in the fate of Indochina; and by 1943 he was visualizing some sort of trusteeship for the peninsula, in which the United States would partic- ipate. None of these ideas, however, was written into an international agreement at Yalta or thereafter. In fact, by the beginning of 1945 Roosevelt seems to have lost much of his anti-imperialist zeal. He still talked vaguely of a trusteeship arrangement for Indochina, but this may have been a reflection more of his dislike of the French than of his anti-imperialism. At any event the United States took no step at this time to bring about such a regime, and its contribution to the shape of postwar Southeast Asia was minimal. Reasons for this dwindling enthusiasm can only be speculated, but one fundamental factor seems to have been the United States government's reluctance to consider political questions for countries in which American forces were not involved in any significant way. "I dislike making detailed plans for a country we do not yet occupy," said Roosevelt in October 1944.15 This meant that while he would push for an American empire in the Pacific, the influence of the United States would be limited elsewhere in Asia.

Finally, American and British officials and strategists saw no reason why the Soviet Union should not regain South Sakhalin and the Kuriles from Japan. Since Russia already had the Komandorski Islands and Kamchatka close to the Aleutians and Alaska, the addition of the former Japanese lands would not alter the strategic picture in the Northern Pacific vis-à-vis the United States. Soviet forces would occupy them at any event, and this was not objectionable so long as the United States retained the Pacific islands it occupied. As Secretary of War Stimson wrote in a candid memorandum, the Yalta accord on the Far East "should not cause us any concern from a security point of view, assuming always we keep clear our control over the Pacific islands."16 As for the British, the Foreign Office simply accepted the proposition, as stated in a memorandum shortly after Yalta, that "acquisition by Russia of South Sakhalin and the Kuriles would not affect any direct British interest."17

The Yalta Conference arrangements for the Asia-Pacific region after the war, then, were comparable with those reached in such earlier conferences as those at Versailles and Washington. Just as one sometimes refers to the Versailles system or the Washington system as a definer of a structure of international relations, it is possible to talk of the Yalta system, which involved some outlines of the postwar world structure as defined by the United States, Great Britain, and the Soviet Union. As far as the United States was concerned, it confirmed the developments after 1941 that the country would maintain its power and position in the Western Pacific. In Europe and the Middle East, on the other hand, the postwar role of the United States was not clearly articulated at Yalta. In these areas of the globe Britain and Russia were pictured as the two major powers to establish and maintain some sort of equilibrium. It was only in the Pacific that the United States definitely departed from the pre-1940 position of retrenchment and retreat to pan-American regionalism. The situation has lasted to this day. "After all," said Richard M. Nixon in March 1971, "We are a Pacific power. . . . The United States, as I said earlier, is a Pacific power."18 This was the legacy of Yalta.

American supremacy in the Pacific Ocean has not been challenged since 1945. Neither Britain nor the Soviet Union has sought to undermine drastically this part of the Yalta formula. Nor has there been a serious threat to the Soviet position in the former Japanese possessions, although during 1945-46 some Americans expressed unhappiness about their transfer to the Soviet Union. The greatest departure from the Yalta system came about in Southeast Asia. Instead of the region's reverting to the prewar regime, it plunged into colonial wars and political instability, which have not abated. In the development of the United States as an Asian-Pacific power, it should be stressed that American intervention in the area was not envisioned at the time of the Yalta Conference. Had the United States adhered to the Yalta system, there might still have been colonial struggles but there would have been no American involvement in Southeast Asia. To understand why the United States went beyond the arrangements of early 1945, it is essential to turn to another aspect of those arrangements that also was soon subjected to transformation— China.

CHINA'S POSITION IN 1945

China was not one of the great powers at the end of the war. Whatever the degree of President Roosevelt's infatuation with the image of China as a great power, his private thoughts and public action in the winter of 1944-45 belied any such notion. To be sure, he wanted China as one of the permanent members of the prospective United Nations organization; but this was primarily to convince the American people that the United States was not joining an exclusively European club and that the United Nations would be a truly international body worthy of American participation. In the context of Asian-Pacific politics, Roosevelt's view of China was reflected in the Yalta agreements; he considered that the Big Three would be the major partners for the new order after the war. Russia, rather than China, would assume the burden of fighting the Japanese army; and for doing so the Soviet Union would be offered a prize at the expense of China. Manchuria would, in effect, be turned into a Russian sphere of influence. Neither the Soviet Union nor Great Britain, it is true, seemed likely to extend control over China proper; and it was not expected that China would revert to the pre-1941 status of a semicolonial country. But it would not, for the foreseeable future at least, act as a major power. Peace, order, and stability in postwar Asia depended, according to official American thinking represented by Roosevelt before his death, on the new balance of power being established among the Big Three, not among the mythical "four policemen."

Russia and Britain could not have agreed more with the American position. Although concrete evidence of Soviet thinking is meager, it appears that the Russians considered China a prize for exploitation by the Big Three, especially by the United States, whose preponderant influence and position in Chinese politics and economy continued to be conceded by Moscow well after 1945. As for themselves, Soviet officials were more anxious to retain what they were promised in Manchuria than to encourage the growth of a strong China. British disdain for the idea of China as a great power is too well known to require comment. Churchill's private words were even less complimentary to the Chinese than his public attitude. "It is quite untrue to say that China is a world power equal to Britain, the United States, or Russia." "The idea that China . . . should be rated . . . above France or Poland or whatever takes the place of Austria-Hungary, or above even smaller but ancient, historic and glorious states like Holland, Belgium, Greece and Yugoslavia—has only to be stated to be dismissed." "That China is one of the world's four great Powers is an absolute farce."[19]

China was not going to be recognized by the Big Three as a power of equal status and importance in the postwar Asian scene. Implicit in the Yalta accord, however, was the symbolic significance of China as a unified, independent, and sovereign nation. China was not seen as a power; it was perceived as an idea. This was because the Big Three did not want merely to discuss joint strategy against Japan and agree on their respective prizes in the event of victory. The Asian-Pacific order they were visualizing was essentially a new balance of power based on the anticipated distribution of their respective positions and strengths. But the wartime leaders of America, Britain, and Russia had given their alliance an ideological and idealistic character by signing the Atlantic Charter; and at the Teheran Conference they had issued a ringing declaration: "We shall seek the cooperation and active participation of all nations . . . whose peoples in heart and mind are dedicated, as are our own peoples, to the elimination of tyranny and slavery, oppression and intolerance. We will welcome them . . . into a world family of democratic nations." It is not surprising, then, that at the Yalta Conference, where the three leaders sought to define the shape of the postwar world, they should have tried to provide some ideological underpinning for the new order. They did so in their joint declaration on liberated Europe and in the final communiqué, in which they spoke of the need for "continuing and growing cooperation and understanding among our three countries and among all peace-loving nations" so that "the highest aspirations of humanity [may] be realized—a secure and lasting peace."

It was all very well to talk of continuing "cooperation" among the three, but what did it entail in the Far East? It could not possibly involve their dedication to anti-imperialism or self-determination, since these principles were being violated at Yalta. China provided the answer. It was China that offered a specific context in which "cooperation and understanding" might be achieved. According to the Yalta agreements, the United States, Britain, and the Soviet Union would accept the principle of China's territorial sovereignty, refrain from interfering with Chinese domestic politics, and continue to deal with Chiang Kai-shek as the government of Free China. These were vague ideas, but at least they served to give specific and substantive content to the notion of Big Three cooperation in an ideological sense. By somehow adhering to these principles, it was felt that the wartime alliance would be perpetuated into the postwar years. China was to be the symbol of their cooperation in the transition period; it would give an ideological underpinning for the structure of international relations that was being erected. Whether the Big Three would in fact "cooperate" in China would determine whether their alliance was more than a sheer marriage of convenience.

For the United States such an approach to China had several important implications. First, it was perfectly in accord with the traditional policy of befriending the Chinese. America had always stood for Chinese integrity and the Open Door; and, as noted earlier, the idea of Sino-American friendship had constituted a basis of America's self-perception as an Asian power. The Yalta agreement confirmed this tradition, implying that the role of the United States would have a strong ideological component. Second, for this reason there was no departure at Yalta from the long-standing policy of the United States that ideals such as the Open Door and territorial integrity in China would not be realized through the use of American force. No direct military involvement by the United States in China was foreseen in the postwar period. Third, America would act within the framework of collaboration with Russia and Britain in solving Chinese problems. Fourth, none of these powers would establish a position of preponderance in China after the war. Finally, in view of these considerations, America's primary interest in China would continue to be economic. The Yalta agreement seemed conducive to creating a favorable environment for promoting trade and investment activities by foreigners, especially Americans, after the war, now that Japan, which had kept China under its exclusive control, would be ejected from the continent. It is obvious that in terms of American aspirations toward China, there was no real departure from prewar policy. This was in marked contrast with desires and designs in the Pacific, where the United States was bringing about a new structure of power relations.

THE U.S. ROLE AFTER 1945

Events after the Japanese surrender were soon to show, in China as much as in Southeast Asia, that the assumptions underlying the Yalta agreements would not long define effectively the limits of American power on the Asian continent. There were forces within and without the United States that tended to militate against the continuance of these agreements. The result was that American involvement in Asia steadily deepened and its power extended far beyond what had been visualized in early 1945. Any discussion of the United States as an Asian power in the postwar era must take this crucial development into consideration.

First of all, the framework of American-British-Russian cooperation in China was undermined by the willingness of Britain and the Soviet Union to act unilaterally in their own interests. The direction of their policies was different, however. The Soviet Union was anxious to establish at least temporary hegemony over Manchuria in order to confiscate and remove food and industrial equipment. These acts were no different from what the Russians were doing in Germany, and they were considered part of Russia's claim to Japanese reparations. Nevertheless, they were conducted without consultation with the other allies; moreover, they implied that the Soviet Union wanted to keep Manchuria weak and impoverished. Soviet assistance to Chinese Communist forces had the further effect of keeping China in turmoil. While there was no policy of massive intervention in China, these instances did demonstrate the Russian tendency toward unilateralism, notwithstanding the idealistic language of the Yalta accord.

British policy moved in the opposite direction. After the war the London government was not interested in playing an active role in international affairs involving China. It was not so much that Britain no longer wished to count as one of the Big Three as that it was acutely aware of its inferior position vis-à-vis the other two. As Churchill stated at the War Cabinet meeting in April 1945, "How could the British Commonwealth, as the third of the three Great Powers, match the power and influence which would be wielded after the war by Russia and the United States? In material resources we could not hope to equal either of these Powers." The only hope, he said, lay in "our superior statecraft and experience and, above all, [in] the unity of the British Commonwealth of Nations."[20] Britain's statecraft and experience might have been put to good use in China so as to retain the framework of Big Three cooperation. Instead, London adopted an almost exclusively economically oriented policy in postwar China, seeking trade and investment opportunities wherever possible but refraining from taking the initiative to coordinate action among the Big Three.

British abstention left only the Soviet Union and the United States as the two great outside powers in China. Instead of Big Three cooperation, there now had to be collaboration between America and Russia. In Europe and the Middle East there was a transition period, during 1945-47, in which Britain gradually gave up its role as a great power and turned to the United States to assume part of its functions. There was no comparable transition in China, and the United States was confronted with the presence of 70 Soviet divisions in Manchuria at the end of the Pacific War. Under the circumstances it was extremely difficult to consider how the Yalta framework of big-power cooperation could be maintained. According to the original scenario, the United States would have had to refrain from military and political involvement in China, withdraw all its forces, and concentrate on economic activities. At least one key official, John Carter Vincent, director of the Far Eastern Office of the State Department, persisted in this view throughout 1945 and beyond. Shortly after the Yalta Conference, he wrote to Ambassador Patrick J. Hurley that "in spite of the reports on Rumania and Poland . . . we can reach an understanding with Russia in regard to China on which we can rely."[21] In his view such an understanding called for evacuation of both American and Russian troops from China and their pledge not to interfere in the Communist-Kuomintang struggle for power. When, after the Japanese defeat, officials in Washington decided to augment American troop strength in China, partially as a response to the Soviet presence in Manchuria, Vincent sharply rebuked them, saying, "We should have in mind possible political and international reactions to determine whether, in seeking to provide for military security in this manner, we have not disturbed our international political relations to a point that might negate the assumed security advantages of our military position in China."[22]

As Vincent clearly understood, if the United States were to maintain the framework of cooperation with the Soviet Union in the Far East—an assumption that underlay the Yalta system— it was important to pursue a hands-off policy in China. The Yalta formula was in a sense a restrictive ordinance for the two powers; it defined the limits of Soviet rights and concessions in Manchuria, but it also confined American involvement on the Asian mainland to economic interests and ideological influence. If such an understanding had been scrupulously maintained by both Moscow and Washington, there might not have been a Cold War in Asia. The story of Asian international relations for a quarter century after 1945 was that of a progressive deterioration of the Yalta system as the Soviet Union and the United States both went beyond its restrictive limits and involved themselves in Chinese affairs. With Great Britain no longer acting as a great Asian power, such a situation inevitably invited an atmosphere of Cold War confrontation between the Big Two.

Paradoxically, American intervention initially was justified in the name of the Yalta agreements. While John Carter Vincent stressed cooperation with Russia as the key to postwar Asia, others felt that the development of a unified China was the essence of the Yalta accord. Both viewpoints were right, of course, but they led to diametrically opposite proposals for American policy. Whereas Vincent considered Big Two cooperation as an end in itself, the second group viewed it as merely a means to attain Chinese unification. From such a point of view, the occupation of Manchuria by Soviet troops was deeply disturbing and necessitated some bold response by the United States. As is well known, there were three alternative policies the latter could adopt in such a situation: assistance to the Kuomintang, support of the Communists, or the promotion of a coalition government through America's good offices. But whatever policy was adopted, it implied deepening involvement of the United States in Chinese affairs. In that process the United States might conceivably bring about a unified China; just as likely it might provoke Chinese resentment and cause deterioration in Sino-American relations. Chances for American-Soviet cooperation would certainly diminish no matter what alternative was followed. But those who called for bold initiatives by the United States maintained that unless it did something, the situation in China was bound to worsen and the ideal of a unified and independent China would never be materialized. Since the ideal was to be the symbol of American-Soviet cooperation to begin with, there could be no cooperation among these two without a unified China. This was the ultimate dilemma. The delicate synthesis of power politics and idealism that seemed to have been attained at Yalta began to break down. While the Yalta system had postulated a new balance of power in the Far East and American-Soviet cooperation to encourage the growth of an independent China, neither of these objectives was to be achieved in the immediate postwar years. Instead, the United States and the Soviet Union extended their spheres of influence in Asia and directly confronted each other in an atmosphere of suspicion and hostility.

THE SITUATION IN THE 1970s

This much historical background helps provide some perspective for the understanding of what has been happening in Asian-Pacific relations since the early 1970s, a quarter centruy after Yalta. "The historic opportunity for this generation," declared Henry Kissinger in his New York address of April 23, 1973, "is to build a new structure of international relations for the decades ahead." The speech was compared by James Reston to the Marshall Plan of 1947 as a major policy enunciation. Yet in inspiration and content the Kissinger statement really harked back to the Yalta Conference. It sought to put an end to the period of Cold War confrontation and herald the coming of the age of "a new structure of peace, less geared to crisis and more conscious of opportunities, drawing its inspirations from its goals rather than its fears." Just as the Big Three at Yalta talked of postwar cooperation, so did Kissinger emphasize the need for post-Cold War "cooperation," a word that appeared with almost monotonous regularity in the speech. Echoing the three wartime leaders' rhetoric of idealism, tying them together in peace as well as in war, Kissinger asserted, "We must identify interests and positive values beyond security in order to engage once again the commitment of peoples and parliaments. We need a shared view of the world we seek to build."[23]

For over 25 years after 1945 there was no "shared view of the world" in the Asia-Pacific region. The wars in Korea and Vietnam were but the most visible evidence of that failure. The United States grew in power and influence as an Asian-Pacific power to an extent never visualized at Yalta, and it may even be argued that there were "interests and positive values beyond security" accompanying the growth of American power. The United States involved itself on the Asian mainland in the name of freedom, anti-Communism, and self-determination. American forces fought in Vietnam, said President Nixon in his address before the South Carolina legislature on February 20, 1973, "for the most selfless purpose that any nation has ever fought a war. . . . They went for a very high purpose, and that purpose can never be taken away from them or this country."[24] But this was not "a shared view of the world," accepted by other nations and peoples. After the collapse of the Yalta system, each power went its own way, justifying its action in unilateral terms, without bothering to consider international cooperation. Actually, quite often national security alone seemed sufficient reason for involvement in Asia. As Everett F. Drumwight, chief of the Division of Chinese affairs of the State Department, wrote as early as November 1945, in direct contradiction to the views of his chief, John Carter Vincent, "the promotion of the security of the United States" necessitated a massive commitment of American forces in China to assist the Chiang Kai-shek regime. "Considerations of our own security interests," he said, should come before anything else, and they justified turning China virtually into an American protectorate.[25]

The Sino-American détente since 1972, then, can be seen as part of the search for a new structure of peace, as an alternative to the postwar pattern of international relations. In a sense it implies a return to the Yalta system; the United States, instead of entrenching its power on the Asian continent, would retreat to the limits foreseen in 1945 and concentrate its armed strength in the Pacific Ocean. On the continent its interests and activities would take a more economic than military shape. It would respect the sovereignty and independence of China. As President Nixon declared in Shanghai, "Never again shall foreign domination, foreign occupation, be visited upon this city or any part of China." Moreover, the United States would reaffirm that Taiwan is part of China—a proposition that goes back to the Cairo Conference of 1943.

The emerging structure of Asian-Pacific relations, however, would not be a replica of the Yalta system. The Yalta conception of China, as noted above, was somewhere between a weak, divided, foreign-controlled country and a strong, vigorous power. The Nixon visit to the People's Republic of China amounted to acknowledging that the United States now considered China a great power. Moreover, Japan too would be a key member of the emerging international system. Shortly before the trip, James Reston, who had traveled to Peking and Tokyo, wrote that the "problem now is to . . . try to bring all the major powers—the U.S., the U.S.S.R., China and Japan—together to create a new order in the Pacific."[26] These four, instead of the wartime Big Three, would now be the major architects of the new structure of peace in the Asia-Pacific region. The historic significance of the Nixon trip lay in giving official recognition to such a notion. Although President Nixon was accused of ignoring Japanese sensitivity by unilaterally revising policy toward China, the Sino-American détente in fact had the effect of encouraging the thought that Japan too was a great power.

This was brought about in a number of ways. China's repeatedly expressed opposition to the revival of Japanese militarism gave the impression, as the columnists Rowland Evans and Robert Novak wrote, that "What really underlies Premier Chou En-lai's assaults on Japan is big-power rivalry. Much more quickly than Washington, Peking has perceived Japan's return as a world power."[27] In the United States, on the other hand, strong concern was voiced over the Nixon administration's alleged neglect of Japan in favor of China. As the New York Times editorialized in September 1971, "The United States prior to 1941, and again today, is proceeding on the assumption that the critical relationship in Asia is that between the United States and China. . . . Neither in trade nor in any other field is China likely, in the measurable future, to become as important to the United States as Canada, Western Europe or Japan."[28] In Japan too the Sino-American rapprochement provoked a self-conscious assertion that it too was a great power, an aspiration that was extremely vague in specific content but that seemed to be fulfilled when the Chinese government shifted its policy in 1972 and welcomed an official visit by the Japanese prime minister. The Chou-Tanaka joint statement contained a passage that was virtually identical with that in the Shanghai communiqué: "Neither of the two countries should seek hegemony in the Asia-Pacific region and each country is opposed to efforts by any other country or group of countries to establish such hegemony." Japan had clearly reentered Asian politics. An insignificant factor in the Yalta scheme, it would now be a member of the "Pacific quadrilateral."

Under the circumstances, the United States would be one of the four major Asian-Pacific powers, instead of being one of the Big Three or being the greatest power in the region. Whether a new balance of power will in fact develop among the four and contribute to peace, order, and stability remains to be seen.

Power considerations alone, however, will not be sufficient to consolidate a new order in the Asia-Pacific region. For one thing, the constituent elements of the "Pacific quadrilateral" are not equal in military strength, political influence, or economic resources. The position of Japan seems particularly ambiguous. It alone of the four powers does not possess nuclear weapons; its defenses are tied almost exclusively to an alliance with one of the other three; its people are divided over the future direction of the country; and its ever-expanding economy makes its position extremely vulnerable to world conditions because of the dependence on other countries for energy resources. Japan would provide a key to the stability or instability of the Asia-Pacific balance.

More fundamentally, however, a structure of international relations based upon balance-of-power considerations without economic, cultural, and ideological underpinnings would remain unstable, as the history of the Yalta system clearly demonstrates. If the United States were to contribute to the making of the new order in Asia and the Pacific, it would have to be concerned with these other aspects of foreign affairs. This is not an easy task. Unlike Europe, countries of the Asia-Pacific region do not share a common tradition, and they have not participated in international relations as equal members. It is much easier to speak of a new Atlantic Charter, as Henry Kissinger did in his April 24 address, since America's values, goals, and basic interests "are most closely identified with those of Europe." It is difficult to find any such commonality among Americans, Russians, Chinese, and Japanese. It is by no means clear that they can develop "a shared view of the world we seek to build." Kissinger did stress that "The Atlantic community cannot be an exclusive club. Japan must be a principal partner in our common enterprise." Although Japan and the Western nations do not derive from common cultural roots, it is not difficult to conceive of their overlapping goals and interests. As Gerard Smith has put it, "The United States, Western Europe and Japan face a common condition. They are the major industrial areas of the world, and they share common concerns about the problems of environment and modern industrial society as well as common security concerns."29 But what common values and concerns does China have with the other countries? Can there really be cultural and intellectual ties that bind the Asian-Pacific powers?

"If we succeed in working together where we can find common ground," said President Nixon in his toast at Shanghai, "if we can find common ground on which we can both stand, where we can build the bridge between us and build a new world, generations in the years

19

ahead will look back and thank us for this meeting that we have held in this past week. Let the Chinese people and the great American people be worthy of the hopes and ideals of the world, for peace and justice and progress for all." The history of American-Asian relations is too full of instances where words like "peace," "justice," and "progress" have meant different things to different governments, to enable one to find comfort and assurance in such rhetoric. Nevertheless, one has to begin somewhere to find an ideological and intellectual basis for the new balance of power. The Shanghai communiqué mentioned the desirability of broadening cultural contact between the two peoples. It is to be hoped that by means of such contacts Chinese and Americans would develop a sense of interdependence so that they, together with Russians, Japanese, and other peoples of the area, would contribute to the definition of a new internationalism through which alone the Asian-Pacific balance of power could be transformed into an Asian-Pacific community of nations.

NOTES

1. Christopher Thorne, The Limits of Foreign Policy: The West, the League and the Manchurian Crisis of 1931-1933 (London, 1972), p. 254.
2. New York Times, Apr. 20, 1973.
3. Public Opinion, June 21, 1900, p. 774; Independent, July 12, 1900, p. 1655; Literary Digest, July 28, 1900, p. 74. For the most recent discussion of America's China policy at the turn of the century, see Richard D. Challener, Admirals, Generals, and American Foreign Policy, 1898-1914 (Princeton: Princeton University Press, 1973).
4. Thorne, op. cit., p. 195.
5. D. Clayton James, The Years of MacArthur, vol. 1. (Boston, 1970), p. 591.
6. Lord Halifax to Anthony Eden, Dec. 6, 1941, Foreign Office archives, FO 436, Public Record Office.
7. Charles Bateson, The War with Japan: A Concise History (East Lansing, Mich.: 1968), p. 150.
8. New York Times, Mar. 17, 1972.
9. British delegation (San Francisco) to Foreign Office, May 12, 1945, Prime Ministers' papers, PREM 4, 31/4, Public Record Office.
10. Churchill to Eden, Dec. 31, 1944, ibid.
11. Far Eastern Committee memo, Mar. 30, 1945, Cabinet papers, CAB 96/5, Public Record Office.
12. Churchill to Eden, Dec. 31, 1944, Prime Ministers' papers, PREM 4, 31/4, Public Record Office.

13. Eden to Churchill, Jan. 8, 1945, PREM 4, 31/4, Public Record Office.

14. Hamilton memo, Jan. 6, 1942, State Department archives, 740.0011PW/2030 1/2, National Archives.

15. Arthur Layton Funk, Charles DeGaulle: The Crucial Years, 1943-1944 (Norman, Okla., 1959), p. 303. For a good discussion of American and British policies in Southeast Asia during the war, see Russell H. Fifield, Americans in Southeast Asia: The Roots of Commitment (New York, 1973).

16. Henry L. Stimson to Harry Truman, July 16, 1945, Foreign Relations of the United States: 1945, vol. 7 (Washington, 1969), p. 943.

17. Foreign Office draft memo, Feb. 19, 1945, CAB 96/5, Public Record Office.

18. New York Times, Mar. 10, 1971.

19. Churchill to Alexander Cadogan, Mar. 22, 1943, PREM 4, 100/8; Churchill memo, Apr. 1943, PREM 4, 30/11; Churchill to Eden, Aug. 23, 1944, ibid., Public Record Office.

20. Churchill's statement at War Cabinet meeting, Apr. 3, 1945, CAB 65, vol. 52, Public Record Office.

21. John Carter Vincent to Patrick J. Hurley, Apr. 2, 1945, Foreign Relations of the United States: 1945, vol. 7, pp. 323-25.

22. Vincent to James F. Byrnes, Nov. 12, 1945, ibid., 614-17.

23. New York Times, Apr. 24, 1973. It is interesting to note that Leonid I. Brezhnev echoed Kissinger's remarks when he visited the United States in June 1973. In his radio and television address to the American people, the Russian leader stressed the theme of "peaceful and mutually advantageous cooperation" between the two countries. He recalled the wartime alliance, which, he said, "could have been expected to usher in a new era of broad peaceful cooperation between the Soviet Union and the United States." Thus, he too was recalling "the spirit of Yalta." As he remarked, "Mankind has outgrown the rigid 'cold war' armor which it was once forced to wear. It wants to breathe freely and peacefully. And we will be happy if our efforts to better Soviet-American relations help draw more and more nations into the process of détente." (For a text of the speech, see New York Times, June 25, 1973).

24. New York Times, Feb. 21, 1973.

25. Drumright memo, Nov. 16, 1945, Foreign Relations of the United States: 1945, vol. 7, pp. 629-34.

26. New York Times, Dec. 3, 1971.

27. Chicago Sun-Times, Oct. 4, 1971.

28. New York Times, Sept. 24, 1971.

29. Ibid., Mar. 2, 1973.

2

THE CHANGING STRATEGIC
BALANCE IN ASIA
A. Doak Barnett

The basic strategic balance in Asia* has been undergoing major changes for several years. The Nixon-Chou summit meeting in early 1972 highlighted this fact in a fairly dramatic fashion. Although in many respects this meeting simply gave added impetus to trends already underway for some years, it nevertheless clearly symbolized the start of a new period in Asian international relations.

What has been emerging, in terms of big-power relations in Asia, is a new "four-power balance" fundamentally different from the bipolar situation that characterized the 1950s and early 1960s. The new situation is a complex one, characterized by overlapping patterns of quadrilateral, as well as bilateral and triangular, relationships among the major powers involved in the region. These relationships have by no means crystallized in "final" form, and some further changes are certain to occur. By its very nature, in fact, the new situation is one that may well involve considerable fluidity and continuing adjustments. Nevertheless, one can identify some of the main directions of recent changes, and it is important to assess their possible consequences. To what extent is the new situation likely to contribute to stability or instability? Is a new equilibrium now emerging, or will the changes increase the potential for conflict? What are some of the principal problems and dangers inherent in the situation?

Although the Nixon-Chou summit meeting in 1972 was in many respects a historic turning point, it was the product of forces and events that can be traced at least to the early 1960s—and in some respects to the 1950s; they came to a head, however, only in the late

---

*The discussion of "Asia" here has been arbitrarily restricted to East Asia—the region roughly from Burma to Korea. If South Asia were to be included, a range of other issues would have to be considered.

1960s. Several converging trends were most important: the growing
conflict between China and the Soviet Union, the pressures on the
United States to withdraw from Vietnam and reduce the American
military presence in Asia, and the reemergence of Japan into a position
of increasing influence in the region.

THE SINO-SOVIET SPLIT AND THE U.S. REACTION

The Sino-Soviet split was without doubt the most important single
cause of the change from a bipolar to a multipolar situation. The
complex story of growing Sino-Soviet tensions is well known and need
not be recapitulated here. Suffice it to say that strains in relationships
between Peking and Moscow began to grow in the 1950s, steadily increased in the 1960s, and reached a climax during 1968-69. The end
result was a situation that convinced Peking that its security was
threatened in such a way that it should pursue more flexible policies
toward much of the rest of the world. It also finally convinced the
other powers—including the United States—that it was both possible
and desirable to deal with Peking and Moscow separately, rather than
as parts of a single bloc.

The policies of both Peking and Moscow contributed to the growing
antagonisms and tensions between them, but it was probably above all
the Soviet military buildup around China that created a situation that
convinced the Chinese that their security demanded major changes
in their policies toward the other major powers. This buildup took
place on a large scale in the second half of the 1960s, at a time when
China was experiencing widespread internal turmoil during the Cultural Revolution. To a certain extent it doubtless reflected genuine
concern in Moscow about a potential "Chinese threat" to Russia's
security and interests—even though one can easily argue that because
of its overwhelming military superiority the Soviet Union should not
have feared such a threat as much as it apparently did. Some Russian
leaders seemed to take very seriously (more so, at least, than most
foreign observers elsewhere) Chinese hints that they might press
claims to large portions of Soviet territory. Moscow watched with
considerable apprehension the progress the Chinese were making,
from 1964 on, in developing an independent nuclear capability. It was
also angered by Peking's relentless ideological and propaganda attacks
and its efforts to compete against and undermine Soviet influence
throughout the world. Over time, moreover, the Russians apparently
became increasingly uneasy (or so some of their private statements
appeared to suggest) about the seemingly "irrational" behavior of
Chinese leaders, especially during the Cultural Revolution. There
is little doubt, however, that "irrational" factors on the Russian

side—including deep historical memories of the Mongol "hordes," oversimplified geopolitical thinking (Chinese overpopulation plus Siberian underpopulation = a major threat), and emotional anti-Chinese feelings—contributed to an exaggerated Soviet assessment of the "Chinese threat" (comparable, in some respects, with that which prevailed in the United States in the 1950s) and to Moscow's decision to carry out a huge military buildup on China's borders.

From the Chinese perspective the Soviet buildup was viewed, understandably, with increasing alarm; and by the late 1960s the "Soviet threat," as perceived in Peking, was unquestionably the major foreign policy preoccupation of the Chinese leadership. Whether or not Peking took seriously the hints of possible Soviet attack against China's nuclear and industrial centers—and it well may have—Chinese leaders clearly became increasingly concerned not simply about the possibility of overt military conflict but also about the possibility of increased Soviet pressures and the potential for Russian "meddling" in Chinese domestic politics. In 1968 Soviet intervention in Czechoslovakia (and Moscow's articulation at that time of the so-called Brezhnev doctrine, justifying intervention in the internal affairs of other socialist nations) heightened Chinese fears. And the small but bitter Sino-Soviet border conflicts along the Ussuri River in 1969 greatly intensified passions on both sides and brought the two countries close to war.

These events, occurring as the Cultural Revolution in China drew to a close, highlighted the liabilities and dangers of the extreme isolationism that had characterized China's foreign policy during 1966-68. It was immediately thereafter, during 1968-69, that Peking began to look outward once again, started to evolve a more flexible and pragmatic approach in its foreign relations generally, and undertook to broaden its relationship with the entire non-Communist world.

Ever since that time national security concerns, rather than ideological or other considerations, appear to have been the most important single factor shaping Peking's foreign policy (although economic considerations have probably been of some significance too), impelling the Chinese to adopt more flexible approaches designed to increase their room for maneuver and leading them to alter their policies toward both the United States and Japan. A prime Chinese aim since the late 1960s has been to develop new relationships with the other major powers in Asia in such a way as to counterbalance the Soviet Union and create new constraints on Moscow.

During the period when Peking was considering new policies (its first post-Cultural Revolution feelers toward the United States came in late 1968), the United States also began a major readjustment of its policies. Under strong domestic pressures, Washington started to move cautiously but steadily toward disengagement from Vietnam, especially from 1968 on, and in 1969 a newly elected President articulated his "Nixon Doctrine." Although the precise meaning of this doctrine was not immediately clear—it is still, in fact, subject to debate—there was no question that it represented a new general trend toward reducing rather than increasing the American military presence in Asia, and indicated a desire to develop more flexible political and diplomatic policies in part to compensate for the planned changes in the U.S. military position in Asia. This doubtless reinforced the views of those in Peking who argued that it was now the Soviet Union, rather than the United States, that posed the greatest immediate security problems for China, and that Chinese policy should be adapted accordingly.

President Nixon and his principal foreign policy adviser, Henry Kissinger, reassessed U.S. policies on the premise that a new multipolar big-power relationship was emerging (a pentagonal one, globally, involving the United States, the Soviet Union, China, Japan, and Western Europe), and began to reevaluate and adjust U.S.-China policy in this context. As early as 1969 the Nixon administration started to take some steps that showed increased flexibility and a desire to broaden contacts with the Chinese. There is no doubt that Peking was alert to these changes and was inclined to be responsive to them, just as Washington was increasingly alert and responsive in this period to the changing nature of intra-Communist relations and Peking's "feelers." In short, a process of cautious interaction between the United States and China developed gradually during 1968-70 and laid the groundwork for the dramatic development that subsequently occurred.

JAPANESE REEMERGENCE AND ITS RESULTS

Another major development during this same period was the reemergence of Japan into a role of increasing independence and influence in Asia. The agreement to return Okinawa to Japan in 1969 was a milestone in this process, but the rise of Japan's economic influence in the region was the most important measure of its changing role. By the late 1960s it was already becoming clear that the Japanese were rapidly establishing a position of economic predominance throughout much of Asia. It was also clear that the Japanese government was under continuing pressure to reassess and redefine Japan's broad international role and foreign policy in the changing overall situation.

For many years Japanese leaders had been urged by influential segments of public opinion to normalize relations with Peking and had been deterred from doing so mainly, at first, by U.S. attitudes and, later, by the unavoidable complications posed by the Taiwan problem. Peking had not made it easy for Japan to change its policies; in fact, throughout much of the Sato period, it maintained a generally hostile and rigid posture toward the existing Japanese leadership, setting preconditions for establishing formal relations that were difficult for Tokyo to meet. As Peking watched Japan's influence grow, however, it was impelled to reexamine its policy toward Tokyo as well as Washington, but it did not immediately adopt a more flexible or conciliatory stance. In fact, in part because they were disturbed by the seeming implications of the Nixon-Sato communiqué in 1969 (which suggested the possibility that, as the U.S. military role in Asia diminished, Japan might assume regional security responsibilities, in particular with regard to Korea and Taiwan), the Chinese mounted an intense propaganda campaign highlighting the dangers of Japanese remilitarization. Obviously Peking greatly exaggerated the dangers for political effect, but the campaign nevertheless reflected genuine Chinese concerns. The situation changed, however, when it became clear to Peking not only that some improvement in U.S.-China ties would be possible but also that Eisaku Sato would soon be replaced as Prime Minister. At that point the Chinese switched their propaganda line and made it clear that they were prepared to adopt a more flexible posture and normalize relations with Sato's successor—whoever the might be—if Japan would agree to alter its position regarding Taiwan.

During this same period the Soviet Union, motivated in large part by its desire to compete against the Chinese, increased its political activities in much of Asia and attempted, to the extent possible, to expand its influence and presence. The Russians' attempts to broaden their trade and diplomatic contacts, their growing naval role, and diplomatic initiatives such as Brezhnev's 1969 proposal for an Asian security pact were all part of this process. However, although Moscow's efforts bore considerable fruit in South Asia, where Soviet-Indian ties were significantly strengthened, in East Asia the Russians' real leverage was fairly limited.

These were among the major trends that lay behind, and help to explain, the dramatic developments in 1971-72 that resulted in major changes in both Sino-American and Sino-Japanese relations and hastened the emergence of a new pattern of four-power relations. Peking's invitation in April 1971 to an American ping pong team to visit China—in itself an act not seemingly of world-shaking importance— set things in motion, and events then moved rapidly. Henry Kissinger made his famous secret trip to Peking in mid-1971, followed by a second trip in the fall, and laid the groundwork for President Nixon's visit in early 1972 (and probably also for Peking's entry into the UN in the fall of 1971). The resulting Nixon-Chou summit meeting captured the imagination of the world and produced a major document—the Shanghai communiqué—that called for U.S.-China trade, cultural exchanges, and, most important, improved diplomatic contacts. In effect,

26

both sides agreed to lay aside the Taiwan issue, temporarily at least, in order to make progress toward "normalized" relations.

IMPACTS OF THE SHANGHAI COMMUNIQUÉ

The greatest immediate impact of the Shanghai communiqué was symbolic, but it was followed by concrete steps to begin building a new U.S.-China relationship. Nonofficial exchanges soon got under-way, and trade grew fairly rapidly. (By the end of 1972, in fact, it appeared that Sino-American trade in 1973 might approach $400 million, in which case the United States would probably become China's second largest trading partner, after Japan, if one excludes Hong Kong.) In early 1973 the United States and China agreed to establish liaison offices—embassies in all but name—in Peking and Washington.

As these events unfolded, efforts to "normalize" Sino-Japanese relations were also intensified and accelerated. Peking greatly moderated its propaganda line concerning Japanese remilitarization, from late 1971 on, and indicated through various channels that it was eager to discuss establishing formal relations with Sato's successor. In Japan the pressures to recognize Peking, even at the cost of cutting formal diplomatic ties with Taiwan, were greatly increased by the 'Nixon shock" produced by the President's dramatic switch of China policy without prior consultation with Tokyo. So too were the pressures to reexamine Tokyo's broad relationship with the United States and Japan's basic role in the world. When Kakuei Tanaka replaced Sato as Prime Minister in 1972, a Japan-China summit meeting in Peking was quickly arranged; it produced a statement in which Japan agreed to go considerably further than the United States had—cutting official ties with Taiwan and establishing full diplomatic relations with Peking.

The repercussions of all of these events were immediate and far-reaching. Virtually all nations in Asia, large and small, were compelled to reassess their positions and their policies. The Soviet Union, on its part, not only continued to strengthen its military position in Asia; it also stepped up its political and economic activities on a broad front to try to compete against the Chinese. Most important, Moscow soon gave evidence of being more flexible in its approaches toward both the United States and Japan. In mid-1972 the first U.S.-Soviet summit ever to be held in Moscow took place, at which the Russians agreed to some new arms control measures and attempted to promote expanded U.S.-Soviet economic relationships. In Soviet-Japanese relations the issue of a formal peace treaty was reopened, and discussions of possible joint economic enterprises in Siberia were intensified. The changing Asian balance was probably also a factor impelling the Russians to show increased interest in steps toward

27

détente in Europe and to press for a European security conference; the Chinese, in any case, gave evidence that they believed these moves were a sign of Moscow's shift of concerns from West to East.

Throughout Asia the repercussions were widely felt. In Northeast Asia the decisions by North and South Korea to open direct bilateral negotiations for the first time were generally interpreted, and probably rightly so, as a response to the changing big-power balance. In Southeast Asia not only was added impetus given to settlements that would facilitate the withdrawal of American forces from Vietnam; many smaller Asian states began taking steps to accommodate to the new situation and to increase contacts with China. Virtually every nation in Asia was impelled to reexamine its security requirements and relationships with all four major powers in the region, in the context of the new multipolar situation that was emerging.

The overall impact of the Nixon-Chou summit meeting, in sum, was to accelerate processes of change that had been underway since the 1960s, highlight the need for all nations to adjust to the emerging pattern of four-power relations, and create a new atmosphere of fluidity, détente, accommodation—and, one must add, uncertainty—that affected, in varying ways and degrees, almost all existing relationships in the region.

CHARACTERISTICS OF THE NEW PATTERN OF RELATIONSHIPS

What are likely to be the characteristics of the new pattern of relationships that is now taking shape? And how is it likely to affect the prospects for peace and stability in the region in the period immediately ahead?

It is not easy to characterize the new situation—or at least not easy to describe it in simple terms. Not only is it very different from the bipolar situation in Asia of a decade or more ago; it is also different from traditional European Models of the balance of power. Even though there are clearly four big-power actors in Asia now, there obviously are major disparities and discrepancies among them, and the existing relationships are by no means equilateral. In military terms there are two superpowers (the United States and the Soviet Union) that in ultimate strategic terms are in a class by themselves, one emerging nuclear power (China), and one major nation (Japan) that is still weak and dependent in purely military terms. In economic terms, however, the situation is very different. Three of the major powers (the United States, the Soviet Union, and Japan) are highly advanced countries, while one (China) is still essentially a developing nation. Moreover, Japan, the nation in the region that is weakest in military terms, is now the one that is rapidly achieving a position of economic predominance. Politically the influence of the four obviously varies also, with the United States and China exercising the largest political roles in the region at present—although Japan's political influence is growing—while the Soviet Union is clearly, so far, in a secondary position.

The complexity of relationships is underlined by the fact that although many of the actions of each of the major participants can now be best understood in terms of interactions among all four members of the quadrilateral, others can be analyzed most fruitfully in terms of triangular relations—including the U.S.-China-Russia, China-Japan-Russia, Japan-U.S.-China triangles—while some obviously must still be examined in bilateral terms.

Another characteristic of the situation, which (together with the existing disparities in military power) leads some to argue that it should not be labeled or viewed as a "balance" at all, is that the quality of bilateral relationships among the four major nations involved is obviously very different. While the United States and Japan are still closely linked by a mutual security pact, China and the Soviet Union (despite their 1950 alliance, which is now a dead letter) are locked in hostile confrontation, while the other bilateral relationships (U.S.-Soviet, U.S.-Chinese, Chinese-Japanese, and Japanese-Soviet) are characterized by varying mixtures of competition and cooperation.

Some critics of current U.S. policies in Asia have argued that if Washington were to view Asia in terms of a four-power "balance" and shape its policies accordingly, this could lead the United States to treat the other three powers in the region, without discrimination, as of equal importance to its interests, in which case the U.S.-Japanese relationship could soon deteriorate, to the great detriment of both U.S. interests and the general stability of the region. There is no intrinsic reason, however, why the concept of "balance" must be defined in such a limited and literal fashion.

What is emerging, whatever labels are used, is a new multipolar situation, different in basic respects from the pattern of the past, in which four major nations will clearly play the key roles. The roles of all four will be extremely important. The future of general peace and stability in the region will depend to a very large degree on their interrelationships and interactions. Other powers will have to adjust to this new pattern of four-power relationships and will be compelled to search for means to protect their own interests and security in its overall context. Whether minor conflicts remain essentially local or spread and threaten the region will depend to a large extent on the relationships among the big four and their responses to such conflicts.

Whether one describes this new situation as a "four-power balance" or "four-power equilibrium," or simply (more neutrally) a "four-power relationship" (or with some other term, for that matter) is not of great significance, so long as one defines what one means— and understands what the realities of the situation are.

EFFECTS OF THE NEW PATTERN

What will the effects of this new pattern be? A good case can be made that, despite all the elements of fluidity and uncertainty, the new four-power relationship, in the general form that now appears to be evolving, could well create a dynamic equilibrium or balance (use of either term is acceptable, in my opinion) that should tend to reduce rather than to increase the chances of big-power conflict in the region and to enhance rather than to detract from the prospects for regional peace and stability—if certain foreseeable problems and dangers that would clearly be destabilizing can be dealt with effectively. Such a dynamic equilibrium should be preferable to the tense bipolar division of Asia in the recent past. However, the "if" in this judgment is important, and it is therefore essential to identify and analyze major problems and dangers inherent in the situation and to consider what is required to cope with them.

What will such an equilibrium, if it in fact emerges, be like? First of all, each of the four powers will pursue its interests with a fairly higher degree of independence (more so, certainly, than in the past); this will be unavoidably true to a considerable degree of the United States and Japan, as well as the others, even if a close special relationship between Washington and Tokyo is maintained. (It will be argued below that a close U.S.-Japan tie is essential in order to main- tain the kind of four-power equilibrium that is now taking shape; and if it is not retained, a very different, and almost certainly less stable, four-power or three-power pattern would probably emerge.) In this situation each power will find it necessary and desirable to respond to most of the actions of the others, and virtually everything that each does will have important implications for and repercussions on the others. All four can be expected to show greater flexibility and man- euverability in their policies than in the past, yet each will almost certainly also confront new and complicated limitations and constraints. While military factors will continue to be important in relationships in the region, the relative importance of diplomatic, political, and economic factors will grow—and in fact the basis of a new "balance" will be more political and economic than military.

There is no doubt that this situation will involve major elements of fluidity, maneuver, and uncertainty. Some changes and adjustments in relationships may occur fairly frequently, and shifting patterns of parallelism and cooperation as well as competition will develop. Yet in a basic sense there will probably be severe limits on the extent to which any of the four powers can manipulate the balance to its advantage, and an increasingly complex net of cooperative as well as competitive economic and political links seems likely to develop across old lines of political division.

Even more important, the dangers of major big-power conflict should, one hopes, be reduced. In any situation in which one of the powers might be tempted to threaten attack on a second, all the other powers would almost certainly oppose such action; and even if the others were not disposed to become directly involved in a military sense, the threatening nation could expect them to react, politically and economically, in ways that doubtless would be costly to it. This should operate to help, at least, to deter major conventional conflicts.

The possibility of nuclear conflict seems small. Deterrence is already effectively operative in the relationships involving the United States and Japan and the Soviet Union (and this will continue to be the case, even for Japan, so long as the U.S.-Japan security treaty is maintained), and clearly it will not be very long before China also acquires a minimal credible deterrent (some might argue that it already has acquired it). Also, the nuclear element and dangers of escalation already reinforce other deterrents to major conventional conflicts. Although nuclear blackmail is still theoretically conceivable, in practice it will probably be avoided (at least in any crude form) because of the costs and risks that could be involved, which are already great and clearly will increase rather than decrease over time.

In general, even though military-strategic factors will still be of great importance in shaping both attitudes and policies, the possibility of actual military conflict among the major powers (except, as will be discussed below, between the Soviet Union and China) appears to be fairly remote in the period immediately ahead; competition for influence will almost certainly be conducted, therefore, mainly by political and economic rather than military means. As relationships have changed, especially since 1971, the patterns of competition have increasingly involved rivalry to reduce tensions and improve relations, both among the major powers and between them and the smaller nations; here again, the Sino-Soviet relationship has been a notable exception so far. Conceivably this could change in the period ahead, and whether or not it does could greatly affect regional stability.

Despite many elements of fluidity in the situation, which doubtless will create numerous uncertainties and could well create an impression and atmosphere of instability, on balance the emerging pattern seems likely to be fairly stable in one very fundamental respect. At present the possibility seems small that, at least in the foreseeable future (let us say the remainder of the 1970s), there will be any

31

dramatic changes in alignments of a kind that could upset and seriously destabilize the present general pattern of relationships. The biggest question marks in this respect concern the Sino-Soviet and U.S.-Japan relationships; and therefore the future of the balance will depend greatly, as will be noted below, on the future of these two relationships.

Finally, the emerging pattern seems likely to operate, at least to some extent, to reduce (though not necessarily eliminate) the likelihood of big-power military confrontations in localized conflicts in Asia. Most such conflicts are likely to seem less threatening to the overall balance than was the case when the balance appeared to be both bipolar and fragile; and the competition among all four powers should operate, in most situations, to reinforce other constraints against direct big-power military intervention. To the extent that this is true, and that the big powers pursue policies toward the major potential conflict areas in Asia that stress political, diplomatic, and economic competition and maneuver rather than military involvement, this may well help to reduce the frequency of such local conflicts and to limit and contain the scope of those that do occur.

Whether or not one believes that a projection of trends along the lines suggested above—that is, the emergence of a somewhat fluid but nevertheless relatively stable equilibrium that should reduce rather than increase the dangers of large-scale military conflict in Asia in the period immediately ahead—is likely to be correct must depend on a fairly wide range of judgments about how specific relationships are likely to develop and how specific problems are likely to be dealt with in the next few years. It simply is not possible within the confines of this chapter to discuss all of these. Suffice it to say that while I accept the fact that such a projection must be based on some optimistic assumptions, I nevertheless am inclined to believe—at this time, at least—that the emergence of an equilibrium roughly of the kind described is not only possible but also likely—and is, furthermore, desirable.

PROBLEMS AND DANGERS OF THE NEW PATTERN

But even if one believes that cautious optimism on this score is now justifiable, it is nevertheless clear that there is no certainty about such a course of events; and there is no doubt that the emerging situation has inherent in it a number of problems and dangers that could conceivably result in a very different outcome. Some of these, if the worst were to happen, could produce major conflicts or major shifts and/or realignments that could seriously destabilize the situation and destroy the hope for the kind of equilibrium described above.

Sino-Soviet relations probably pose the greatest potential dangers to peace and stability in Asia in the period immediately ahead. One theoretically possible change in these relations that would have destabilizing effects would be a dramatic shift in Peking's and Moscow's policies leading to a far-reaching rapprochement, that is, to the reestablishment, in effect, of a close Sino-Soviet alliance. If this were to occur, many present trends would probably be reversed; and the general thrust of forces in the region would doubtless be once again toward greater bipolarity, increased tension, and possible confrontation. Both the United States and Japan would be compelled, in these circumstances, to reassess their basic foreign policies in Asia, as would most smaller nations.

Is this a real, as well as a theoretical, possibility? There is considerable evidence that over the years some Chinese leaders—including some major military leaders—have opposed chairman Mao's hostile approach to the Soviet Union and have urged greater moderation and flexibility—and at least some steps toward a Peking-Moscow détente. One cannot rule out the possibility that, at the time of succession, leaders with such views might come to the fore again. Yet, on balance, it does not seem likely that any far-reaching Sino-Soviet rapprochement will occur in the foreseeable future. After more than a decade of dispute, there are now numerous conflicts of interest between the two nations, as well as deep mutual suspicions, that make it very unlikely. Moreover, to the extent that improved Sino-American and Sino-Japanese relations can be consolidated before the succession occurs in China, the chances of any sudden, far-reaching, and destabilizing Sino-Soviet rapprochement occurring will be further reduced.

The greater danger, actually, lies in the possibility of open Sino-Soviet military conflicts. The uncertainties of the succession period in China may well increase this danger, especially if the succession were to produce a period of confusion and conflict in China and if Soviet leaders at that time were tempted to intervene, exert new pressures on Peking, or meddle in Chinese politics in an attempt to influence the outcome. If open Sino-Soviet military conflict on a sizable scale were to occur, the impact on both the United States and Japan, as well as other nations—and on the stability of the entire region—could be enormous, even if other nations avoided direct involvement. Such a conflict, perhaps even more than a Sino-Soviet rapprochement, would necessitate basic reassessments of the situation in Asia by all nations involved, which would doubtless lead to some very basic policy changes. (It might well, for example, stimulate major remilitarization in Japan.)

While a major Sino-Soviet conflict is a real danger, on balance it seems unlikely to occur, since both Moscow and Peking will probably be constrained by the huge potential risks and costs that would be involved and the likely effects on other nations. However, both the United States and Japan should nevertheless do all they can to minimize the possibility of open Sino-Soviet conflict. Although their direct leverage is not likely to be great, they can make wholly clear their opposition to such a conflict and the fact that it would, in their view, have far-reaching adverse consequences, to which they would be compelled to respond politically and economically (and in their own military-security policies), even if they avoided direct military involvement.

Whereas either an open Sino-Soviet military conflict or a sudden major rapprochement between Peking and Moscow would tend to alter the basic character of the now-emerging four-power balance in such a way as to increase the likelihood of instability, tension, and conflict in the region, a limited Sino-Soviet détente that lowered the existing level of tensions and reduced the dangers of conflict between the two countries would not necessarily have such an effect. On the contrary, it could well contribute significantly in a positive sense to the emergence of a more stable equilibrium in Asia. There is definitely a possibility that gradual steps toward such a limited détente could occur at some point, after chairman Mao's death if not before. If so, such a development should be welcomed, rather than greeted with dismay, by the other powers. The aim of achieving increased stability in the emerging balance can best be served, in short, by a Sino-Soviet relationship that is neither one of close alliance nor one of tense confrontation and conflict but, rather, one of correct, restrained relationships. What is to be hoped for, in sum, is a Sino-Soviet relationship that will not be dominated solely by hostile competition (though competition will almost certainly continue) but one that will permit at least some cooperation involving China and the Soviet Union, as well as the other major powers in the region, in devising international solutions for the most critical regional problems. (The level of Sino-Soviet hostility today is obviously a major barrier to such cooperation.)

Another potential development that could seriously destabilize the situation in Asia in the period ahead would be a deterioration of the U.S.-Japanese relationship. The kind of equilibrium now emerging requires the continuation of a special relationship between the United States and Japan— and, specifically, the continued maintenance of a U.S.-Japanese security pact for one all-important reason: to reinforce Tokyo's confidence in Japan's security and thereby obviate the need for Japan to embark on major remilitarization and to develop an independent nuclear capability. A serious deterioration of U.S.-Japanese relations, leading to termination of existing security agreements, would not only be a major blow to the U.S. interests, in both security and economic terms (it would almost certainly necessitate a fundamentally different U.S. approach to Asia), but would also probably have far-reaching effects on both China and the Soviet Union that would contribute to increased instability in the entire region.

In theory, if Japan's security ties with the United States were cut, Tokyo might opt for alignment with some other nation—China, for example, or even the Soviet Union—but in reality this seems very unlikely, for numerous historical, economic, and political reasons. More possible might be the creation of a situation in which Japan decided to opt for unarmed neutrality; but even this does not really seem probable, in the light of the leadership's security concerns and latent nationalism. The most likely consequence of a deterioration of U.S.-Japanese relations would be the emergence of a Japan that decided it was essential to remilitarize—and to acquire its own nuclear weapons. Such a development probably would significantly increase the uncertainties and the tensions in both Sino-Japanese and Soviet-Japanese relations—and very possibly in U.S.-Japanese relations as well.

At present both Peking and Moscow appear to have some awareness of the potentially adverse consequences that trends of this sort could produce, and currently both maintain a relatively moderate and tolerant posture toward the U.S.-Japan security treaty. It is a striking fact that, since the recent improvement of its relations with Washington and Japan, Peking has in effect indicated that under existing circumstances it not only accepts the treaty's continuation but apparently tends to favor it as a useful counterweight to Moscow and as a deterrent to increasing Japanese remilitarization.

Since 1971 there have been serious strains in the U.S.-Japanese relationship. Some of these may well have been unavoidable, in the sense that in attempting to assert a more independent role in world affairs, as they were inevitably destined to do, the Japanese have been impelled to raise important questions about past policies—and most particularly about the basic nature of the Tokyo-Washington relationship. Economic differences and growing trade competition also have probably been unavoidable. The seriousness of the strains, however, has clearly been increased by the U.S. government's insensitivity to Japanese concerns and by the lack of adequate U.S.-Japanese consultation and cooperation concerning both China policy and economic problems.

At present there is no reason to believe that the damage done has been irreparable. Because of the stake that both countries have in the continuation of close economic relations, and because of the firm commitment of Japan's dominant leadership to the maintenance of the existing security relationship (and continuing Japanese reliance on the U.S. "nuclear umbrella"), the likelihood is that, despite the existing strains, a close and special relationship will continue. Yet there is no absolute certainty that it will, and whether it does will depend on the effort made by both sides to resolve existing problems. (In time this will almost certainly require some significant changes in the detailed arrangements involved in the existing security pact, especially in regard to U.S. bases in Japan, as well as mutual compromise on the most divisive economic issues.) Moreover, it will depend fundamentally on whether the Japanese continue to have confidence in the dependability of U.S. defense commitments—and on whether the Japanese believe they can play a major new international role, as they are now striving to do, without acquiring a larger independent military capability.

The two main dangers discussed above—a Sino-Soviet military conflict and a serious deterioration of U.S.-Japanese relations—are probably, in real terms, the most potentially destabilizing developments that could occur and upset the equilibrium in Asia in the period immediately ahead. But there are many other foreseeable problems that will affect the degree of stability or instability in the region. It is not possible to discuss—or even list—them all in the brief space available here, but it is desirable at least to mention a few of them.

Major Chinese military intervention in Southeast Asia is obviously one theoretical possibility that cannot be ignored. Some years ago it would clearly have been at the top of almost any list of potential threats to regional security in Asia. There are many reasons today, however, to rate it fairly low as a danger in the period ahead. The history of the 1950s and 1960s does not suggest that the Chinese Communist leaders have not been prone to high-risk military adventures in the region, and Peking's present preoccupation with both the potential threat to its security in the north and very pressing domestic problems—and with the consequent need to bolster its position by improving relations with the United States, Japan, and other non-Communist countries—probably makes large-scale Chinese military intervention in neighboring areas of Asia even less likely than in the past.

However, Peking, in addition to giving moral and material support to its allies and clients in the Indochina area, may well continue giving low-level indirect support to revolutionaries in a number of other countries in the region—for example, Thailand and Burma. At present, Peking's stress on expanding normalized state-to-state relations suggests that its backing of revolutionaries abroad will almost certainly be deemphasized in the period immediately ahead. How much this facet of its policy will be deemphasized, and how long its present policies will continue, remain to be seen. But as long as the Chinese continue to avoid major military intervention outside Chinese borders, cautious Chinese support of clients or revolutionaries in areas such as Southeast Asia is not likely to threaten to upset or reverse the basic trend toward a new four-power balance in Asia. However, the degree to which they emphasize the importance of state-to-state relations or support for revolutionaries abroad obviously will significantly affect the prospects for regional stability.

A sudden, dramatic and far-reaching withdrawal of the U.S. military presence from Asia is another theoretical possibility that would have seriously destabilizing results and would compel policy reassessments and adjustments by all other nations in the region. Such a U.S. "withdrawal" would basically change the character of the situation. This does not seem likely to occur in the period ahead, however. What is likely is a gradual reduction of the level of American forces maintained in the region and a step-by-step cutback in U.S. bases. This probably will not have seriously adverse effects on the regional balance if it is carried out, as now seems likely, at a fairly gradual rate (although precisely how and under what circumstances it is done will be important, particularly in Korea and Thailand). In fact, the majority of nations in the region appear to have accepted and to be adjusting to the fact that a reduced U.S. military presence in the region is almost certain to occur over the next few years. There is no doubt, however, that the effects of this trend will depend to a considerable extent on the pace and manner in which it occurs, and the consequent reactions of other nations to it. A carefully executed reduction of direct U.S. military involvement is now generally expected and could well contribute positively to the new equilibrium that is emerging. However, if other nations were to conclude that the United States was in fact "withdrawing" from the region and totally disengaging from any military responsibility for helping to maintain regional security, the impact would clearly be destabilizing. Many Asians would then begin thinking about the problems of the region not in terms of a four-power balance but in terms of a very different kind of three-power China-Japan-Soviet relationship, and they almost certainly would regard this situation as more unstable and potentially dangerous than a four-power balance involving the United States. Continued U.S. security involvement in some form is therefore a prerequisite for the kind of equilibrium that is now evolving.

Another basic prerequisite for peace and stability, regionally as well as globally, is the maintenance of a stable U.S.-Soviet strategic relationship. There is no doubt that the Russians have been uneasy about the new four-power pattern of relationships that is emerging in Asia. In particular they appear to be apprehensive that the United States will try to manipulate China or that China will try to manipulate the United States in such a way that Soviet interests will be harmed. Some Russians seem to fear that what will take shape is, in effect, an anti-Soviet U.S.-China alignment.

To date, in adjusting its policies the United States has generally been successful in avoiding the worst dangers inherent in this situation. By stressing that it is determined to develop viable and improved relationships with both Moscow and Peking, Washington has acquired increased leverage in relations with both without provoking strong hostile reactions from either. It is essential, however, that as the situation evolves, Washington be extremely sensitive to the need to continue dealing evenhandedly with both the Russians and Chinese and attempt to moderate the fears of both that potentially hostile alignments directed against them could emerge. This will require considerable diplomatic skill, but it should certainly be possible. To the extent that the United States is able to convince both Peking and Moscow that their fears of collusion against them are unfounded, this should contribute to the evolution of a more stable four-power balance; to the extent that the United States fails to do this and arouses fears of crude manipulation, this could intensify apprehensions and tensions in ways that could endanger stability.

Looking ahead, it is possible to foresee many other problems, some of which clearly will involve important risks and dangers, that could affect the stability of the region. At present, for example, both Sino-Japanese and Sino-American relations are, in a sense, in a honeymoon period; but it would be unrealistic to ignore the potential for increased strains in both relationships in the future.

At present Peking and Tokyo are both eager to expand economic and other ties between their two countries, and this seems likely to continue in the period immediately ahead because of the indisputable benefits to both. Yet even today Chinese leaders are probably quite ambivalent about Japan's growing influence in Asia, and there is a high probability that a strong and growing competitive element will affect Sino-Japanese relationships in the future. Peking doubtless will continue to have anxieties about the possibility of Japanese remilitarization and will view with unease the development of expanded Japanese-Soviet economic ties (it has already openly expressed its opposition to Japanese desires to build a major pipeline in Russia that would run close to China's borders); but, most important, it almost certainly will view with apprehension Japan's growing economic role throughout the region—in Korea, Taiwan, and Southeast Asia—and probably will feel compelled in time to compete against the Japanese influence in most of these areas. Exactly how such Sino-Japanese competition might develop is difficult to predict, since for some time at least the instruments for increasing Japanese influence will be mainly economic while the Chinese will of necessity have to rely primarily on political means; nor is it clear how such competition will affect bilateral Sino-Japanese relations. But the present honeymoon period is not likely to last indefinitely, and further Sino-Japanese relations probably will be characterized by a complicated mixture of competitive and cooperative elements.

In U.S.-China relations, the problem of Taiwan has so far simply been shelved, not solved, and one cannot assume that it could not again become an issue of contention in the future. This will depend on what occurs on Taiwan itself and on the reactions not only of Peking but also of Washington (and Tokyo) to future developments. For the present both the United States and China appear to be determined to set the Taiwan issue aside, in order to improve Sino-American relations. Both seem prepared to allow time for further changes to occur, and to hope that these will occur peacefully. Moreover, since 1971 the Nationalist regime on Taiwan appears to have adjusted fairly success- fully to the altered circumstances affecting it. In the light of all this, the immediate prospect is probably for the maintenance of the status quo. But over time pressures may well increase for changes, and no one can predict today whether these will operate to move Taiwan toward peaceful reunification with or accommodation to the mainland, or toward permanent separation and ultimate independence. There clearly will be pressures working in both directions. Conceivably the processes of change could be so gradual that they will not pose intolerable dilemmas for the major powers involved in this situation or any sudden new dangers that could seriously destabilize the region. But no one can be sure this will be true. Over the long run, stability in the region will require changes that are acceptable, or at least tolerable, to both Peking and Taipei, and to Washington and Tokyo as well; obviously this will be easier said than done. One certainly can imagine developments, in whichever direction Taiwan may move, that could pose difficult dilemmas and create new strains in the emer- ging pattern of four-power relations.

THE FOUR MAIN POWERS AND THE
SMALLER POWERS

This discussion has focused primarily on the evolving relation- ships among the four major powers in Asia, not because the concerns and interests of the smaller powers are unimportant but because the larger issues of war and peace, regional security, and general stability clearly will depend above all on what the big powers do. There is almost no question, however, that there will continue to be tensions, instabilities, and conflicts affecting the smaller powers—in both North- east and Southeast Asia. Clearly some of these could pose threats to regional security and stability—although how serious such threats may be will depend to a considerable extent on how the major powers respond to them.

In the period ahead all four major powers in Asia will be involved, and in a sense competitive with each other, in both Northeast and

Southeast Asia. At present, however, all four seem predisposed, in varying degrees, to try to limit rather than expand conflicts in these regions and to avoid situations that could lead to major confrontations. A crucial question for the future is whether, or to what extent, the four principal powers, while continuing to compete with each other for political and economic influence in these areas, can agree—tacitly or explicitly—to avoid military intervention, develop new forms of cooperation and competition, and use their influence to increase the local prospects for stability and limit the dangers of potential conflicts. If, over time, cooperative—or parallel—efforts among the big powers in their approaches to these areas can evolve, this would obviously increase the prospects for general stability in the region. If not, there clearly will be a continuing danger that local conflicts could escalate, lead to increased big-power intervention, and raise the possibility of military confrontation that could threaten the overall pattern of four-power relationships.

In Northeast Asia the process of political interaction between North and South Korea that has recently begun could theoretically lead to genuine détente, reduced tensions, and increased stability. But it is apparent that, at best, the process will be prolonged and extremely difficult. The Korean Peninsula is still one of the most heavily armed regions in the world; and because of the persistence of deep suspicions in both North and South, the situation remains potentially volatile. The situation is unique because the security concerns of all four of the major powers in Asia intersect there to an unusual degree, and there is little doubt that each of the four would be likely to regard a major conflict—or sudden drastic political change—on the peninsula as a threat to its security and other interests. This situation therefore contains substantial dangers, as well as significant opportunities. The main danger is that if major conflict were to break out, it could soon involve all four of the interested powers, directly or indirectly. However, this fact may well give all four a large stake in encouraging developments that can prevent conflict and stabilize the situation, and this creates important opportunities for cooperation.

At this stage perhaps the major powers can do no more than urge the Koreans in both the North and the South to work seriously to explore the possibilities for mutual compromise and accommodation. However, if and when some real progress is made in direct North-South negotiations, there will be strong arguments in favor of big-power cooperation at some point—either through explicit or tacit agreements or through mutually understood parallel actions—to reinforce the steps taken by the Koreans themselves in order to help stabilize the situation. Among the kinds of agreements or understandings that might be desirable for the four major powers to consider would be ones guaranteeing the nonuse of force between North and

South, limiting the arms flows to the peninsula, and, perhaps, making Korea a nuclear-free zone. Such possibilities deserve serious study and discussion now, even though it obviously will be some time before conditions develop to the point where they might be realistic and practical.

The situation in Southeast Asia is more complex than that in Northeast Asia, and the problem of achieving real stability there is therefore intrinsically more difficult (although one might argue that in some respects conflicts in Southeast Asia may be less explosive or dangerous, because the major powers now are not likely to view them as being so threatening to their security interests). Here too the trend, in the broadest sense, has been toward détente in the recent period; as compared with the recent past, all of the major powers now seem to be predisposed to try to reduce the level of conflict in the region and forestall big-power confrontation. On balance, also, the gradual trend toward increasing four-power political and economic involvement—which seems likely to grow in the period ahead—may well work slowly to transform contests for influence in and over the region from military rivalries to political and economic competitions. However, the continuation of fighting in the Indochina states, and of American military involvement (especially through the use of air-power) in the region, as well as Chinese and Soviet assistance to their Communist allies, obviously underlines the possibility of renewed conflicts that could involve the major powers.

What is to be hoped for in this situation is the gradual evolution of a new situation in which the major powers—and especially the United States and China—will feel impelled to use their influence to dampen overt military conflicts in the region or at least to contain them and prevent them from spreading. The prospects for stabilizing the military situation in the Indochina states continues to be, as it has for a long time, highly problematic. But if and when fighting there dies down (probably whatever the outcome, I would be inclined to believe), the prospects then for reducing the danger of conflicts elsewhere in the region, and for developing tacit or explicit cooperation among the major powers to stabilize the situation (and to limit the scope of local conflicts if and when they occur), could well improve.

Neutralization

A desirable long-term goal would be the "neutralization" of Southeast Asia. (This is admittedly a somewhat elusive and elastic term, capable of being defined in many different ways; without trying to define it precisely, I use it here to mean essentially a situation in which the major powers abstain from maintaining significant military forces of their own within the region and avoid direct military intervention in local conflicts that do occur.) For neutralization to be effective, in such a way that it would increase rather than decrease the likelihood of stability in the region, a number of preconditions would doubtless have to be met. One would be a gradual emergence of tacit or explicit understandings among the major powers limiting both military and subversive political activities in the region. Another would probably be the development of more effective mechanisms for regional cooperation among those countries within the region that now feel most vulnerable to external threats.

Whether a situation in which "neutralization" seems to be a practical and desirable possibility evolves slowly in the period ahead remains to be seen. Perhaps it is overly optimistic to believe that it can, at least in the near future. Even if it does not, however, the new four-power relationship in Asia may well impose new constraints on all the major powers that will reduce the danger that local conflicts will grow into larger ones involving big-power confrontations that could threaten regional stability—especially if, as currently seems to be the case, the major powers genuinely recognize the liabilities and dangers that major conflicts in the region would involve.

Looking ahead, there are several other kinds of problems whose handling will have very significant effects on the evolving four-power relationship and on the prospects for regional stability. Two categories of particular importance are problems of arms control and problems relating to the ocean areas of Asia.

Arms Control

To date Asia has been very little involved in any important arms control measures. In the period ahead, however, it will become increasingly important to try to devise arms control agreements applicable to the region. There is no question, for example, that if it were possible to reach either tacit or explicit understandings about conventional arms control measures applicable to Korea and/or Southeast Asia—such as measures to reduce the present levels of forces or to limit external arms supplies—the prospects for stability would improve.

In terms of big-power relations, moreover, a question that will become increasingly urgent over time will be whether—and if so how— China can be involved in nuclear arms control. (The need to prevent proliferation in the region will also become more, rather than less, important in the future; and a successful nonproliferation policy will depend greatly on China's stance and policies.) Up to the present Peking has generally taken a strongly negative stance toward the major nuclear arms control measures agreed upon or proposed by the United States and the Soviet Union. Both of the nuclear superpowers, more-over, have tended to believe that, because of China's relative weakness in nuclear terms, there has not been any great urgency about involving it in existing discussions or agreements; it has also been felt, with some justification, that China's involvement might simply complicate and delay the process of reaching U.S.-Soviet agreement.

As China's nuclear capabilities grow, however, the urgency of involving China will clearly increase; and there will come a point when the continued stability of the nuclear balance could well depend on whether Peking is involved in the arms control dialogue. Before long, moreover, the prospects for further meaningful nuclear arms control agreements will probably depend to a considerable extent on Peking's willingness to endorse them.

It may well be unrealistic to hope that Peking will abandon its past views on nuclear arms control and show an active interest in taking part in the process until it achieves what it believes to be a much more dependable and credible deterrent (a more reliable second-strike capability) than at present. It is nevertheless important at least to try to initiate a dialogue now with the Chinese, starting with problems of nuclear stability. Such a dialogue, once begun, could well center at first on discussion of questions relating to the command and control of nuclear weapons and the problems of preventing nuclear accidents. Questions relating to no-first-use and nuclear-free zones also deserve consideration in the near future. Even though China has shown no evidence of willingness to join in any dialogue, even con-cerning such issues, continued efforts should be made to induce it to do so. Over the long run the maintenance of a reasonably stable stra-tegic situation in Asia will become increasingly difficult unless Peking can be convinced that it, like the other nuclear powers, must concern itself with and become involved in efforts to achieve progress in arms control.

Freedom of the Seas

Problems relating to the ocean areas in Asia are relatively new (at least as a major concern to the principal powers); but they have recently come increasingly to the fore, and they will probably become even more important in the period ahead. Like a number of the other problems already discussed, disputes over ocean areas could lead to serious frictions and even conflicts in Asia, yet they could also become a focus for international cooperation in the region; in short, they create both dangers and opportunities. The problems arise because of the chaotic situation that currently exists in relation to the laws of the seas, and the fact that several nations in Asia have put forth conflicting claims regarding the limits of their territorial seas, fishing-rights areas, and exploration rights in continental shelf areas.

One important issue concerns the major straits in Southeast Asia (especially the Malacca Straits), where the conflicting demands of the littoral nations (Malaysia and Indonesia in particular) and the major maritime nations pose a potentially serious problem. The Japanese especially, because of their great dependence on oil from the Middle East, believe that it is of extreme importance to reach agreements that ensure free transit of tankers through the straits. If use of the straits were to be placed in doubt, this conceivably could have far-reaching—and not entirely predictable—effects. As far as the Japanese in particular are concerned, any threat to close the straits might stimulate pressures to reexamine Tokyo's entire security posture. (Some Japanese officials state privately that free transit through the straits is really Japan's most "vital interest" in Southeast Asia—far more important to Tokyo than any existing economic interests in the region itself.)

The most complicated conflicts of interest relating to ocean areas in Asia concern the Yellow and East China Seas, where China, Japan, Korea, and Taiwan have conflicting claims regarding continental shelf areas. These conflicts are important, and could become increasingly so, because of the large deposits of oil (and probably other important resources) that are believed to be located in these areas. The United States is also involved because a number of American oil companies have begun exploration under contract in the area. Because of the large economic stakes involved, there is clearly a potential for serious conflicts over competing claims that could affect the entire pattern of regional relationships. On the other hand, the logic of the situation argues for efforts to reach new kinds of international agreements, involving new forms of regional cooperation, in exploiting oil and other resources in these areas. (The United States, because it possesses the most advanced technology for exploiting under-sea oil resources, conceivably may be able to exert some leverage in the direction of regional cooperation; it should certainly try to do so.) If steps toward practical international cooperation could be taken—for example, among China, Japan, and the United States, and perhaps some of the other claimants as well—this might well have a very positive, constructive impact on broader patterns and relationships in the region. If, instead, there are bitter conflicts over competing claims, the adverse political impact could be substantial.

To sum up, the new four-power balance that is currently evolving in Asia is fundamentally different from anything that had existed in the past. There are a good many reasons to believe that, while it is likely to be fairly fluid in some respects, it could well prove to be reasonably stable in a basic sense and that it may help to create a new situation in which dangers of large-scale military conflicts are less than they were in the bipolar situation that existed in the past. As the discussion above indicates, however, one certainly cannot view the future with complacency. There are numerous dangers and problems that will continue to pose threats to regional stability and security. Some of these could upset the evolving balance and lead to major conflict if they are not dealt with intelligently and skillfully. As in all human situations, the actual course of events will depend upon crucial policy decisions made by key leaders in the major countries involved. Despite the many existing uncertainties, however, there is reason to be cautiously optimistic about the prospects for stability, at least in the period immediately ahead, partly because the kind of four-power relationship that now seems to be evolving probably will operate—more than the bipolar situation did—to impose constraints on all the powers that should, one hopes, help to deter major military conflicts.

3

IMPLICATIONS OF THE DÉTENTE
FOR SINO-AMERICAN TRADE
Jerome Alan Cohen

Although the gradual reduction of U.S. trade restrictions was one of the Nixon administration's principal means of publicly communicating its desire for détente with China, the American decision to seek a new relationship was based primarily on political rather than economic grounds. To be sure, as the 1960s unfolded and China reversed its trade pattern of the previous decade to do roughly three-quarters of its foreign trade with Western Europe and Japan rather than with the Communist world, certain segments of the American business community had begun to press the government to relax trade barriers. Belatedly the Kennedy and Johnson administrations did make certain modest gestures to signal a possible willingness to do business with the PRC, but this was mere tokenism amid the overall conduct of American foreign policy and particularly increasing U.S. involvement in the Vietnam conflict. Essentially those unrequited gestures, like the more successful strategy subsequently masterminded by Henry Kissinger, were made for political and not economic reasons.

Neither Democratic nor Republican administrations succumbed to to the age-old myth of a vast China market. And few knowledgeable businessmen were as naively euphoric as their Australian counterpart who, giving new expression to an idea that has long inflamed the Western imagination, pointed out that "if every Chinese person used one woolen article a year, it would absorb the whole of the Australian wool clip."[1] Economists had driven home the lesson that, whatever the reopening of trade with the mainland might mean for importers of items such as hog bristles, specialty foods, and handicrafts and for a few exporters of grain and machinery, statistically it would amount to a drop in the bucket compared to the total volume of U.S. foreign trade.

The reasons advanced in support of this prediction are by now familiar. Ever since the break with the Soviet Union and the withdrawal from China of Soviet experts in 1960, the PRC has pursued a policy of autarky designed to make itself relatively free of dependence on the outside world. Unlike its rival on Taiwan, which has sought to flourish by taking advantage of the international division of labor and by becoming an integral part of world trading patterns, the People's Republic has allocated a minor role to foreign trade. It seeks to satisfy most of the needs of its largely agrarian population through domestic production and tends to restrict imports to whatever technology and essential goods it cannot produce.

Moreover, it was pointed out, no matter what economic strategy it adopts, China will be severely limited in the amount it can import because of foreign exchange problems. Although China's trade tends to show a favorable balance of modest proportions each year, its accumulated foreign exchange reserves (currently in excess of U.S. $725 million) cannot finance a major increase in imports. Also, it was argued, the advent of trade with the United States, while eliminating barriers that previously precluded China from buying many things that it needs, would not substantially increase the export sales necessary to finance such purchases, because China sells few things that Americans desire. In addition, internal demands would make it difficult for China to increase export production of those items that could be sold to the United States.

Of course slender foreign exchange reserves and export sales would not preclude a significant increase in Sino-American trade were the PRC willing, as Taiwan is, to accept medium- and long-term credits. But, mindful of old China's domination by foreign lenders and of new China's unpleasant experience with its Soviet creditors in the early 1950s, the PRC has proudly proclaimed one of the principles of its policy of self-sufficiency to be the refusal to accumulate foreign debt. Therefore, economists argued, whatever the PRC's objective needs from an outsider's point of view or whatever its import desires according to its own economic strategy, it would not generate a large volume of trade with the United States in the foreseeable future.

Yet one of the most surprising things about the détente—other than that it happened at all—is the substantial impact that it has already had upon Sino-American trade. If in April 1971, when ping-pong diplomacy stunned the world, anyone had predicted that in 1973 the United States and the PRC would do over U.S. $900 million in trade (as American officials were estimating in September 1973), he would have been dismissed as irresponsible. Indeed, in the immediate post-ping-pong period it was far from clear that there would be any Sino-American trade worth mentioning, despite the advent of cultural and political contacts between the two countries.

We should remember that, after years of vainly attempting to interest the United States in trade, tourism, and the exchange of correspondents and cultural groups, in 1960 the PRC had announced that it would no longer seek such contacts "so long as the United States Government still persists in its policy of hostility and aggression against China, still persists in occupying China's territory of Taiwan by armed force, and continues to scheme to create 'two Chinas'. . . ."[2] In 1964 an important Chinese trade official had stated that there could be no "normal trade" until "normal relations are established between our two countries."[3] And as late as April 1970 Chou En-lai had said that trade with the United States was a minor matter about which nothing could be done until the Taiwan problem was settled.[4] In 1971 Chinese officials made it clear that, despite the lack of "normal" relations— that is, diplomatic relations at the ambassadorial level—and despite the failure to settle the Taiwan problem, the invitation to the U.S. ping-pong team was intended to introduce an era of "people-to-people" diplomacy. But they were reluctant to say whether trade would be considered "people-to-people" diplomacy.

Conversations with officials of the then newly established PRC embassy in Ottawa, for example, plainly indicated that trade might be treated differently from cultural exchange. I recall being shocked at the vehemence with which ordinarily pleasant trade officials attacked the American embargo when I succeeded in turning our discussion from politics to trade. "You Americans tried to strangle our revolution," one said, almost shouting. "You tried to use trade to kill the new China." All my attempts to elicit information about trade prospects were parried with the observation that it would be "premature" to focus on "details" until there had been a "fundamental change" in American policy toward Taiwan. The outburst that my inquiries triggered was reminiscent of the harsh statements with which the PRC had rejected American trade overtures in the 1960s.[5]

As late as June 1972, three months after President Nixon's visit, I encountered similar reticence about trade details on the part of officials of the China Council for the Promotion of International Trade (CCPIT) in Peking, even though some direct Sino-American trade had begun and even though the Shanghai communiqué that culminated the President's visit had stated:

> Both sides view bilateral trade as another area from
> which mutual benefit can be derived, and agreed that
> economic relations based on equality and mutual benefit
> are in the interest of the peoples of the two countries.
> They agree to facilitate the progressive development of
> trade between their two countries.[6]

Whenever I asked about trade agreements, modes of protecting industrial property, and other devices for facilitating economic relations, I was told: "Everything depends on the future development of political relations." The director of the Legal Affairs Department of the CCPIT expressed interest in gathering material about the legal aspects of trade and particularly about such technical subjects as international arbitration, trademarks, admiralty, and commodity inspection; but it was too early to talk about the construction of an infrastructure for Sino-American trade, he said. The Chinese attitude seemed to be that we Americans were lusting after the China market and that before the PRC let us have our way, it wanted to be sure that we would give China the political satisfaction that it has so long sought from us.

In addition to demanding changes in American policy toward China as the price for developing trade, at least at certain times the PRC also seemed to be linking trade prospects to termination of American involvement in the Vietnam conflict. In April 1972, for example, Vice Premier Li Hsien-nien reportedly stated that Sino-American trade could not be greatly expanded so long as the United States "continues its bombing of North Vietnam."[7]

Of course, for most of the first year after ping-pong it remained uncertain to what extent the United States itself would take steps to facilitate Sino-American trade. It was not until February 14, 1972, that the gradually evolving U.S. policy placed trade with China on substantially the same basis as trade with the Soviet Union, authorizing American firms to export a broad range of nonstrategic commodities to the PRC without obtaining Department of Commerce permission for each transaction.[8] And it was not until the summer of 1972, with the approval of the sale of Boeing aircraft and RCA permanent earth satellite ground stations, that it became clear that in those transactions for which a specific license was still required, the Commerce Department would not unreasonably prohibit exports on the ground that they might prejudice national security.

Moreover, prior to the July 15, 1971, announcement of Henry Kissinger's secret trip to Peking and of President Nixon's projected visit, most major American businesses had shown little overt interest in the China trade. This was not only because they believed the China market to have a limited potential but also because they were extremely concerned about the possibility of unfavorable domestic reactions to any news of their doing business with "Red China." Some of the largest U.S. corporations were still unhappy about episodes in which their negotiations for large-scale ventures in the Soviet Union or certain East European countries had aborted because of the pressure of public opinion. I recall that at a 1963 meeting convened in San Francisco's World Trade Center by former Congressman Charles Porter, who was hoping to mobilize a business lobby to open up the China trade, virtually all of the major corporations represented were reluctant to go on record. Even in the spring of 1971, after ping-pong raised the possibility that trade might follow, most of the major corporations, far from vigorously probing the China market, continued to play the role of reluctant dragons. More than one executive echoed the sentiments of the company president who told me: "I've been burned before. If the U.S. Government wants us to do business with China, I want a letter from the Secretary of State telling me that it is in the national interest for us to do so. That will give me something to show the stockholders and irate citizens who descend upon me. Otherwise, I don't want to get involved."[9]

In February 1972, Secretary of Commerce Maurice Stans predicted that Sino-American trade would develop at a much slower rate than Soviet-American trade.[10] Yet during 1971, almost four decades after normalization of relations and after half a century of trade, the United States did less than $220 million of business with the Soviet Union.[11] And trade with China that year—all of it indirect—had amounted to less than $5 million.[12] The most elaborate academic estimate of the total volume of direct Sino-American trade that could be anticipated by 1980 predicted that, although it might conceivably rise as high as $900 million per year, it would probably remain well below that figure.[13] The consensus of economists continued to be "that—except under most optimistic assumptions—the level of commercial interchange between the United States and China is likely to be of rather modest proportions, even if all restrictions on the movement of nonstrategic goods were removed by both sides."[14]

By 1973, however, the picture looked rather different. As Henry Kissinger somewhat puckishly noted at the end of February, when announcing the decision by Peking and Washington to establish liaison offices in each other's capital, the development of Sino-American trade had outstripped the predictions of economists.[15] Figures for 1972 had revealed an impressive rise to $93.5 million, almost two-thirds of it American exports, and the initial projections of U.S. government analysts for 1973 anticipated a jump to perhaps $300 million.[16] By the end of May the evidence suggested that the total for the year might in fact reach $500 million, and Undersecretary of State William J. Casey, instead of echoing Assistant Secretary Marshall Green's "note of caution" of the previous October, referred to "the huge Chinese market" and recognized that economic relations had developed "at a rapid rate . . . presenting the possibility that the United States will become one of the top two or three trading partners of the People's Republic of China."[17] By midsummer, although U.S. Bureau of the Census reports of shipments and arrivals for the first few months of the year seemed inexplicably low, State Department specialists were predicting that total trade for the year would surpass $700 million. And by September they were estimating more than $900 million.

If consummated transactions do indeed approach that figure, this will be a staggering development, especially since Washington and Peking have not yet even constructed the framework that will eventually boost their bilateral trade to a higher level. The diplomatic liaison offices opened only recently; the U.S. Commerce Department and the American business community are still organizing to meet the new situation; and the PRC and the United States have only begun to discuss matters such as trade, maritime, civil aviation, and consular agreements, most-favored-nation treatment, and credits.

How should one account for this surprising development? Obviously many factors have played a role, including the devaluation of the dollar, which makes American goods more competitive abroad. A continuing improvement in Sino-American political relations during the 18 months following the Nixon visit was, of course, the prime factor. Especially significant was the termination of American involvement in the Vietnam conflict in early 1973, which removed a major obstacle to trade expansion. Although full normalization of relations between Washington and Peking must await some resolution of the Taiwan problem, the PRC has plainly abandoned the policy of making normalization a prerequisite to substantial trade.[18] It had been assumed that when the opportunity arose, China would purchase from the United States both high-level technology and high-quality agricultural commodities that were unavailable elsewhere. But China has also begun to buy from America when the equivalent is available elsewhere, and it has not even insisted on limiting its trade with individual American companies to those that abstain from participation in Taiwan's booming economy. For example, Peking could have purchased telecommunications equipment from over 20 firms other than RCA, half of them non-American. Not only did it choose an American firm, but one that enjoys a large investment in Taiwan. Similarly, the PRC recently selected the Chase Manhattan Bank to be the first American bank to maintain correspondent relations with the Bank of China, although Chase has established a branch in Taipei and an office in Moscow. "No questions asked" is frequently reported to be the Chinese attitude about the activities of American companies in Taiwan and other places, and various American traders shuttle back and forth between Taiwan and the mainland with only the most perfunctory efforts at concealment.

On the American side we have also witnessed a rapidly increasing desire to expand the China trade. The present Secretary of Commerce, Frederick B. Dent, has bluntly stated that it is the intention of his department to engage "in a no-holds-barred effort to make the American businessman more competitive and to facilitate his entry into this market of growing importance to the total U.S. trade picture."[19] This has been visible in the sympathetic hearing that the

Commerce Department's Office of Export Control, after initial pressure from the White House and State Department, has given to applicants for validated licenses for the export of products that might be regarded as "strategic." Indeed, the scope of what exports may be considered detrimental to national security is now so diminished that the Chinese are currently exploring the acquisition of nuclear power plants, the export of which will require approval by the Atomic Energy Commission (AEC). It should be noted that although the PRC, unlike some East European countries, has thus far refused to fill out Commerce Department forms provided for the purpose of identifying the end user and the use to which potentially strategic U.S. exports are to be put, increasingly it has been providing the information in substance without cooperating in form. AEC approval of the sale of nuclear power plants would, of course, involve the Chinese in a greater degree of cooperation than anything yet encountered, raising such questions as end-use safeguards and on-site inspection.

The attitude of American businessmen also has changed dramatically within a two-year period. No longer is there much fear of courting an adverse reaction from stockholders or the public by demonstrating interest in the China trade. On the contrary, doing business with the PRC has become the "in" thing. At a symposium on the subject in October 1972, I was astounded when the executive vice-president of a well-known manufacturer asked whether Chinese state trading representatives would mind if during a negotiation the American side released publicity concerning the negotiation "in order to maintain a progressive image with its stockholders and the public." At a more recent conference Secretary of Commerce Dent assured the multitude assembled to discuss "this new national commercial initiative" that "[a]s you serve your stockholders in this respect, please be assured that you are also serving the national interest."[20] The proliferation of China trade symposia also testifies to the fresh interest of the business community, as does the fact that many thousands of American businessmen have besieged the PRC with requests to attend the Chinese Export Commodities Fair in Kwangchow, popularly known as the Canton Fair. As a new image of the People's Republic takes shape, American traders are beginning to describe their counterparts on the mainland in the same terms as they do those on Taiwan. As one speaker put it at a recent symposium, "they're very much like us—honest, hard-working, smart, punctual, clean, and humorous."

A broad segment of American business has rather quickly become involved in the China market. In addition to Boeing, RCA, and Chase Manhattan, some of the other well-known early entrants are Monsanto (sale of man-made fibers), SOHIO (licensing of fiber technology), M. W. Kellogg (construction of complete ammonia plants), Weyerhaeuser (sale of liner board) Western Union International (satellite telecommunications sale), Continental Grain (wheat sale), and Macy's and Nieman-Marcus (handicraft imports). Many other well-known companies are now negotiating; a host of major oil companies have begun to vie for China's attention; a large number of lesser known companies have already concluded transactions; and export-import firms, some especially created for the new China trade, have become very active.

Where will this whirlwind end? Plainly enough, one cannot expect a continuation of anything like the rate of growth that Sino-American trade has experienced since the beginning of 1972, even assuming, as I do, a continuation of the present favorable political climate. In fact, it is possible, though I believe unlikely, that 1973 may not be equaled in 1974. After all, the substantial grain and cotton purchases that have unexpectedly swelled this year's total may not recur. Economic developments within both China and the United States, including the evolution of domestic policies unconnected with Sino-American relations, clearly will have an important effect; but I profess no competence to forecast them. Yet institutional factors and policy questions specifically pertaining to Sino-American relations will also be important and deserve our consideration.

NEW INSTITUTIONS FOR THE CHINA TRADE

The establishment of liaison offices represented a first step toward building the infrastructure of Sino-American trade, for they are charged with handling commercial as well as other problems. The extent to which the new offices will foster trade, however, remains uncertain. Thus far only a few staff members in each office have been assigned to commercial matters, and both the Chinese and American offices have been at pains to emphasize the limitations this imposes. In a speech delivered shortly after the opening of the U.S. office in Peking, Alfred Jenkins, one of its two deputy chiefs, described its functions relating to trade:

> At the outset these officers will be working to build rela-
> tionships at all levels with the Ministry of Foreign Trade,
> Chinese state trading corporations, the China Council for
> the Promotion of International Trade, and other organiza-
> tions concerned with China's foreign commerce. As in all
> our endeavors, the aim of these contacts will be to create
> an atmosphere of mutual understanding and cooperation
> between the Chinese trading corporations and ourselves
> and our businessmen, in which there can be a smooth,
> effective and expanding interchange of people and informa-
> tion between our two trading communities. We want to

help the Chinese side learn more about American ways
of doing business, and to bring to their attention the full
range of goods and services which the United States has
to offer. At the same time we need to learn more about
those products and processes of greatest interest to the
Chinese, so that we can go back to our own businessmen
with trade opportunities on which to base specific initiatives. We want also to make available to the Chinese as
much information as possible about our own market, so
that they can expand their exports to the United States.
It will take time, of course, to develop the optimum range
of working contacts, but we will need to move forward
with this multifaceted task. We have already met a number of top officials in the state trading corporations and
have been pleased to note their expressions of interest
in working with the Liaison Office. We are hopeful that
we can succeed in building a climate in Peking in which
there can be easy access for U.S. businessmen in their
initiatives to the Chinese trading community.

We are also at work on another important aspect of
our commercial activities in Peking, that of meeting with
and assisting Americans when they come to China for
business discussions. In the past several weeks we have
seen quite a number of U.S. business representatives. I
hope we have succeeded in providing useful advice and
information during the course of their discussions with
the Chinese. Once again our aim here is to promote
mutual understanding between our businessmen and their
Chinese counterparts, so that what we Americans have to
offer gets clearly across to the other side, and that what
comes back from the Chinese is clearly understood. Too
often, when there are such great cultural and linguistic
differences between American businessmen and their
Chinese opposite numbers, it is all too easy for innocent
misunderstandings to arise, with opportunities lost as a
result. We do not want this to happen in Peking. Within
our resources, we want to be as much involved in your
efforts as you find it useful for us to be, so that we can
help insure that this does not happen. We will be happy,
when called upon, to provide advice and other appropriate
and feasible support; we will be willing, when the occasion calls for it, to accompany businessmen to the state
trading corporations; we might even be persuaded from
time to time to join in those wondrous Peking banquets
which are so happily a part of Chinese business negotiations. In short, we will assist you in any way we can,

taking into account the limitations imposed upon us by our small numbers and also, of course, the desires and interests of our Chinese hosts.

Another aspect of our work which I might mention is our hope to have officers on hand at every Canton Fair, to help our businessmen assess trends, and again to provide advice, assistance, and other support to our traders as they go through the sometimes exhausting experience of the month-long fair routines.[21]

Although Jenkins indicated willingness to help individual firms once their representatives reach China, he said the liaison office did not have the resources to become the forwarding point for either requests for visas or for invitations to enter China, nor could it forward brochures or other information to China's state trading corporations. He advised businessmen to address themselves directly to the Chinese corporations but to keep the Peking liaison office apprised of their initiatives, perhaps by sending it copies of correspondence. My conversations with the economic officers of the PRC's Washington liaison office suggest that they view their functions in a similar way. Because of their limited resources, they too emphasize the desirability of direct contacts between American firms and Chinese corporations and suggest that copies of correspondence be sent to their office.

Unless the staff of the American office is enlarged, it seems unlikely that it will long be able to render much in the way of assistance on individual negotiations in China. Moreover, it may be undesirable for it to attempt to do so, exposing the office as it would to charges of conflict of interest or favoritism toward one firm rather than another in the allocation of its scarce resources. The really valuable potential of the commercial staff would seem to lie in the more generalized services outlined by Mr. Jenkins and especially in collecting, analyzing, synthesizing, and presenting to the Chinese trade organization, on the one hand, and to the American government and business community, on the other, the perceptions, problems, and suggestions of the other side. In this respect both liaison offices can play a very useful catalytic role in facilitating trade.

The U.S. government has recently taken a number of other steps to develop its institutional capability for coping with the centrally controlled state trading monopolies of the socialist states. In March 1973 the President established the East-West Trade Policy Committee (EWTPC), with Secretary of the Treasury and Assistant to the President George Shultz as chairman and Secretary Dent as vice-chairman, in an effort to centralize government trade policy more effectively than in the past. It is not yet clear what role, if any, the EWTPC will play in China trade. In the fall of 1972, the Commerce

Department established the Bureau of East-West Trade "to focus more sharply on the problems of dealing with monolithic foreign trade corporations."[22] Although the Bureau has been largely preoccupied with Soviet and East European developments and has lacked sufficient expertise relating to China, it is gradually becoming prepared to meet the new challenge.

Apart from disseminating information and reviewing applications for export licenses, the Bureau's effort to date in the China field has been concentrated upon the creation of the National Council for United States-China Trade, a private, nonprofit corporation. According to the Council's own description:

> The National Council will provide a focal point for the initiation of trade contacts, including those with the China Council for the Promotion of International Trade (CCPIT) and appropriate officials and state trading agencies of the People's Republic of China. It will promote the dissemination of commercial information to interested members of the United States business community and appropriate entities in the People's Republic of China. The National Council will also provide a forum for the discussion of trade issues with the appropriate officials of the People's Republic of China, and where appropriate, act in an advisory capacity to the United States Government on issues which may affect trade, economic cooperation and other relations between United States firms and the appropriate entities in the People's Republic of China.[23]

More specifically, the Council plans to exchange visits with the CCPIT; sponsor the visits of U.S. trade missions and other specialized delegations to China; assist businessmen in obtaining invitations to China and after they arrive there; help Chinese trade missions and specialized delegations visit the United States; facilitate trade exhibitions; provide China with comprehensive data on the American economy and on manufacturers, agricultural exporters, fairs and exhibits, industrial and trade associations, and pertinent laws and regulations; obtain similar information from China; provide a China market research service; conduct seminars; and publish a bulletin.[24]

At the Council's organizational conference on May 31, 1973, Secretary Dent frankly explained that "[t]he necessity for government to intercede so deeply in affairs normally the preserve of the private sector results from the fact that foreign trade is a monopoly of the state in the East." He noted that "this centralized state control politicizes commercial relations with the socialist states to a degree unknown with our other major trading partners" and pointed out that "[w]e have responded with measures of our own."[25]

The Council, of course, is the creation of the White House as well as the Commerce and State Departments and, as such, bears some of the marks of politicization. Its chairman and several other members of the Board of Directors, which was constituted only after much political tugging and hauling, are old friends of the President. The White House even controlled the selection of an academic "China watcher" to address the Council's organizational conference, vetoing not only specialists who had a trace of a McGovern connection but also anyone from the Brookings Institution.

The original 20-man (no women) Board of Directors consisted of 16 businessmen, 3 bankers and a lawyer. At the time of their appointment in March 1973, few directors had any experience in the China trade, although their acceptance of the coveted directorships obviously implied an eagerness to enter the field. Shortly after the Council's organizational conference, for example, one of its two vice-chairmen, David Rockefeller of the Chase Manhattan Bank, went to the PRC for the first time and established the first American banking relationship there. The Board reflects a very strong export orientation even though perhaps the principal problem in Sino-American trade is how to increase American imports. Only one of the original 16 businessmen-directors represents a company that is an importer, and he resigned soon after his appointment for reasons unrelated to the Council.

Although the Council was slow to get organized and appeared to be floundering in its earliest phase, it has recently begun to show signs of offering more than promises. Christopher H. Phillips, a former state senator, diplomat, banker, and President of the United States Council of the International Chamber of Commerce, has taken office as President and Executive Director. Phillips, who has no special acquaintance with China, played a role in Sino-American relations when, as U.S. Deputy Representative at the United Nations, he announced that the United States would no longer oppose PRC representation in the UN but would seek to retain a seat for the Republic of China on Taiwan.[26]

Both the PRC and the United States regard the Council as the counterpart to the CCPIT in Peking, which, despite its nongovernmental form, is clearly part of China's foreign-trade organization. The CCPIT informs foreign business groups about China's foreign trade, acquires information on foreign markets on behalf of Chinese enterprises, invites foreign firms and delegations to China and sends similar Chinese representatives overseas, organizes trade fairs at home and abroad, and provides facilities for the mediation and arbitration of disputes and for the registration of foreign trademarks. The Council, as its first move, plans to send a delegation to the PRC in November to open discussions with the CCPIT and to visit the autumn Canton

Fair. In an effort to demonstrate the potential value of Council membership (initial membership fees of $2,500 for corporations with sales or gross income of $50 million per year or more and $1,000 for others, plus annual dues as yet undetermined, appear to have inhibited applications), the Council announced that it hoped to secure admission to the Canton Fair for many members and to arrange other visits to China.27

One of the Council's more important domestic tasks will be to develop satisfactory working relationships with the genuinely private American trade organizations such as the National Association of Manufacturers, the East-West Trade Council, and the China Trade Association that can usefully supplement the Council's activities.

Another challenge facing the Council will be to demonstrate its interest in serving small businesses as well as the big companies — which, after all, have the resources to undertake independent exploration of the China trade. And the Council will have to be sensitive in dealing with organized labor, consumer groups, and other organizations. The Council, which needs expertise, will also have to decide the extent to which it should draw upon the considerable reservoir of academic talent in the field of Chinese studies and whether in doing so it should continue to allow politics to take command.

The Chinese have made it very plain that the Council is their chosen instrument in the American business community and that other American organizations interested in the China trade should cooperate with the Council. Yet perhaps because internal developments in China required delay until establishment of a new Communist Party line and consolidation of the leadership at the Tenth Party Congress, the Chinese, while generally encouraging and very genial, have been quite vague in responding to the Council's specific requests. A frequently heard reply is: "When you meet with the CCPIT, you can arrange these matters." Unfortunately, because of the Party Congress the initial Council meeting with the CCPIT was postponed from mid-summer to November. It is also noteworthy that the PRC has sent ping-pong players, acrobats, scientists, doctors, gymnasts, journalists, and water conservation specialists to the United States but no trade delegations, even though Chinese trade delegations frequently visit all the other major industrial countries as well as many smaller ones. The Boeing Company has had over 50 Chinese airline officials, engineers, technicians, flight crew members, and trade representatives in residence at Seattle for varying periods in connection with the PRC's purchase of jet aircraft.

In view of this satisfactory experience, the successful visits of other Chinese groups to this country, and the PRC's burgeoning interest in trade with the United States, one can probably anticipate the arrival of trade groups in the near future. Peking may simply be waiting for the appropriate host organization, the National Council, to make arrangements with CCPIT. This would be consistent with the rough overall understanding that seems to have been worked out between Peking and Washington, whereby the Committee on Scholarly Communication with the People's Republic of China will invite academic, scientific, and professional groups to the United States; the National Committee on United States-China Relations will invite athletic and cultural groups; and the Council will invite trade groups.*

CRITICAL DECISIONS FOR THE FUTURE OF TRADE

A certain amount of time undoubtedly will be required to establish cooperative trading relationships between two countries that have been bitter enemies for two decades and that have very different cultural and historical backgrounds and political, social, and economic systems. In the near future a large number of complex and controversial decisions must be made by elites in Peking and Washington within the broader context of substantive problems not directly related to Sino-American relations and through domestic political processes that are being redefined under the stress of internal tensions. The decisions that gradually emerge will determine the full implications of the détente for Sino-American trade.

Some questions are already being negotiated by the two governments. Early in 1973 they "agreed in principle" to settle the problems of American private claims for property of U.S. citizens taken by the PRC (totalling almost $200 million plus interest) and of PRC claims for assets blocked by the United States (roughly $78 million). No

---

*The spring 1973 Canton Fair offered an example of what may be Chinese ambivalence toward Sino-American cooperation on trade. In addition to permitting participation by well over 100 American businessmen and a visit by one of the commercial officers of the U.S. liaison office who was en route to Peking, the Chinese also allowed the U.S. Consulate-General in Hong Kong to send one of its commercial specialists. Yet officials of the Ministry of Foreign Trade, the state trading corporations, and the CCPIT studiously avoided responding to the specialist's requests to call upon them. This treatment contrasted sharply with the warm reception that the PRC has accorded to officials of the liaison office in Peking. The explanation may lie in the Chinese perception of the niceties of diplomatic protocol, in view of the fact that the Hong Kong Consulate-General, unlike the liaison office, has no official relation to the PRC. Or this may simply have been another phenomenon of the transitional period.

normal trading relations can occur until these issues are settled. In the current circumstances, if a Chinese trade exhibit, ship, or airplane arrived in this country, some private claimants might seek to attach the property in an effort to satisfy their claims through litigation, creating considerable political embarrassment as well as difficulty for expanding trade relations. And Peking is understandably reluctant to allow American banks to play their customary role in financing purchases until PRC assets that many of them hold are released.[28] Although reaching a settlement has already taken a good deal longer than Washington anticipated, these issues may well be disposed of before this essay appears. U.S. public claims against the PRC for government property seized in China presumably will be handled as part of the larger financial settlement that can be expected to accompany the establishment of formal diplomatic relations between Washington and Peking. Until that time they may constitute an obstacle to the extension of Export-Import Bank credits and other government financing.

Also on the agenda in the immediate future will be a variety of topics upon which agreements will be required if an appropriate framework for Sino-American trade is to be erected. A trade agreement will probably be concluded between the two governments, although it is possible that an "unofficial" agreement might be made between the CCPIT and the National Council for United States-China Trade. The subject matter of a trade agreement may be narrow or broad and its provisions vague or precise. A Sino-American agreement might cover most of the problems dealt with in the 1972 Soviet-American trade agreement as well as many others presented by the very newness of the relationship.[29] Given the pluralistic nature of American life, the agreement is likely to be suggestive rather than specific about the total trade to be conducted within a certain period and the types and volumes of particular goods to be traded, stating goals in a general way and pledging best efforts to achieve them. Among the subjects for which it may provide are reciprocal most-favored-nation (MFN) treatment; protection against market "disruption" by imports; currency payments in U.S. dollars or any other freely convertible currency; reciprocal establishment of official commercial offices; establishment of offices by private American firms in China and visa, housing, travel, and import privileges for their employees; reciprocal recognition of corporate entities as legal persons that can sue and be sued in domestic courts and that can have their property seized in satisfaction of court judgments; specified procedures and guarantees for the arbitration of contract disputes in third countries and the enforcement of arbitration awards; reciprocal protection of patents, trademarks, and copyrights; reciprocal commodity inspection and certification arrangements; and the extension and guarantee of credit facilities.

Although the PRC ordinarily has awaited the establishment of formal diplomatic relations before concluding bilateral maritime and civil aviation agreements, it is anticipated that Washington and Peking will soon negotiate such agreements. We can also expect the United States to make an effort to win Chinese acceptance of a consular agreement that would spell out reciprocal protections for the personal security of their nationals who are visiting the other country, in order to guarantee American officials at least prompt access to detained nationals; or it may be that such a guarantee will become part of the code of diplomatic privileges for the liaison offices that is already being discussed.[30] It is also possible that a joint U.S.-China commercial commission, similar to the commission that the United States and the Soviet Union established in 1972, may soon be organized to oversee and facilitate the implementation of the various agreements.

Plainly enough, this network of agreements would not only make Sino-American relations considerably more intimate but would also integrate the PRC more closely into the international economic arena and significantly affect its domestic polity. Yet many other difficult decisions also confront the leaders in Peking. For example, to what extent should they adopt the many suggestions now being received about how to sell more to the United States and thus increase foreign exchange earnings to finance requisite purchases? It is one thing to adjust the label on canned goods and the goods themselves to meet U.S. Food and Drug Administration (FDA) requirements, but should the PRC agree to market its products under "private label" so that what usually is sold as "Great Wall mandarin oranges" is instead sold as "Safeway Stores mandarin oranges"? Of course, resort to private label would enable China to sell much larger quantities in the United States in the near future than it otherwise would, but this would require PRC economic planners to allocate proportionately greater resources to the export market and away from domestic consumption or to divert exports from old trading partners—both unattractive choices. It would also demand some curbing of national pride and a willingness to slow the process of familiarizing the American market with Chinese brand names.

One can easily tick off a host of similar questions that have arisen during recent negotiations at the Canton Fair. Should the PRC allow would-be purchasers of frozen seafood to visit the freezing plants to discuss possible technical improvements that would make the seafood more acceptable to the American market? To what extent should American equipment salesmen have an opportunity to meet the technicians, engineers, and management of the prospective end users rather than negotiate through the less-informed middlemen of the state export-import corporation? Is the PRC willing to enter into long-term sales contracts so as to guarantee purchasers a steady source of supply?

Will its manufacturers adapt to American styles, packaging, and quality control? Moreover, to what extent will Peking seek to increase the processing of raw materials prior to export rather than continue the less lucrative export of unprocessed materials? How these questions are answered could have an important cumulative impact upon Chinese society as well as upon Chinese trade.

Legal questions also abound. Should the PRC acquiesce in the request of American shrimp importers to draw the contract so that they have no obligation to pay if upon arrival the shrimp fail to meet FDA standards? Such a provision is a familiar one in American contracts with other countries but is unknown to the Chinese. An American importer who accommodated to Chinese practice suffered a heavy loss as a result. More broadly, will the PRC develop an identifiable civil and commercial law upon which foreign traders can rely? Or, in lieu of that, will its corporations specify in their contracts that the law of a given foreign country should govern the transaction? Many American businessmen are concerned by the legal vagaries of dealing with China, and their concern has been magnified by awareness of the difficulties that some businessmen from other countries have recently encountered in persuading the Chinese to fulfill contracts and to honor arbitration clauses.

Pricing is obviously a critical problem and came to the fore at the spring 1973 Canton Fair, when most traders were stunned by the large price increases in many export items. I recall my own shock upon confirming the rumor that the PRC was indeed asking $14 per bottle of mao-tai CIF New York. (It's good, it's strong, but Remy-Martin it isn't.) Various explanations have been offered for the increases. There is widespread agreement that the PRC, seeking to maximize its foreign exchange earnings at a time when it was experiencing shortages in many export commodities, sought to charge what the traffic would bear. Some observers believe that in certain instances China may have resorted to very high prices to "save face" by making the commodity so unattractive that buyers would not discover how inadequate stocks were. The entry of American buyers was also noted as a factor by jaded Europeans, who openly pined for the good old days before the newcomers had "spoiled" the market. My lengthy conversations with Chinese trade officials at the fair suggested that several other factors were at work. One was a feeling that China had been exploited at past fairs by traders who bought cheaply in Canton and then reaped unduly high profits, especially during the recent vogue for things Chinese. At a time when world market prices have been rising steadily, the Chinese also seemed to be experiencing the inconvenience of making so many of their export contracts during a semi-annual one-month period; they often explained price increases in terms not only of recent world market rises but also of ones that were anticipated prior to the next fair. Finally, in certain cases pricing practices appeared to reflect lack of familiarity with the structure and functioning of the American marketing system. Whatever the explanation, the bloom came off the rose at the spring 1973 fair, as few businessmen got the impression that the PRC was adhering to its maxim of "friendship first, trade second" and many returned home without having made projected purchases. A much greater effort to understand the American market would seem to be called for so that the PRC can arrive at an optimum pricing policy.

Of course, whatever steps the PRC takes to increase its exports will be insufficient to finance the purchase of the capital equipment imports required for modernization. One of the principal decisions confronting the PRC in these circumstances concerns the extent to which it should modify its policy of refusing medium- and long-term foreign credits and return to its policy of the early 1950s of accepting foreign assistance, this time from the major capitalist states rather than the Soviet Union. Although the Chinese have not yet decided to go into long-term foreign debt, they are reconsidering the matter. The first sign of a new Chinese attitude toward credit came with the negotiation of agreements that euphemistically called for medium-term "deferred payments." Indeed, I have seen a sophisticated Chinese diplomat smile broadly while reiterating that credits were unacceptable but deferred payments might be possible. More recently, the PRC has openly negotiated intermediate-term loans. It is very difficult to predict the amount of long-term borrowing from abroad that Peking might prove willing to absorb, but one informed estimate suggests that it would not be unreasonable to anticipate a figure of $2.5 billion for a five-year period.[31] If China should opt for credits in a substantial way, it would have to decide many detailed questions, among them how much to accept from a given country and whether this aid should be "tied" to trade with that country. The determination of Chinese leaders never again to allow foreigners to gain control over China through the extension of loans and never again to rely heavily on any single country makes it likely that the PRC would prefer relatively modest amounts of aid from a number of different countries rather than look to only one source. The desire to foster friendly relations with all the capitalist states and to secure an optimum bargaining position would also lead to this conclusion, although it is possible that other factors might make massive loans from the United States alone attractive. In any event the acceptance of American loans would give Sino-American trade a further boost.

A decision to resort to long-term borrowing will not be easy for China's leaders, who derive considerable satisfaction from the economic and political independence of their "self-reliance" policy. An alternative that permitted them to enhance foreign exchange reserve substantially while maintaining the posture of self-reliance should seem attractive to them. Such an alternative appears to be available if the PRC is willing to cooperate with foreign firms in extracting and marketing China's vast, previously untapped mineral and fuel resources. In addition to natural resources, China has skilled, disciplined, inexpensive labor. What it lacks is the high-level technology and capital necessary to make the most of its advantages. The United States and other industrialized nations have the requisite technology and capital, as well as an insatiable appetite for natural resources and an appreciation of Chinese labor. These circumstances would seem to make cooperation highly probable if the PRC is bent upon becoming a strong, modern nation. Indeed, one might expect the PRC to emulate the strategy of its Soviet rival, which has been energetically seeking to enlist the United States, Japan, West Germany, and other countries in precisely this kind of cooperation in an effort to develop its great economic potential.

Yet again ideological considerations, especially the preoccupation with national independence, complicate China's decision-making. Certain forms of cooperation with foreign firms are beyond the pale. China is unlikely to follow the example of some of the East European Communist countries, particularly Rumania and Hungary, by authorizing its state agencies to enter into joint production ventures. Foreigners may not make direct investments in China. Chou En-lai has emphasized to American visitors that not only wholly owned foreign subsidiaries but also joint ventures will not be tolerated. The Chinese did not require the Soviet Union to liquidate its interest in the Sino-Soviet joint stock companies of the early 1950s in order to clear the way for American equity ownership. Nevertheless, it should be possible to work out other forms of cooperation that will not involve foreign investment in China, at least in name. China is not the first developing country to have to accommodate the spirit of nationalism to the facts of national interest and international interdependence. For example, production-sharing agreements have authorized certain American oil companies to make what is functionally equivalent to, but still distinct from, investment in Indonesia in return for prescribed rights to a share of the oil extracted on terms that respect equality and mutual benefit. Imaginative businessmen and their lawyers are currently exposing the Chinese to the possibilities of production-sharing, service contracts, management fees, licensing arrangements, and a variety of other devices. One should also not overlook the possibility that companies owned or controlled by the PRC in Hong Kong, Singapore, Macao, and other places may be willing to join American firms in marketing PRC products abroad.

Although the PRC has not yet yielded in any significant way on its frequently expressed refusal to allow outsiders to participate in the development of its resources, it plainly is reexamining the question. There have been a few encouraging signals, and the logic of cooperation may ultimately prevail. As Undersecretary of State William J. Casey recently summarized the situation:

> [The Chinese] are realistic enough to perceive that the advantages in price and other advantages in [the sale of] consumer goods may become increasingly fleeting as the mobility of equipment and technology increases. On the other hand, trade advantages based on resources and established transportation and marketing patterns remain. Within the framework of these realities, with China's willingness to employ talent, pay for technology and sell raw materials I believe American business will find a way to work out mutually profitable development projects which will accelerate China's ability to bring specialized American products to the huge Chinese market. One of the important interests of our liaison mission in Peking will be to explore and assess the way the Chinese are prepared to proceed to utilize American technology and skills in their effort to develop their resources.[32]

Should this optimism prove warranted, one can foresee the possibility that before long China, which is already self-sufficient in oil, may be marketing in the United States and Japan large surpluses extracted with American cooperation, thereby raising the China trade to new dimensions.

In the interim Peking will have to resolve a number of questions relating to the wise expenditure of existing foreign exchange reserves. For example, to what extent should it seek to acquire technology and "know-how" through licensing agreements such as the few that were recently concluded with American firms?[33] Should it attempt to make licensing a more attractive option by abandoning its refusal to permit the licensor to verify compliance with contract restrictions by monitoring manufacture? Again one runs into Chinese sensitivity to foreign interference. Lucian Pye has stated:

> I have heard the most powerful officials in the Chinese foreign office speak of China's determination not to allow foreigners through trade and the sale of technology to control China in any manner. This fear of being dominated through the presumed leverage of trade has manifested itself in the extraordinary lengths the Chinese have gone to purchase spare parts and not enter into maintenance agreements. One might hope that one of the early effects

of expanding trade with American firms would be to convince the Chinese that they do not need to follow their current practice of purchasing up to three years of stocks in
spare parts, and that it would be more prudent to spend
the money that would be so tied up in buying further productive machinery. At present the Chinese, ever mindful
of the damage they experienced to their economy when
the Soviets arbitrarily cut off all further dealings with
them, feel that they must protect themselves against the
danger of comparable behavior from other quarters. Their
calculation is that extensive stocks of spare parts will
give them not only a cushion against such an eventuality,
but also models for copying so as to speed the realization
of Mao's goal of "Self-Reliance."[34]

Of course, not all of China's future decisions affecting Sino-
American trade will arise in a bilateral context. The PRC must also
arrive at an optimum multilateral economic posture that will be reflected in its relations with the United States. It has already begun
to take part in the United Nations Commission on Trade and Development (UNCTAD) and in the UN Economic Commission for Asia and
the Far East (ECAFE), and it probably will adhere eventually to relevant multilateral treaties such as the Universal Copyright Convention
and the UN Convention on the Recognition and Enforcement of Foreign
Arbitral Awards. It is less clear whether the PRC will emulate Rumania in the near future by participating in the General Agreement
on Tariffs and Trade, the International Monetary Fund, and the World
Bank, although even these possibilities, once thought out of the question, seem to be more likely.
    Our earlier discussion indicated that the United States will also
have to make a number of decisions that will affect the growth of Sino-
American trade. For example, what kind of trade agreement should
it conclude? Should the United States grant China MFN treatment
with respect to customs duties, export-import rules and formalities,
and other matters? Should it make available Export-Import Bank
loans and guarantees and other credit arrangements? Should it restrict
the export of grain and other commodities that are in short supply at
home? To what extent should it allow national security considerations
to interfere with exports? How should the United States deal with the
problem of restricting the entry of Chinese textiles?
    American firms also will have to decide how much in the way of
resources they should allocate to exploring the China trade and how
flexible they should be in adapting to its peculiarities. I previously
mentioned the shrimp importer who gambled—and lost—by not insisting on a contract provision that conditioned his obligation to pay upon

FDA approval. Boeing had to decide whether a "confidentiality clause" in the contract was likely to prove an adequate substitute for the usual measures for the protection of its technology. SOHIO had to decide whether licensing without monitoring arrangements would be worth the risk. RCA had to decide whether to accept contracts that failed to specify the law that would govern any dispute. Virtually every China trader has to decide whether to take a chance on the uncertainties of Peking's preferred modes of settling disputes, and an increasing number of companies may have to decide whether to expose their employees to the risks of residing in China. Space precludes analysis here of the pros and cons of these and many other public and private decisions facing the United States, but I cannot resist a word about MFN treatment and related problems.

The dramatic 1973 increase in Sino-American trade consists almost entirely of American exports, so that the United States currently sells to the PRC roughly a dozen times what it buys. This presents a serious problem. Although China does not insist on maintaining an evenly balanced relationship with each of its trading partners, it has become concerned about developing a gross and long-run imbalance in its trade with the United States. For example, at the recent Canton Fair, officials who were negotiating China's acquisition of foreign machinery frankly said:

> We would like to purchase large amounts of capital equipment from the United States, but we are worried about our balance of payments. What are you going to buy from us to help us pay for our purchases? We don't say that you must buy from us as much as you sell to us, but we would like you to make a good-faith effort to do what you can to correct the existing situation.

The PRC has also registered this concern at the diplomatic level, making it clear that the United States may not be paying sufficient attention to the Shanghai communiqué's reference to "equality and mutual benefit" in economic relations.[35]

The extension of MFN to China would cease the existing discrimination against Chinese goods by granting them the same access to the world's largest market that the goods of most other countries enjoy. This would enable the PRC to sell its goods at substantially lower prices than at present, when a number of Chinese manufactures and even some primary products are unsalable because of high duties. Thus the PRC would increase its sales significantly and earn more dollars with which to purchase American goods. In urging Congressional authorization of MFN for China, Eugene Theroux, consultant to the National Council on United States-China Trade, said in March 1973:

If allowed to compete fairly with other exporters to the
U.S., it has been estimated that with improvements in
styling, quality control and marketing techniques, China
could generate $300 to $500 million in export earnings
from sale to the U.S. of labor intensive manufactures.
This is a measurable increase from the currently estimated level of some $50 million.[36]

Unless the United States takes affirmative steps to facilitate
the entry of Chinese goods to its markets, Peking will probably try
to reduce the growing imbalance by purchasing less from the United
States than it otherwise would. We must bear in mind that many of
China's purchases to date could have been made from other countries.
If America does not wish to lose future orders, whether for airplanes,
telecommunication equipment, cotton, or grain, it ought to grant Chinese
goods tariff treatment equal to that conferred on most other countries.
This is not to say that the elimination of discriminatory tariffs
alone will suddenly reverse the present trend. As the earlier discussion indicated, MFN is only one of many problems that need to be
solved as the very different, long-separated Chinese and American
economic systems seek to adjust their institutions for doing business.
Yet MFN is an important factor. It is also a highly visible symbol of
American goodwill, about which Peking is understandably sensitive for
historical reasons. Not only did America discriminate against Chinese
goods by continuing to ban all trade with the PRC for almost two decades after the end of the Korean war, but also in the nineteenth century, after the European powers used armed force to exact MFN treatment for their exports to China without granting China reciprocity, the
United States shared in the benefits of this unequal arrangement for
many years. Chinese officials of today have told American diplomats
that the PRC stays out of many American markets because it considers
the absence of MFN treatment unfair.[37]
The trade legislation that the Administration has proposed to
the Congress would grant the President authority to conclude international agreements extending MFN treatment for renewable three
year periods to any Communist country, subject to a ninety-day Congressional veto procedure and subject to the President's right to sus-
pend or withdraw MFN at any time.[38]
At this writing, prospects for passage of the President's trade
bill are uncertain. In addition to the anticipated opposition of organized
labor, protectionist industry and dedicated anti-Communists, a new
and formidable obstacle to the bill has arisen in the widespread Congressional determination not to confer trade benefits upon the Soviet
Union so long as it continues to restrict the emigration of its Jewish
nationals. This has led to the introduction of a bill in the House of

Representatives entitled the "Act for Freedom of Emigration in East-West Trade" and a similar proposal in the Senate.[39] The House bill (1) prohibits the extension of MFN to "any non-market economy country" that denies its citizens the opportunity to emigrate or imposes significant financial impediments to emigration; (2) prevents such a country from receiving U.S. government credits and credit and investment guarantees; and (3) precludes the President from concluding any commercial agreements with such a country. The Senate version is virtually identical except that it does not prohibit conclusion of commercial agreements.

These proposals, which the press has compendiously dubbed "the Jackson-Vanik amendment," represent an effort to persuade the Soviet Union to terminate its so-called "education tax" and other barriers to free emigration that have worked particular hardship on Jews wishing to leave, and public discussion has focused upon their impact on Soviet-American trade. Nevertheless, the language of the proposals is not limited to the Soviet Union but embraces every "non-market economy country" that restricts emigration. Furthermore, neither the proposed statutory language nor the statements of its sponsors limit the applicability of these bills to situations where a nonmarket-economy country discriminatorily restricts emigration on the basis of race, religion, ethnic origin, or similar factors. Rather, the proposals appear to prohibit MFN treatment and other commercial benefits if the country in question restricts emigration for any reason whatever. Although their sponsors frequently allude to the right to free emigration enshrined in the Universal Declaration of Human Rights adopted by the UN in 1948, the proposals themselves go beyond the Declaration, which contains a general escape clause that subjects the right to emigrate "to such limitations as are determined by law solely for the purpose of securing due recognition and respect for the rights and freedoms of others and of meeting the just requirements of morality, public order and the general welfare in a democratic society."

In these circumstances this proposed legislation would necessarily apply to the PRC. It is a nonmarket-economy country that plainly restricts emigration, although its restrictions are not designed to discriminate against any racial, religious, ethnic, or other subgroup of its society, nor do they appear to have such a discriminatory effect.

Adoption of the proposed legislation in either of its present forms would deal a devastating blow to the gradually developing, vitally important Sino-American reconciliation. It would deny both the United States and the PRC the previously mentioned benefits of MFN treatment for Chinese products. More important, and virtually unknown to the American public, it would prevent the U.S. government from directly or indirectly extending credits or credit guarantees to the PRC at a time when the PRC might at long last accept credits from Western countries in order to increase its purchases abroad substantially. It would also prevent the government from in any way

69

guaranteeing any indirect American investments that the PRC may eventually come to accept. For example, before obligating itself to spend millions of dollars drilling for oil under a production-sharing agreement, an American company would presumably wish to obtain a U.S. government guarantee against subsequent Chinese interference with what would be tantamount to an investment in China. But the proposed legislation would not permit such a guarantee. Finally, the House version would prevent the President from even concluding a commercial agreement with the PRC, although a bilateral agreement is badly needed to establish an appropriate framework for trade.

MFN, credits, credit and investment guarantees, and commercial agreements are all instruments that the world's other industrialized countries are prepared to employ in competing with the United States for the China trade. If the United States denies itself these instruments, it will lose out on a significant share of that trade and damage its political relations with the PRC.

No adequate reason has been advanced for applying the so-called Jackson-Vanik amendment to the PRC, and indeed little attention has been devoted to its bearing upon China. In the existing circumstances, it would make no more sense to apply this prohibition to China than to the many market-economy countries that enjoy MFN and other commercial benefits despite their severe restrictions upon emigration.

Indeed, we ought to consider whether it is possible for the United States, without hypocrisy, to insist that the PRC let down its barriers to emigration. If millions of Chinese were permitted to leave their country, one wonders how many of the proponents of free emigration in the Congress would vote to admit them to the United States, even assuming that the racial attitudes underlying the Oriental Exclusion Acts expired together with that obnoxious legislation. The record of other countries in this regard also fails to inspire confidence. We should recall that when, during the spring of 1962, the PRC did relax emigration barriers for a brief period, the United Kingdom sealed Hong Kong's border with China because it could not absorb the exodus. Viewing the matter in this light, one can argue that the People's Republic has actually assisted the rest of the world by not permitting the departure of millions of its nationals but instead adequately feeding, clothing, and housing one-fourth of humanity for the first time in China's history.

In any event, even if free emigration from China is an objective that the United States sincerely wishes to achieve, continuing denial of mutually beneficial economic advantages surely is not going to pressure Peking into yielding. The PRC will only regard such an attempt as an unfriendly gesture that is both politically and economically foolish.

Moreover, given the intense Sino-Soviet rivalry, if the United

States should extend MFN and other economic benefits to China before resolving its difficulty with the Soviet Union, it will be providing the latter with an even more powerful stimulus to permit the emigration of Soviet Jews in order to obtain the long-awaited comparable benefits for Soviet-American relations. Therefore, if Congress deems it necessary to enact the so-called Jackson-Vanik amendment, it would be desirable to narrow the scope of the legislation to avoid application to China. As Senate Majority Leader Mike Mansfield has wisely recommended, the development of commercial relations with China should not be delayed pending resolution of the Soviet emigration dilemma.[40]

CONCLUSION

This essay began with the observation that the American motivation for détente with China was essentially political rather than economic. Yet it is apparent that the implications of the détente for trade are profound. It is also apparent that the implications of trade for détente are profound. Although trade was not a major factor in determining the American desire for a new relationship with China, it is beginning to play a vital role in nourishing that relationship. A broad segment of American business now appreciates the idea that it is acceptable and even desirable and profitable to trade with China. This influential and increasingly large stratum of American society has begun to learn about China, to diffuse its newly acquired knowledge in the community, and to acquire a vested interest in expanding contacts with the People's Republic. No longer will Americans be dependent upon a small group of diplomats, journalists, and academic specialists for their impressions of new China. Moreover, U.S. policy-makers are operating on the assumption that "[t]rade fosters habits and attitudes of adaptation, accommodation and agreement which, hopefully, will be carried over into political and security relationships."[41] They may be right, and in any event it is essential to explore the possibility.

Peking has also demonstrated its sensitivity to the value of trade. The past two years of contacts with American businessmen have been a period of intense information-gathering for the PRC. This exposure seems to have enhanced its awareness of how useful high-level technology can be to China's modernization, and business transacted to date has shown the Chinese that it is possible to deal with Americans on a satisfactory basis. The Chinese have also taken advantage of trade contacts to acquire a broader perspective of American society than has been available through scanning the media and through meeting diplomats and cultural exchange groups. Peking knows full well that through trade it is building an important constituency in the United States that will contribute to the normalization of Sino-American relations; and, like Washington, it is betting that economic cooperation will foster cooperation in other areas. It knows too that by forging strong

71

commercial links with the United States it further demonstrates to the Soviet Union the solidity of its American connection.

Plainly, both Peking and Washington can take some satisfaction in the conduct of their trade to date. How quickly they progress during the next few years will depend upon how hard they try. Yet even skeptics will have to concede that prospects are bright.[42]

NOTES

1. Henry S. Albinski, Australian Policies and Attitudes Toward China (Princeton, N.J.: Princeton University Press, 1965), p. 267.

2. "Red China Limits Talks with U.S.," New York Times, Sept. 14, 1960, p. 11.

3. "Interview with Ch'en Ming," Far Eastern Economic Review (FEER) 44, no. 8 (May 21, 1964): 366.

4. See "Chou En-lai Statement," Kyodo (Peking), Apr. 20, 1970, in Foreign Broadcast Information Service, 1, no. 76 (Apr. 20, 1970): A 10.

5. For a review of China's attitude toward trade with the United States from 1949 to 1970, see Jerome Alan Cohen, "Chinese Law and Sino-American Trade," in A. Eckstein, ed., China Trade Prospects and U.S. Policy (New York, Washington, and London: Praeger Publishers, 1971), pp. 137-39. See also Oliver Lee, "U.S. Trade Policy Toward China: From Economic Warfare to Summit Diplomacy," in Arthur Stahnke, ed., China's Trade with the West, A Political and Economic Analysis (New York: Praeger Publishers, 1972), p. 33. Even today this anger over U.S. trade controls continues. For example, when the PRC agreed to purchase American equipment from RCA and Boeing, it refused to allow the seller to write into the force majeure provision of the contract a stipulation that the denial of an export license by the U.S. government would free the seller from its obligation.

6. For the complete text of the joint communiqué, see Department of State Bulletin (hereafter DSB) 66 (1972): 435.

7. Washington Post, Apr. 24, 1972, p. A-8, quoted in Robert Starr, "Developing Trade with China," Virginia Journal of International Law 13, no. 1 (Fall 1972): 32, n. 72.

8. See Starr, op. cit., pp. 24-25.

9. For comparable American corporate reactions to trade with the Soviet Union, see Harold J. Berman, "East-West Trade: Business Before Pleasure," Nation 216, no. 20 (May 14, 1973): 620-21.

10. Richard Phalon, "Stans Sees Slow Growth in China Trade ," New York Times, Feb. 3, 1972, p. 13.

11. In 1971 U.S. imports from the Soviet Union were $56,811,247. See U.S. Bureau of the Census, U.S. General Imports—World Areas, Country, Schedule A Commodity Groupings, and Method of Transporta-

tion, report FT 155, 1971 Annual (Washington, D.C.: Government Printing Office, 1972), p. 292. In 1971 U.S. exports were $160,464.621. See U.S. Bureau of the Census, U.S. Exports—World Areas, Country, Schedule B Commodity Groupings, and Method of Transportation, report FT 455, 1971 Annual (Washington, D.C., 1972), p. 381.

12. See William J. Casey, Undersecretary of State for Economic Affairs, "Trade as a Factor in Improving United States-PRC Relations," an address to the National Council for United States-China Trade Conference, May 31, 1973 (this conference is hereafter cited as "Conference" and this speech as "Address by Undersecretary Casey").

13. See Robert F. Dernberger, "Prospects for Trade Between China and the United States," in Eckstein, ed., op. cit., pp. 185 ff.

14. Alexander Eckstein, "Introduction," ibid., p. xxvii. See also Dwight H. Perkins, "Is There a China Market?" Foreign Policy no. 5 (Winter 1971-72): 88, 105-06.

15. See "Presidential Assistant Kissinger Visits Asia: Transcript of News Conference, February 22, 1973," DSB 68 (1973): 316.

16. See Dick Wilson, "Breaking the Ice," FEER 80, no. 13. (Apr. 2, 1973): 43. See also Lucian W. Pye, "The Prospects for Development of Commercial Relations Between the United States and China," Conference (hereafter cited as "Address by Professor Pye").

17. Address by Professor Pye. See Marshall Green, "Trade in the Context of United States Relations with the People's Republic of China," Oct. 9, 1972; DSB 67 (1972): 491. See also Address by Undersecretary Casey.

18. See Jerome Alan Cohen, "When Will China and the United States Complete the 'Normalization' of Relations?" in Francis O. Wilcox, ed., China and the Great Powers, to be published by Praeger.

19. Address by Secretary of Commerce Frederick B. Dent, Conference (hereafter cited as "Address by Secretary Dent").

20. Ibid.

21. Alfred LeS. Jenkins, speech before the National Council for United States-China Trade, May 31, 1973.

22. Address by Secretary Dent.

23. The quotation is from an undated summary distributed by the National Council for United States-China Trade.

24. Report by Thornton A. Wilson of the National Council for United States-China Trade's Board of Directors, on behalf of the Program and Liaison Committee, Conference (hereafter cited as "Report by Thornton A. Wilson").

25. Address by Secretary Dent.

26. Henry Tanner, "U.S. Eases Stand in Debate at UN on Seating Peking," New York Times, Nov. 13, 1970, p. 1.

27. Report by Thornton A. Wilson.

28. Address by Undersecretary Casey. See also Stanley B. Lubman, "Trade with China Enters a New Stage," New York Times, June 10, 1973, sec. III, p. 3. For a brief discussion of the background

of the private claims and blocked assets problems, see John J. Fitz-patrick, Jr., and Toby B. Prodgers, "Blocked Assets and Private Claims: The Initial Barriers to Trade Negotiations Between the United States and China," Georgia Journal of International and Comparative Law 3, no. 2. (1973): 449.

29. For the text of the Sino-American trade agreement see "U.S. and USSR Sign Agreements on Trade and Lend-Lease," DSB 67 (1972): 595-604. For a PRC scholar's view of trade agreements, see Wang I-wang, "What Are the Differences Between Commercial Treaties and Trade Agreements," Kung-ming jih-pao (Enlightenment daily), May 12, 1950, p. 3; English translation in Jerome Alan Cohen and Hungdah Chiu, People's China and International Law: A Documentary Study (Princeton, N.J.: Princeton University Press, 1974), item 31-13. For an authoritative study of PRC practice, see Gene T. Hsiao, "Communist China's Trade Treaties and Agreements (1949-1964)," Vanderbilt Law Review 21, no. 5 (1968): 623.

30. For analysis of the problems of assuring the security of foreigners in China, see Jerome Alan Cohen, "The Personal Security of Businessmen and Trade Representatives," in Victor H. Li, ed., Law and Politics in China's Foreign Trade (Seattle: University of Washington Press, 1974). For background on the Chinese legal system, see Jerome Alan Cohen, The Criminal Process in the People's Republic of China, 1949-1963: An Introduction (Cambridge, Mass.: Harvard University Press, 1968).

31. See Dernberger, op. cit., pp. 272-73.

32. Address by Undersecretary Casey. See also Address by Professor Pye.

33. See "SOHIO, Mainland China Set Royalty Agreement," Wall Street Journal, May 7, 1973, p. 6.

34. Address by Professor Pye.

35. Address by Undersecretary Casey.

36. Eugene A. Theroux, "A Long March to Expanded Trade?" Congressional Record 119, no. 56 (Apr. 10, 1973): S6863. The extent of discrimination against Chinese imports can be seen from the fact that hand-knotted carpets from Iran, for example, are subject to an 11 percent duty while comparable Chinese carpets are subject to a 45 percent duty. See David C. Buxbaum, "American Trade with the People's Republic of China: Some Preliminary Perspectives," Columbia Journal of Transnational Law 12, no. 1 (1973): 46, n. 32.

37. Address by Undersecretary Casey. For a PRC scholar's view of MFN, see Wang Yao-t'ien, Kuo-chi mao-i t'iao-yüeh ho hsieh-ting (International trade treaties and agreements; Peking: Financial and Economic Press, 1958), pp. 25-33; English translation in Cohen and Chiu, op. cit., item 33-2.

38. See Title V of H.R. 6767, Trade Reform Act of 1973, 93rd Congress, 1st session, introduced Apr. 10, 1973.

39. H.R. 3910, 93rd Congress, 1st session, introduced Feb. 7,

1973. Amendment on East-West Trade and Freedom of Emigration, 93rd Congress, 1st session, introduced Mar. 15, 1973. See Congressional Record 119, no. 41 (Mar. 15, 1973): S4822.

40. Sen. Mike Mansfield, "China and the US: The New Congress and the New China—An Agenda for Action," in Francis O. Wilcox ed., op. cit.; see note 18.

41. Address by Undersecretary Casey.

42. Since this essay was written, there have been a number of encouraging developments. Representatives of the National Council for United States-China Trade completed a very successful visit to China. They arranged for the CCPIT to send the PRC's first trade delegation to the United States in 1974 and to follow this with an exchange of trade exhibitions between the two countries, exchanges of selling and purchasing missions, and exchanges of trade, economic, and technical information. In addition to the regularly scheduled discussions with CCPIT and government foreign trade officials, members of the National Council delegation also met with representatives of the Bank of China and with the Legal Department of the CCPIT to review specialized questions of mutual interest. The latter meeting dealt with conciliation and arbitration procedures, protection of patents, trademarks and copyrights, standard trade contract and insurance clauses, and governmental regulation of imports and exports.

The autumn Canton Fair offered further evidence of China's desire to expand trade with the United States. The number of American businessmen participating (over 200) again doubled, as it has at every fair since they became welcome in the spring of 1972. They made record purchases of roughly (U.S.) $25 to 30 million in Chinese goods, and sold at least $15 million in U.S. goods. Representatives of a dozen American firms were subsequently invited to Peking to continue negotiations relating to exports to China. The PRC also announced, among other purchases, an order for five more ammonia plants from the M. W. Kellogg Co., at a cost of some $130 million. Moreover, Chinese pricing practices at the fall fair were far more reasonable than they had been at the previous fair, and trade officials made it clear that the PRC had decided to make an effort to comply with United States Government regulations relating to imports and with the needs of the American market. This explicit resolve, which the National Council delegation also noted, appears to be related to a high-level policy decision to take the necessary technical steps to allow foreign trade to flourish. The recent appointment of Li Ch'iang, a veteran commercial expert, to replace Pai Hsiang-Kuo as Minister of Foreign Trade seems to reflect this new policy.

Thus as of mid-December 1973, although American transportation difficulties were slowing grain deliveries to the extent that 1973 Sino-American trade figures might fall somewhat below the projected $900 million estimate, bilateral trade developments continued to look bright.

4

AMERICAN NEWS MEDIA
AND CHINA
Stanley Karnow

Walter Lippmann once noted that we are living in the "age of publicity," and his observation could be applied to the role played by the U.S. media in both reflecting and shaping American attitudes toward China. The People's Republic of China and the United States have used the media in the course of developing their new relationship. The Chinese invited a cross section of the American media into China at the time of the ping-pong breakthrough in order to publicize that event. President Nixon similarly stage-managed his visit to China as a television spectacular in order to publicize that event in the United States and throughout the world.

PROBLEMS IN U.S. COVERAGE OF CHINA

In my estimation, the quality of U.S. coverage of China has not matched its importance. From the rise of the Communists to power in 1949 to President Nixon's trip, the American media have generally tailored their views of China to fit the fashion of the moment.

This is not to suggest that American journalists have been manipulated to express certain viewpoints. Yet, in scanning their reports on China since the 1950s, it seems to me that they have lacked balance. Having frequently magnified the Communist regime's shortcomings in the past, they now appear to be swinging to the other extreme of portraying China in excessively euphoric terms. The danger in this, as Doak Barnett has pointed out, is that "well-meaning illusions . . . leave almost as much room for misunderstandings" as hostile ones.[1] Thus the risk is courted of substituting one bias for another and, in the process, limiting the possibility of perceiving realities.

The Chinese themselves have contributed significantly to America's narrow perceptions of China. For many years China was closed to the American media. Those of us who served in Hong Kong managed, I think, to keep abreast of trends. But Hong Kong, for all its value as an observation post, is no place from which to attempt to grasp the physical magnitudes and human dimensions of China. A recent train trip across the North China plain illustrated to me the Chinese agricultural problem far more dramatically than the piles of statistics I had read in Hong Kong over the years. So there is a net improvement in the fact that some American newsmen can occasionally enter China. Here again, however, serious pitfalls loom. The foreign traveler in China these days is on a guided tour. He is taken to show-case communes, factories, schools, and other enterprises, where the Chinese he sees are carefully selected shills. Last year at Peking University, for instance, a couple of colleagues and I thought we were chatting with students chosen at random when one of them, in reply to a question, began: "As I told Mr. Reston last summer. . . . "

Americans are therefore subjected to news management inside China, and in some ways this may be no better, and possibly worse, than not going to China at all. For many journalists who visit China are, in my opinion, misled by the notion that seeing is believing. Editors add to the tendency to equate presence and credibility by attaching enormous weight to datelines. I recall a television debate several years ago in which Han Suyin cut short Joseph Alsop's critical comments with the devastating question: "When was the last time you were in China, Mr. Alsop?" Since then Mr. Alsop has been in China, and his glowing accounts surpass anything Dr. Han has ever written. Perhaps, then, we can expect Mr. Alsop to deflate a critic with the same question Dr. Han asked of him.

But if the Chinese have curbed or controlled the American media's perceptions of China, I think the media themselves have been even more responsible for their failings. I would attribute these failings to two main factors that, it is important to emphasize, the media share with the American public. In the first place, the media and the public share that peculiarly American feeling about China that has been characterized as a "love-hate" syndrome, which prompts them both to swing from extremes of affection to extremes of hostility. Second, the media and the public share a profound ignorance of China—and this ignorance often reduces their skepticism and increases their gullibility.

American emotional attitudes toward China reach back to the days when American missionaries were trying to convert the "celestial heathen," and American children contributed pennies to save the starving Chinese. These emotions rose in pitch during the Japanese invasion of China, when Time named Chiang Kai-shek Man of the Year and Harold Isaacs, viewing that period in retrospect, later wrote that "the image-makers in their simple-minded enthusiasm had turned China at war into a movie set and had made the Chinese into plaster saints."[2] The American sense of responsibility for China continued even after the Chiang and his persuasive wife began to show signs of corruption and ineptitude. In mid-1946, assuming that Americans held the key to China's destiny in their hands, Time asserted that if the United States "cannot somehow bring a liberal revolution within the Kuomintang, then it had better clear out" of China.[3]

The take-over by the Communists and their subsequent anti-American posture disappointed and confused Americans. They could not believe that the Chinese, their Chinese, had turned against them. This view was implicit in Dean Rusk's celebrated description of the infant People's Republic of China as a "slavic Manchukuo." The New York Times also took the position that the Communist Chinese were merely Soviet puppets. "It is both our right and our duty to wait for further evidence before we recognize the Communist regime as a genuinely sovereign government," intoned a Times editorial at the time.[4]

I personally observed this mixture of disappointment and confusion in Henry Luce, the Time mogul, with whom I traveled in Asia in 1960. Having been born in China, his concern was special. Yet he did influence the public, and he was torn between his love for the Chinese and his inability to conceive of them as Communists. If you told him that the Communist Chinese were successful, he exploded that "Communists can't do well." If you told him that the Communist Chinese were doing badly, he exploded that "Chinese can't do badly."

Luce's outlet for his love of the Chinese was his veneration of Chiang Kai-shek. During a visit to Taiwan in the spring of 1960, he sent a memorandum back to his editors in which he said that he "did not probe energetically into the question of what if anything is wrong with Taiwan" because, he wrote, "I was in the home of my friends." He then went on to describe Chiang as radiating "vitality and confidence," concluding that the Nationalists had done a "wonderful job." I suspect that had Luce lived long enough to visit China, he might have sent a similar memorandum from there.

The change in attitudes toward China since Peking's reconciliation with the United States has been astounding. Back in 1961, for example, the columnist Joseph Alsop was writing that the Chinese diet averaged 600 calories per day, and that this "methodical and rationed" starvation was a deliberate policy designed to lower the population and thereby ease the pressure on available resources.[5] But after a visit to China, during which he was treated regally, Alsop ecstatically praised Chinese agricultural progress and estimated Chinese farmers to be among the richest in Asia.[6] The usually perceptive New York

Times columnist James Reston underwent a similar transformation. He asserted in 1962 that the Chinese had "made such a ghastly mess of their revolution" that they were attacking India in order to "halt the more democratic development of that country."[7] Reporting from China in 1971, however, Reston likened the Chinese revolution to an old-fashioned "cooperative barn-raising" that ought to make Americans "outrageously nostalgic and even sentimental."[8] Even a seasoned correspondent like Harrison Salisbury, also of the New York Times, was carried away during his China tour. Quoting a Chinese official as saying that labor reform had been "the great experience of my life," Salisbury commented that he knew the man was telling the truth "from the emotion in his voice, the reverence with which he spoke."[9]

It is now clear that even observers who were able to get into China before the present détente often failed to perceive the country's realities. No American was closer to China and its leaders than the late Edgar Snow. Yet in The Other Side of the River, published in 1962, Snow minimized the food problem even though subsequent information contained in such documents as the Kung-tso t'ung-hsun (Work bulletins) of the People's Liberation Army have proved that the crisis was real. Although Snow traveled extensively in China and had better access to Chinese officials than most foreigners, he did not perceive the tensions inside the Communist Party at the time and caught up with them only when a revised version of his book, entitled Red China Today, appeared in 1970. A random selection of his revisions indicates that ignorance was not limited to those who were barred from entering China. In the original, for instance, Snow described Liu Shao-chi as Mao Tse-tung's successor and stated that he "today works as closely with him as formerly."[10] That sentence is omitted from the 1970 edition, replaced by a footnote saying that "by 1966 it became clear that Mao by no means did or ever had viewed Liu Shao-chi as his logical successor."[11] Snow had also asserted in the earlier work that Liu's "writings show no significant deviation from Maoism,"[12] but that observation is absent from the revised edition.

The ignorance of the American media about China stems largely, in my estimation, from the disinclination on the part of media managers to train or hire specialists. Only a few journalists are familiar with the Chinese language, and equally few know much about either ancient or modern Chinese history. Specialists are frequently regarded as suspect by media executives. In Hong Kong a few years ago, a rare correspondent who was fluent in Chinese and had traveled in China failed to impress his editors because, as one of them put it, "He can't cover anything else."

That comment reflects the short attention span of media managers toward the China story. They are interested, indeed excited, when the Cultural Revolution is convulsing the country or when President Nixon visits Peking. But they quickly turn off as the subject loses its drama. After all, accounts of grain production or birth control or esoteric political rivalries among people with unpronounceable names do not thrill newspaper readers or television audiences. The result is a lack of continuity in China coverage. Moreover, the failure to follow China on a consistent basis leaves the media unprepared to report fully when a major development does occur. The Lin Piao crisis, although a sensational event that could not have been predicted, nevertheless caught many journalists off base because the media had lost interest in China during the lull that followed the storm of the Cultural Revolution.

Before the thaw in Sino-American relations, Americans widely felt the need for more information about China. In his book The American People and China, A. T. Steele quotes numbers of editors, newspaper readers, and television viewers as saying that they desired more and better-balanced reports on China.[13] During that period, according to Steele, the New York Times devoted an average of one column per day to events related to China—half the space alloted to the Soviet Union but three times the amount given to Japan.[14] The invitation to the American ping-pong team to enter China in April 1971 changed all that. The Chinese carefully issued visas to representatives of the U.S. media in order to publicize the ping-pong team's tour. At the same time they made another move that was to be extremely significant for the invitation to President Nixon that would follow. They authorized Edgar Snow to publish in Life an interview with Mao Tse-tung, made the previous December, in which the Chairman expressed a desire to have Nixon visit China.[15] Not long afterward, at an editors' convention in Washington, Nixon replied to chairman Mao that he looked forward to the trip. Thus the media were used to promote the rapprochement.

THE MEDIA AND THE PRESIDENT'S VISIT TO
CHINA

The effort to improve relations between the United States and China proceeded along two tracks, one secret and the other open. Starting in early July 1971, Henry Kissinger proceeded along the secret track with his initial visit to Peking. Simultaneously, selected American journalists began to enter China, and the tone of their reporting differed radically from what the press had taken earlier. No longer did the New York Times refer to the Communist Chinese government as "the most totalitarian regime of the 20th century," as it had in 1959.[16] Instead, it published articles affirming that chairman Mao's doctrines had "propelled China into a continuing revolution that

80

is producing a new society and a new 'Maoist man.'"[17] Harrison
Salisbury even contended in his book that this new "Maoist man" presented a spiritual challenge to decadent Americans: "When would the
New American Man and the New American Woman walk the earth,
proud and confident, making the oceans boil and the continents
shake?"[18]

As preparations for the President's trip went ahead, administration officials sought to discourage any news about China that might
compromise the visit. State Department sources suddenly dried up
and even refused to divulge such innocuous information as the extent
of Chinese aid to Syria. Nixon himself even ceased to refer to the
Chinese regime as Communist. Underlying this blackout was the fear
that the Chinese might be prompted to cancel the President's visit on
the grounds that the U.S. government was interfering with internal
Chinese affairs. When news about Lin Piao filtered into the American
press, for example, there was talk inside the White House of Adminis-
tering lie detector tests to certain officials in an attempt to discover
"leaks."

The President was greatly preoccupied by press and especially
television coverage of his China visit as time for the trip approached.
This would be an unprecedented voyage and, he calculated, it would
have a tremendous impact on his popularity at home. Thus American
negotiators worked hard to persuade the Chinese to authorize the networks to invade China with vast amounts of television paraphernalia,
and it was considered a U.S. victory when they acceded. The television
coverage itself, according to many critics, was rather thin. Television
stars like John Chancellor of NBC and Walter Cronkite of CBS were
reduced to talking about their breakfast menus, and Barbara Walters
found an "air of disappointment" in the fact that Nixon was not greeted
at the airport with gongs and cymbals. On the strength of a single
visit to a single commune, CBS's Dan Rather reported that industrialization was "the central failure of Mao-style Communism so far."

Some journalists have argued that coverage of the Nixon trip
was weak because the President and the Chinese exercised strict
control over the media. I have argued, however, that the media themselves were at fault for failing to cover the trip with their available
specialists. The networks could have given more play to their own
Asian veterans, such as Bernard Kalb of CBS and John Rich of NBC,
or they could have included in their crews academic experts such as
Ross Terrill, James C. Thomson, Jr., and Allen Whiting instead of
using them as "analysts" in their studios at home. The newspapers
and magazines, similarly viewing the trip as a prestige exercise,
generally chose to send their Washington bureau chiefs or White
House correspondents rather than their specialists. Indeed, the only
newspaper reporters on the visit who had concentrated on Chinese

affairs within recent years were Henry Bradsher of the Washington Star, R. H. Shackford of the Scripps-Howard chain, Robert Keatley of the Wall Street Journal, and myself as representative for the Washington Post. Hence the media indirectly colluded with the White House in treating the episode as a "spectacular." In the process, I believe, they were captivated by appearances while losing sight of realities.[19]

I also believe that the presence of the American media on the trip influenced the negotiations between President Nixon and Premier Chou En-lai. The role of the media in this instance must be seen against the background of the negotiations themselves.

One of Nixon's main objectives, we were told in Honolulu as we laid over on our way to Peking, was to set up an "ongoing communications belt" with the Chinese. Even earlier I had been told that the President would try to persuade the Chinese to agree to something like the liaison offices that were subsequently established in Peking and Washington in 1973. Chou En-lai, in contrast, apparently wanted concessions from Nixon on the Taiwan issue, and he said as much in his first banquet speech. In that speech Chou urged the President to recognize the "five principles of peaceful coexistence," one of which is mutual respect for "territorial integrity." During the negotiations that went on that week, Nixon finally acceded to Chou's demands by pledging, with qualifications, to withdraw U.S. troops and military installations from Taiwan and by acknowledging the Taiwan issue to be an internal Chinese matter. In my estimation the Chinese used the American media as leverage to make their gains.

If the Chinese cooperated in the President's unusual publicity spectacle, it was essentially because it offered them the chance to promote their own interests. In their view the more Nixon's presence in China was publicized in the United States, the greater would be domestic American expectations for the President to return home with some kind of accord. Thus the Chinese deliberately inflated Nixon's image so that unless he acquiesced to their demands, he would leave China empty-handed. The President stayed awake until 5 A.M. on Saturday, February 26, in an apparent effort to break a deadlock that had developed between the Chinese and himself. His anxiety to discourage reports that such a deadlock existed was evident in the fact that his press secretary, Ronald Ziegler, announced in Hangchow later that day that "basic agreement" had been reached. His announcement was carefully calculated to reach the East Coast of the United States in time for the late editions.

It is in vogue to be an American interested in Chinese affairs these days, and the prospect is that increasing numbers of journalists from the United States will be given visas. So far the Chinese have profited from their new flexibility. The reporting has been favorable.

Journalists who would resist guided tours at home have been willingly and even happily taking them in China. There is a long way to go, therefore, before Americans are told by the media that China is neither as bad as its critics have claimed nor as good as its sympathizers assert. When we reach that point, some measure of real Sino-American understanding will have been achieved.

NOTES

1. New York Times, Apr. 8, 1973.
2. Harold Isaacs, Scratches on our Minds (New York, 1958), p. 176.
3. Quoted in Felix Greene, A Curtain of Ignorance (London, 1965), p. 38.
4. Quoted in ibid., p. 91.
5. New York Herald-Tribune, Sept. 3, 1961.
6. New York Times, Apr. 18, 1973.
7. Ibid., Oct. 21, 1962.
8. Quoted in Sheila K. Johnson, "To China, with Love," Commentary, June 1973.
9. Quoted in ibid.
10. Edgar Snow, The Other Side of the River (New York, 1962), p. 148.
11. Edgar Snow, Inside Red China (New York, 1970), p. 327 n.
12. Snow, The Other Side of the River, p. 339.
13. A. T. Steele, The American People and China (New York, 1966), pp. 141 ff.
14. Ibid., p. 157.
15. Life, Apr. 30, 1971.
16. New York Times, Oct. 1, 1959.
17. Ibid., June 25, 1971.
18. Quoted in Johnson, op. cit.
19. Stanley Karnow, "Playing Second Fiddle to the Tube," Foreign Policy, Summer 1972.

5

PROSPECTS FOR SINO-AMERICAN
SCHOLARLY EXCHANGE
Stephen Uhalley, Jr.

The newly emerging pattern of international relationships is a
welcome relief after so many years of the bipolar standoff and atmosphere that had victimized Sino-American relations. At long last
there is again hope that this reviving relationship will allow for useful
scholarly exchanges as well. Some such exchange, in fact, now appears
to be inevitable. Nevertheless, we are in no position to be unduly
optimistic about the amount and depth of such interchange, particularly
in certain areas of study. We need only remind ourselves that beneath
the novelty and enthusiasm of the current, initial contacts between
the United States and China there remain fundamental and enormous
differences between the respective political systems, ways of life,
and societal objectives. These differences cannot be underrated or
underestimated. They will continue to cause problems, and these
should be accepted realistically. Our task will be to make the most
of the new opportunities despite the problems.

POSSIBLE IMPEDIMENTS

Fear is expressed in some quarters, particularly by many
younger and politically radical or dissident scholars, that an effort
is being made to create a mechanism that would monopolize the handling
of Sino-American scholarly exchanges.[1] Certainly it would not appear
to be in the best interests of American scholars to be constrained
by a monopoly. Nor would there appear to be any real need for such
a monopolized exchange mechanism. The lessons of the experience
of the Soviet-American exchange program over the years are not
completely relevant to the U.S.-China relationship, and certainly
should not be used to argue for a similar institutionalization of exchanges.[2] However, this particular apprehension may not be fully

justified. The Committee on Scholarly Communication with the People's Republic of China, for example, is not supposed to be exclusive or monopolistic. As long as such an organization does its work fairly, diplomatically, and effectively, there should be no problem. In fact, such a nonexclusive agency on the American side as this Committee appears to be, or some such facilitating organization, may correspond to what the Chinese themselves would like to work with. There seems to be an understandable eagerness on the part of the Chinese to entrust the handling of exchanges on the American side to reputable and re'iable agencies. At the very least the Chinese will want to have such an option among others, for it is likely, and proper, that other channels for exchanges and communications will remain.

More serious and more fundamental are the limitations on inquiry that will bedevil the visits to China of scholars in certain fields, and the unlikelihood of Chinese scholars being able to visit the United States in large numbers or with the objectives of testing rather than confirming hypotheses, approaches, and methodologies. One could dwell on these negative aspects of the topic at some length. However, I think that little purpose would be served in the end. It might be better simply to acknowledge their seriousness and then resolve to make the best of the situation.

It might help to remember that we should not overreact to the new turn in international relationships that makes this topic now worth pursuing. Adjustments in global realpolitik alignments do not necessarily reflect value transformations. They do not in this case. China and the United States are still at loggerheads in many respects, despite the current politeness, friendly rhetoric, and multiple cultural exchanges and mutual visitations. There is an understandable reluctance to raise serious questions at this point, for the novel sensation of cordiality is still too pleasant to seriously threaten or to undermine. However, we do realize that beneath the surface the weightier differences exist. Many of the bourgeois values and behavior patterns of the American people are anathema to the Chinese. They must certainly be concerned about the danger that such influences will undermine their own revolutionary resolve. This apprehension will account for some of the barriers that obstruct the realization of truly meaningful exchange programs. The term "meaningful" here is meant to connote experiences of free and open discourse between Chinese and Americans that result in genuine mutual insights and understanding.

It is also advisable to avoid viewing the present rapproachement from a perspective that is too narrow or too ethnocentric. Americans are prone to this error, even though it may be understandable because of the position and power of the United States and because of the opportunities Americans now present to the Chinese. All of this, one might imagine, should result in a special relationship with China that, despite differences, will afford special opportunities to Americans. Unfortunately, this is not the case. The Chinese may recognize all too well the role and power of the United States, and they will seek to exploit all available opportunities that will benefit them. Nevertheless, rather than evolve a new, special, or privileged kind of relationship with the United States, China is likely to fit relations with the United States into an already established framework of relationships with foreign countries (regardless of the Taiwan complication) and will follow policies for dealing with Americans that have already been applied to other foreigners. In other words, there is not likely to be very much unique about the Sino-American exchange experience. This means that Americans can hardly expect anything more in the way of treatment or opportunities than have already been given to Europeans and others who have been visiting China regularly over the years.* Of course few peoples have been as persistently determined to study China in the face of obstacles as Americans have. There is the possibility that, given this attitude, Americans might do more with the opportunities that may be given to them. In general, however, prospects for Americans in China are prefigured in the experience of others.

OPPORTUNITIES FOR SCHOLARS IN CHINA

In looking back at that record, and at what others are still doing, we see that while not many scholars have spent time profitably in China, there are some who have done so. Before the Cultural Revolution there were dozens of students, mostly from other socialist countries, who studied at Peking University, some for several years. Some scholars did research in Chinese archives. Some foreign legations in Peking have included scholars among their staffs, although the amount of actual scholarship these individuals could accomplish is debatable. It is apparent that Marxist identification or orientation was an asset. In certain fields that are less sensitive politically, such as linguistics, a congenial political orientation seems to have been unnecessary. Today there is even a non-Marxist Swedish scholar studying labor history in Nanking. McGill University will soon be

---

*However, there have been reports from Peking in mid-1973 that some Europeans are resentful of the special treatment being given Americans, including the making available of housing for which others had become accustomed to wait for long periods. This could be a temporary phenomenon.

sending several students to China for protracted periods of study. The Chinese are preparing to send students to England for study in several disciplines.

On the basis of this range of experience, there are then grounds for expecting that at least similar opportunities will be presented in the Sino-American relationship. This is a reasonable expectation, especially since the liaison offices are in place and Sino-American relations are being further regularized. The opportunities would seem to become more promising too as China's domestic politics continue the current swing to more moderate or centrist positions and policies that reflect the current foreign policy of accommodation.

Of course, the tone of China's domestic political-ideological atmosphere is a changeful and relative quantity. While we discern an increasingly moderate atmosphere today, the political-ideological climate is further to the left as a whole than it was in the years preceding the Great Proletarian Cultural Revolution. This is true at least to the extent that revisionism and bourgeois restorationist tendencies in those days were gaining ascendancy, as was claimed, as well as to the extent that such backsliding has been arrested as a result of the Cultural Revolution. This suggests that even though moderation may be the order of the day, the level of receptivity to certain kinds of scholarship proposals may not be, or come to be, particularly high. The Cultural Revolution affirmed a more revolutionary domestic orientation.

Ironically, one might speculatively regard the current rapprochement as poorly timed for the most effective scholarly exchanges. If revisionists were more concerned with expertise, with professionalism, as well as with status and its prerogatives, than with ideological purity or revolutionary zeal, then they might have been relatively more receptive to notions of traffic with Western scholars, especially had they decisively secured dominance. Take the educational system as an example. The Chinese educational system before the Cultural Revolution had many points of similarity with the educational system of the United States. Although before 1967 the Chinese had a so-called two-track educational apparatus—a mass education track and an elitist education track—the latter received far more emphasis than did the former. This elitist track stressed high-quality academic training in the general Western sense and produced well-trained technicians and professionals in many fields of specialization. Academic excellence and professional specialization were stressed over political education, over the instilling of socialist values, and over the stressing of respect for physical labor. Students who were selected for and who generally succeeded in this system usually came from professional or official families, most of them urban-based. They spent long years of training, during which performance was judged by competitive examinations. Increasingly, the critics reported, graduates assumed a life style and privileges that they believed accorded with their elevated status, setting them apart from the general population. Socialist on the surface and in intent, the system in fact reflected many Western educational concepts and values.

Of course, there is no way of telling how such similarities or latent points of congeniality might have resulted in the Chinese revisionists' receptivity to closer, including scholarly, relationships with the United States in, say, the early 1960s. There were also differences between the systems, including the widely differing ultimate objectives of the respective societies. However, these were the years when, following the withdrawal of Soviet specialists and aid, China was in uncertain straits. And given the alleged willingness to compromise of the ascendant revisionists—who, we are led to believe, pragmatically and rationally approached solutions to problems (as opposed to Mao's alleged "ideological" and "romantic" approach)—it may not be unreasonable to speculate that they might eventually have been receptive to the notion of taking leaves from more Western books to hasten economic development in their country. The irony is, of course, that these were years when despite the superficial overtures of the Kennedy administration, the United States certainly did not seem disposed to scout out and follow up opportunities seriously.

The purpose of this speculation about possible past missed opportunities is merely to emphasize that the present opportunities may not be nearly as good in terms of developing meaningful scholarly relationships with the Chinese system because the Cultural Revolution has occurred. Consider the results thus far of the attendant revolution in education alone. The elitist track has been largely dismantled. Social revolution is emphasized, not features and values that are suggestive of Western models. This has made a considerable difference, chiefly in terms of revolutionary determination, which seems to have been strongly renewed, and in accompanying attitudes toward potentially compromising practices and values. Hence the Chinese are more likely than ever to be on guard against influences that they suspect will be harmful to their revolutionary enterprise or that will be detrimental to their supporters in the next rectification campaign. Another product of China's success is a revolutionary pride and confidence that express themselves in a new openness to foreigners. This confident openness can be misleading, for it is not likely to signal a readiness to accept serious criticisms or suggestions. However, for the purpose of making the most of the current rapprochement, it is an attitude that makes friendship or at least friendly interpersonal relationships much easier.

This new self-confidence reflects a psychological change of profound significance on the part of China vis-à-vis the world. For while China may still speak humbly of learning from others, which is an honest enough sentiment as far as it goes, it is also clear that she is assuming a role of teacher as well. It is this self-conscious view of herself as having become a model, although such a definition is subject to many qualifications—with all that this may suggest in the way of images from her traditional past—that provides an unprecedented opportunity relevant to our concern. It means that a confident China is in a communicative mood and that real communication among scholars, may be possible. But communication is a two-way affair and requires a common wavelength.

NEW APPROACHES TO STUDY IN CHINA

In order to gain the most possible in these new communications with an attitudinally transformed China, Americans might resolve to make some desirable changes of their own. There has been a need of some changes for some time, and not just to establish ourselves on the necessary wavelength at this time. Conventional scholarship on China has not been outstanding in producing genuine understanding and useful insights in recent decades. It should not cause too much regret if we now set aside many conventional assumptions and methodologies, in favor of thinking and tools more appropriate to the task. Change does not come easily, but today there are great incentives to do so. The greatest of these incentives is the fascination that contemporary China awakens in most who have heard something of developments there. Even the most conservative Western medical doctors are taking a more serious look at the wonders of acupuncture, and the use of such medical techniques is part of the revolutionary ethos of new China. Hence, it might follow that even Cold War-minded and conservative scholars are being led to ask questions that old assumptions and modes of analysis are unable to answer satisfactorily.

China today is undeniably a fascinating phenomenon. Its people are grappling with fundamental human problems in bold new experiments that are of universal interest. A proper appreciation and comprehension of China challenges us. Obviously, if we cannot understand it according to old formulas, then we must find new ways to do so. There is no suggestion here that American scholars should accept anything at face value, nor be uncritical, nor "ideologically compatible," nor starry-eyed. We merely need to be open-minded and receptive to new ideas, new conceptions, new ways of looking at objects of study.

What is needed ultimately is a new disposition to learn, and to learn what we can by the means available. A new disposition to learn might translate itself in terms both of new attitudes and purposes and of new techniques and methodologies. The new attitudes might include, beyond open-mindedness and receptivity, a willingness to identify more closely with the object of study. Chinese, Communists or not, would be regarded more as fellow human beings confronted with very real problems that are met with the means at their disposal in ways consonant with their well-being and the realization of their societal objectives. Their achievements, and the why and the how of them, might receive at least as much attention as the failures. The positive features of their programs and the humane values they are seeking to instill should get at least equal billing with the less appealing programs and practices. Shortcomings and failures should not be ignored, but they should not be blown out of proportion. Genuinely balanced assessments are in order.

Once many of the more conventional scholarly approaches are set aside, at least provisionally, as having proved of limited value and as not particularly appropriate to the available opportunities, and once the new disposition to learn is determined, it may be that alternative techniques and methodologies will be found at hand or may evolve as situations permit and suggest. There are already examples of experimental techniques that have proven exciting and fruitful, and these suggest the way for others. These must be schemes that fit into the Chinese framework and that the Chinese find compatible with their own practice and purposes. In this respect I would like to emphasize one approach in particular, the cooperative group approach. It is practical and has promise inasmuch as cooperating collectivities are comprehensible and familiar to Chinese thinking and planning. If the work of such groups is properly planned by American organizers, it may yield a great deal that would not normally be expected from the present limits placed on visitations to China.

One avenue of group effort was experimented with by the second Committee of Concerned Asian Scholars (CCAS), which visited China in March-April 1972. It will be worth reviewing here. This delegation of American visitors was privileged to receive some interesting concessions from their Chinese hosts, including extended stays in both an agricultural commune and an urban setting. The second CCAS delegation, which numbered 30, divided into two groups of 15, each of which followed a separate itinerary for most of the visit. One group followed a mostly coastal itinerary and had its extended stays in Shanghai and near Tangshan; the other followed an inland route and had its extended stays in Linhsien, Honan, and in Shenyang, Liaoning.

The visit to Linhsien is a good example of how a great deal can be made of a visit of four or five days to an agricultural commune. After arriving at the county seat of Linhsien, following a long, jolting bus ride from the train station at Anyang, the group of 15 Americans formulated the basic strategy. It was decided that four members of the group would stay at the county's administrative headquarters for much of the visit in order to observe top-level administrative organs and to get a comprehensive picture of the much-lauded Red Flag canal system. The rest of the group went to a production team of the Ta Ts'ai Yuan production brigade of Cheng Kuan commune. This commune is an extraordinarily large one, comprising some 90,000 members, and is located close to the county seat. The designated production team, one of six in the brigade, was composed of 47 families. The 11 American visitors arrived at midday and were distributed in groups of two or three to various families. The Americans had been invited to China as a friendship delegation and, in keeping with the spirit of friendship, a special policy was followed for the rest of the first day with the production team. Soon after the initial billeting the group headed out to the communal fields for a stint of labor. This gesture, consisting of a couple hours of weed-pulling and manure-spreading, followed by an hour of sitting conversation, must have effectively derailed serious production for the team by some hours. Nevertheless the gesture was well-taken. Throughout the entire first day no cameras were displayed, no "hard" questions were posed, and no notes were taken. Complementing the effort to make friends was a late afternoon of frisbee flipping, first with the children and then gradually with numbers of adults, and a hilarious evening of recording and playing back villagers' voices and songs on tape recorders, which they had neither seen nor heard of before. Sleeping that cold night, the first of four on an unheated k'ang (brick bed), was a mixed experience consisting of equal parts of misery and the gratification that accompanied the feeling that one could communicate with these people.

Such a conscious emphasis on friendship has positive implications for subsequent efforts to study people. The soft approach did much in this case to allay suspicions and apprehensions, and to induce the villagers to be responsive to subsequent questioning. This is not to imply, of course, that there was a conscious design to lull or to deceive respondents. It was quite clear all along that the purpose of the Americans was to learn something about life in this agricultural environment, and not just to be friendly.

The real advantage of the cooperative group approach is seen in the experience of the next three days. Instead of the group of visitors being subjected to a common schedule of places to see and persons to interview, there was considerable scope for smaller groups to go in different directions. This enabled them to accomplish much more in the limited time available and to make a number of useful informational cross-checks. There were collective visits to the production brigade's medical clinic, the tailor shop, the noodle factory (which made noodles from sweet potatoes), the granaries, the piggery, the store, and the meeting room. Smaller groups and individuals visited the primary and lower middle schools and had lengthy interviews with various individuals in the brigade. These included the brigade chairmen, the vice-chairman of the Poor and Middle Peasants Association, the People's Militia commander and his political instructor, the accountant, the school principal, the doctor, and various farmers and their families. One small group followed the routine of the manager of the production team's seedling bed, listening to his descriptions and asking questions as he related his tasks from beginning to end. This particular interview was conducted at the seedling bed itself and moved to the communal field as required by the descriptive explanations; much of it was committed to film, both motion and still, and to the tape recorder. Women members of the American group were especially interested in the life of the women of the commune and made a number of interviews in pursuit of this interest. Naturally interviews with host families continued pretty much throughout the entire stay, in the evenings and at mealtimes. Some enterprising visitors rose early with their host family and worked in the fields before breakfast.

Approaching this experience in this way not only enabled the visitors to absorb the subjective feelings that such immersion in the life of the community made possible but also maximized the amount of data they could gather in the short stay. The amount of information gathered by the group as a whole is probably more than a single individual might have gotten had he stayed with the same production team for a month or more.

The same approach was applied during a stay at a factory that was part of the urban experience. The Shenyang transformer factory had been visited before, but never so intensively. The usual visit is for a single afternoon. In this case most of the group of American visitors lived for two nights in one of the workers' dormitories. Once again there was the opportunity to experience the life of Chinese in this kind of setting and to receive many impressions and insights not otherwise available to outsiders. But living arrangements aside, the approach to an analysis of how this factory operated is the object of our interest here. Following the usual introductory remarks about the factory over tea in the reception room, the group of 15 broke into smaller groups that spent the rest of the time at the factory pursuing more specialized investigations.

One group held a series of discussions with the plant's top-level management and asked searching questions of the revolutionary committee. This proved to be a relatively rewarding effort because the chairman of that committee was an articulate, knowledgeable authority who spoke with great self-assurance. Another group observed practices at the shop level, and another studied such ancillary services as the health clinic and nursery.

A similar pattern was followed by this group of Americans at Peking University, where they spent one night at a student dormitory. Again there were the common elements—the reception, a campus tour, and an evening cultural performance—and the experience of eating, conversing, and sleeping with Chinese student hosts. And again the Americans dispersed into groups that explored more particular interests. One group visited the department of history, another the department of English, and another the department of philosophy.

The methodology employed by this particular group is suggestive of what can be done to make the most of the available opportunities. It was an imaginative and a productive approach, but it might have been applied even more effectively. With improvements future groups will accomplish much more. Improvements would include, first, better and more thorough planning of the journey as a whole and of particular visits within China. Ideally such planning might be done as part of a more comprehensive scheme that would encompass several such projected group visits. The composition of the groups could be improved by better selection or selection with a particular eye to the objectives of the visit. And attention should be given to the cooperation factor, for success is largely dependent on members working together and sharing experiences and information. A group of radical economists has already provided an example of disciplinary concentration, and they did in fact adopt the general approach I have outlined. More can be done in the way of improving interview techniques under essentially informal circumstances. This is also part of planning and might be partially resolved by disciplinary specialists, but lines of questions could be made more systematic and purposive. Built into the planning and organization of the group visits could be a clearer understanding of writing and publishing expectations and responsibilities. Prior understanding would result in fewer ruffled feathers and better publications. Much of the information gathered by the second CCAS group circulated satisfactorily among the members of the group, but publication has not been systematic.

The obvious rejoinder to this suggested approach is that visitors such as the CCAS or radical economists are given advantages or sympathetic and preferential treatment for what may be essentially political reasons. The point, of course, is well taken. Nevertheless, I suggest that future group visits, especially those lacking any particular political coloration, might plan to use the cooperative approach to the greatest extent possible. Even if long stays are not granted to such groups, some of the techniques can still be applied. For example, when visiting a factory or school even for a single day or an afternoon, it ought to be possible to break into small groups to talk to various Chinese respondents separately. The main idea is to break up the large reception room treatment as much as possible, so as to encourage greater candor and to enhance the solicitation of more discrete data.

We don't want to get carried away with expectations from this or any other conceivable approach during a China visit. There are, after all, certain restraints, and they are likely to remain. These are among the essential differences between their system and ours. But we owe it to the Chinese and to ourselves to test the possible in all given circumstances. When the suggested approach can be implemented, it is likely to be more productive than not. Ideally it has enormous potential.

Of course, the information made available by means of such cooperative group approaches should not be seen only in isolation. What is produced in this way is merely another input into our growing knowledge of contemporary China, knowledge that is continuously being augmented from other sources. This includes the observations of individual scholarly or journalistic and other visits to China, and unofficial information made available by Chinese during their own visits abroad. All of this information collectively should be seen as supplementing (certainly rather than supplanting) the more traditional sources. Thus radio monitoring, Chinese newspapers and other publications and documentation, and refugee interviewing are still necessary, although it is to be hoped that the use of this material will become better as our insights result in the maturation of assumptions and lead to more sophisticated methodology and exercise of humanity and balance in interpretation. What the visits to China do provide, even when the suggested cooperative approach cannot be used, is an opportunity to meet Chinese personally and to get a personal feel—however circumscribed and artificial in many respects—for the environment in which they live, work, and play. At the very least this personal dimension helps provide balance to the Chinese equation and fleshes out details.

The cooperative group approach fits into the Chinese scheme of things and may prove to have an appeal for the Chinese. Whether it is used by economists, industrial relations specialists, or anthropologists it could prove to be a valuable tool. The concept could be utilized by other areas of academia as well. For example, it is conceivable that a class or seminar could be organized into such a cooperative group. The class might emanate from one or from a consortium of universities or colleges and be led by one or more professors. The class would study intensively a single theme or a single or several related types of institutions or practices. Each member might be made responsible for a particular aspect of the overall theme. The appropriate assignment of research topic would be made prior to arrival in China, as a necessary part of the comprehensive planning for the course. It would be highly desirable, of course, if students selected for such a class have appropriate academic background preparation and a knowledge of the Chinese language.

Remembering that the prospects of meaningful scholarly exchange can hardly be expected to thrive under the circumstances of the current Sino-American rapproachement, considering the real differences in the respective systems and goals, and considering the leftward gravitation of China's revolutionary orientation compared with a decade ago, there nevertheless are grounds for guarded optimism. American scholars may have many of the same kinds of opportunities that others have had as they come to fit into the established Chinese framework and practices for dealing with visiting scholars. In response to their own need the Chinese are certainly anxious to extend opportunities to scholars in the sciences and in engineering and related fields. There may be programs developed for language training; interest was expressed to me at Wuhan University about such an exchange with the University of Hawaii. Historians at Wuhan University and at Peking University expressed a desire to visit the University of Hawaii when they might have the opportunity to go to the United States. The University of Hawaii has made a standing invitation to such scholars. There are indications too that soon Chinese students may be able to study in the United States on an experimental basis. This is in line with the reasoning of some Chinese that exposure to outside influences is a necessity of life. It may result, they feel, in some attrition; but it is something that must be faced. There may be breakthroughs here and there for American scholars, particularly in linguistics and other comparatively apolitical disciplines in the humanities and social sciences. One American scholar has already received a one-year visa to do research in modern Chinese literature. An occasional historian, political scientist, or anthropologist may also qualify for an extended stay. An educational television crew from the University of Hawaii recently returned from visit to China where it did intensive filming for a documentary on children. But short of these special kinds of opportunities there does seem to remain the possibility of achieving more within the limited scope of the normal type of China trip and whatever modest modifications that can be sometimes arranged for such a trip. The cooperative group approach can be improved to yield more than the information and insights that are currently being obtained.

Therefore, despite the problematic prospects ahead and the pervading negative features of the subject, it is helpful to look at the positive side and make the best of it. After all, for the first time in a generation Americans have access to China. The much-desired dialogue has finally begun. We should seek to promote this dialogue, and to this end we should do what is possible. If this requires imagination, inventiveness, and the adoption of a new readiness to learn, this will not be harmful. The purpose of dialogue is to communicate for the purpose of achieving greater understanding and the wisdom understanding brings. Thus we need to eschew the unrealistic pan-egyrics of the ideologue and avoid the equally unrealistic and distorting views of the cynic. Only genuine efforts to achieve the balanced view will produce worthwhile learning. Insights generated by such learning may help us not only to understand the whys and hows of developments in China today but also may move us to salutary critical self-evaluations. By the same token, the dialogue may yet be a vehicle for demonstrating to the Chinese a more realistic appreciation for some of the sound features, values, and accomplishments of our own system, regardless of the blemishes and deficiences that we too must acknowledge and remedy. On both sides there are worthwhile values to be discovered and rediscovered. Scholars and others will want to make the most of the limited opportunities before us.

As this paper was completed, it was gratifying to hear reports of agreements reached in Peking that promise stepped-up scientific and scholarly exchanges. The agreements were negotiated during a 17-day visit by a delegation of 21 American scientists, scholars, and staff, representing the National Academy of Sciences, the Social Science Research Council, and the American Council of Learned Societies. Reportedly there are to be a dozen or more groups a year of up to 10 scientists from the two countries. Soon individual scientists from both countries will be able to work in each others' laboratories for several months at a time. Americans will study Chinese medicine, horticulture, seismology, and archaeology. Significantly, contemporary Chinese political history remains off limits. The Chinese are most interested in American technological advances. Interestingly, Dr. Glenn Seaborg, former chairman of the Atomic Energy Commission, who was part of the delegation, was impressed by China's emphasis on applied research "to serve the people," reportedly stating that a move in this direction "might be useful in America too."[3]

NOTES

1. See "A Statement on U.S. China Exchanges," Committee of Concerned Asian Scholars Newsletter (Jan. 1973), pp. 16-20.
2. For an estimate of prospects based on Soviet-American exchange experience see Robert F. Byrnes, When the Academic Door to Peking Opens, Subcommittee on National Security and International Operations of the Committee on Government Operations, United States Senate (Washington, D.C.: U.S. Government Printing Office, 1970).
3. San Francisco Chronicle, June 15, 1973, p. 13.

6

CHINA AND THE UNITED NATIONS
John G. Stoessinger

China's entry into the United Nations in late October 1971 occurred at a moment when the world organization itself was undergoing a profound transformation. The Soviet-American bipolar world had come to an end. Old alliances had begun to loosen and new ones were about to form. The old cleavage between Communists and capitalists was slowly being superseded by a new cleavage between the haves and have-nots of the world. It was almost as if a kaleidoscope had been shaken vigorously and the old patterns had disintegrated to form an entirely new constellation. A new generation had come into its own, with its own political priorities and its own definitions of what constituted a viable world order. In short, the postwar world had definitely ended. China's entry at that very moment served as a catalyst that both reflected and accelerated a systemic change in the international order.

Efforts to describe the global system in terms of mathematical models must remain metaphoric. U Thant, shortly before his retirement, had spoken of the emergence of a five-power world: the United States, the Soviet Union, China, Japan, and the emerging Western Europe. This seems to be the view also of the present American administration. Within the United Nations, however, the most basic power configuration at this time is a triangular one: the uneasy relationship among China, the Soviet Union, and the United States. Machiavelli would have taken great delight in this constellation, since each of these three powers is afraid of being "ganged up on" by the other two and each aspires to the role of the "lady" in the triangle, to be wooed by the other two men. In world politics, as in love, triangles are inherently unstable; and this configuration may not endure for long. At this time, however, it constitutes a useful analytical tool.

After almost two years of membership in the United Nations, China has a remarkable record of participation. In this paper I shall examine this record with particular attention to the main problems on the agendas of the Security Council and of the General Assembly on which China has taken positions. On the basis of this objective record I shall make an attempt to evaluate China's role in the United Nations.

CHINA'S RECORD IN THE SECURITY COUNCIL

The main problems that have been the concern of the Security Council since China's entry have been five: the war between India and Pakistan; a broad range of African matters; peace-keeping, on Cyprus in particular; the continuing crisis in the Middle East; and the dispute over the Panama Canal.

China's debut in the Security Council occurred during the Indo-Pakistan war. On that occasion the Security Council was paralyzed, not because of the usual Soviet-American deadlock but because of a confrontation between the Soviet Union and China. The three vetoes that were cast by the Soviet Union on behalf of her ally, India, were cast in essence against China and her ally, Pakistan. The level of discourse between the delegates from China and the Soviet Union reached levels of vituperation rarely matched in the history of the Security Council. Ironically enough, the delegate from China accused the delegate from the Soviet Union of the very transgressions of imperialism and colonialism with which the very same Soviet delegate 20 years earlier had castigated the United States. It became clear on that occasion that the gulf between the two great Communist powers, China and the Soviet Union, was a great deal wider than that which separated China from the United States or the Soviet Union from the United States. Several months after this fateful meeting, China cast her first veto, against the admission of Bangladesh.

On the occasion of the Security Council's meeting in Addis Ababa, Ethiopia, in order to underline the rising importance of Third World problems, China made her first concerted and powerful bid for the ideological leadership of the smaller nations of the Third World. She vigorously supported all the resolutions that were adopted, or initiatives that were taken by the Council, against the white minority governments of South Africa, Rhodesia, and Portugal. She emphasized again and again that she had nothing in common with the reprehensible behavior of the two superpowers and that she, too, had suffered—as most of the nations of the Third World had suffered—from the yoke of Western incursions in the 19th century. Although the Soviet Union and China found themselves voting on the same side on many of these resolutions, China always took great pains to disassociate herself from the other Communist power.

98

There was considerable anxiety in the United Nations that China's entry would mean the death of the last remaining major United Nations peace-keeping force still in existence, that in Cyprus. The Cyprus force was under the exclusive jurisdiction of the Security Council and depended for its life on extensions of its mandate, which had to be renewed every six months. Since the main beneficiaries of the Cyprus force—Greece and Turkey—were both members of NATO, there was some anticipation that China, not particularly interested in making peace within NATO, would veto the operation. When the vote came, however, China abstained, and has done so on every succeeding occasion, with the result that the Cyprus force continues to exist on the basis of an uneasy triangular consensus among China, the Soviet Union, and the United States.

China's appearance in the Security Council has not helped the quest for a solution to the continuing crisis in the Middle East. In fact, the spectrum of discord has widened. For the first time since their active participation in the Middle East conflict, the Palestinians found themselves a great-power sponsor: China. China's support of the Palestinians must be seen in the context of the triangular constellation mentioned earlier. China's greatest fear in the Middle East is the possibility of "collusion" between the two "establishment super-powers," the United States and the Soviet Union, with China frozen out. A Soviet-American compromise solution in the Middle East is the one China fears most, and hence she has decided to back the political entity that is absolutely opposed to such a compromise, the Palestinians.

The recent Security Council meeting in Panama afforded China another opportunity to underline her support for the Third World. On that occasion the United States was isolated in its position that the dispute over the Panama Canal was a bilateral affair between itself and Panama. The third American veto in the history of the Security Council was cast on that occasion. The other members of the Council felt that the problem was one of colonialism in the Western Hemisphere and therefore deserved the multilateral attention of the United Nations. China supported this view with passion and once again, though voting on the same side as the Soviet Union, took pains to separate herself from Russia. Her objective to be the leader of the Third World became particularly clear on that occasion.

CHINA'S RECORD IN THE GENERAL ASSEMBLY

China's main interest in the General Assembly, with special attention to the 27th session, has focused on seven major problems: disarmament, development, the environment, the seabed, terrorism, finances, and a United Nations University.

China's position on disarmament has been plagued by a measure of ambiguity. On the one hand, she has found herself unable to oppose a Soviet initiative for a world disarmament conference openly because that would injure her position in the eyes of the Third World. On the other hand, to accede to radical disarmament would have frozen China's nuclear inferiority vis-à-vis the Soviet Union. It was difficult for China to escape from this dilemma, but finally she decided in favor of her right to continue nuclear tests, a position that was greeted by considerable displeasure in the Third World. In fact, a measure of support that the Chinese had gained among the smaller nations by virtue of her previous position on questions of colonialism was now canceled. China has not adhered to the three main instruments of arms control that have been signed under the aegis of the General Assembly: the Outer Space Treaty, the Nuclear Nonproliferation Treaty, and the Seabed Treaty. It is interesting to note, however, that China had not violated any of these treaties; and should she decide to accede to any of them de jure, such a decision would not entail a major shift in policy.

Ambiguity has also marked China's position on the various UN programs concerning economic development. In a sense one can describe China's dilemma in this respect as an identity crisis, since, on the one hand, she is an atomic power in good standing but, on the other, is still a poor and developing nation. China attempted to resolve this dilemma by supporting all initiatives taken by the Third World majority in the Assembly to enhance development programs and, by herself, pledging close to $2 million to the United Nations Development Program.

China's role in the newly established UN Environment Program has been truly catalytic. She virtually stole the spotlight at the Stockholm Conference in June 1972 because the Soviet Union was absent and the United States showed a relatively low profile. Once again China supported the position of the Third World countries, which defined environmental needs in developmental terms. The slogan "The polluter must pay" was of Chinese origin and was aimed with equal vehemence at both the Soviet Union and the United States. In this context China also raised a fundamental philosophical question by pointing out that the United States, which has approximately 6 percent of the world's population, consumes over 50 percent of the world's ecological resources. The world, in China's view, could afford only one United States of America.

But what if China decides to emulate the industrial model? The planet would not be able to sustain it. The spectacle of 700 million poor Chinese may be a national tragedy, but the spectacle of 700 million rich Chinese would be a planetary catastrophe. By raising these fundamental questions, China underlined the urgency of the environmental crisis and the need for a global approach to it. When the question of the location of the new Environmental Secretariat arose in December 1972, China strongly supported the Third World position of placing it in Nairobi, Kenya, which the United States opposed and on which the Soviet Union abstained. It was dramatic to note how, on that occasion, the old cleavage between the capitalist and Communist states was eclipsed by a new cleavage between the rich and the poor.

Similar fundamental questions were raised by China on the question of terrorism. The Chinese stated quite bluntly that national liberation groups, including the Palestinians, were justified in the use of force against the "establishment" powers such as South Africa, Rhodesia, Portugal, and Israel, which were decided by China to be the real terrorists. In this connection the Chinese resuscitated the old Scholastic doctrine of the "just war" but conveniently sidestepped the thorny problem of definition.

In her quest to become the major spokesman of the smaller nations, China supported their ambitious claims to territorial waters extending, in some cases, up to 200 miles. On this occasion the Chinese once again took the opportunity to chastise the superpowers. Perhaps the most interesting new initiative taken by China on this topic, however, was her position that the United Nations itself, rather than any single state, should have access to the resources of the seabed.

China played a constructive role in the bitter dispute between the Soviet Union and the United States over the American move to reduce the U.S. assessment for the regular budget from 31 percent to 25 percent. The Soviet Union had taken the position that the American contribution should be raised to 38 percent instead of being lowered. In the context of this debate, the Chinese came forward with an unprecedented offer to raise their contribution gradually over the next few years from 4 percent to 7 percent. When taken together with the expected contributions of the two Germanys, which should amount to approximately 9 percent of the budget, it seems that the American reduction will be more than made up by contributions from China and the two Germanys.

In December 1972 the General Assembly approved a resolution to establish a United Nations University. The vote was overwhelming, and only the Soviet Union and several Eastern European States found themselves in the opposition. China, partially because the Soviet Union opposed the resolution and partially because Japan had played a large role in initiating it, voted in favor.

CHINA'S ROLE VIS-À-VIS THE
SECRETARY-GENERAL AND THE SECRETARIAT

China's entry into the United Nations coincided with the election of the fourth Secretary-General. On legal grounds alone, had China chosen to do so, she could have vetoed the election of a new Secretary-General. Not only did she acquiesce in the election of Kurt Waldheim but she also displayed considerable sensitivity to the fate of a large number of Chinese nationals who were recruited into the Secretariat over the period of 23 years during which China was represented by the Nationalist government. Most of the staff members are still in the Secretariat and continue to perform their duties with a minimum of friction. The PRC government, in turn, is slowly bringing its own people into the Secretariat. For the time being, one of the places in the world where Chinese Communists and Chinese Nationalists manage to coexist in the same physical location without any upheaval is the UN Secretariat.

In their approach to the office of the Secretary-General, the Chinese have pursued a fairly restrictive policy. They acquiesced in the participation of the Secretary-General in the Paris Peace Conference on Vietnam. Together with the North Vietnamese, they opposed a more active role of the Secretary-General, which would have included his signature on the documents that were signed in Paris. Instead, on China's insistence, the compromise that was reached determined that the documents were signed "in the presence of the Secretary-General."

An overall perspective of China's role in the United Nations demonstrates that she, like most other members of the world body, has pursued her national interests, tending to employ the United Nations as yet another instrument toward that objective. In that pursuit her behavior had been pragmatic rather than ideological. It is interesting to note, for example, that although Maoist guerrillas were active in East Pakistan, China chose to support the government of West Pakistan in its civil war. In that sense China has placed Machiavelli above Mao Tse-tung.

It is useful to remember that of all the members of the United Nations, China probably has the least experience with a multilateral organization and the innumerable compromises and accommodations that membership in such a body entails. In light of this fact, China's diplomats have done remarkably well, learning the arts of negotiation and compromise in a relatively short time. Like many other members they have found themselves at times on the horns of dilemmas from which they have had to extricate themselves. The conflicting objectives of wooing the Third World and of pursuing nuclear development were cases in point. China managed to deal with these dilemmas with a fairly high degree of sophistication.

On balance, the overall record suggests that China has managed to fit into the structure of the United Nations without excessive turbulence. One may justly wonder today whether the 23-year fight led by the United States to keep China out of the United Nations was justified. Certainly on several issues China's impact has been negative, but on many more the effect has been constructive. There is little doubt that on the balance sheet, the credits exceed the debits. Perhaps most significantly, China drew the world's attention to the urgency of the ecological problem. In the light of the fact that most member states have a tendency to bring their problems to the United Nations at a very late stage, and indeed make the United Nations a kind of receiver in bankruptcy, subsequently blaming it for that bankruptcy, China's initiative in this regard must be considered as a major contribution. Moreover, since the great powers continue to relegate the United Nations to the sidelines, and negotiate the great policy issues outside of it, the fact that at least one major power has taken up the cause of smaller nations, which feel more and more ignored on the current global scene, is an auspicious development. Finally, from China's point of view, it is important to remember that for 2,000 years she has considered herself to be the center of the universe, superior to all other nations, which she regarded as "barbarians." Then, in the 19th century, the scales were suddenly reversed: the "barbarians" invaded China and parceled her out among themselves. China's entry into the United Nations signifies the first time in her history when she is compelled to deal with other states on the basis of sovereign equality.

7

THE PARTICIPATION OF THE PRC
IN THE UNITED NATIONS
William R. Feeney

INTRODUCTION

The seating of the People's Republic of China (PRC) in the United Nations (UN) in October 1971 as the sole legitimate representative of China marked the beginning of a new era for the world organization. For the first time since the establishment of the PRC 22 years earlier, the de facto government of the world's most populous nation was accorded the full privileges of membership and the Nationalist government on Taiwan was expelled. This important shift in credentials can best be described as an accommodation with reality that has very far-reaching implications for the organization, its membership, and the PRC. Not only has one of the last major barriers to universality been breached but the UN now provides, for the first time in many years, a common arena for meaningful great power diplomatic contact, interaction, and negotiation.

Any analysis of PRC participation in the UN, however, would be incomplete without a brief review of the process by which Peking entered the world body. The resolution of the Chinese representation issue was a protracted and at times caustic affair.[1] The question first arose as the result of the Communist victory over the Nationalists in the Chinese civil war. Since China was an original UN member and one of the five great powers, the fundamental question was legally not one of admission but of deciding which government, Peking or Taipei, had the better credentials to represent China in the world body. Although a number of governments had already recognized Peking or were prepared to do so soon, the United States, while indicating its willingness to abide by the verdict of the majority, took a stand opposing a Soviet resolution in the Security Council to expel the Nationalists. The Soviet proposal was rejected and set the stage for a 21-year struggle.[2] Thus, because of political considerations, the question of PRC participation was practically transformed from a question of credentials to one of membership.[3]

The outbreak of the Korean War in June 1950 constituted a crucial turning point for the Chinese representation question. The voluntary absence of the Soviet Union from the Security Council, ironically in protest against the continued Nationalist presence, enabled the United States to secure UN endorsement for a collective, but heavily American dominated, "police action" to oppose first the North Korean invasion of South Korea and later the armed intervention of Chinese "volunteers." The UN role in this confrontation, the extent to which the United States dominated the organization, the Security Council rebuff of the presentation by a PRC delegation of Peking's position on Korea and Taiwan, and the passage of two U.S.-backed anti-Chinese resolutions that branded the PRC an "aggressor" and recommended a trade embargo against it compounded the initial estrangement between Peking and the world organization.[4]

By drawing upon its virtually automatic majority in the General Assembly, the U.S. devised the so-called Moratorium Formula whereby any consideration of the issue was systematically postponed on a yearly basis. Saddled with the onus of the Korean intervention, Peking fared poorly in the early years. But after the 1953 Armistice the PRC began to make inroads on the margin of exclusion by gaining the support of many of the newer UN member states. This trend was particularly pronounced in the 1960 vote. (See Attachment A, Table 1.) To offset growing support for Peking, the United States adopted a new parliamentary tactic by which the matter would be considered an "important question" under Article 18 of the UN Charter, thus requiring a two-thirds vote. The large initial margin of support accorded the U.S. position in 1961 was gradually eroded with the further expansion of UN membership and by the defection of a number of earlier supporters. By 1965 although the United States was still able to win on the "important question" resolution, the vote on the main resolution to seat the PRC ended in a tie. (See Attachment A, Tables 2 and 3.)

This ground swell of support for the PRC was temporarily interrupted by the Great Proletarian Cultural Revolution. Massive internal turmoil, excessive xenophobia, and strong U.S. and Nationalist lobbying among key African states produced a temporary reversal in the pro-Peking tide. However, the emergence of more moderate Chinese leadership during the Ninth Chinese Communist Party Congress; the election of President Nixon, who had earlier urged that U.S. policy come to grips with the reality of China; the implementation of a number of concrete political and economic steps designed to ease Sino-American tensions; the phasing out of U.S. involvement in Indochina; and the dramatic announcement of a Nixon visit to China significantly influenced subsequent UN voting on the Chinese representation issue. In 1970, though not decisive because of the two-thirds requirement, an Assembly majority went on record for the first time as favoring the seating of the PRC.

As additional nations extended diplomatic recognition to the PRC, the U.S. position was modified according to the recommendations of the Lodge Commission, made public in April 1971, which advocated the adoption of a "two Chinas" policy. Peking's right to UN representation was recognized in both the General Assembly and the Security Council; but the expulsion of Taiwan from the UN, as demanded by the PRC, would be treated as an "important question" requiring a two-thirds majority vote.[5] Although it was felt in many quarters that no serious U.S. effort would be made to save Taipei, a series of intricate parliamentary maneuvers was organized and intensive pro-Taiwan lobbying efforts were mounted.* The essence of American strategy, in the words of one European diplomat, was to turn the vote into a "worldwide plebiscite for or against the United States." Although the United States succeeded in winning priority for its procedural resolution making expulsion of Taiwan an important question, the all-important key vote on the question itself was lost by a narrow 59-55-15 margin. Certainly the presence of Henry Kissinger in Peking and the defection of a number of earlier supporters, especially in Europe, proved to be decisive.† The last vote on the main resolution to seat the PRC and to expel the Nationalists, which needed only a majority, was anticlimatic and passed by an overwhelming 76-35-17 margin.[6]

The PRC performance in the UN since then has clearly demonstrated that Peking has consistently sought to achieve three major goals; national unification, enhanced national security, and Third World leadership. Throughout its tenure in the world body, both predictable and unexpected issues have arisen. Because parliamentary diplomacy demands immediate and public commitment, often in an ad hoc fashion, Peking is no longer able to enjoy the luxury of delay before announcing its position and the rationale for it. Rather, like other UN participants, the PRC has had to make difficult choices in the full glare of world publicity. Long-term gains have had to be weighed against short-term

---

*Interestingly, though the Albanians and the Soviet bloc supported the PRC, they did not engage in active lobbying on Peking's behalf.

†For a comparison of the 1970 and 1971 roll call votes, see Attachment B. Only 4 allies backed the United States—Greece, Luxembourg, Portugal, and Spain—while 18 including, the United Kingdom and the Scandinavian countries, voted against the United States and 7 abstained.

losses, consistency and principles against the prospects of voting defeats, and, most important, the goal of Third World leadership against the interests and demands of national security. Occasionally concessions to expediency have had to be made.

The presence of the PRC in the world organization, though undoubtedly complicating UN politics and decision-making, has belied many of the earlier alarmist fears and predictions of its traditional opponents. Indeed, the seriousness of Peking's UN intentions has been evidenced not only by a carefully controlled policy of pragmatic self-interest, with a minimum of recrimination for its protracted exclusion and past policy differences with the organization, but also by the large size and high caliber of its delegation, which recently numbered some 49 diplomats.[7]

From the outset if the PRC has vigorously pursued its own national interests, careful efforts have also been made to adopt appropriate tactics to achieve those ends. For nearly a year the Chinese presented a dualistic attitude within the organization. In the initial general debate in the General Assembly, Peking's spokesmen assumed a tough, succinct, and uncompromising line in attacking China's enemies and appealing to potential supporters. But in the subsequent multilateral diplomatic process, the relatively inexperienced Chinese proved to be much more cautious, no doubt because of the pitfalls posed to the uninitiated by the problem of assuming recorded public positions on a wide array of divisive issues. After the autumn of 1972, as Peking's delegates gained greater knowledge and familiarity with the complexities of UN policies and procedures, this initial circumspection gave way to increased confidence and assertiveness in all phases of their UN activities.

But for the most part, if Peking, which was able to enter the UN on its own terms, has not strayed very far from its original positions and goals, it has certainly elaborated upon them at length in response to changing international circumstances. Even more important, it has also forged a voting record by which its UN participation can be compared and evaluated. The purpose of this paper is to review the performance and voting record of the PRC on a number of key issues during the 26th and 27th General Assembly sessions, periodic meetings of the Security Council, and in the several other UN bodies of which Peking is a member. These matters include Taiwan, the Indo-Pakistan war and Bangladesh, disarmament, the Middle East and international terrorism, colonialism, Vietnam, peace-keeping, the selection of a new Secretary-General, the law of the sea, and economic development.

TAIWAN

One of Peking's foremost foreign policy objectives has been to consolidate its claim to "the province of Taiwan" and to eliminate any residual presence at the UN of what was termed "the Chiang clique." Encouraged by the early ouster of two UN-accredited Nationalist newsmen employed by the Taipei government-controlled Central News Agency of China, the Peking delegation intensified its pressure for full implementation of the General Assembly resolution of October 25, 1971. This resolution recognized the PRC as the only legitimate representative of China and called for the expulsion of the "representatives of Chiang Kai-shek."[8] In a formal note to Secretary-General Kurt Waldheim in January 1972, Huang Hua, PRC permanent UN Ambassador, demanded that the UN cease all contacts with and assistance to Taiwan.[9] Accordingly, some $32 million worth of UN Development Program assistance was ended by the following June, though no similar request was made for 19 WHO projects on Taiwan totaling nearly $200 million.[10] Two months later all references to Taiwan were dropped in UN publications and documents.

Similar demands were voiced for an end to Nationalist representation in the UN specialized agencies and a halt to all UN assistance "instigated by the United States, the Chiang clique, and India" to Tibetan, Hong Kong, and Macao refugees. The specialized agencies are largely autonomous from the UN and several employ a system of weighted voting. As of May 1973 Taiwan had withdrawn or been ousted from all but the World Bank Group (IBRD, IMF, IDA, IFC), and the PRC has been formally admitted to seven agencies (ILO, UNESCO, WHO, WMO, ICAO, IMCO, and FAO). However, Peking has not yet assumed an active role in most of these organizations, largely because of a shortage of trained personnel and the need for adequate preparations. As for the latter demand, though Peking at the July 1972 session of the Economic and Social Council (ECOSOC) insisted that the office of the UN High Commissioner for Refugees halt all aid to the "so-called Tibetan refugees and Chinese refugees in Hong Kong and Macao" and delete all references to them, no final General Assembly action has been taken.[11]

A further step in repudiating Taiwan was announcements that Peking would neither honor UN resolutions adopted during the Nationalist tenure nor assume any share of the $28.6 million debt owed by Taipei when it was expelled.* At the close of the 27th General

---

*Prior to the entry of the PRC about 2,750 resolutions had been adopted by the General Assembly, 1,650 by ECOSOC, and 300 by the Security Council.

Assembly session in December 1972, a resolution was adopted deleting all of Taiwan's unpaid assessed contributions from the PRC account.[12] In contrast with this hard line, however, Peking has demonstrated a moderate and understanding attitude toward some 150 Chinese employees of the UN Secretariat, most of whom hold Nationalist passports. Strong efforts have been made, with some apparent success, to win their loyalty. Finally, as of May 1973, some 92 governments have either recognized or have restored diplomatic relations with the PRC, an increase from 68 at the time of its entry. On balance, therefore, Peking has been able to remove most of the remaining vestiges of a Nationalist presence in the UN and has increasingly isolated Taiwan from its membership.

THE INDO-PAKISTANI WAR AND BANGLADESH

Of far greater immediate concern to the PRC was the issue of the Indo-Pakistani war, which erupted in December 1971, shortly after Peking's UN debut. The 1969 Ussuri River clashes, Moscow's subsequent military buildup along the Sino-Soviet border, and strong Soviet diplomatic and military backing for India in its latest confrontation with Pakistan induced Peking to lend strong support to the latter, which had become a tacit South Asian ally in recent years.[13] Perhaps even more important, if the PRC mutely acceded to the secession of East Pakistan, the same precedent could well be applied to Taiwan or to China's potentially restive nationalities, which might want to assert their separate national identities.[14] Taken together, these considerations triggered an acrimonious confrontation during a three-day emergency session of the Security Council (December 4-6).

During the course of that debate Ambassadors Huang Hua and Yakov Malik engaged, in true Cold War style, in several vicious rhetorical slugging matches that soon became personal and concerned more with national and ideological differences than with the issue at hand. In speeches on December 5 and 15, Huang Hua accused the "Soviet social-imperialists" of "carrying out aggression, interference, subversion and expansion everywhere" and likened Moscow's role in the current dispute to "Soviet military aggression and armed occupation of Czechoslovakia in 1968." Referring to the Soviet delegate as "Mister Malik," a supreme insult among Communists, the Peking representative denounced the "renegade features" of the Soviet leadership for betraying Marxism-Leninism and for seeking to set up a "Manchukuo"-type government in East Pakistan in order to gain control of the continent, encircle China, and strengthen its position in contending with the other superpower for world hegemony.[15]

In supporting Pakistan, the PRC went far beyond the U.S. position and, for reasons of national security, chose to back completely the claims of General Yahya Khan's military regime that it was fully entitled to keep its grip on East Pakistan by all available means, including the savage repression of an unmistakable demand for self-determination.[16] On the one hand, it could not be denied that China was on fairly safe international legal ground in opposing the extra-legal Indian attack against its neighbor, which was designed to force the repatriation of the Bengali refugees and bring about the dismemberment of a perennial rival in South Asia. But in so doing, Peking selectively repudiated a long-held doctrinal position that accorded unreserved support for popular wars of national liberation and the right to national self-determination.[17] Moreover, the PRC placed itself squarely in opposition to the views of the vast majority of the Third World, which was appalled by West Pakistani atrocities.

In the Security Council the PRC and the United States found themselves voting together, though for somewhat different reasons, on three draft resolutions, each of which in varying terms called upon the belligerents to take immediate steps to cease hostilities, withdraw their troops, and assist in the return of the East Pakistani refugees.[18] Each of these proposals was summarily vetoed by the Soviet Union.[19] A Soviet counter draft resolution, calling upon the Pakistani government to cease all acts of violence in East Pakistan and to reach a political settlement, was rejected when it failed to receive the requisite nine affirmative votes.[20] Recognizing the impasse of great power disunity, the Security Council referred the question to the General Assembly, where a resolution was passed recommending, rather than ordering, steps similar to those contained in the vetoed U.S. proposal.[21] The impending collapse of Pakistani resistance led to the adoption of a belated Security Council resolution that merely called for a cease-fire (by that time already largely in effect) until troop withdrawals could take place.[22]

The application of Bangladesh for admission to the UN the following autumn renewed Peking's initial embarrassment vis-à-vis the Third World. In opposing Bangladesh's request, the PRC representative argued that Dacca was in flagrant violation of two earlier UN resolutions that called for the repatriation of all prisoners of war and civilian detainees taken during the war and for the removal of all foreign (Indian) troops from Bangladesh.* Not only did the issue lead to a caustic repetition of Sino-Soviet name-calling, but the defeat of

---

*At the time approximately 80,000 Pakistani soldiers and 10,000 West Pakistani civilians remained in Indian hands contrary to S/RES/307 (1971) and A/RES/2793 (XXVI), December 7, 1971.

a PRC proposal to postpone any consideration of the question until the resolutions were fully implemented prompted Peking to resort to casting its first Security Council veto.[23] In justifying this action, Huang Hua cited Article 4 (1) of the UN Charter, which states that UN membership is open to "peace-loving states which accept the obligations contained in the present Charter and, in the judgment of the Organization, are able and willing to carry out these obligations." Paradoxically, the United States for years had used this very argument, based on resolutions regarding Korea, Tibet, and India, to bar the PRC from the world body.[24] Though Peking has thus far succeeded in excluding Bangladesh from the UN, this has been accomplished at the price of considerable Third World displeasure.[25]

DISARMAMENT

The issue of disarmament, and especially the question of nuclear weapons, has placed Peking in a difficult position with much of the Third World, but with considerably less damage to its leadership designs. Broad support for a Soviet proposal for a world disarmament conference and an end to nuclear testing in the atmosphere has come from many smaller and middle-sized Third World countries, thus confronting the PRC with a dilemma. If China agreed to participate in the conference, strong pressure against further Chinese nuclear weapons testing could be expected at a time when the goal of developing a moderately effective nuclear deterrent had not been achieved. If Peking declined to take part, the Soviets would use this refusal to depict the PRC as callous of Third World opinion and guilty of both sabotaging world peace and polluting the atmosphere with radioactive fallout.[26]

During the 26th General Assembly session, a bitter Sino-Soviet clash ensued over this issue. Responding to a Soviet draft resolution proposing a world disarmament conference,[27] Ch'iao Kuan-hua, PRC Vice Foreign Minister, argued that China had always favored disarmament but was compelled to develop nuclear weapons because of the nuclear threat posed by the two superpowers. Accordingly, Chinese participation was made contingent upon three demands: (1) that the conference have the clear aim of discussing the question of the complete prohibition and thorough destruction of nuclear weapons; (2) that both superpowers publicly pledge not to be the first to use such weapons; and (3) that all nuclear bases on the territories of other countries be dismantled and all nuclear armed forces and means of delivery be withdrawn.[28]

This counterproposal triggered a bitter exchange between Ambassador Malik and Ch'iao. The former emotionally accused the

Chinese of pouring out a "flood of slander and monstrous inventions against the Soviet Union" and, noting American reservations on the conference, charged the PRC with "teaming up with the imperialists" in a "duet of negativism."[29] Not to be outdone, Ch'iao responded by calling Malik's remarks a "splendid self-exposure" and inquired who was "singing a duet with the U.S. imperialism" when

> . . . to the north of China, large numbers of Soviet armed forces including rocket forces are stationed in the People's Republic of Mongolia; to the east of China, the United States is maintaining a large number of military bases and nuclear bases in Japan proper and Okinawa. . . . In Europe, the Middle East, the Mediterranean, the Indian Ocean and other parts of the world, the Soviet leadership considers that the final say rests only with an agreement between the Soviet Union and the United States.[30]

Apart from rhetorical subterfuge, the PRC was able to take advantage of Third World desires for conference participation by all the great powers, careful advance preparation, and the U.S. preference for a smaller negotiating forum. Though Peking voted against three resolutions urging the cessation of nuclear testing, the PRC was able to avoid embarrassment by supporting several other disarmament resolutions. These included a Mexican-Rumanian substitute for the original Soviet proposal that left the conference date, place, and agenda to be fixed by the next Assembly and a resolution favored by much of the Third World declaring the Indian Ocean a zone of peace.[31]

At the UN Conference on the Human Environment in Stockholm (June 5-16, 1972) and the general debate at the 27th General Assembly session, the PRC was less successful in avoiding the embarrassing onus of its position on disarmament. At the former, Peking tried to seize the initiative by demanding that the industrial powers compensate the developing nations for "colonialist and neo-colonialist exploitation," by insisting that responsibility for environmental pollution be fixed on "the imperialist, colonialist and neo-colonialist policies of the superpowers," and by promoting a number of anti-superpower disarmament resolutions.[32] Despite the absence of the Soviet Union from the 114-nation conference, the PRC failed to make good on its claims to Third World leadership when many of its proposals were either omitted from the final document or considerably watered down. But most damaging of all, the PRC found itself in a distinct minority position, along with France and Gabon, in opposing a strongly worded, Third World-backed resolution condemning atmospheric nuclear testing and urging its abandonment.[33]

In New York the following autumn Peking was forced into the even more compromising position of voting with such Third World nemeses as Portugal and South Africa in opposing a Soviet-backed proposal on the nonuse of force in international relations and the permanent prohibition of the use of nuclear weapons.[34] The extent of PRC isolation was reflected in Ch'iao Kuan-hua's description of the proposal as "a downright fraud" and in his denunciation of the Soviets for "sophistry," "nuclear blackmail," and trying to make people believe that they had "laid down their butcher's knives."[35] In addition to losing little time in calling Third World attention to the identity of China's voting partners, the Soviets retorted by pointing to PRC opposition to three resolutions aimed against atmospheric nuclear testing, in which they were joined this time by France, Portugal, and Albania.[36] Since Peking was able to support only one other significant disarmament proposal during the session (deploring the use of napalm), the Chinese were indeed hard-pressed.[37]

To avoid further offense to the Third World, the Chinese were anxious to work out a compromise that would allow them to vote for the world disarmament conference proposal without any specific commitment. Peking agreed to support a resolution that provided for a special 35-member committee to be named by the UN General Assembly President, Stanislaw Trepczynski, from candidates suggested by regional groups to examine the conference views and suggestions of all governments.[38] However, when Trepczynski, presumably under strong Soviet pressure, appointed the committee at the last minute, seats were left vacant for the nuclear powers. If the PRC response was swift in denouncing the Assembly President for abusing his authority, it also provided Peking with the perfect excuse for not participating, thereby largely scuttling the committee and perhaps even the conference itself.[39]

Thus the PRC, despite considerable obstacles, has been able to weather the disarmament storm fairly well. In fact, it should be noted that a fair number of Third World countries tend to share Peking's views on the military dominance of the two superpowers because of their nuclear capabilities. Also, since the feeling is fairly widespread that the PRC is the Third World representative in the nuclear club, Peking's recalcitrance on disarmament questions has not been as damaging to its Third World leadership pretensions as otherwise might be expected.

THE MIDDLE EAST AND INTERNATIONAL TERRORISM

On the Middle East question the PRC from the beginning has pursued a vigorous pro-Arab policy in the UN. From a strictly national

security perspective, the Chinese have much to gain from keeping
the Middle East dispute simmering. First, any settlement of the issue
would eventually lead to the reopening of the Suez Canal, thus affording
the Soviets easier access to the Indian Ocean and jeopardizing PRC
lines of communications with its Arab and African friends.[40] Second,
tension in the Middle East, particularly if it led to an expanded Soviet
military presence in the area, would mean fewer Soviet forces stationed
on the Sino-Soviet frontier. Finally, continued conflict in the Middle
East would tend to undermine the evolving Soviet-American détente,
especially in Europe; reduce in turn the chances of success of both
the mutual and balanced force reduction talks and the Conference on
Security and Cooperation in Europe; and once again limit Moscow's
ability to expand its military presence on the Chinese border.

In view of these considerations, the PRC has assumed a persistently hard-line approach toward what it describes as "Israeli
Zionist aggression." But in assessing responsibility for the absence
of peace in the area, Peking's representatives have laid the bulk of
the blame squarely on the shoulders of the superpowers. In the PRC's
first detailed UN policy statement, Ch'iao Kuan-hua charged that the
superpowers were "acting in collusion" at the UN to prevent the recov-
ery of the lost Arab territories and were

> . . . taking advantage of the temporary difficulties facing
> the Palestinian and other Arab peoples to make dirty
> political deals in their contention for important stra-
> tegic points and oil reserves at the expense of the na-
> tional rights and territorial integrity and sovereignty
> of the Palestinian and other Arab peoples.[41]

He went on to characterize the superpowers as "paper tigers" and
advocated the outright use of force to settle the question. Thus, from
the outset it was abundantly clear that Peking had no intention of joining
the other great powers to seek a peaceful solution.

As this issue developed, the PRC position became comparatively
more anti-Soviet if not less anti-American. This tendency was first
apparent in the omission of any concerted condemnation of the United
States in Peking's Security Council response to Israeli attacks on
Lebanon in February 1972 and on Lebanon and Syria the following
September.[42] When the issue was debated at the 27th General Assembly session, comparatively perfunctory criticism of the United
States for "undisguised support and encouragement to Israeli aggression" was overshadowed by a vehement denunciation of "the other
superpower," which was

> . . . masquerading as a friend of the Arab people . . .
> taking advantage of the temporary difficulties of the Arab

countries to carry out large-scale infiltration and expansion in the Middle East under the signboard of "help eliminate the consequences of aggression" and "assist the Arab people." It is more deceptive and more dangerous than old-line imperialism. . . . They want to realize the old tsar's long-cherished ambition for control of the Mediterranean Sea and the establishment of hegemony in the Middle East.[43]

This intensified anti-Soviet line led to several significant variations between the PRC and the Soviet Union in voting performance. On each occasion the Chinese opted for a much harder line against Israel than the Soviets were willing to support. In the General Assembly in both December 1971 and the following year, while the Soviets voted in favor of draft resolutions aimed against Israel, Peking abstained, on the ground that the condemnations were not sufficiently strong.[44] The two Communist giants parted company for much the same reason over Security Council action following the February 1972 Israeli attack on Lebanon.[45] The only instances of Sino-Soviet voting cooperation were on a July 1972 Security Council resolution calling on Israel to return without delay all Syrian and Lebanese military personnel abducted from Lebanon in a June raid and several General Assembly resolutions dealing with Palestinian refugees adopted in December 1972.[46]

Somewhat the same kind of Sino-Soviet rivalry occurred at least initially over the closely related problem of international terrorism. This issue had become increasingly compelling following a wave of aerial hijackings, bombings, kidnappings, and assassinations of diplomats, and the cold-blooded killing of 26 people at the Tel Aviv airport and 11 Israeli Olympic athletes in Munich. The major difficulty inherent in this question is the political motivation for many of these acts and the tendency almost invariably for them to become part of the ongoing confrontation between revisionist and status quo forces. Thus, any international effort to control terrorism is likely to become highly subjective and may well be regarded as detrimental to revisionist goals and favorable to the status quo.

As supporters of revolutionary activities, both the PRC and the Soviet Union could therefore be expected to oppose UN efforts to impose curbs on terrorism. Accordingly Peking, along with the Arab states, argued in September 1972 in the General Committee to exclude the issue from the General Assembly agenda. Ch'en Ch'u, PRC deputy permanent representative, went so far as to declare: "It is perfectly just for the oppressed nations and peoples to use revolutionary violence against the violence of imperialism, colonialism, neo-colonialism, racism and Israeli Zionism,"[47] In contrast, while the Soviet delegate ob-

115

served that antiterrorist measures could be used by neocolonialists "to suppress the liberation movements" and that "no one has the right to deprive people of the right to fight for their rights", the Soviet Union, along with Czechoslovakia, abstained on the vote to consider the issue.[48]

During the ensuing debate in the General Assembly's Legal Committee (November 9-22), the PRC defended the "just struggles" of the Palestinians and African liberation movements and claimed such acts were "not terrorism at all."[49] Moreover, Peking insisted that terrorist acts should be dealt with by the countries in which they occurred and not by international treaty. The Soviets, on the other hand, initially suggested that the International Law Commission meet in May 1973 to draft a treaty, a proposal supported by the United States and the other Western powers.[50] But when the Arabs were able to convince the African states that mesaures directed against terrorism might be used to outlaw African national liberation movements, the Soviets quickly mobilized Communist bloc support to scuttle the issue, lest the Chinese upstage them in Third World eyes. In a vote in the Legal Committee, later confirmed by the entire General Assembly, an Arab-African-Communist coalition adopted a resolution that condemned "repressive and terrorist acts by colonial, racist and alien regimes" but took no action except to study the causes of terrorist acts and ways of eliminating them.[51] In strongly supporting much of the Third World from the beginning on this issue, Peking was able to force a change in Soviet policy, gain an important propaganda advantage, and shift the blame for terrorism from the actual perpetrators to selected Western regimes.

COLONIALISM

For both security and ideological reasons, the PRC from the outset has adopted a strong anticolonial UN posture. First, by lending strident vocal support in the world body to the anticolonial cause, particularly in southern Africa, and also by granting modest military and economic assistance to selected nationalist movements, Peking could expect to reap considerable long-term political advantage should the forces of African nationalism prevail in the Portuguese colonies, Namibia, Rhodesia, and the Republic of South Africa. Second, even if African nationalism is contained, Peking's prestige would be higher in the eyes of many Black African and other newly independent states. Third, in a strategic sense a rise in Chinese influence in Africa would help to counter Soviet expansion into South Asia and the Indian Ocean, especially if bases could be acquired on the African east coast. Fourth, should Moscow begin to intensify pressure along the Sino-Soviet border, Peking might well expect important reciprocal support both in and out of the UN from the anticolonial bloc. Finally, since China, unlike the Soviet Union, was an early victim of colonialism and imperialism and was able to achieve freedom from foreign domination by revolutionary means, the anticolonial issue provides a useful propaganda vehicle to promote throughout the Third World the alleged superiority of Mao's brand of revolutionary Communism in successfully coping with "colonialism, neo-colonialism, and imperialism."

Like the Middle East question, this issue has provided another occasion for spirited Sino-Soviet competition for Third World favor. Not only have the two Communist states tried to outdo one another in denouncing the colonial policies of the Western powers, but each has occasionally questioned the authenticity of the other's anticolonial commitment. Thus during the special UN Security Council meetings in Addis Ababa (January 28-February 5, 1972), Huang and Malik openly jousted for rhetorical advantage, competition which sharpened considerably soon after when the PRC was elected to join the Soviet Union as a member of the Special Committee on Decolonialization.[52] Particularly indicative of this rivalry was the General Assembly speech of Huang Hua on October 20, 1972, in which he indirectly castigated the Soviet Union for

> . . . masquerading as a friend of the Asian, African, and Latin American peoples by flaunting the signboard of "anti-imperialism and anti-colonialism" while professing to give so-called "aid," while it is perpetuating the same colonial evils. That is a newest type of colonialism.[53]

The colonialism issue is one of the few matters on which the PRC and the Soviet Union have consistently voted together. The two major exceptions have been (1) the question of Namibia and the creation of a three-member group (Argentina, Somalia, and Yugoslavia) to initiate contacts with South African authorities over the future of the old League mandate and (2) the granting of UN economic assistance to Zambia, which recently cut all remaining trade and communication ties with Rhodesia. Because many African states favored the former initiative, the Soviets somewhat hesitantly backed Security Council resolutions in February and August 1972 and abstained the following December on establishing a "dialogue" with South Africa. But Peking charged that it was a "trick" to create "confusion" and refused to participate in the voting.[54] Though neither power made reference to the other, it was clear that in opting for the hard-line approach despite current African feelings, China expected to benefit considerably should no progress be made on the issue. Sino-Soviet competition was also apparent on the latter question. While the PRC joined with the other Western powers in supporting economic assistance for Zambia, the

Soviets initially charged that the resolution failed to condemn those states that were responsible for the racist regime in Rhodesia, particularly the United Kingdom, and abstained on the resolution. Since Moscow soon backed a stronger resolution, it is likely that the Soviets wished to demonstrate their ability to take a hard line on behalf of the African cause while indirectly expressing their concern over growing Chinese influence in East Africa, which stems from PRC aid in the construction of a $750 million railroad linking Zambia to Tanzania, to be completed in 1974.[55]

One interesting sidelight to the PRC position on the colonial issue is provided by the cases of Hong Kong and Macao. In a March 8, 1972, letter to the Special Committee on Decolonialization, Huang Hua objected to the inclusion of these coastal enclaves in the official UN list of nonself-governing territories. Instead, he argued that Hong Kong and Macao are "part of Chinese territory occupied by British and Portuguese authorities" and that since these areas were "entirely within China's sovereign right," the UN had no right to discuss the question. The letter concluded by asking that the "erroneous" categorization as "colonial territories" be "immediately removed" from all UN documents.[56] By suggesting that these areas were not really colonies but a part of China, the PRC denied that each might have the future right to choose independence rather than Chinese rule. But in doing so, Peking came very close to appropriating some of the domestic jurisdiction arguments propounded in an earlier era by the former colonial powers. Although a Decolonialization Committee majority recommended the adoption of the PRC position in June 1972, the General Assembly has not yet taken any action.

Compared with other issues, colonialism has proved to be extremely valuable in winning support for Peking among the Afro-Asian portion of the Third World. By strongly supporting Panama's claim to sovereignty and jurisdiction over the Panama Canal and the Canal Zone at the Security Council meeting in Panama City (March 15-21, 1973), the PRC has been able to broaden its appeal on this question to the Latin American states. Of particular satisfaction to Peking was the lopsided pro-Panama vote, against which the United States was forced to cast a rare veto.[57] Though the issue has proved less useful against the Soviet Union than the West, the Chinese to a large extent have been able to supplant the white and relatively affluent Soviets as the foremost champion of anticolonialism in the eyes of much of the Third World.

VIETNAM, PEACE-KEEPING, AND THE SELECTION OF A NEW SECRETARY-GENERAL

In contrast with Peking's combative positions on the above issues, a relatively low-key and even accommodative approach has marked the questions of Vietnam, peace-keeping, and the selection of a new Secretary-General. In the case of Vietnam, Peking's public statements in the UN up to the time of the cease-fire were infrequent and rather perfunctory condemnations of U.S. policies. The one real exception was the May 1972 blockade of North Vietnam. At that time, in response to a U.S. letter seeking to justify these actions, Huang Hua sent a sharply worded letter of protest to Secretary-General Waldheim and U.S. Representative George Bush, President of the Security Council for that month.[58] In addition, though the Vietnam question had been on the Security Council agenda since 1966, the Chinese flatly rejected Secretary-General Waldheim's May 1972 initiative to bring the war question before the Council. While it was likely that the other four great powers would not have objected, Peking did so to demonstrate support for the North Vietnamese and Viet Cong contention that since the struggle was basically a civil war, it was a matter of domestic jurisdiction and thus had "nothing to do with the United Nations."[59]

Likewise, despite long-time opposition to the UN's peace-keeping role dating from the Korean War, Peking on three occasions has abstained in voting on resolutions extending for six-month periods the mandate of the UN force in Cyprus.[60]

Finally, while there was considerable haggling among the Big Five over a successor to U Thant, there was no sustained deadlock. Even though the PRC would have preferred an Asian or African and appeared to support Max Jacobson of Finland as its second choice, the Chinese were willing to accept Kurt Waldheim, who had strong Soviet support. Thus, at least on some issues, Peking has proved to be pliable and pragmatic.

THE SEA AND THE SEABED

An increasingly important issue before the United Nations in recent years has been that of the sea and the seabed. This question, which includes such matters as fishing rights and marine conservation, territorial water limits and the rights of coastal and other states therein, transit through narrow straits, peaceful uses of the international seabed, and the creation of an international authority to administer the international seabed, has enormous political, military, and economic implications.[61]

Ever since its entry into the UN, and especially after its selection to the Committee on the Peaceful Uses of the Sea-Bed and the Ocean Floor beyond National Jurisdiction in December 1971, the PRC has leaned very heavily on this issue to attack the superpowers, enhance its own economic and strategic interests, and advance its claim as the only big power protector of the Third World. By supporting the claims of several Latin American states for sovereignty up to 200 miles from their coasts, Peking seeks to gain the goodwill of all under-developed coastal states, which might then claim control over such important sources of wealth as fisheries, petroleum, and mineral deposits. Not only would this development render the latter more independent of the superpowers, but the rejection of this claim by both the United States and the Soviet Union affords China an excellent opportunity to exploit a popular Third World issue, especially in the Western Hemisphere. In a strategic sense such a claim, if upheld, would go very far in expanding PRC security, in that foreign warships, including submarines and military aircraft, would have to obtain permission from coastal nations to sail in waters or through international straits that fall within their jurisdictions or to fly over them. Finally, since the 200-mile limit would extend from the coasts of Taiwan, Peking could claim for itself a sizable part of the vast wealth of the East China and Yellow Seas if that limit is internationally accepted for jurisdiction over fishing, petroleum, and mineral resources.

Accordingly, in major speeches before the Sea-Bed Committee in March and July 1972 and March 1973, Chinese representatives stated the following themes: (1) each country has a sovereign right to decide the scope of its rights over territorial seas; (2) all coastal countries have the right of disposal of the natural resources in their coastal seas, seabed, and its subsoil; (3) the seas and submarine resources beyond the limits of territorial jurisdiction are in principle commonly owned by all peoples of the world, and their use and exploitation should be settled through joint consultation of all states; (4) the right of innocent passage through territorial waters and international straits lying within the latter is subject to the regulation and prior consent of the coastal state affected; (5) the international seabed should be used only for peaceful purposes, with the specific prohibition against the activities of nuclear-powered submarines; and (6) coastal states have the right to exercise jurisdiction and control marine pollution over areas adjacent to their territorial areas.[62]

If the U.S. was the principal initial target of Peking's attack against the superpowers on this question, the Soviet Union was soon equally denounced in the Sea-Bed Committee for "plundering ocean resources," attempting to "partition and control the seas," and "slandering the just stand of small and medium countries."[63] Japan also came under fire for its claims to a number of islands and the surrounding waters in the East China Sea. In a particularly forceful declaration, Representative An Chih-yuan asserted:

> I hereby reiterate: China's Taiwan Province and
> all the islands appertaining to it, including Tiaoyu Island,
> Peihsiao Island, etc., are part of China's sacred territory.

The sea-bed resources of the seas around these islands
and of the shallow seas adjacent to other parts of China
belong to China. . . . No one whosoever is allowed to
create any pretext to carve off China's territory and
plunder the sea resources belonging to China.[64]

With the exception of the Sea-Bed Arms Control Treaty signed in
February 1971, before the PRC entry, no significant action on this
question can be expected until the 3rd Sea Law Conference scheduled
for April-May 1974. Nevertheless, by vigorously challenging the
superpowers, ostensibly on behalf of the Third World, the PRC has
been able to gain a significant propaganda advantage.

ECONOMIC DEVELOPMENT

The question of economic development has also been of particular importance for the PRC in the UN in several ways. First, in
keeping with its goal of Third World leadership, Peking has made
strong efforts to articulate the widely shared grievances of the underdeveloped states against the wealthier nations. Chinese denunciations
of such alleged practices as excess profiteering; plundered resources;
inequitable trading relationships; control of national monetary systems,
shipping, and insurance; and the use of economic aid and technical
personnel to control and subvert the recipient state have been particularly well received. Second, the PRC has cited the continuation of
these policies as one more compelling reason for forging a solid,
Chinese-led Third World bloc capable of effective resistance, especially
against the "imperialistic superpowers." Finally, by consistently
stressing the need to achieve political and economic independence
through the principle of self-reliance, Peking has sought to minimize
superpower influence in the underdeveloped world and, implicitly,
to proselytize on behalf of the Maoist road to those objectives.
In pursuing these goals the PRC has met with mixed success.
At the Third UN Conference on Trade and Development (UNCTAD III),
held in Santiago, Chile (April 13-May 21, 1972), the Chinese not only
emphasized these themes but also indicated their desire to join the
Third World-dominated "Group of 77." But when it was discovered
that the latter regarded China as a great power rather than a poor
and struggling nation, Peking's representatives quietly dropped the
matter.[65] At the October meetings in Geneva of the Trade and Development Board of UNCTAD, the PRC again attacked the developed countries for their exclusion of the developing states in handling the world
monetary crisis, which had "inflicted great losses" on the latter.[66]

In December 1972 the PRC somewhat surprisingly agreed to serve a 3-year term as one of the 45 members of the UN Industrial Development Organization (UNIDO), which is the principal executing agency for UN Development Program (UNDP) industrial projects in the less developed countries. Finally, China attended its first meeting of the Economic Commission for Asia and the Far East (ECAFE) in Tokyo in April 1973, where the same Third World themes were sounded.[67] While it is too early to determine the ultimate impact of these moves, Peking will probably be able to gain considerable leverage against the developed nations by pressing for higher development funding levels for the Third World.

CONCLUSION

Like all other member-states, the PRC has sought to make use of the United Nations as a forum for articulating its foreign policy views and as one vehicle for implementing its objectives. Entry into the world body with the elite status of a great power has substantially strengthened Peking's international prestige and has led increasingly to the isolation of Taiwan. This process seems to be gathering momentum and is aided by China's generally pragmatic and skillfull UN performance. Thus Peking has been able to move a considerable way toward its eventual goal of national unification.

Another PRC objective in the UN has been to maximize its national security against foreign threats and potential aggression. On the one hand, strong fears of Soviet encirclement and preemptive nuclear attack have induced Peking to take unpopular positions on such questions as the Indo-Pakistani war, Bangladesh, and disarmament. While the results have not been as detrimental as expected, Peking, in playing the great power game a of realpolitik, has experienced occasional slippage in its Third World influence and appeal. On the other hand, if the Nixon visit, the winding down of the American military presence in Vietnam and the rest of Asia, and the Tanaka visit have enhanced Chinese national security on its southeastern and eastern borders, Peking has also seen fit to depart occasionally from the theme of a plague equally on both the superpowers to a more pronounced anti-Soviet bias. Thus, to a large extent American-Soviet conflict in the world body has been replaced by Sino-Soviet confrontation.[68]

To date the PRC has made only limited use of the UN to further its national power and security through economic development. Though periodic protests are made against the World Bank Group and the paternalistic role of the developed, contributing nations in the UNDP, Peking has preferred to limit its reliance on these agencies for

ATTACHMENT A: ROLL CALL VOTES ON CHINA
REPRESENTATION ISSUE, 1951-70

Table 1: Votes on U.S. Proposal not to Place the Question
of Chinese Representation on the Agenda, 1951-60

Year	Total U.N. Membership	To Consider		Not to Consider		Abstention	Absent
1951	60	11	(18.7%)	37	(61%)	4	8
1952	60	7	(11.7%)	42	(70%)	11	0
1953	60	10	(16.7%)	44	(73.3%)	2	4
1954	60	11	(18.3%)	43	(71.7%)	6	0
1955	60	12	(20%)	42	(70%)	6	0
1956	79	24	(30.4%)	47	(59.4%)	8	0
1957	82	27	(32.9%)	48	(58.6%)	6	1
1958	81	28	(34.6%)	44	(54.3%)	9	0
1959	82	29	(35.4%)	44	(53.7%)	9	0
1960	99	34	(34.7%)	42	(42.9%)	22	1

Table 2: Votes on Soviet Motion (1961-62) and on Albanian Motion
(1963-71) to Seat the PRC

Year	Total U.N. Membership	For		Against		Abstention	Absent
1961	104	36	(34.6%)	48	(46.2%)	20	0
1962	110	42	(38.2%)	56	(50.9%)	12	0
1963	111	41	(36.9%)	57	(51.4%)	12	1
1964				No Vote Taken			
1965	116	47	(40.2%)	47	(40.2%)	20	2
1966	121	46	(38%)	57	(47.1%)	17	1
1967	123	45	(36.6%)	58	(48.3%)	17	3
1968	126	44	(35%)	58	(46.4%)	23	1
1969	126	48	(38.1%)	56	(44.4%)	21	1
1970	126	51	(40.2%)	49	(38.6%)	25	1
1971	131	35	(26.7%)	76	(58%)	17	3

Table 3: Votes on U.S. Proposal to Regard the Matter of Chinese
Representation as an "Important Question" Requiring a
Two-Thirds Majority, 1961, 1965-70

Year	Total U.N. Membership	For	Against	Abstention	Absent
1961	99	61	34	2	2
1965	116	56	49	11	0
1966	121	66	48	7	0
1967	122	69	48	4	1
1968	126	73	47	5	1
1969	126	71	48	4	3
1970	126	66	52	7	1

Source: Compiled from UN Yearbooks and the New York Times.

123

	Important Question		Main Resolution	
	1970a	1971b	1970c	1971c
Afghanistan	Against	Against	PRC	PRC
Albania	Against	Against	PRC	PRC
Algeria	Against	Against	PRC	PRC
Argentina	For	For	ROC	Abstain
Australia	For	For	ROC	ROC
Austria	For	Abstain	PRC	PRC
Bahrain*	—	For	—	Abstain
Barbados	Abstain	For	ROC	Abstain
Belgium	For	Abstain	Abstain	PRC
Bhutan*	—	Against	—	PRC
Bolivia	For	For	Abstain	ROC
Botswana	For	Abstain	Abstain	PRC
Brazil	For	For	ROC	ROC
Bulgaria	Against	Against	PRC	PRC
Burma	Against	Against	PRC	PRC
Burundi	Against	Against	PRC	PRC
Byelorussia	Against	Against	PRC	PRC
Cambodia (Khmer Republic)**	For	For	ROC	ROC
Cameroons	Against	Against	Abstain	PRC
Canada	For	Against	PRC	PRC
Central African Rep.	For	For	Abstain	ROC
Ceylon (Sri Lanka)**	Abstain	Against	PRC	PRC
Chad	Abstain	For	ROC	ROC
Chile	Against	Against	PRC	PRC
Colombia	For	For	ROC	Abstain
Congo (Brazzaville)	Against	Against	PRC	PRC
Congo (Kinshasa) (Zaire)**	For	For	ROC	ROC
Costa Rica	For	For	ROC	ROC
Cuba	Against	Against	PRC	PRC
Cyprus	For	Abstain	Abstain	Abstain
Czechoslovakia	Against	Against	PRC	PRC
Dahomey	For	For	ROC	ROC
Denmark	Against	Against	PRC	PRC
Dominican Republic	For	For	ROC	ROC
Ecuador	For	Against	Abstain	PRC
El Salvador	For	For	ROC	ROC
Equatorial Guinea	Against	Against	PRC	PRC
Ethiopia	Against	Against	PRC	PRC
Fiji	For	For	Abstain	Abstain
Finland	Against	Against	PRC	PRC
France	Against	Against	PRC	PRC
Gabon	For	For	ROC	ROC
Gambia	For	For	ROC	ROC
Ghana	Against	For	PRC	PRC
Greece	For	For	ROC	Abstain
Guatemala	For	For	ROC	ROC
Guinea	Against	Against	PRC	PRC
Guyana	Abstain	Against	Abstain	PRC
Haiti	For	For	ROC	ROC
Honduras	For	For	ROC	ROC
Hungary	For	For	PRC	PRC
Iceland	For	Against	Abstain	PRC
India	Against	Against	PRC	PRC
Indonesia	Not Voting	For	Not Voting	Abstain
Iran	For	Abstain	Abstain	PRC
Iraq	Against	Against	PRC	PRC
Ireland	For	Against	Abstain	PRC
Israel	For	For	ROC	PRC

	Important Question		Main Resolution	
	1970[a]	1971[b]	1970[c]	1971[c]
Italy	For	Abstain	PRC	PRC
Ivory Coast	For	For	ROC	ROC
Jamaica	For	For	Abstain	Abstain
Japan	For	For	ROC	ROC
Jordan	For	For	ROC	Abstain
Kenya	Against	Against	PRC	PRC
Kuwait	Against	Against	Abstain	PRC
Laos	For	Abstain	Abstain	Abstain
Lebanon	For	For	Abstain	Abstain
Lesotho	For	For	ROC	ROC
Liberia	For	For	ROC	ROC
Libya	Against	Against	PRC	PRC
Luxembourg	For	For	Abstain	Abstain
Madagascar	For	For	ROC	ROC
Malawi	For	For	ROC	ROC
Malaysia	Against	Against	Abstain	PRC
Maldive Is.	Absent	Absent	Absent	Absent
Mali	Against	Against	PRC	PRC
Malta	For	Abstain	ROC	ROC
Mauritania	Against	Against	PRC	PRC
Mauritius	Abstain	For	ROC	Abstain
Mexico	For	For	ROC	PRC
Mongolia	Against	Against	PRC	PRC
Morocco	Against	Abstain	PRC	PRC
Nepal	Against	Against	PRC	PRC
Netherlands	For	Abstain	Abstain	PRC
New Zealand	For	For	ROC	ROC
Nicaragua	For	For	ROC	ROC
Niger	For	For	ROC	ROC
Nigeria	Against	Against	PRC	PRC
Norway	Against	Against	PRC	PRC
Oman*	—	Absent	—	Absent
Pakistan	Against	Against	PRC	PRC
Panama	For	For	ROC	Abstain
Paraguay	For	For	ROC	ROC
Peru	Against	Against	Abstain	PRC
Philippines	For	For	ROC	ROC
Poland	Against	Against	PRC	PRC
Portugal	Abstain	For	Abstain	PRC
Qatar*	—	Abstain	—	Abstain
Rumania	Against	Against	PRC	PRC
Rwanda	For	For	ROC	PRC
Saudi Arabia	For	For	ROC	ROC
Senegal	For	Abstain	Abstain	PRC
Sierra Leone	For	Against	ROC	PRC
Singapore	Against	Against	Abstain	PRC
Somalia	Against	Against	PRC	PRC
South Africa	For	For	ROC	ROC
South Yemen	Against	Against	PRC	PRC
Spain	For	For	ROC	Abstain
Sudan	Against	Against	PRC	PRC
Swaziland	For	For	ROC	ROC
Sweden	Against	Against	PRC	PRC
Syria	Against	Against	PRC	PRC
Tanzania	Against	Against	PRC	PRC
Thailand	For	For	ROC	Abstain
Togo	For	Abstain	ROC	PRC
Trinidad-Tobago	Abstain	Against	Abstain	PRC
Tunisia	Against	Abstain	Abstain	PRC

(Continued)

	Important Question		Main Resolution	
	1970[a]	1971[b]	1970[c]	1971[c]
Turkey	For	Abstain	Abstain	PRC
Uganda	Against	Against	PRC	PRC
U.S.S.R.	Against	Against	PRC	PRC
Ukraine	Against	Against	PRC	PRC
United Arab Republic	Against	Against	PRC	PRC
United Kingdom	For	Against	PRC	PRC
United States	For	For	ROC	ROC
Upper Volta	For	For	ROC	ROC
Uruguay	For	For	ROC	ROC
Venezuela	For	For	ROC	ROC
Yemen	Against	Against	PRC	PRC
Yugoslavia	Against	Against	PRC	PRC
Zambia	Against	Against	PRC	PRC

Totals:

1970 Important Question

For: 66	Against: 52	Abstain: 7	Absent: 2
		Present but not voting:	1

1971 Important Question

For: 55	Against: 59	Abstain: 15	Absent: 2

1970 Main Resolution

PRC: 51	ROC: 49	Abstain: 25	Absent: 1
		Present but not voting:	1

1971 Main Resolution

PRC: 76	ROC: 35	Abstain: 17	Absent: 3

*These states were admitted as new members after the 1970 roll call vote.
**These states have changed their official names to those listed in parentheses.

[a]This resolution—UN Doc. A/RES/2642 (XXV), Nov. 20, 1970—stipulated that any change in Chinese representation was an "important question" requiring a two-thirds vote for passage. Thus, a "for" vote indicates support for the U.S. position while an "against" vote expresses support for the PRC.
[b]This resolution—UN Doc. A/L. 632, Sept. 29, 1971—was revised from the 1970 version and declared that any proposal that would result in depriving the Republic of China of representation in the United Nations was an "important question" requiring a two-thirds vote for passage. Once again a "for" vote supports the U.S. position and an "against" vote supports the PRC.
[c]These resolutions—UN Doc. A/L. 605, Nov. 20, 1970; UN Doc. A/RES/2758 (XXVI), Oct. 25, 1971—would restore all rights to the People's Republic of China, recognize the representatives of its government as the only lawful representatives of China to the United Nations, and expel forthwith the representatives of Chiang Kai-shek. For purposes of clarity the "for" and "against" votes have been recorded as "PRC" and "ROC" votes, respectively.

Sources: New York Times, Nov. 21, 1970; Oct. 26, 1971.

development assistance both to avoid damage to its pride and image vis-à-vis the Third World and to remain commited to the doctrine of economic self-reliance. Hence, PRC participation in UNIDO and in ECAFE will provide Peking with propaganda sounding boards aimed at the Third World rather than conduits for its own development. However, it should be noted that Peking has not been averse to utilizing the UN as a supplementary negotiating arena for trade expansion and cultural exchange.

By far the major thrust of the PRC's UN participation has been to become the undisputed champion of the Third World. While its great power status has occasionally been an embarrassment, Peking has met with increasing but by no means complete success. Initially cool, many Third World states have recently begun to respond favorably to China's generally sophisticated advocacy of many of their favorite causes, especially colonialism, the Middle East, economic development, and the future of the oceans. It seems unlikely, however, that such a variegated lot as the underdeveloped world will ever be able to forget the PRC's great power status and accept Chinese leadership unequivocally. On balance, however, China has done remarkably well, considering its brief tenure in the UN, with most of its gains coming at the expense of the superpowers.

As to the future of China's participation in the world body, it is likely that, barring dramatic shifts in policy, Peking will continue to advocate the Third World cause vis-à-vis the superpowers and the developed nations. To its benefit, the course of events has already disposed of the embarrassing issue of the Indo-Pakistani war and in all probability will soon resolve the question of Bangladesh's entry into the UN. To the extent that the disarmament impasse is superseded by the press of issues considered more vital to Third World interests, the PRC will be in an enviable position to capitalize even further in building a broad UN base of support. Regardless of the outcome, all must agree that neither China nor the UN will ever be quite the same.

NOTES

1. By far the best single source currently available is Byron S. J. Weng, Peking's UN Policy: Continuity and Change (New York: Praeger Publishers, 1972). Although most of the following works are dated in varying degrees, many do provide useful information, insight, and analysis on this issue (they are listed chronologically): Herbert W. Briggs, "Chinese Representation in the U.N.," International Organization 6, no. 2 (May 1952): 192-209; G. G. Fitzmaurice, "Chinese Representation in the U.N.," 1952 Yearbook of World Affairs

(London), pp. 36-55; Benjamin Brown and Fred Green, Chinese Representation: A Case Study in United Nations Political Affairs (New York: Woodrow Wilson Foundation, 1955); Stanley K. Hornbeck, "Which Chinese?" Foreign Affairs 34, no. 1 (Oct. 1955): 24-39; David Brook, The U.N. and the China Dilemma (New York: Vantage Books, 1956); David Brook, "The Problem of China's Representation in the U.N.," Journal of East Asiatic Studies (Manila) 5, no. 1 (Jan. 1956): 43-68; Sheldon Appleton, The Eternal Triangle? Communist China, The United States and the United Nations (East Lansing, Mich.: Michigan State University Press, 1961); A. Appadorai, "The Question of Representation of China in the United Nations" (Ph. D. diss., University of Minnesota, 1961); William Boyer and Neylan Akra, "The United States and the Admission of Communist China," Political Science Quarterly 76, no. 3 (Sept. 1961): 332-53; Sheldon Appleton, "The United Nations 'China Tangle,'" Pacific Affairs 35, no. 2 (Summer 1962): 160-67; F. B. Schick, "The Question of China in the U.N.," International and Comparative Law Quarterly 12, no. 4 (Oct. 1963): 1232-50; Roderick C. Ogly, "Decision-Making in the United Nations—The Case of the Representation of China," International Relations (London) 2, no. 9 (Apr. 1964): 588-608; A. G. Mezerick, ed., China Representation in the United Nations (New York: International Review Service, 1965); A. Neylan Akra, "Some Aspects of the Problem of Chinese Representation in the United Nations" (Ph.D. diss., University of Pittsburgh, 1965); Lincoln P. Bloomfield, "China, The United States, and the United Nations," International Organization 20, no. 4 (Autumn 1966): 653-76; Byron S. J. Weng, "Communist China's Changing Attitudes Toward the United Nations," ibid., pp. 677-704; Myres S. McDougal and Richard M. Goodman, "Chinese Participation in the United Nations: The Legal Imperatives of a Negotiated Solution," American Journal of International Law 60, no. 4 (Oct. 1966): 671-727; Lung-chu Chen and Harold D. Lasswell, Formosa, China and the United Nations: Formosa in the World Community (New York: St. Martin's Press, 1967); Hungdah Ch'iu, assisted by R. R. Edwards, "Communist China's Attitude towards the United Nations: A Legal Analysis," American Journal of International Law 62, no. 1 (Jan. 1968): 20-50; Winberg Chai, "China and the United Nations: Problems of Representation and Alternatives," Asian Survey 10, no. 5 (May 1970): 397-409; Jerome Alan Cohen, "Chinese Participation in the United Nations: Changing Realities and the Imperatives of New Policy," American Journal of International Law (sixty-fifth annual meeting of the American Society of International Law) 65, no. 4 (Sept. 1971): 1-8; Richard M. Goodman, "Chinese Participation in the United Nations: The Imperatives of a Negotiated Settlement," ibid., pp. 9-16; Evan Luard, "China and the United Nations," International Affairs (London) 47, no. 4 (Oct. 1971): 729-44; R. G., "China, Divided States and Mini-States," International Conciliation no. 584 (Sept. 1971): 13-16; William J. Cunningham, "The

Communist Party of China and the United Nations, 1943-1950," Asian Quarterly no. 3 (1972): 191-201; and Byron S. J. Weng, "Some Conditions of Peking's Participation in International Organizations," in Jerome Alan Cohen, ed., China's Practice of International Law: Some Case Studies (Cambridge, Mass.: Harvard University Press, 1972), pp. 321-43.

2. The vote was 6-3-2. In favor: Soviet Union, Yugoslavia, India; opposed: China, Cuba, Ecuador, Egypt, France, United States; abstain: Norway and the United Kingdom. Weng, Peking's UN Policy . . . , pp. 247-48, n. 9.

3. For a discussion of the "credentials," "representation," and "membership" schools of thought, see Goodman, "Chinese Participation in the United Nations: The Imperatives of a Negotiated Settlement, " pp. 10-12.

4. See UN Doc. A/RES/498 (V), Feb. 1, 1951; and UN Doc. A/RES/500 (V), May 18, 1951.

5. The texts of the U.S. resolutions can be found in New York Times, Sept. 14, 1971.

6. For the texts of the various resolutions, see New York Times, Oct. 26, 1971. A review of the PRC entry into the world body can be found in Peter Cheng, "Peking's Entry into the United Nations," Asian Forum 4, no. 4 (Oct.-Dec. 1972): 16-29.

7. This compares favorably with the United States (72), France (70), and the Soviet Union (67). Louis Halasz, "Another Chance," Far Eastern Economic Review 78, no. 50 (Dec. 9, 1972): 24. For a detailed listing, see United Nations, Delegations to the General Assembly, Twenty-seventh Session, November 1972 (New York: United Nations, 1972), pp. 39-42.

8. UN Doc. A/RES/2758, Oct. 25, 1972.

9. For the text of the letter, see Peking Review 16, no. 3 (Jan. 21, 1973): 15.

10. Japan Times, Apr. 7, 1972.

11. For PRC action in ECOSOC, see Peking Review 15, no. 31 (Aug. 4, 1972): 18.

12. See UN Doc. A/RES/3049C (XXVII), Dec. 19, 1972. The vote was 92-9-24. UN Monthly Chronicle 10, no. 1 (Jan. 1973): 97-98. Earlier in October the PRC voluntarily offered to raise its budget assessment from 4 percent to 7 percent over the next five years. However, Peking refused to pay for the following items: (1) the UN presence in Korea; (2) expenses of the UN High Commissioner for Refugees for refugees from Tibet and the China mainland; and (3) financing costs of the UN bond issue for peace-keeping operations in the Middle East and the Congo.

13. Best recent estimates indicate that Soviet military strength on the China border had tripled from the 15 divisions in place in 1968

and now constituted nearly one-third of the entire Soviet army. New York Times, Sept. 10, 1972.

14. For a brief discussion of this possibility, see Cheng Huan, "China's 'No' to Dacca," Far Eastern Economic Review 77, no. 36 (Sept. 2, 1972): 11-12.

15. Excerpts of these speeches can be found in ibid., p. 23; Peking Review 14, no. 50 (Dec. 10, 1971): 8-10; ibid., no. 52 (Dec. 24, 1971): 16. In his response Ambassador Malik labeled Huang "that slanderous man from the socialist betrayal camp" who was "aspiring to the role of an imperialist jester" and accused China of wanting to become a "super-super-super Power of super-Powers." For excerpts of this speech, see UN Monthly Chronicle 9, no. 1 (Jan. 1972): 21.

16. Andrew Boyd, "China in a Hot Seat," Vista 8, no. 1 (July-Aug. 1972): 37.

17. For a discussion of past PRC positions and policies on these matters, see James Chieh Hsiung, Law and Policy on China's Foreign Relations; A Study of Attitudes and Practice (New York and London: Columbia University Press, 1972), pp. 79-82, 289-96.

18. For the texts of the three resolutions, two sponsored by the United States and the other by an eight-power group, see UN Doc. S/10416, Dec. 4, 1971; UN Doc. S/10446 and Rev. 1, Dec. 12, 1971.

19. In each case the vote was 11 (PRC, United States)-2 (Poland, Soviet Union)-2 (France, United Kingdom). For the vote breakdowns, see UN Monthly Chronicle 9, no. 1 (Jan. 1972): 13, 20, 33.

20. See UN Doc. S/10418, Dec. 4, 1971. The vote was 2 (Poland, Soviet Union)-1 (PRC)-12 (France, United Kingdom, United States). Ibid., p. 19.

21. The Security Council resolution referring the question to the General Assembly was UN Doc. S/RES/303 (1971). The resolution passed by the latter was UN Doc. A/RES/2793 (XXVI), Dec. 7, 1971. The vote on the latter was 104-11 (Soviet Union)-10, with both the PRC and the United States siding with the majority. Ibid., p. 89.

22. UN Doc. S/RES/307 (1971). The vote was 13-0-2 (Poland, Soviet Union). Ibid., p. 26. For the PRC version of these proceedings, see Peking Review 14, no. 51 (Dec. 17, 1971): 10, 13, 16.

23. In his speech before the Security Council, Huang Hua accused the Soviet Union of acting with "honey in mouth but dagger in heart" and of "committing aggression and subversion in the name of assistance to third-world countries." New York Times, Aug. 26, 1972. The vote on the PRC draft resolution (UN Doc. S/10768, Aug. 21, 1972) was 3-3-9. The four-power draft resolution (UN Doc. S/10771, Aug. 23, 1972) recommending UN membership for the People's Republic of Bangladesh was defeated 11-1 (PRC)-3 (Guinea, Somalia, Sudan). The four other great powers voted in favor. UN Monthly Chronicle 9, no. 8 (Aug.-Sept. 1972): 24.

24. For the full text of Huang Hua's speech, see Peking Review 15, no. 35 (Sept. 1, 1972): 6-9.

25. This was particularly evident when Bangladesh was overwhelmingly voted into UNESCO in the autumn of 1972. Louis Halasz, "Another Chance," p. 25.

26. For Soviet views of the PRC position, see V. Rybakov, "The People's Republic of China and the Disarmament Problem," International Affairs (Moscow) no. 9 (Sept. 1972): 26-32.

27. UN Doc. A/L. 631, Nov. 3, 1971.

28. Peking Review 14, no. 49 (Dec. 3, 1971): 14-16.

29. New York Times, Nov. 27, 1971.

30. Peking Review 14, no. 49 (Dec. 3, 1971): 17-18.

31. The three resolutions against nuclear testing were UN Doc. A/RES/2828 A, B, C, (XXVI), Dec. 16, 1971, the votes on which were 74-2-36; 71-2-38; and 91-2-21, respectively, with the PRC and Albania alone in opposition. UN Monthly Chronicle 9, no. 1 (Jan. 1972): 116-17. For the Mexican-Rumanian proposal adopted by acclamation, see UN Doc. A/RES/2833 (XXVI), Dec. 16, 1971. The Indian Ocean Peace Zone Declaration, UN Doc. A/RES/2832 (XXVI), Dec. 16, 1971, was passed by a vote of 61-0-55, with the other four great powers abstaining. Ibid., p. 119. For an explanation of the PRC position on the latter question, see Peking Review 14, no. 50 (Dec. 10, 1971): 8-9.

32. For the general PRC position as outlined at Stockholm, see Peking Review 15, no. 24 (June 16, 1972): 5-8, 13. See also "In the Beginning," Far Eastern Economic Review 77, no. 27 (July 1, 1972): 24.

33. New York Times, June 13, 1972. The final vote was 56-3-29, with the United States and United Kingdom abstaining. For Peking's reaction to the "Declaration on the Human Environment," its suggested revisions, and the resolution prohibiting and condemning nuclear tests, see Peking Review 15, no. 25 (June 23, 1972): 8-11.

34. The vote on A/RES/2936 (XXVII), Nov. 29, 1972, was 73 (Soviet Union)-4 (PRC, Albania, Portugal, South Africa)-46 (France, United Kingdom, United States). UN Monthly Chronicle 9, no. 11 (Dec. 1972): 41-42.

35. For the text of the speech, see Peking Review 15, no. 46 (Nov. 17, 1972): 5-6.

36. UN Doc. A/RES/2934 A, B, C (XXVII), Nov. 29, 1972. The votes were 105-4-9, 89-4-23, and 80-4-29, respectively. UN Monthly Chronicle 9, no. 11 (Dec. 1972): 50-51. For excerpts of the Sino-Soviet verbal exchange, see ibid., pp. 42-46.

37. UN Doc. A/RES/2932 (XXVII), Nov. 29, 1972, adopted by a vote of 99 (PRC, Soviet Union)-0-15 (France, United Kingdom, United States). Ibid., pp. 48-49.

38. UN Doc. A/RES/2930 (XXVII), Nov. 29, 1972.

39. Louis Halasz, "Crippled Committee," Far Eastern Economic Review 79, no. 5 (Feb. 5, 1973): 24-25. For PRC views on this development, see Peking Review 16, no. 3 (Jan. 19, 1973): 8-10.

40. Richard C. Hottelet, "What New Role for the People's Republic of China?" Saturday Review 59, no. 38 (Sept. 18, 1971): 30.

41. New York Times, Dec. 9, 1971. For the full text of the speech, see Peking Review 14, no. 51 (Dec. 17, 1971): 7-9.

42. Cf. Peking Review 14, no. 51 (Dec. 17, 1971): 9, with excerpt of speeches by Huang Hua before emergency meetings of the Security Council. See ibid. 15, no. 9 (Mar. 3, 1972): 17; and ibid., no. 37 (Sept. 15, 1972): 13.

43. For the text of Huang Hua's speech, see ibid. no. 50 (Dec. 15, 1972): 5-6.

44. UN Doc. A/RES/2799 (XXVI), Dec. 8, 1971. Interestingly, the United States also abstained, believing that the measures went too far, while the other three great powers voted in favor.

45. UN. Doc. S/RES/313 (1972). The vote was 8 (United States, United Kingdom, France)-4 (PRC)-3 (Soviet Union). UN Monthly Chronicle 9, no. 3 (Mar. 1972): 66. In the case of the September 1972 Israeli raids on Syria and Lebanon in reprisal for the Munich Olympic killings, the United States vetoed a draft resolution calling on all parties to cease all military operations immediately. UN Doc. S/10775, Aug. 25, 1972.

46. UN Doc. S/RES/317 (1972) and UN Doc. A/RES/2963 A, B, C, D, E (XXVII), Dec, 13, 1972.

47. New York Times, Sept. 23, 1972.

48. Ibid. The vote was 15-7-2. One clue to Soviet motives was a reference by Ambassador Malik to a number of terrorist acts carried out by "Zionist extremists" against the Soviet UN mission in New York.

49. See Peking Review 15, no. 49 (Dec. 8, 1972): 12.

50. New York Times, Nov. 22, 1972.

51. UN Doc. A/RES/3034 (XXVII), Dec. 18, 1972. The key vote in the Legal Committee was 76 (PRC, Soviet Union)-34 (United States, United Kingdom)-16 (France). New York Times, Dec. 12, 1972. When Assembly President Trepczynski appointed a 35-nation committee in April 1973 to report on measures to combat international terrorism, the PRC was the only great power that refused to participate.

52. For excerpts of the Huang-Malik exchange at Addis Ababa, see UN Monthly Chronicle 9, no. 3 (Mar. 1972): 20-21, 23-25, 59-60, 63-64.

53. See Peking Review 15, no. 44 (Nov. 3, 1972): 22. See also PRC anti-Soviet views expressed over the issue of Rhodesia and the Soviet response denouncing these charges as "slanderous anti-Soviet fabrications." UN Doc. A/8663, Mar. 3, 1972; UN Doc. A/8664, Mar. 10, 1972.

54. The vote on S/RES/313 (Feb. 1972) and S/RES/319 (Aug. 1972) was 14-0-0; on S/RES/323 (Dec. 1972) it was 13-0-1 (Soviet Union). UN Monthly Chronicle 9, no. 3 (Mar. 1972): 3; ibid. no. 8 (Aug.-Sept. 1972): 20-24, passim.

55. Cf. UN Doc. S/RES/327 (Feb. 1973) and UN Doc. S/RES/329 (Mar. 1973). For the texts of the resolutions, see UN Monthly Chronicle 10, no. 3 (Mar. 1973): 8-9, and ibid., no. 4 (Apr. 1973): 15. In the first instance the vote was 14-0-1 (Soviet Union), in the latter it was unanimous.

56. New York Times, Mar, 11, 1972. For the text of the letter, see UN Doc. A/AC. 109/396, Mar. 9, 1972.

57. For excerpts from Huang Hua's speech, see Peking Review 16, no. 12 (Mar. 23, 1973): 8-11. By a vote of 13 (PRC, Soviet Union, France)-1 (United States)-1 (United Kingdom), the Security Council failed to pass a resolution that called for the abrogation of the 1903 treaty and the conclusion of a "new, just and fair treaty" based on Panamanian sovereignty. New York Times, Mar. 23, 1973. See UN Doc. S/1093, Rev. 1, Mar. 22, 1973.

58. For the text of the U.S. letter of May 8, see UN Doc. S/10631, May 9, 1972. For the PRC letter of May 11, see UN Doc. S/10638, May 11, 1972, reprinted in New York Times, May 12, 1972. Since neither the General Assembly nor the Security Council was in session during the intensive Christmas 1972 bombing of Hanoi and Haiphong, the PRC was unable to mount a UN protest prior to the January cease-fire announcement.

59. For an interesting insight into the relationship between the UN and the war, see Cornelius F. Murphy, Jr., "The United Nations and the Vietnam Settlement," Vista 8, no. 5 (Apr. 1973): 14-15, 46-47.

60. The resolutions were S/RES/305 (1971); S/RES/315 (1972); S/RES/324 (1972). In each case the vote was 14-0-1 (PRC).

61. For a brief review of recent developments in the UN on this issue, see R. Z. [Ralph Zacklin] and E. T. H. [E. Theodore Hedding], "The Sea," in "Issues Before the 26th General Assembly," International Conciliation no. 584 (Sept. 1971): 79-88; and Eugene B. Skolnikoff, "A Technological World: Can the UN Meet the Challenge?" Vista 8, no 2 (Sept.-Oct. 1972): 68-69.

62. See speeches by PRC delegates in Peking Review 15, no. 10 (Mar. 10, 1972): 14-16; ibid. no. 32 (Aug. 11, 1972): 14-15; and ibid. 16, no. 13 (Mar. 30, 1972): 9-12.

63. UN Monthly Chronicle 9, no. 4 (Apr. 1972): 36-37.

64. See Peking Review 15, no. 10 (Mar. 10, 1972): 16. The catalyst for this sweeping claim was the inclusion of these islands in the "reversion zone" in the return of Okinawa from American to Japanese control. For an elaboration of the Peking position, see the PRC letter of May 20, 1972. UN Doc. S/10653, May 20, 1972.

65. Louis Halasz, "Getting to Know You," Far Eastern Economic Review 77, no. 27 (July 1, 1972): 14. For the PRC position at UNCTAD III, see Peking Review 15, no. 17 (Apr. 28, 1972): 11-14.

66. Peking Review 15, no. 42 (Oct. 20, 1972): 11-12.

67. For the speeches of PRC representatives at ECAFE and the May meeting of UNIDO in Vienna, see Peking Review 16, no. 16 (Apr. 20, 1973): 13-15; ibid. no. 17 (Apr. 27, 1973): 16-17; and ibid. no. 20 (May 18, 1973): 4-6.

68. For recent Soviet views on Peking's challenge, see G. Apalin, "Peking and the 'Third World,'" International Affairs (Moscow) no. 12 (Dec. 1972): 28-34; and V. Rybakov, "China in the United Nations: A Barren Policy," ibid. no. 3 (Mar. 1973): 48-52.

II

THE SPECIFIC
RELATIONS

8

MOSCOW'S REACTION TO
NIXON'S JAUNT TO PEKING
George Ginsburgs

Whether or not the Kremlin was literally stunned, as claimed by Western analysts, by the disclosure of Henry Kissinger's secret trip to the PRC and the accompanying announcement of Nixon's prospective visit to mainland China remains a debated issue. In theory, of course, the Russians ought to have received the news with equanimity, since for some time they had been dropping ominous hints concerning intensified contacts between Peking and Washington and warned about the likely consequences of an impending Sino-American rapprochement. To be sure, the suddenness, speed, and magnitude of the unfolding events might still have caught the Soviet leadership flatfooted, regardless of their belief in the accuracy of their own prognosis. Or the people involved could simply have been whistling in the dark, in the hope of exorcising the very specter that presently confronted them and whose appearance, which they had predicted in good faith that the contingency would not materialize, now confounded all their real expectations.

Be that as it may, the fact is that even prior to Kissinger's first excursion to Peking, the Soviets had publicly expressed skepticism concerning the purity of the motivations animating both parties in their recent moves to establish a more intimate dialogue. Hence they viewed with a jaundiced eye the sequence of steps initiated by their chief rivals signaling a more cordial mood in their mutual relations and caustically commented on most of the features of the current phase of "smiling diplomacy." Soviet sources noted, for instance, that the American authorities had lifted all restrictions on travel by U.S. citizens to the PRC but that these curbs stayed in effect vis-à-vis Cuba, North Vietnam, and North Korea, where, the State Department had allegedly declared, the situation was quite different—sufficiently so as not to warrant lowering the bars. Furthermore, U.S.

companies had been permitted to sell nonstrategic goods to China and U.S. oil corporations were allowed to fuel merchant ships calling at Chinese ports. Evidence mounted that a change in Washington's attitude toward the question of seating the PRC in the United Nations was being contemplated, and American interest in resuming the bilateral talks in Warsaw had been privately conveyed to Peking. The Chinese had reciprocated by buying Italian trucks equipped with General Motors engines and U.S. telephone equipment, had sent out feelers concerning the possible purchase of Boeing jets, and in mid-April 1971 had gone so far as to invite a U.S. table tennis team and three American journalists to tour the mainland.

If these developments had been, as one Soviet writer put it, merely a "pragmatic prologue to normalization of relations between the two countries,"[1] the phenomena could raise few objections. What upset the Russians, however, was some of the static that they sensed behind the overtures, such as the frank delight attributed to certain American circles with the Chinese leaders' political and ideological break with the countries of the "socialist community" and the gradual reorientation of China's trade to Western markets. China's deliberately bellicose posture on her northern frontiers was said to encourage the idea that together the United States and the PRC might gain more leverage against the Soviet Union. The Kremlin also charged Sino-American collusion over the Vietnam conflict and accused China of giving confidential assurances to the United States that it would not intervene in the Vietnam war, which prompted the latter to escalate its belligerent activities in the area.[2] Peking had presumably decided that, in order to obtain the desired concessions on Taiwan, Washington had to be persuaded of the chances of striking an advantageous political deal; the United States duly responded by easing naval patrols in the Taiwan Straits. What were all these maneuvers intended to accomplish? Nothing less, according to the Russians, than to pull China away from the Soviet Union, an old dream of Eisenhower and Johnson that, the Soviets concluded, the current White House incumbent, whose anti-Communist views have long been common knowledge, fully shared.

I have quoted the indictment at length because it illustrates both the durability of many of the themes since sounded by official Soviet outlets concerning the prevailing tenor of Sino-American liaisons and the inherent ambiguity of the Soviet reflexes to these stimuli. For, as the preceding shows, the Soviet approach to the problem is a mixed one: obviously, Moscow cannot impugn the propriety of Sino-American contacts per se, especially when the Soviets have insisted throughout on the legitimacy of their ties with the United States; at the same time, the Russians either conveniently profess or genuinely believe that the precise nature of the negotiations between the PRC and the United States is or tends to be directed against the vital interests of the Soviet

Union and so deserves outright condemnation. The duality has persisted to this day, although the manner of its exact formulation has varied, depending on the commentator and the occasion.

Fundamentally, all Soviet observers agree that, in pursuing their present flirtation with the PRC, the "capitalist" powers wish to complicate Sino-Soviet affairs. Thus, we are told, the United States seeks to "unfreeze" its trade relations with China, in the hope of getting the PRC further from the world socialist system and involving it in the political intrigues of American imperialism against the forces of socialism, peace, and progress. Conversely, impelled by its own anti-Soviet sentiments and seduced by the notion that the price of Western assistance is the manifestation of overt hostility toward the policies associated with the Soviet Union, Peking has stepped up its efforts to split the "socialist" fraternity and redoubled its attempts to discredit the Soviet Union on the international scene. In striving to sell their services to the "imperialist" bloc in exchange for its favors and meanwhile fulfill their personal ambitions for global hegemony, Mao Tsetung and his entourage have at last reached the point of open betrayal in proclaiming that the moment has finally arrived to deal with the Soviet Union and the United States in an "equal way." Such a course, the Russians contend, has long been dear to Mao's heart and may well be in the nationalist interest of the Maoist leadership; but it certainly has nothing in common either with the authentic national interest of the Chinese people or with the interests of socialism in China, not to speak of the interests of world socialism and the anti-imperialist movement.

Inasmuch as these machinations are intended to injure the Soviet Union and its close allies, they constitute the PRC's quid for the expected quo of Western political and economic aid to China to replace the help and backing once supplied by the "socialist" community, which Peking so shortsightedly and self-destructively chose to reject when it consciously spun off on its separate trajectory. The above notwithstanding, the Soviets do not yet venture beyond simply suggesting that the paths of the PRC and its new-found Western friends here run parallel—that is, they have not, at least to date, gone so far as to impute that the respective tracks intersect or converge. On the contrary, from the very outset Soviet observers have appeared to derive a large measure of satisfaction from the conviction that sundry objective and subjective limitations effectively preclude the current liaison's developing from a mere ad hoc accommodation to a stable substantive consensus. To begin with, each principal had his particular agenda and schedule that on individual items might match the corresponding article in the other side's plans but that did not coincide on the essentials. Next, while the Chinese could be of considerable value to the "capitalist" world by virtue of their willingness to engage in propaganda and disruptive tactics aimed at the "socialist" states, in the positive sense they had little to offer their Western clientele. In the opinion of Soviet analysts, for example, the PRC's sparse resources drastically circumscribed the economic opportunities available to Western businessmen and caused the latter to wonder aloud how profitable the Chinese mainland market was likely to be in actual practice.[3]

The West was in better shape to meet China's exigencies, the Russians pointed out, but whether it was ready to do so and to what extent was something else again. A few Russian commentators seemed to think that the United States might unbend to a marked degree, including the possibility of acceding to proposals for the "demilitarization" of the Taiwan Straits and the withdrawal of U.S. troops from the island. The majority, however, aired a more sober appraisal and stressed the alternative of Washington's maintaining a relatively rigid attitude in this sector, at least in the near future, on the grounds that the United States could frankly afford to adopt a more independent behavior vis-à-vis the PRC than vice versa. Token concessions to indicate appreciation of Peking's "naked anti-Sovietism and its labors to undermine the unity of the world anti-imperialist front" were to be expected, of course; but, the Soviets took care to add, the relaxation would never entail, for instance, the weakening of "U.S. imperialism's" positions along the Chinese perimeter or the initiation of massive American assistance to promote the industrialization of the PRC. In similar vein the probable political consequence of the rapprochement between Peking and Washington would be not a change in the pattern of U.S. diplomatic behavior but, rather, the continued conversion of the Mao regime into an instrument of imperialism, since anti-Sovietism was recognized ex cathedra as the sole rationale for the current Sino-American meeting of the minds. Basically, what marked Washington's relations with Peking at this stage, as the Soviets claimed to understand them, was the desire of the U.S. leadership to get more out of Peking than it would have to give in exchange, in evidence of which Soviet spokesmen cited the obvious lack of any intention in American government circles to return Taiwan or renounce the "two-China" concept or revise previous policies on any single key issue affecting the PRC.[4]

On balance, therefore, none of what the Soviets said or wrote in this connection proves that they had any foreknowledge of the imminence of Kissinger's flight to Peking or the arrangements for Nixon's trip to the PRC. Rather, the thrust of the contemporaneous Russian analysis would seem to suggest that the Kremlin figured on a protracted spell of modest incremental progression in Sino-American contacts, perhaps peaking at some comparatively distant future date in an experiment in quasi-summit diplomacy. If true, then history overtook Moscow and the subsequent turn of events caught it completely unaware.

Nevertheless, even assuming that the Russians did expect something to happen here, they might still have been unprepared for the dramatic situation with which they were next faced. To the extent, however, that they had previously played Cassandra, they were now spared the embarrassment of pretending not to be surprised and, in fact, did refer to their earlier prophecies in support of the assertion that they were neither flustered nor discomfited by what had just occurred.

SOVIET RESTRAINT

So much for the theoretical prologue. When confronted with the fait accompli, Moscow greeted the news of Kissinger's expedition to Peking with stony silence. The reaction may very well have been due, as alleged by Western Kremlinologists, to the Russian leadership's sense of total bewilderment at such a rapid improvement in Sino-American relations. Not having foreseen this contingency, presumably the Soviet authorities had not formulated a suitable response and, unable to improvise on the spur of the moment, they chose after a brief initial delay to release a bare report of the event without speculating on its potential meaning.[5] However, other explanations are equally logical. Since the announcement of Kissinger's journey to the Chinese mainland said nothing specific about the nature of his business there, the Soviets may simply have felt that substantive comments were premature and idle remarks were pointless, tacitly reserving the right to reply when more had been divulged about what had occurred during the Peking talks. Or rushing into press with rebuttals at the first sign of activity by the competition may have been thought to be inadvisable lest it be apprehended abroad as a symptom of excessive anxiety. Or assuming an air of public indifference might be calculated to rob the episode of its dramatic quality and dampen the mood of the occasion by implying that whatever the opposition was portraying as a major coup was neither very significant nor especially noteworthy.

At the time informed Western circles already guessed that when the Soviets decided to voice an opinion on the subject, they would probably echo the earlier theme that the Soviet Union favored the normalization of relations between all countries so long as that policy did not pursue anti-Soviet goals. The statements emanating from the East European capitals hard upon the heels of the disclosure of Kissinger's trip while Moscow kept mute tended to confirm this prediction, since these accounts also attempted to preserve a judicious balance between acknowledgments that Nixon's planned visit to China might serve the cause of peace and warnings that the Maoist regime might thereby be encouraged in the prosecution of its anti-Soviet aims and, counting now on the friendship of the United States or at least expecting thus to buy its complaisance, be apt to broaden the scope of the ideological and diplomatic warfare it persisted in waging against the "socialist camp."6

When criticism was expressed, the target almost invariably was the PRC, whose ulterior motives in this connection apparently struck the Kremlin's East European confidants as more suspect than those of the Nixon administration or whose conduct was among them a pet target for denunciation at this time, compared with the more selective practice of local evaluation of U.S. behavior in international affairs in recent years. To the extent that Washington officials took pains in the following days to stress at every opportunity Nixon's own assurances that his move toward Peking "is not directed against any other nation," that "we seek friendly relations with all nations," and that "any nation can be our friend without being any other nation's enemy," they appealed to the latter phenomenon by inviting an appraisal on the positive merits of the documented record instead of inciting contrary conclusions based on a priori doctrinal deductions. Peking made no such placatory gestures and, hence, fanned further antagonism in quarters quite predisposed to look upon it with marked hostility, with the result that among the latter it was branded as the primary culprit to whom was forthwith assigned the bulk of the blame for this cavalier upsetting of the established apple cart.

Meanwhile, Moscow held its tongue. Even the next tentative step did not modify the situation, for what the Soviets did was to reprint on July 21, 1971, in the weekly Literaturnaya Gazeta, an article originally distributed by the official Bulgarian Telegraph Agency that recapitulated the gist of the earlier news bulletins on the topic but in a more strident tone. Nixon's pledge that his plans to travel to China would not adversely affect the interests of third parties was contrasted with Peking's silence on that score, which ostensibly put Nixon's professions in a different light. On that ground the Sino-American rapprochement was assailed in harsh terms as reflecting the anti-Soviet positions of the two principals. According to the Bulgarian script, repeated by Moscow:

> On one side, it is the purposeful, anti-Communist policy of the United States which, like the policy of imperialism as a whole, appears aggressive in its relations with the socialist commonwealth, especially in relations with its leading detachment, the Soviet Union.
> On the other side, it is the policy of the Chinese leaders, characterized by unbridled anti-Soviet propaganda, introduction of a split in the international Communist and workers' movement, in the ranks of the socialist countries, and by attempts to weaken the anti-imperialist front.

> The goals that both Peking and Washington pursue
> and their suddenly expressed desire to normalize rela-
> tions cannot but call for serious questions from all people
> interested in peace.
> There are no signs that either the United States or
> the Chinese leaders have changed or are prepared to
> change in any basic way the policy carried on up to now
> or to alter in a positive way their attitude toward pre-
> serving peace in the world.

The final verdict was that the joint Sino-American announcement of
July 15, 1971, which memorialized Nixon's projected trip to Peking
quite clearly showed that the Chinese had engaged in "secret collusion
with imperialism."[7]
Resort to the device of indictment by proxy is not rare in the
Soviet political repertoire. Indeed, the technique has much to recom-
mend it. In this case, the artifice allowed the Kremlin to deliver a
stinging rebuke to both the United States and China, especially the
latter—censure that, in the eyes of Moscow, they amply earned for
trying to get together behind Russia's back or, at any rate, without
asking the Russians to attend the festivities. At the same time, however, attributing the condemnation to a Bulgarian source in principle
meant that the Soviets themselves, no matter how much they may have
approved or how strongly they may have shared their associate's
indignation, were not responsible for these views and were not formally committed to that thesis, thereby leaving them free, if need be,
subsequently to adopt another line.
In effect, having forcefully yet tactfully registered their displeasure over the incident, that is precisely what the Soviets soon
proceeded to do. The tenor of the first overt Soviet response to the
publicity surrounding the latest turn of events in Sino-American diplomacy impressed foreign analysts as more sophisticated and conciliatory than the verbal style of its Bulgarian predecessor, although on
most of the essential aspects they resembled each other to a singular
degree.[8] The main effort seemed to be directed at making sure that
the Soviet Union was not excluded from the emerging Sino-American
dialogue. Despite what had occurred, the Soviet Union now served
official notice on both its rivals that it remained ready to cooperate
vigorously with all states, the PRC and the United States included,
"for the sake of strengthening universal peace, for the sake of freedom,
independence, progress and prosperity of all peoples."
The Soviet government's own position on this issue allegedly
had not changed and could still be described as an uneasy mixture of
hope and uncertainty as to what the current trend would produce. The
Soviet Union, we are told, operated on the assumption that the political

decisions of states must be aimed not at complicating the international situation but, rather, at easing tensions. "Undoubtedly," the author of the article then added,

> the long-term interests of the people of the People's Republic of China and the United States, just as the interests of all the peoples of the world, require decisions promoting stronger peace and security and not political intrigues aimed against other states, for such intrigues, as historical experience teaches, in the long run turn against their initiators.

At this point no one could tell whether the United States and the PRC were prepared to take the lesson to heart, and the assessment confined itself to noting that only the further development of events would reveal the "true intentions" of Peking and Washington. Meanwhile, the Soviet leadership would, of course, have to take into account all the possible consequences of the Chinese-American contacts, with our informant scoffing, "Needless to say, any designs to use the contacts between Peking and Washington for some pressure against the Soviet Union, on the states of the socialist community, are nothing but the result of a loss of touch with reality."

Next an offer was extended to the PRC to restore friendly relations between the Russian and Chinese nations, coupled with criticism of Peking's anti-Soviet platform and its constant attempts to disrupt the solidarity of the "socialist commonwealth" in the face of the imperialist threat. A parallel invitation to develop mutual relations on the basis of the principle of peaceful coexistence was addressed to the United States, along with an unequivocal reiteration of the Kremlin's determination to oppose the "aggressive actions" of the American government. Washington's claim that Nixon's planned visit to China was an expression of its "peace-making line" did not, in Moscow's opinion, square with U.S. conduct elsewhere in the world, particularly in Vietnam. "It is not by chance," the Russians declared, "that the contacts with Peking are also regarded by many in the United States as a continuation of precisely this reactionary, anti-Communist course." To people of this stripe a successful Sino-American flirtation held out the prospect of the PRC drawing even closer to the capitalist countries, especially the United States, and thereby commensurately weakening the viability of the international Communist movement. The "progressive press," on the other hand, hoped that better Chinese-American relations would induce a relaxation of tensions but was in no way persuaded that Peking and Washington could indeed be trusted, since their past performance afforded adequate ground for serious misgivings about their real objectives.

144

Hence, the Soviet message can be summed up as follows: the Soviet Union was not rattled by the growing intimacy between the United States and the PRC, but it plainly favored improving its own ties with both of them; on balance, the Kremlin viewed the normalization of Sino-American relations as a positive manifestation, provided neither side sought to capitalize on the goodwill of its new friend at the expense of other countries, above all the Soviet Union and its socialist partners. The Russians had reason to believe that warmer relations between Peking and Washington did not automatically spell abandonment by either one of its hegemonial aspirations which endangered global peace and security, and therefore counseled universal exercise of unflagging vigilance to guard against a unilateral bid to dominate the world or a joint U.S.-PRC conspiracy to divide it among themselves. Any such enterprise, the Soviets asserted, was doomed to failure; and the only practical solution was for both Peking and Washington to come to terms with Moscow and thus forge a solid basis for future cooperation among all three, an arrangement from which, according to the Soviet canon, the rest of the international community was bound to profit.

Except for an occasional minor adjustment in wording and emphasis, the Soviets have since tenaciously clung to this stock formula, which, on the whole, has served their tactical purposes well enough.[9]

RELATIONS WITH INDIA AND PAKISTAN

The first opportunity to test the concrete application of Soviet intentions in this sphere presented itself that summer, in connection with the events on the Indian subcontinent, ranging from the signature of the Soviet-Indian treaty of friendship on August 9, 1971, to the Soviet Union's foreign policy tack during the ensuing Indian-Pakistani conflict over Bangladesh. To be sure, the preliminary work on the pact itself had stretched over the preceding two years, so that its conclusion at this time was not attributable solely to the power realignment then in progress in the region, in key with the waxing U.S.-PRC courtship. Even so, there is no gainsaying that the quickening pace of the Sino-American thaw played a crucial role in these matters. India, fearful that a Peking-Washington entente might bolster Pakistan's military capacity and whittle down India's armed superiority, sought tangible reassurance through closer association with the Soviet Union, America's and China's rival on the scene, while looking for a safe moment to settle the score with Pakistan once and for all—whenever New Delhi could firmly count on Peking, Washington, and Moscow mutually checkmating their respective ambitions in this theater of operations for the required span of time. Clearly, India's drift toward

the Soviet Union was also thoroughly welcome to the latter. In this
game of musical chairs, the Kremlin saw a unique chance to increase
India's dependence on the Soviet Union and coincidentally undermine
the influence of both China and the United States in this area.

The net outcome of the melee confirmed India as the big winner
in the contest. By the same token, the Soviet Union achieved its primary aim of eliminating an effective local Chinese and American
political presence. However, the very totality of India's victory dim-
med any serious hope the Soviets may have had of henceforth exerting
routine control over India's diplomatic record, a fact that incited the
Russians to move to redress the shattered geopolitical equilibrium
in some measure by helping to get Pakistan back on its feet after its
searing defeat. By hedging its bets, the Soviet Union guaranteed an
element of choice on the premises, kept at least a minimum of options
open, and carved out a niche for itself as an accepted arbiter of the
myriad petty differences that continued to feed the flames of the Indian-
Pakistani feud. In a negative sense, then, the Russians had gained the
upper hand over their American and Chinese competitors by depriving
them of a solid foothold in the area. What, to a significant degree,
made this possible was the congruency in the Sino-American display
of solidarity with Pakistan, which made India, confident of Russian
assistance, seek an early showdown with its ancient foe that promptly
led to the latter's undoing.

On the positive side, though, the value of the political dividends
that accrued to the Soviet Union in the process is much harder to fix:
neither India nor Pakistan is tied to Russia's apron strings; China and
the United States may be temporarily eclipsed here, but both may yet
mend their fences with India and reenter the tourney. The one major
accomplishment the Russians have to their credit is that if the Chinese
and the Indians remain at loggerheads, the Chinese will have less
opportunity in the future to stir up trouble between India and Pakistan,
whereas India will be in better shape to withstand Chinese pressure
and more likely to run to Russia for succor against any perceived
threat from China alone or a China that seemingly enjoys a special
place in the affections of Washington.

In the ranks of the opposition, Pakistan and China sustained the
worst losses, while for the United States the experience chiefly dealt
a blow to its pride and prestige. The discrepancy meant that the
Russian leaders could derive added satisfaction from knowing that they
had administered a severe setback to the Peking regime without having
to worry that the incident might drive a sharp wedge between the Soviet
Union and the United States, with which they still hoped to engage in
businesslike dialogue in order to prevent the ad hoc U.S.-PRC liaison
from coalescing into a quasi-matrimonial status that would leave
Moscow out in the cold. Indeed, the Soviet mass media clearly adopted

146

a double standard in their treatment of the United States and the PRC during this period. As a rule the United States was approached in a conciliatory vein, and such criticism as there was, relatively mild in any event, was largely confined to intramural debates or discussions in private or semi-private forums. The official attitude toward China was more mixed: offers of cooperation and invitations to let bygones be bygones and to turn over a new leaf in Sino-Soviet relations alternated with stern denunciations of various aspects of Peking's foreign and domestic performance.

Thus, statements made by top U.S. government figures to the effect that Washington did not want its overtures to Peking to jeopardize its contacts with Moscow received prominent billing in the Soviet central press.[10] In the next breath the Chinese were charged with having maliciously fabricated rumors of an impending Soviet invasion of China so as to justify their appeasement of the "imperialist" states and abjectly curry favor with the members of the "capitalist" world, principally the United States, and were accused of deliberately torpedoing the Sino-Soviet border talks with the same objectives in mind.[11] The effort appeared to be motivated by the desire both to tarnish the PRC's reputation in general and to render it less attractive as a public consort to the United States, whose attention would presumably then be deflected to the items featured on the Soviet-American agenda.

THE CAMPAIGN AGAINST CHINA

The virulence of the Soviet verbal attacks on China mounted in proportion to the progress registered by Moscow's campaign to improve its own relations with Russia's "capitalist" neighbors. The search for a modus vivendi in East-Central Europe, symbolized by the ratification of the 1971 treaty between the Soviet Union and the Federal Republic of Germany and the conclusion of the four-power agreement on Berlin, doubtless owed much of its success to the dramatic developments in the Far East. If Washington and Peking could bury the hatchet, so could Bonn and Moscow. Chancellor Willy Brandt's government certainly found it easier to vindicate the thrust of its Ostpolitik by evoking the prima facie example of the Nixon administration's pilgrimage to Peking. The Soviets took due advantage of Brandt's commitment to this proposition to wring sundry concessions from the West German authorities; but deep down the Russians were probably just as eager as the West Germans to bring this chapter of history to a satisfactory end, secure their European flank, and be free to attend to urgent business elsewhere. Compromise was inevitable under the circumstances and, of course, the Chinese could not resist the temptation to tax the Russians with selling out the interests of the socialist community for a mess of capitalist pottage.

Picking on the Chinese in these conditions fulfilled several functions. By hurling insults at Peking, for instance, the Soviets expected
to counter the latter's jibes at Moscow for reportedly "toadying" to
the "imperialist" bloc. They also sought to make light of the Chinese
claim that the Kremlin was willing to normalize the situation in Europe
at almost any price to permit it to focus all its energies on organizing
a widespread crusade against the PRC in Asia and the Pacific basin.
The very fact that the Soviets repeatedly cited these allegations only
to deride them (in rather clumsy fashion, one might add) as products
of an overheated imagination and in turn flailed at Peking for conspir-
ing with all sorts of unsavory elements on the European political scene,
neo-Nazis not exempted, to agitate in Russia's front yard and divert
its attention from what was going on in other parts of the world is a
fair sign that the Chinese had hit on a sore spot and in this case had
correctly interpreted Soviet calculations.[12]

The problem of how to deal intelligently with the challenge now
posed by the Chinese created a bit of a procedural dilemma for the
Russians. To persist in sniping at the Chinese for acting in the international arena virtually as the Russians did would make little sense.[13]
Hence, the Russians switched tracks and gradually shifted from the
international to the internal plane, where they could zero in on the
peculiarities of the Maoist domestic blueprint without tarring themselves with the same brush.[14] That stratagem also enabled the Russians to signal the sister parties that the current splurge of Gemütlich-
keit did not mean that China had ceased to be an ideological persona
non grata or that it was all right for orthodox Communists to rush
into Peking's embrace because a mood of "fraternization" hovered
in the air. The Kremlin already had sufficient cause to be concerned
about recent Chinese inroads in Yugoslavia and Rumania,[15] made
considerably easier by the general lowering of diplomatic barriers
and relaxation of sectarian tensions triggered by news of the establishment of direct contacts between Peking and Washington and the positive
response of most other countries to this major development. This
seemed a fitting method to cool the ardor of some of the Soviet Union's
East European allies for the notion of renouncing forthwith all the
ancient quarrels and starting afresh, without appearing to be deliberately sabotaging the widespread enthusiasm for détente that the Sino-
American initiative had kindled.

Thus, a favorite target of Soviet criticism was the militarization
of Chinese society, the imposition of drastic economic sacrifices on
the Chinese workers in order to hoard resources for military preparations, and the fostering of a climate of war psychosis in the country
by constant propaganda on the theme of an impending Soviet invasion.
In this connection the Soviets even referred to the existence of a
faction within the top Chinese leadership that allegedly opposed the

dominant role of the armed forces in the nation's life and the policy of cultivating friendly relations with the United States. True or not, the story that among the Chinese themselves there were people who were unhappy at the course pursued by their government would be calculated to discourage outsiders from indiscriminately endorsing the whole scheme. At the same time, perhaps in an effort to prettify their image by advertising an abiding benevolent attitude toward the PRC and their reliability in honoring prior commitments, the Russians reiterated their rejection of the "two-China" concept and demanded that the PRC alone be seated in the United Nations as the legitimate representative of the Chinese people without further delay. Whether the Russians really wanted to see the PRC in the world organization and how useful were Moscow's official exertions there on the latter's behalf are a different matter. What is significant is that the Russians thought it prudent to maintain that posture in public, even while stepping up their attacks on the Peking regime on other grounds.

INVOLVEMENT OF OTHER COUNTRIES

The next step in the Kremlin's global campaign to neutralize the potential consequences of the Sino-American thaw involved Japan; and in January 1972 Andrei Gromyko was dispatched to Tokyo in a bid to forge closer Soviet-Japanese ties that was described by Western analysts "as a transparent display of warmth to balance the growing contacts between China and the United States."[16] The purpose of the mission was presumably to reconnoiter current Japanese views on the United States and China, plumb the depths of Japanese resentment over the Nixon administration's secretive tactics in approaching the PRC, investigate the possibility of exploiting Japanese pique over the incident to the advantage of the Soviet Union, and block the PRC's moves to woo Japan. Unsure of what the Japanese proposed to do in the emerging four-way power game in the Far East, the Russians tried hard to win the Japanese over to their side, dangling the bait of an early peace treaty, commercial and economic inducements (in particular, the prospect of cooperation in tapping the vast wealth of Siberia), and better treatment of Japanese fishermen plying their trade in the northern waters adjacent to Soviet shores. Clearly, the expansiveness of the mood the Soviets sought to communicate in their talks with the Japanese matched the degree of anxiety they felt over the possibility of a Sino-Japanese axis and the importance they attached to keeping Japan out of Peking's "clutches," plus fear that they might not succeed in doing so. In other words, heroic gestures were appropriate for the occasion to prevent a crisis situation from arising; they were consciously exaggerated because the Soviets were not certain what kind of competition they now faced, how far they should go to deal with it effectively, and how much risk they could afford to run. Even then, however, Moscow stuck to intangibles, holding out a promissory note, as it were, but not revealing the actual size of its stake until the other contenders had tipped their hands.

Nor were the lesser Communist states neglected in the process, with Moscow lavishing special attention on North Vietnam, whose response was quite gratifying. Worried about the likely implications of the Sino-American dialogue for their own future, confronted with a sharp escalation of American military operations in Indochina, and, hence, dependent to an ever increasing degree on the sophisticated weaponry supplied by the Soviet Union, Hanoi and the Viet Cong took extra pains to publicize their communality of interests with the Soviet Union and the harmonious nature of Soviet-North Vietnamese relations. Whatever the position hitherto occupied by the North Vietnamese vis-à-vis the Sino-Soviet dispute, Peking's willingness to play host to Nixon at a time when the conflict in Indochina was reaching new levels of ferocity put a chill on North Vietnamese-Chinese affairs from which Soviet-North Vietnamese contacts only benefited.

The preceding survey does not, of course, chronicle each diplomatic move made by the Soviet Union during this period that may in some way be attributed to the impact of the Sino-American rapprochement. The Soviet "counteroffensive" ranged far wider. The agenda included important discussions with the political leaders of West Germany, France, Canada, and the Scandinavian countries and a quiet campaign to sell the governments of Malaysia, Singapore, and Indonesia on the virtues of neutralism. In many respects, however, the link between these episodes and the Sino-American experience is at best a tenuous one; and this flurry of activity is related to the Chinese-American rapprochement solely in the sense that it was designed to steal the thunder of the Washington-Peking extravaganza and, instead, glue the spotlight to Moscow's performance.

After having taken these elementary precautions, the Kremlin made a few final mildish remarks about both the United States and the PRC[17] and settled back to await the outcome of Nixon's encounter with the Chinese leadership. Soviet press reporting on Nixon's arrival in Peking was cryptic. As might have been expected under the circumstances, the brunt of Soviet comments fell on Peking's shoulders, for receiving Nixon at a time when American bombing in Vietnam was at a peak, betraying the Communist camp, and concocting the "most pernicious consequences" for the Communists of Indochina. Although the United States was once again warned against attempting to use the Maoist regime's desertion from the international Communist movement for its own purposes and to extract a profit from the latter's avowed anti-Sovietism, Russian criticism of U.S. policy was in a comparatively moderate tone. The reason would seem to lie in the Kremlin's determination to retain an open channel of communication with Washington and not to scuttle Nixon's planned trip to the Soviet Union in May 1972. The Soviets had no objections to rapping American knuckles over the China affair when necessary; but, they saved the vitriol for the "renegade" Chinese comrades, apparently in the belief that with enough skill and patience the United States could somehow be swayed, bribed, or bamboozled away from its transient fascination with China and brought back to the realization that its long-term interests required a lasting accommodation with the Soviet Union while the Chinese were immune to such techniques.

Meanwhile, the Russians were busy behind the scenes. There have been allegations that Moscow encouraged the North Vietnamese to launch a military drive to coincide with the Nixon visit to Peking, in order to wreck any hope of a Sino-American agreement on ending the war in Indochina. The Soviet mass media kept up a drumfire of hostile commentary on recent events in China, charging Peking, inter alia, with earmarking unprecedented sums from the national budget for military items and accusing Western nations of supplying the Chinese with strategic materials even for the production of nuclear weapons. They also missed no opportunity to aggravate the note of constraint that had crept into North Vietnamese-Chinese relations as an accompaniment to the growing Sino-American flirtation.

The grand coup, however, was the scheduling of a visit by a North Korean delegation to the Soviet Union to coincide with Nixon's stay in Peking. Thus far Pyongyang had stubbornly resisted all Soviet blandishments and, while deftly straddling the fence in its dealings with Moscow and Peking, had lent a more sympathetic ear to the PRC than the Soviet Union in their doctrinal and diplomatic polemics. Nevertheless, with the Chinese now ensconced in cozy chatter with the hated American foe, the North Koreans could no longer afford the luxury of "leaning to one side." The trip to Moscow served a dual purpose: to show Peking that the North Korean regime did not depend wholly on its support and had other friends in the world on whom it could count, and to obtain Soviet assistance in exchange for taking a more middle position in the Sino-Soviet controversy. If the Soviets genuinely thought that this was an opportunity to enroll the North Koreans on their team, the gambit failed, for Pyongyang persisted in steering an autonomous course despite all Soviet efforts to buy its allegiance. On the other hand, the experiment was not in vain, since the North Koreans henceforth held themselves more aloof from their Chinese colleagues than before.

RESPONSE TO THE SHANGHAI COMMUNIQUÉ

The initial Soviet response to the Shanghai communiqué sounded quite hostile. The Soviet mass media tended to dwell on certain items that the Russians apparently found rather disturbing. Stress was laid on the secrecy surrounding the talks themselves and the scanty language of the printed text concerning the contents of the discussions. The passage asserting that both the United States and China are "opposed to efforts by any other country or group of countries to establish" hegemony in the Asia-Pacific region seemed to irritate the Russians particularly, as though it confirmed earlier Soviet suspicions of an existing or impending Sino-American collusion in Asia and perhaps elsewhere. Anxiety on that score seemed to have prompted the Soviets to put extra stress in their public pronouncements on the wisdom of their own proposals for "collective security" arrangements in Asia,[18] which Washington had long labeled as a vehicle for extending Soviet influence in the area.

By the next day, however, after having had more leisure to study and ponder the wording of the Shanghai document, the first outburst of truculence subsided and the Soviet leadership switched to a milder and more relaxed tone. The Chinese were now given credit for having opposed the American position on the Vietnam war, a rare phenomenon indeed. Instead of pushing the conspiracy theory, the Tass commentary took express note of the statement in the joint declaration that there remained "essential differences between China and the United States" on foreign policy issues and in their social systems and reported that, in lieu of indicating consensus on a variety of other topics, each party had registered its separate views.

On the whole, the impression one gets from looking at the public record is that in the beginning the Soviets felt considerable apprehension about what the meeting might portend in terms of potential Sino-American cooperation and the possible adverse effects of any such understanding on the interests of the Soviet Union and, hence, reacted skeptically to the relatively bland account released by Washington and Peking regarding what they had purportedly discussed and agreed on. In fact, judging by this episode, the standard Soviet reflex when unsure is to act nasty and then to backtrack if, on second thought, the occasion is deemed not to have warranted the snappishness. But the original "loss of temper" is controlled enough that nothing irrevocable is uttered "in the heat of the moment" that could prevent a subsequent shift to a more moderate attitude. In this case, once the Kremlin had decided that it faced no immediate danger from the Sino-American tête-à-tête, it dropped its angry mask and composed a more amiable visage that hinted at the prospect of constructive bilateral contacts with the United States as well as China; took care not to slam the door on any chances of Soviet maneuvering between Peking and Washington to keep the two apart and guarantee that the three-handed diplomatic game did not degenerate into a two-handed contest, with the Russians reduced to the role of idle kibitzer; and served to maintain a propitious atmosphere for Nixon's proximately scheduled visit to the Soviet Union.

Having thus set the stage, Moscow stayed comparatively quiescent until the "climax" of Nixon's trip to the Soviet Union and meeting with the Russian leaders had been satisfactorily consummated. How much the Soviets had counted on this opportunity and how handsomely their forbearance paid off may be gauged from the number and substantive thrust of the accords signed by the two governments to celebrate the event and in the months that followed. Whatever crisis the Soviets may have feared from the unfolding Sino-American dialogue has yet to materialize. Meantime, Soviet-American relations have vastly improved, in part because of a desire by Washington to demonstrate its impartiality toward both giant Communist powers and in part because the Russians too have conducted themselves in more civil fashion vis-à-vis the United States precisely in order to counter China's seductiveness, convince Washington that it had more to gain by being friendly to Moscow, and make certain that if a Sino-American coalition was ever contemplated, the scheme would be stillborn.

The Soviets may have safeguarded their American flank, as it were; but the Sino-Soviet dispute showed no sign of abating and Peking was logging palpable progress in its overtures toward Tokyo, which furnished the Russians with additional food for worry. All of this further stimulated Soviet interest in advertising their "collective security" blueprint for Asia,[19] which they touted as an efficient antidote to the American "Guam doctrine" and the PRC's dreams of exercising political supremacy in South and Southeast Asia. Though the United States was mentioned in this connection, the reference to Washington's activities in the region was almost perfunctory, while the Chinese had to absorb the brunt of the Soviet attack. As often happens in situations of this sort, the Kremlin here resorted to the old diversionary tactic of mounting a great show of indignation over alleged Chinese insistence that the United States must retain its military role in Europe and Asia and continue to underpin the various "imperialist, anti-Communist" blocs that had been erected at the height of the Cold War.[20]

In short, the Soviets were again trying the old ruse of crying "Stop, thief!" to divert world attention from the patently anti-Chinese business they themselves engaged in and to focus it on the "pro-imperialist" ingredients of the foreign policy program they ascribed to Peking. Or they figured that by bluntly chastizing the Chinese for a certain type of conduct, they would be able to throw a smoke screen over their own operations. Or they fell back on the old tu quoque technique or pretended that they were merely responding in kind to prior Chinese provocation. Whatever the motives, the Kremlin was definitely seeking practical ways and means of fortifying its "defenses" athwart China's southern perimeter so as to be able to exert, if only by proxy, adequate pressure on its rival for local leadership while making sure that if the United States did pull its forces out of the region, the Chinese, or even the Japanese, would not inherit the mantle by default and the power "vacuum" that an American withdrawal would leave would be properly filled by an organized group of "nonaligned" states enjoying full Soviet support and capable of escaping the gravitational tug of the PRC or Japan.

For that matter, one likewise detects at this stage a gradual stiffening of the Soviet attitude toward Japan. The billing and cooing that had preceded Nixon's trip to Peking had helped Japan overcome the initial difficult stage of readjustment following the sudden unveiling of the Sino-American liaison. Japan had not done anything reckless or foolish on the spur of the moment, such as hurling itself into China's arms. But neither had Tokyo succumbed to Russian blandishments, which doubtless annoyed the Kremlin. On the other hand, while the Chinese and Japanese were slowly moving toward a mutual accommodation, the Japanese evinced no more urge to be hooked by Peking than they had shown earlier to swallow the Soviet bait. Seeing that they could not win the Japanese over to their side and that the Chinese were not doing a much better job of it, the Soviets adopted a harder line, accusing the Japanese of reviving militarism at home, spreading their economic and political tentacles abroad, aspiring to a dominant role in South and Southeast Asia, and acting as American imperialism's errand boy while carefully promoting their private ends. Ostensibly, the Russians thus sought to convey their annoyance with the behavior of all parties concerned, alert the Japanese to their displeasure, and persuade them to tread softly in their dealings with China and the United States lest they sorely alienate the Soviet Union and forfeit the unique profits they would presumably reap from an intimate association with the Soviet Union in the economic and political realms.

SUMMARY

A cynic, rereading the saga, might, with good reason, conclude that all this fervor and excitement produced remarkably few concrete changes in the original scenario. As far as the Soviet Union is concerned, its relations with China and Japan have neither improved nor deteriorated to any serious degree in the wake of Nixon's safari to Peking. The normalized situation in Europe would probably have occurred anyway, and the Sino-American experiment accelerated the process but did not create the basic preconditions or generate the underlying impetus. Exactly what the Russians gained on the Indian subcontinent is still unclear, except that they at least posted a symbolic victory over their foreign competitors in that arena. Relatively speaking, the Russians came out ahead of the pack; in positive terms, the question of what substantive dividends accrued to the Russians remains a hotly debated issue.

Paradoxically, the one area in which the Soviets can really claim a solid achievement as a consequence of this experience is in their relations with the United States. My suggestion is that this state of affairs is, by and large, the logical outcome of a deliberate policy decision by the Soviet leadership, in the face of the Sino-American thaw, to concentrate its principal efforts on the United States in order to better Soviet-American ties for their own sake and to prevent a potential Sino-American entente that could adversely affect the interests of the Soviet Union. All the other moves, vis-à-vis Japan, India, Europe, and so forth, fall into the category of minimal precautionary measures and perhaps just plain diplomatic window-dressing, whereas the United States was, I believe, perceived by the Soviet authorities as a pivotal piece in the current power shuffle in the Pacific and thus worthy of special attention for the direct advantages to be derived from a closer involvement with the key partner in the ongoing diplomatic game and for purposes of keeping everyone else, the PRC in particular, from attaining that privileged status.

Indeed, the whole record of Soviet behavior in the aftermath of Kissinger's secret flight to Peking indicates a deep concern to preserve an open channel of communication with Washington. In the running Soviet commentary on the progression of Sino-American contacts, the PRC emerges as the chief villain, while the treatment accorded the United States savors of hostile wariness and anxious appeasement.

On balance, the quality of the official Soviet performance on this occasion must earn high grades. The Kremlin was doubtless quite nervous about the possible implications of the Sino-American détente, yet it betrayed no panic. While they did resort to verbal bravado and handed out many glowing promises on how well they intended to recompense their "true friends" with huge economic and political benefits, the Russians did not let themselves be stampeded into assuming any net liability or giving something away for nothing. Whatever concessions were granted the United States or West Germany, for instance, were neatly offset by profits that the Soviet Union collected in return. In short, the Soviets may have been sincerely worried by the inception and subsequent effervescence of the Sino-American dialogue and did not neglect to adopt the proper safeguards. However, the sentiment was apparently not intense enough to lure the Russians into making any rash gestures in terms of either entangling commitments or unilateral donations.

Furthermore, as the initial uncertainty faded and the world, temporarily diverted by all this pomp and ceremony, resumed its dull routine, the Kremlin too reverted to its staple modus operandi. The pitch now sounded less generous and hard bargaining was again the norm. If Soviet-American contacts continue to thrive and multiply, it is because each side finds the two-way traffic valuable and not out of any sense of altruism and compulsion. To be sure, the Soviets might be more prone to compromise today in dealing with the United States lest their intransigence give the PRC an opportunity to catch the United States on the rebound. Even so, this cannot be more than a subsidiary consideration in the formulation of Soviet plans toward the United States; and once Moscow decides that objective or subjective elements bar the prospect of a genuine U.S.-PRC accommodation within the foreseeable future, an equivalent proportion of the present momentum in favor of cultivating Washington's goodwill likewise will vanish, leaving behind an attitude of sober appraisal of what can be gained from carefully massaging the American ego versus what may be lost by pursuing a correct but not intimate working relationship with the United States.

One question still begs an answer: How badly did the phenomenon of the PRC's full-fledged emergence on the international scene, stemming from the dynamics of the Sino-American rapprochement, actually disturb the Russians? Did Moscow indeed regard the consummation as an irretrievable defeat for its former policy line in China, or is the final assessment of the plus and minus features of the event more complex and ambiguous in character? In my opinion the latter is the case.

What, from the Soviet point of view, was perhaps the most undesirable aspect of the entire business was that China's international debut took place under the auspices of the United States, as it were. It was Washington's imprimatur that gave the PRC the last token of informal recognition it required to become an accepted member of the family of nations. The Soviet Union could neither prevent this nor could it engineer the coup on its own. Hence, should Peking ever feel it owes a debt of gratitude for the boost it received in this connection, the United States alone will reap the reward. And, of course, services rendered could furnish the source from which would flow further consensus, a contingency of which the Kremlin was well aware.

On the other hand, the fact of the PRC's acknowledged entry into world affairs must have filled the Kremlin with mixed feelings. China's past isolation had severely cramped its diplomatic style and had guaranteed the Russians an obvious advantage in that respect, which they would henceforth enjoy on a much more limited scale. To the Russians this particular item spelled a negative component in the equation. If the PRC was destined to become involved in big-time diplomacy anyway, the optimal solution for Moscow, under the circumstances, would have consisted of the Chinese gate-crashing the party over U.S. opposition: in this fashion they would bear whatever stigma attached to being part of the crowd while still being denied automatic access to the prerogatives appertaining to the old elite. However, the Kremlin simply could not stage-manage this.

Conversely, as a maverick Peking could and did propound a radical creed, espouse extreme doctrinal principles, and assert its right to defend the orthodox faith against all attempts to dilute or revise the established canon. In militant circles and with hawkish regimes such as those of North Vietnam and North Korea, Peking's solitary and unbending stand contributed significantly to its local popularity, whereas the Kremlin's revolutionary escutcheon had been sorely tarnished by the innumerable compromises the Soviets had elected to acquiesce in over the years while engaged in an endless series of intricate political maneuvers. From here on, though, Moscow and Peking shared the same burden, with the former cashing in on the latter's fall from grace. To the extent that the leveling effect was due to the PRC's belated immersion in the corrosive waters of realpolitik, the Soviets could derive a certain amount of satisfaction from China's plunge into the diplomatic whirlpool and perhaps even feel grudgingly grateful to the United States for making it possible. At a single stroke Mao Tse-tung and his crew were stripped of their aura of religious innocence, forfeited their senior position as the planet's resident firebrands, and lost their special image of ideological incorruptibility.

Nor did the Russians hesitate to pounce at the chance to repay the Chinese in kind for all the dirt Peking had poured over them earlier. The Soviets mercilessly castigated the Chinese for their role in the Bangladesh affair, pilloried the PRC's performance in the United Nations, and accused the Chinese of serving the aims of Western imperialism in the Third World, betraying the cause of the national-liberation movement, and spearheading the bourgeois-capitalist global crusade against the socialist and nonaligned countries.[21] The opportunity to administer a dose of their own medicine to the Chinese must have given the Russians considerable pleasure. More important, however, the Russians now had the means of effectively countering past and present Chinese criticism of various aspects of Soviet foreign policy merely by turning the tables and imputing to Peking the same base motives that Peking had ascribed to them. Hence, ultima analysi, the Soviets might still have concluded that the price was right, even if it meant admitting China to the international circuit.

Over the long haul, the decision may prove Moscow's wisest move yet in the tortured career of Soviet-PRC relations: shorn of their doctrinal halo, the Chinese will have no choice but to challenge the Soviets on the usual grounds of political and economic power, where the Russians are several laps ahead of them; hitherto, the conflict had been waged primarily on the ideological plane, and in that sector the Chinese had commanded a marked edge over their Soviet comrades. Ironically, the PRC's newly won respectability threatens to eliminate the most potent weapon previously stocked in its anti-Soviet arsenal without offering it any viable alternative method of prosecuting the contest successfully. For the Kremlin this dimension of the problem forms the proverbial silver lining to the cloud of Sino-American accommodation and, in that sense, what started out as a vexing episode may, on balance, prove to be a highly gratifying experience.

NOTES

1. R. Moskvitin, "U.S.-China: 'Smiling Diplomacy,'" New Times, 1971, no. 13: 28.
2. For instance, L. Kirichenko, "Peking's Diplomatic Game," ibid., no. 17: 5.
3. I. Trofimova, "Washington-Peking: Another Step," ibid., no. 27: 13.
4. Cf. A. Nadezhdin, "Metamorphoses of Peking Diplomacy," ibid., no. 22: 22-24.
5. Izvestiya, July 16, 1971.
6. New York Times, July 17, 1971, citing editorials from Eesti Hirlap (Budapest) and Express Wierzocny (Warsaw).
7. Quoted in New York Times, July 22, 1971, which also noted that on July 18 the Warsaw newspaper Zycie Warszawy had lauded Nixon's decision as a long overdue reversal of U.S. attitudes toward Peking and that this Polish commentary had not been mentioned in the Soviet press.
8. I. Aleksandrov, "Po povodu kontaktov Pekina s Vashingtonom," Pravda, July 25, 1971.
9. G. Arbatov, "Voprosy, trebuyushchie prakticheskogo otveta, K planiruemoi Amerikano-Kitaiskoi vstrechi v verkhakh," Pravda, August 10, 1971; L. Trofimenko, "Peking and Washington," New Times, 1971, no. 31: 10.
10. Pravda and Izvestiya, Sept. 2, 1971.
11. S. Tikhvinskii, "Sovetsko-Kitaiskie otnosheniya, storonniki i protivniki ikh uluchsheniya," Pravda, Aug. 20, 1971; Izvestiya, Aug. 25, 1971.
12. Cf. D. Vostokov, "The Foreign Policy of the People's Republic of China since the 9th Congress of the CPC," International Affairs, 1972, no. 1: 23-32, esp. 30; B. Kapchenko, "Maoism's Foreign Policy Platform," ibid., no. 2: 35-41, see 38; V. Pavlov, "Europe in Peking's Plans," ibid., no. 3: 15-21, see 16-17; V. Rybakov, "Behind the Scenes of Peking's 'Peace Strategy,'" ibid., no. 11, 16-21, see 19.

13. I. Aleksandrov, "Lozungi i dela kitaiskogo rukovodstva," Pravda, Sept. 4, 1971.

14. New York Times, Sept. 5, 1971, p. 3, and Sept. 8, 1971, p. 12.

15. For instance, S. Yurkov, "Peking's Policy Towards the Socialist Countries," International Affairs, 1971, no. 11: 17-24; B. Kapchenko, op. cit., p. 37.

16. New York Times, Jan. 24, 1971, p. 3.

17. Yu. Zhukov, "Vopreki deistvitelnosti," Pravda, Feb. 17, 1972; O. Rakhmanin, "K istorii druzhestvennykh svyazei Sovetskogo i Kitaiskogo narodov," Izvestiya, Feb. 17, 1972.

18. Pravda, Feb. 27, 1972.

19. V. Kudryavtsev, "Aktualnaya zadacha," Izvestiya, Oct. 12, 1972.

20. See, for instance, I. Aleksandrov, "O nekotorykh takticheskikh osobennostyakh nyneshnei politiki Pekinskogo rukovodstva," Pravda, Sept. 5, 1972; V. Rybakov, op. cit., pp. 19, 21; G. Apalin, "Peking and the 'Third World,'" International Affairs, 1972, no. 12: 28-34, see 30.

21. For instance, G. Apalin, op. cit.; "Po puti politicheskogo avantyurizma," Pravda, Jan. 3, 1973; V. Rybakov, "China in the United Nations: A Barren Policy," International Affairs, 1973, no. 3: 48-52.

CHAPTER

9

THE SINO-JAPANESE
RAPPROCHEMENT:
A RELATIONSHIP OF
AMBIVALENCE
Gene T. Hsiao

The Nixon administration's new China policy has had many political repercussions in the world. Important among these is the Sino-
Japanese rapprochement. From the vantage point of history, such a
rapprochement would have occurred, regardless of the Nixon policy.
As early as 1951, Prime Minister Shigeru Yoshida made the realistic
remark: "Red or white, China remains our next-door neighbor.
Geography and economic laws will, I believe, prevail in the long run
over any ideological differences and artificial trade barriers."[1]
Nevertheless, the timing of the rapprochement and its ramifica-
tions in international affairs are both significant subjects for analysis.
Three questions are pertinent: To what extent did the Nixon policy
influence Japan's decision to normalize relations with the People's
Republic of China (PRC)? How was the rapprochement actually achieved?
And what has happened since the Chou-Tanaka joint statement of
September 29, 1972? Following, then, is a discussion of these questions
under three subheadings: (1) "Sato's Dilemma," (2) "The Chou-Tanaka
Initiative," and (3) "The Beginning of Normalization."

SATO'S DILEMMA

Prior to the opening of "ping-pong diplomacy" in the spring
of 1971, which happened to take place on Japanese soil, seasoned
Japanese political analysts aready acknowledged the existence of a
multipolar world resulting from the growing Sino-Soviet conflict and

---

A slightly shortened version of this chapter has been published
in The China Quarterly (London) no. 57, February 1974.

the changing American attitude toward China after Mr. Nixon assumed the Presidency.[2] Writing in March 1970, a noted Japanese scholar observed:

> The world will see a three-way struggle, beginning with Peking and involving the United States and the Soviet Union, in the course of which they will enter a period of diplomatic warfare reminiscent of the Three Kingdoms in Chinese history.[3]

The basis of his rationale was that since the United States could not remain "a detached observer on a lofty perch" in an all-out war between the Soviet Union and the PRC, it would have no alternative but to find a pipeline to Peking in order to prevent the upheaval's ever occurring. In other words, A Sino-American détente might act as a deterrent on the Kremlin, whose massive military buildup along the Sino-Soviet borders was already a threat to world peace.[4]

Prime Minister Eisaku Sato was well aware of this situation. In fact, he suggested in October 1970 that the whole China problem should be solved in this decade.[5] However, until the PRC replaced the Taiwan delegation in the United Nations in October 1971, Sato, like all his predecessors, maintained what has been commonly termed a "two China" stance. He repeatedly stressed his interest in improving relations with the PRC without, however, abandoning existing political and economic ties with Taiwan. In reply to critics of the Sato policy, Japanese Foreign Ministry officials were actually proud of the fact that through the regular visit of Liberal Democratic Party (LDP) members to the mainland and the exchange of journalists and semiofficial trade missions, Japan's relations with the PRC were both "wider and deeper" than the tenuous links the United States maintained with Peking through the ambassadorial talks at Warsaw.[6]

It is true that the announcement on July 15, 1971, of President Nixon's planned visit to the PRC came as a shock to Japan and, in the opinion of many Japanese government officials, virtually wrecked the foundation of Japan's postwar foreign policy, which gave top priority to the United States while holding the PRC in relative neglect.[7] But Sato was still not prepared to change his "two China" stance. In a speech to both houses of the Diet shortly after the Nixon announcement, he approved of the President's visit to China for the sake of peace and then declared:

> Needless to say, it is most important for our country to maintain and to promote friendly and amicable relations with the Republic of Korea, the Republic of China and other neighboring countries.

In particular, the China problem is one of the biggest
issues facing our country's diplomacy in the 1970s. The
Government intends to improve the relations between our
two countries with care, based on the understanding that
the attitude of the People's Republic of China will have
great influence on the easing of tensions in the Far East.
I think it is important, for this purpose, for both countries
to respect each other's position and to strive to deepen
mutual understanding through talks between various
quarters.[8]

Dissenters within the LDP and all opposition parties except the
right wing of the Japan Communist Party (JCP) intensified their attacks against the Sato policy and demanded his resignation as well
as Japan's immediate recognition of the PRC.[9] But the question was
how and on what terms? A week before Dr. Henry A. Kissinger's
secret mission to Peking on July 9, 1971, the Komeito (Clean Government Party) delegation to the PRC, in a joint statement with the China-
Japan Friendship Association, announced five principles as conditions
for the normalization of Sino-Japanese relations. The gist of these
principles, which had Premier Chou En-lai's prior approval, reads
as follows:
    1. There is only one China, and the government of the PRC is
the sole legitimate government representing the Chinese people.
    2. Taiwan is a province of China and an inalienable part of
Chinese territory.
    3. The "Japan-Chiang [peace] Treaty" is illegal and must be
abrogated.
    4. The United States must withdraw all its armed forces from
Taiwan and the Taiwan Straits area.
    5. The PRC's legitimate rights in all United Nations organiza-
tions must be restored and the representatives of Taiwan expelled.[10]
    The Chinese side endorsed these principles and held that "In
the event of the Japanese government's accepting the above-mentioned
principles and taking practical steps to this end, the state of war between China and Japan can be ended, diplomatic relations restored
and a peace treaty concluded; and then depending on developments,
a mutual non-aggression treaty between China and Japan can be concluded. . . ."[11]
    The five principles were nothing new, nor was the Chinese offer
to conclude a mutual nonaggression pact at a future time. Both dated
back to 1953.[12] What was new was the fact that the PRC chose to repeat
its demand through the Komeito delegation on the eve of Dr. Kissinger's
visit. Several reasons may be discerned. First, the announcement of
the five principles could have served as a reminder to the American

emissary that the PRC's problem with Japan was part of its larger problem with the United States. Second, Peking's willingness to receive for the first time an official delegation of the Komeito, which is basically an anti-Communist party, meant that the Chinese leadership wanted to settle the issues with Japan regardless of ideological and political differences—an overture that is consistent with the PRC's effort to reach a détente with the United States. Third, acceptance of the principles by the Komeito, which was the second largest opposition party in Japan at the time, could have helped build up popular support for the PRC's cause in Japan and thereby exerted additional pressure on the Sato administration. Last, but not least, announcement of the principles through a third party at this turning point of Chinese diplomatic history suggested that there was room for negotiations.

In fact, the fourth principle, concerning the withdrawal of United States armed forces from the Taiwan area is beyond Japan's sovereign power. Perhaps for this reason, in a subsequent joint statement with the Dietmen's League for Promoting the Restoration of Japan-China Diplomatic Relations on October 2, 1971, the PRC dropped that principle.[13] After the PRC's entry into the United Nations, the fifth principle was also removed. Consequently, only the first three principles were at issue.[14]

Dissenting members of the ruling LDP and all opposition parties, including the JCP left wing, accepted these three principles without reservation, as clearly indicated in their joint statements with the PRC. The "mainstream" faction of the LDP was hesitant, however. The central issue involved here was the question of Japan's peace treaty with Taiwan.

Barring all moral implications—which, in the final analysis, are of secondary importance in international power politics—abrogation of the treaty not only meant acceptance of the first two principles but also could create certain immediate consequences for Japan. Militarily, it could endanger the existing American security structure in the Far East, which is essentially based on the 1960 U.S.-Japan security treaty and supplemented by the 1969 Sato-Nixon communiqué, which specified that "the maintenance of peace and security in the Taiwan area was also a most important factor for the security of Japan."[15] Diplomatically, it could deprive the Japanese residents and corporations in Taiwan of proper legal protection. Economically, it might result in the disruption of a highly profitable trade with Taiwan, which in 1971 amounted to $1,034 million in both ways, with a Japanese export surplus of $500 million.[16] Beyond that, Japan had a net investment of $68 million, or 19 percent of the total foreign investment, in Taiwan, with 352 firms in operation, plus 316 technical cooperation projects with numerous local enterprises.[17] A diplomatic crisis could conceivably jeopardize these assets and the 3,000 Japanese residents on that island.

In addition, if Japan were to admit the illegality of the peace treaty with Taiwan, as Peking had always insisted, then Japan would have to conclude a new peace treaty with the PRC in order to end the state of war and normalize relations. This, in turn, would raise the question of war indemnities, which were estimated at over $50,000 million by the president of the Supreme People's Court in 1951.[18] After a visit to Peking in October 1971, former Foreign Minister Aiichiro Fujiyama reported that the PRC appeared to have no intention of demanding such indemnities from Japan.[19] But the Japanese government was not officially informed of this.

The complexity of the matter was further compounded by the fact that Sato was uncertain about the real objectives of American policy toward China. For 20 years since the conclusion of the San Francisco Peace Treaty, Japan shaped its China policy within the general framework of the U.S. Far East policy.[20] The triangular struggle among Peking, Taipei, and Tokyo was in essence a product of the Cold War confrontation between Peking and Washington. Before the United States made its policy intentions clear, Sato could not change his "two China" stance without risking a diplomatic coup.

Thus, in spite of overwhelming domestic pressure for a drastic reorientation of Japan's China policy and the rapidly deteriorating relationship with the United States after the second "Nixon shock" in August, which involved a host of economic issues, Sato supported the two American resolutions, one for the entry of the PRC into the United Nations and the other designed to preserve membership for Taiwan. His stance was no longer "two China" but "one China and two governments."[21] Yet it was at the very moment that the China issue was being debated in the General Assembly that Dr. Kissinger left for a second visit to Peking.[22] The implication was clear that the American performance in the United Nations was simply a diplomatic exercise.

Earlier, in response to the first two Nixon shocks, Sato had twice expressed his wish to visit the PRC and on one occasion personally asked a PRC official, Wang Kuo-ch'uan, to convey "my best regards to Premier Chou En-lai."[23] Premier Chou ignored Sato's overture, saying that he would welcome a new Prime Minister of Japan who had due respect for "Chinese principles."[24] Then on the eve of Kissinger's arrival in Peking (October 19, 1971), Sato delivered a policy speech in which he for the first time accepted the PRC as the legitimate representative of China and expressed the hope that the fate of Taiwan would be settled "through negotiations between the parties concerned."[25]

The defeat of the American resolutions in the United Nations convinced Sato that this would inevitably lead to Japan's formal recognition of the PRC.[26] Accordingly, he sent another message to Premier Chou, this time in the name of LDP Secretary-General Shigeru Hori in order to avoid another personal embarrassment.[27] Chou's reply

was that Hori had failed to specify that Peking was the "sole" government of China and that Japan would abrogate the peace treaty with
Taiwan. "Even if Sato accepted the three basic principles as the basis
of opening talks with us," Chou was quoted as saying, "we shall not
accept Sato as a negotiating partner. However, any successor of Sato
will be welcome in Peking as long as he accepts the three basic principles."[28] In reply, Sato dropped a hint that Japan would abrogate the
treaty in the process of normalizing relations with the PRC.[29] On the
related question of indemnities, Foreign Minister Takeo Fukuda announced that his government was ready to apologize for Japan's war
crimes in China as a precondition for establishing diplomatic relations.[30]

In the wake of these developments, Sato met with President Nixon
at San Clemente to find, among other things, American intentions in
the forthcoming Peking summit. The result was disappointing. The
Sato-Nixon communiqué of January 7, 1972, revealed no agreement on
the China question.[31] In a statement to reporters, Sato bitterly com-
plained: "President Nixon will go to Peking. But what on earth he is
going to talk about is [the] one thing we are interested in."[32] Recalling
the first two "Nixon shocks," he frankly admitted: "I had not been
able to fully trust the United States since the sudden announcement
of the President's plan to visit China and its dollar defense measures
that included the ten percent import surcharge in spite of its promises
to keep commitments with its old friends."[33] For this reason he requested the installation of a "hot line" between Tokyo and Washington
"so that Japan will not be unprepared to receive shocks."[34] Ambassador Nobuhiko Ushiba expressed his apprehension when he warned
that the Nixon trip might be "the beginning of a process of unraveling
our mutual security in the Far East."[35]

Finally, the Shanghai communiqué produced two results that
were to have a great impact on Japan's decision to normalize relations
with the PRC. One was the U.S. declaration that it had no intention
to challenge the Chinese position on either side of the Taiwan Straits
that "there is but one China and that Taiwan is a part of China." The
other affirmed the "ultimate objective" of the United States to withdraw
all its forces and military installations from Taiwan.[36] Together
these statements removed whatever doubt the Japanese government
might still have about Nixon's determination to reach a rapprochement
with the PRC while leaving the Taiwan question to be solved by the
Chinese themselves.

Had Sato not planned to retire, he probably would have taken the
same move as his successor was to take. However, the San Clemente
communiqué had set the date for the reversion of Okinawa as May 15,
1972, thus making his exit imminent. In his tearful farewell speech,
he left his successor with two instructions on the delicate United

States-China-Japan relations. First, he said, as the world was becoming multipolarized, peace in Asia could be protected through friendly relations between Japan and the United States. Second:

> Like the grass and trees bending before the wind, everybody is leaning towards the Chinese mainland. However, I cannot be in such a frame of mind. The Japan-China [Taiwan] treaty which was signed after the San Francisco peace treaty, that is, the friendly relations with the Nationalist government, has been kept up to the present. I have thought that diplomatic relations with China have to be restored and normalized in any case. However, in what form the existing friendly and goodwill relations with the Nationalist government will be maintained is another question. This, I think, should be borne in mind.[37]

THE CHOU-TANAKA INITIATIVE

When Kakuei Tanaka took over the helm of the Japanese government on July 6, 1972, Japan's recognition of the PRC was already a foregone conclusion, legitimatized as it was by Sato's acceptance of a "one China" policy.[38] The question now was how to translate this policy into concrete action. The Japanese Ministry of Foreign Affairs, on which Prime Minister Tanaka depended heavily for expert advice, maintained the following views:

1. The state of war between Japan and China ended with the signing of the Japan-Republic of China peace treaty. Hence it is unnecessary for Japan to sign a new treaty with the government in Peking. Rather, the Peking government should take over the present treaty.

2. Japan, which has abandoned Taiwan, is not in a position to say anything about the final territorial status of Taiwan, but the Chinese assertion that Taiwan is a part of Chinese territory is "understandable."

3. The government of the PRC is the "legitimate government" of China, but the Ministry would not say that it is the "only" legitimate government.[39]

In line with this position, Tanaka set out to tackle the problem simultaneously in four directions for the purpose of (1) establishing a line of communications with Premier Chou En-lai so that a summit meeting could be arranged to discuss the issues; (2) achieving within his own party a consensus, which was needed in Japanese politics; (3) consulting with President Nixon for his understanding of the Japanese position; and (4) assuring the Taipei government of Japan's continued goodwill and cooperation.

To accomplish the first task, Tanaka sent a message to his Chinese counterpart through Socialist leader and Dietman Kozo Sasaki in mid-July, expressing his desire for a summit meeting.[40] Premier Chou promptly extended his welcome to both Tanaka and his Foreign Minister, Masayoshi Ohira, without mentioning acceptance of the three principles as a prerequisite for the visit.[41]

On the Chinese side, a fortnight before the LDP's presidential election, the PRC sent a ranking official, Hsiao Hsiang-ch'ien, to head the Tokyo liaison office of the China-Japan Memorandum Trade Office for the first time since the Cultural Revolution.[42] This was directly followed by a statement by Premier Chou welcoming Tanaka's China policy.[43] Another immediate consequence was the dispatch to Japan of the Shanghai Dance-Drama Troupe, headed by another ranking official and the former chief of the Tokyo liaison office, Sun P'ing-hua, for a month-long visit.[44] Both Hsiao and Sun actually served as the PRC's semiofficial envoys in Tokyo. Tanaka's formal request for a visit to the PRC was presented to them by Ohira on August 11 and the Chinese Ministry of Foreign Affairs officially announced Chou's invitation the next day.[45] However, no specific date was announced for the visit until about September 20, when Tanaka's two envoys to Peking and Taipei, former Foreign Ministers Zentaro Kosaka and Etsusaburo Shiina, respectively, had informed him of the completion of their missions. Then the date was set for September 25.[46]

This hastily organized summit meeting was made possible by a number of conciliatory overtures from both Peking and Tokyo. First, in an interview with Nationalist Ambassador P'eng Meng-ch'i on July 12, Foreign Minister Ohira revealed that when Japan established diplomatic relations with the PRC, the peace treaty with Taiwan would automatically lose its effect.[47] Second, the Japanese government quietly abolished the controversial eight-year-old "Yoshida Letter" by approving use of state funds to finance the export of a second vinylon plant to the PRC since 1964.[48] Third, the Bank of Tokyo reached an agreement with the Bank of China on the settlement of accounts in both Japanese yen and Chinese yuan—an important issue in Sino-Japanese trade pending since early 1960s.[49] Fourth, the Japanese Ministry of Justice lifted the ban on the reentry into Japan of those Chinese residents who had visited the mainland.[50] Finally, Tanaka and his cabinet members made a series of statements and gestures indicating their sincerity in seeking an accommodation with Peking. These include an unsual audience with Sun P'ing-hua and Hsiao Hsiang-ch'ien by Tanaka at the Imperial Hotel in Tokyo.[51]

On the Chinese side, Premier Chou made an important concession to Tanaka through the Komeito that was to form the general framework of peace talks between the two leaders. First, Chou said, the PRC would waive reparations claims against Japan, which, as

167

indicated earlier, amounted to over $50,000 million. Second, Japan's security treaty with the United States and the Sato-Nixon communiqué of November 21, 1969, would not hinder the establishment of diplomatic relations between Peking and Tokyo. Third, the PRC would propose to conclude a treaty of peace and friendship with Japan to invalidate Japan's peace treaty with Taiwan.[52]

On the economic plane Yoshihiro Inayama, president of the Nippon Steel Corporation, reached an understanding with the Chinese that the PRC would give favorable consideration to acceptance of export credit facilities if terms were on an internationally acceptable level; the PRC would welcome Japanese participation in oil exploration in China, presumably including development of the strategically important Pohai Bay, and would export crude oil to Japan; the PRC would send specialist missions to Japan for talks on trade questions relating to steel, heavy electrical goods, oil, and agricultural products.[53]

Tanaka's second task was to achieve a consensus within his own party, which had been deeply divided over the peace treaty issue between the pro-Taiwan and pro-Peking factions.[54] To this end he established a 312-member Council for the Normalization of Japan-China Relations within the ruling LDP, under the chairmanship of Zentaro Kosaka, on July 24. After hearing countless proposals and counterproposals by the various factions, in late August the Council reached a preliminary five-point decision by which the Tanaka Cabinet should abide in establishing diplomatic relations with the PRC.[55] The pro-Taiwan faction, however, refused to accept the "proviso" attached to the decision, which reads as follows:

> There was strong opinion that in view of the deep relations between Japan and Taiwan, sufficient consideration should be given to maintaining these relations.

In the opinion of the pro-Taiwan Dietmen, a more direct expression should be used in reference to Taiwan.[56] After further debate, the proviso was modified. It states:

> In view of the close relationship between Japan and the Republic of China, negotiations should be conducted giving sufficient consideration to the continuation of that relationship.

The five points, which were also slightly rephrased, called for:

1. Normalization of relations on the basis of the United Nations Charter and the ten Bandung principles of peaceful coexistence adopted by the Afro-Asian conference in 1955 at Bandung, Indonesia.

2. Mutual respect for different political, social, and other systems and noninterference in the internal affairs of the other nations. Relations with other friendly nations also should be respected.

3. Mutual nonuse of force or threat of force.

4. Expansion of economic and cultural exchanges. Neither side should take discriminatory action.

5. Cooperation in the promotion of peace and prosperity in Asia.

The LDP's Executive Council formally adopted the decision on September 8, thus giving Tanaka a mandate to proceed with his plan.[57]

Following a technical advance team and armed with the LDP's five-point decision, Zentaro Kosaka led an official 23-man delegation of the LDP—the first in 22 years—to Peking on September 14. There he explained to the Chinese Tanaka's basic position and the existence of strong opposition in the LDP over the Taiwan Issue.[58] Premier Chou entertained the Japanese mission with a banquet on the 41st anniversary of the Mukden (Shenyang) Incident on September 18—a reminder of the past Japanese militarism—but assured Kosaka of Chinese goodwill to the Japanese people. Kosaka in return apologized for Japan's past war crimes in China. The Chou-Tanaka summit meeting thus became certain.[59]

Tanaka's third task was to meet with President Nixon. Early in August 1971, when the United States had decided to sponsor the "dual representation" formula on the China question in the United Nations, Tanaka commented: "This is good news. Now everything is easier for Japan"[60]—a reference to the U.S. acceptance of the PRC as the legitimate representative of China in the world organization. After assuming power in July 1972, Tanaka's Foreign Minister, Ohira, outlined Japan's China policy in relation to the United States in one sentence: Japan would proceed with normalization of Sino-Japanese relations "at its own discretion" while keeping the United States appropriately informed.[61] In August, Ohira explained to Dr. Kissinger that the improvement of Japan's relations with the PRC would not impair its security treaty with the United States.[62]

At the Honolulu conference Tanaka and President Nixon both "recognized that the President's recent visit to the PRC and the USSR were a significant step forward. In this context they shared the hope that the forthcoming visit of the Prime Minister to the PRC would also serve further the trend for the relaxation of tension in Asia."[63] Although what agreement the two leaders had reached is not known, Dr. Kissinger endorsed Ohira's earlier statement by saying that the Tanaka visit to Peking would not damage the security treaty with the United States even if Japan broke diplomatic ties with Taiwan.[64]

Thus assured, Tanaka's last effort was to seek an understanding from Taiwan. Etsusaburo Shiina, Vice-President of the LDP, accepted this thankless task. Prior to his departure for Taipei, tension was already mounting in the Nationalist capital. Authorities threatened to use every means available to prevent Japan from achieving a rapprochement with the PRC. In the economic area, the Nationalist government adopted, or proposed to adopt, a series of retaliatory and self-defense measures. First, Japanese government offers to help build the Taiwan economy were rejected, including a $40 million nuclear power plant and a $17 million expressway.[65] Second, a ceiling was imposed on imports from Japan: anything that exceeded $20,000 in value must be henceforth imported from America or Europe instead of Japan.[66] Third, as a matter of policy, development of the steel, machinery, petroleum, and chemical industries, which had relied heavily on their Japanese counterparts, was to be emphasized; accessories and spare parts were to be made locally to the extent possible; government assistance was to be extended to small and medium-sized enterprises that had cooperated with the Japanese to solve their capital and technological problems; and entrepreneurs were to be encouraged to establish direct marketing contacts overseas instead of contracting with the Japanese businessmen as their intermediaries.[67]

In the military field, legislators urged the government to extend the limits of territorial waters around Taiwan, obviously in an attempt to pose a threat to the safety of Japan's sea-lanes to Southeast Asia.[68] At the same time, over 400 high-level commanding officers of the armed forces held a three-day meeting in early September to "actively strengthen war preparations."[69]

It was under these circumstances that Shiina and 16 Dietmen arrived in Taipei on September 17 with a personal letter from Tanaka to President Chiang Kai-shek. The mission was greeted by Chinese protocol officers and a group of several hundred carefully organized demonstrators, including some pro-Taiwan Japanese residents.[70]

During his two-day stay in Taipei, the Japanese envoy explained to many civic and government leaders that after breaking diplomatic relations with the Nationalist government, Japan would like to continue existing cultural and economic ties with Taiwan. He did not get to see the ailing President but had a serious interview with Premier Chiang Ching-kuo. According to the latter, Shiina asked: what would the Republic of China ask of Japan? and what would the Premier expect of the Japanese government? To the first question Chiang replied that his government did not have any other demand than that the Japanese government stop "betraying its friends." To the second the Premier said that he had no other hope than that Japan would save itself from being "communized."[71] Then Chiang warned Shiina that since all relations between Japan and Taiwan were based on the 1952 peace treaty, the Japanese government would be held fully responsible for any consequence arising from its abrogation of the treaty; the Nationalist government reserved all rights to take any necessary action;

and Japan's rapprochement with the PRC would be tanamount to "making yourselves our enemy again."[72]

The Shiina mission was not a success, but it did complete the last preparation for Tanaka's historical journey to Peking.

THE BEGINNING OF NORMALIZATION

The Tanaka mission to the PRC (September 25-30, 1972) produced a nine-article joint statement that represented an ambiguous compromise of the principles previously enunciated by both sides.[73] Four points are to be discussed: the peace treaty, the status of Taiwan, the question of "hegemony," and Japan's "reversed" relations with the PRC and Taiwan.

On the first point, as mentioned earlier, Premier Chou proposed to conclude a "treaty of peace and friendship" to invalidate Japan's peace treaty with Taiwan. However, he did not say whether the conclusion of such a treaty was a precondition for the ending of the state of war that, by any standard of international law, is a prerequisite for the establishment of diplomatic relations.

The Japanese, on the other hand, maintained that the state of war had ended with the signing of the peace treaty with Taiwan and consequently, instead of signing a new peace treaty with Japan, the PRC should take over the existing treaty. This argument not only contradicted the PRC's basic principle but also contained a major legal defect: the treaty with Taiwan applied to the territories under Nationalist control only.[74]

As a result, no explicit agreement was reached in the joint statement. A section of the preamble states: "The two peoples ardently wish to end the abnormal state of affairs that has hitherto existed between our two countries. The termination of the state of war, the normalization of relations between China and Japan, and the realization of such wishes of the two peoples will open a new page in the annals of relations between the two counties." (Emphasis added. These two sentences are translated from the Chinese text.) Article 1 of the joint statement, however, specifically provides:

> The abnormal state of affairs which has hitherto existed between the People's Republic of China and Japan is declared terminated on the date of publication of this statement.

"The abnormal state of affairs" is certainly not identical with "the state of war." Nevertheless, Foreign Minister Ohira declared that "the concrete expression" of Article 1 "is the establishment of diplomatic relations between the two countries (Article 4), and as a result Japan's peace treaty with Taiwan was "terminated."[75]

Some observers raised the question as to whether a peace treaty duly approved by the Diet could be legally terminated by the Foreign

171

Minister in a simple press statement. Kenzo Yoshida, Director-General of the Asian Affairs Bureau of the Ministry of Foreign Affairs and a member of the Japanese negotiating team, offered an explanation. In his opinion, both Chou and Tanaka were not concerned about the legal aspect of the problem but about the future relations of their two countries. Consequently, the joint statement has been issued with a "forward-looking attitude" in order to achieve a normal state of affairs and friendly relations between Japan and China.[76]

The Chinese have given no indication about the meaning of Article 1 quoted above. On the surface it seems that they have accepted Ohira's intepretation and do not anticipate "any difficulties in concluding a treaty of peace and friendship with Japan," as provided for in Article 8 of the joint statement.[77] This posture is somewhat analogous to the state of relations between the Soviet Union and Japan, where the state of war was ended by a joint declaration in 1956 but the conclusion of a peace treaty is pending on the settlement of other issues.[78]

Concerning the status of Taiwan, Japan recognized the government of the PRC as "the sole legal government of China" (Article 2)—ostensibly a concession to the Chinese. Article 3 of the joint statement provides:

> The Government of the People's Republic of China re-affirms that Taiwan is an inalienable part of the territory of the People's Republic of China. The Government of Japan fully understands and respects this stand of the Government of China and adheres to its stand of complying with Article 8 of the Potsdam Proclamation.

Since Japan's "understanding and respect" for the PRC's stand is not tanamount to accepting the PRC's claim, there remains the question as to whether the status of Taiwan is actually determined in their bilateral relations.[79] Moreover, the Japanese had not anticipated the inclusion of Article 8 of the Potsdam Proclamation in the joint statement. They agreed to it perhaps upon Chinese insistence. Its implication is that Japan has thus agreed to the restoration of Taiwan to China in accordance with the 1943 Cairo Declaration, on which the said article is based.[80] Kenzo Yoshida stated:

> When it comes to the legal interpretation, Japan is basi-cally in no position to judge the territorial title to Taiwan because it has given up Taiwan under the San Francisco Peace Treaty. Legally it will be strange for us to meddle in something which has ceased to be our belonging. Inas-much as Japan accepted reversion of Taiwan to China politically, it has maintained this position. We do not

judge at this juncture that Taiwan [legally] belongs to
China. Neither are we in a position to say such a thing.[81]

The difficulty of Yoshida's interpretation lies in the fact that
neither the PRC nor the Republic of China before it is a signatory of
the San Francisco peace treaty, by which Japan formally renounced
its claim to Taiwan and other related territories.[82] Moreover, the
PRC has denounced both the San Francisco treaty and Japan's peace
treaty with Taiwan as being "illegal and void."[83] Consequently, it
cannot rely on either treaty to justify its claim. Unless a new treaty
with Japan is concluded, the status of Taiwan will remain a legal
tangle.

On the third point both sides agreed to establish a durable relationship of peace and friendship on the basis of the Five Principles
of Peaceful Coexistence and the principles of the United Nations Charter
(Article 6). In addition, both sides pledged that the normalization of
relations between the two countries "is not directed against third
countries. Neither of the two countries should seek hegemony in the
Asia-Pacific region and each country is opposed to efforts by any other
country or group of countries to establish such hegemony" (Article 7).

But just as the Sino-American détente was achieved in part to
frustrate Soviet ambition in Asia, so the rapprochement between the
PRC and Japan inevitably has implications in their mutual relations
with the Soviet Union and the United States. The first serious issue
that has come to the fore since the signing of the joint statement is
Japan's interest in cooperating with the Soviet Union to develop Siberia.
The Chinese have made it clear that the proposed joint Japanese-Soviet
project to build a crude oil pipeline and a parallel highway from
Nakhodka to Irkutsk, linking the already built pipelines from the latter
point to Tyumen, will be an "unfriendly act" toward the PRC and a
threat to its national security because both the oil and the highway
can be used to support the giant Soviet military complex along the
Chinese border.[84]

To cope with this situation, the PRC took a number of moves in
an attempt to stop the Japanese-Soviet project. These include an
agreement with Japan to supply 1 million tons of Chinese crude oil
per year; an offer to Japan to set up a joint project for the development of Chinese oil resources; support for Japan to negotiate with the
Soviet Union for restoration of the Soviet-controlled northern territories
(Habomai, Shikotan, Kunashiri, and Etorofu); and a popular appeal to
the Japanese that both the pipeline and the highway, once completed,
can also be used against Japanese interests.[85]

Tanaka, however, was determined to cooperate with the Soviet
Union. In a letter to Soviet Communist Party leader Leonid I. Brezhnev
in March 1973, he formally offered to help develop Siberian resources

and requested a second round of negotiations for the conclusion of a peace treaty without mentioning reversion of the northern islands as a precondition.[86] This led to the Tanaka-Brezhnev summit meeting in October. Prior to that, Tanaka sought U.S. participation in the Siberian development projects in order to minimize Chinese reaction, and the Tanaka-Nixon joint communiqué of August 1, 1973, seems to have assured Japan of U.S. cooperation in "exploring and exploiting energy resources" in the Soviet Union.

According to preliminary discussions, Japan will provide the Soviet Union with a $1,000 million loan, mostly from the Export and Import Bank of Japan, for the development of the Tyumen oil fields and the construction of the pipeline and highway mentioned above, in return for an annual supply of 40 million tons of crude oil over a period of 20 years. In addition, development of natural gas in Yakut and of petroleum-natural gas in Sakhalin may require another $3,000 million loan from Japan.[87] The concrete role of the United States in these joint endeavors remains uncertain because of the unpredictability of Soviet promises. In fact, the Soviet Union has so far refused to release any technical information to Japan for the development of the Tyumen oil fields.

As to the peace treaty, Moscow reportedly preferred an agreement patterned on the 1971 Indo-Soviet friendship treaty, which does not rule out a military commitment, whereas Japan hopes to regain the northern islands as a quid pro quo for its economic cooperation and the conclusion of a peace treaty.[88] Thus, the Tanaka-Brezhnev communiqué of October 10, 1973, revealed no agreement on either the treaty or the territorial issue, except that both parties agreed to resume talks in 1974. They also agreed to expedite the development of Siberian resources, which "does not exclude participation by a third country."

The Chinese supported Japan's stand on the territorial issue but cautioned Tokyo to exercise the "utmost vigilance" to minimize the military significance of those economic development projects. Otherwise, the PRC would take "appropriate measures."[89]

Chinese opposition to Japanese-Soviet cooperation does not, however, extend to Japan's military buildup and its continued alliance with the United States, at least for the time being. Premier Chou was reported to have "understood" Tanaka's criterion for the fourth five-year defense program (1972-76), which calls for a total expenditure of $15,400 million and was put into effect immediately after the Chou-Tanaka summit meeting.[90]

The PRC's acquiescence in the Japanese military buildup is probably based on Premier Chou's understanding with Tanaka and Nixon about the new role of the United States-Japan security treaty: to contain Soviet expansion in East Asia and to prevent Taiwan from falling into the Soviet orbit.[91] This leads us to the fourth point, Japan's "reversed" relations with the PRC and Taiwan.

The unilateral termination of Japan's peace treaty with Taiwan resulted in the severance of diplomatic relations. However, it did not disrupt their cultural and economic ties. In fact, the two-way trade between Japan and Taiwan in 1972 reached a new record high of $1,511 million, nearly 50 percent more than the previous year, despite the diplomatic turmoil and the avowed policy of the Taipei authorities to restrict commercial dealings with the Japanese. Taiwan's imports ($1,091 million) exceeded exports ($420 million) by $671 million.[92]

With Taiwan becoming the third largest purchaser of Japanese products after the United States ($8,856 million) and Canada ($1,105 million), realism prevailed and the need to find a substitute for diplomatic and consular missions increased proportionately. The formula that was readily available to Japan and Taiwan was the "reverse separation of politics from economics."* Translated into practice, this means the replacement of the Nationalist embassy in Tokyo by an Association of East Asia Relations (AEAR) and that of the Japanese embassy in Taipei by a Japan Interchange Association (JIA).

The AEAR, which was founded on December 2, 1972, after agreement with the Japanese Ministry of Foreign Affairs, took on the form of a juristic person.[93] It consists of a nine-member board of directors with Chang Yen-t'ien as its chairman and a three-member board of supervisors with Ku Chen-fu as its chairman. Chang is a former Vice-Minister of Economic Affairs and presently board chairman of the government-owned Taiwan Sugar Company; Ku, board chairman of the National Association for the Promotion of Industry and Commerce.[94] Under the AEAR there are three branches. The main branch is in Tokyo, headed by Ma Shu-li, who was a ranking official of the Kuomintang in charge of overseas Chinese affairs. The other two branches are in Osaka and Fukuoka.[95]

The JIA, which was founded on December 1, 1972, with the Nationalist government's agreement, does not have a country or area designation because the word "Republic of China" is offending to the PRC and the word "Taiwan" unacceptable to the Nationalists. It is an incorporated organization with a capital of 20 million yen raised by the JIA itself and an operating budget of 650 million yen for 1973-74 provided by the Japanese state treasury.[96] Teizo Horikoshi, vice-president of the powerful Federation of Economic Organizations, serves as the JIA's president; Osamu Itagaki, former ambassador to Taipei (1969-71), as its board chairman; Hironori Ito, minister of the Japanese

---

*Prior to the rapprochement Japan traded with the PRC theoretically under the principle of "separating politics from economics."

175

embassy in Taipei until September 1972, as director of its main branch in Taipei; and a former consul general in Kaohsiung remains as head of the JIA's Kaohsiung branch.97

The overseas branches of both associations are staffed by diplomats and government functionaries "temporarily on leave." The size of each association's overseas staff is for the time being limited to 30, not including native employees. The functions of these branches are to protect the life, property, and rights of individual citizens and juristic persons in the other country; to conduct activities relating to the education of citizens' children in the other country; to facilitate application for entry or reentry visas and resident certificates; to assist the investigation and mediation of cases involving citizens of the other country; to coordinate with the local authorities concerned for the development of trade; to survey the economy, trade, and tourism of the other country in order to achieve a balanced development of trade; to conclude private agreements on trade, investment, and technical cooperation; to inquire into the payment and repayment of loans made before the severance of diplomatic relations; to handle matters relating to technical cooperation, including approved international projects; to facilitate fishing near the other country's waters and the entry of vessels and aircraft (including their crew members) into the other country's ports; the maintenance of communications and air and surface transport for both cargo and passengers; the interchange of academic, cultural, and athletic activities; and the conduct of other affairs necessary for the achievement of each association's objectives.98

Clearly, then, each association enjoys the status of a quasi legation and performs regular consular functions and some untold diplomatic activities. In addition, a Dietmen's Consultation Committee on Japan-China [Taiwan] Relations consisting of 99 LDP members of the House of Representatives and 53 LDP members of the House of Councillors was established on March 14, 1973, among other pro-Taiwan organizations, to promote ties with Taiwan.99 Just as the AEAR is the Taiwan counterpart of the PRC's Memorandum Trade Liaison Office in Tokyo before the Sino-Japanese rapprochement, so the LDP Dietmen's Committee is a counterpart of the former pro-Peking Dietmen's League for Promoting the Restoration of Japan-China Diplomatic Relations.

Japan's continued close relationship with Taiwan inevitably impeded the progress of its normalization process with the PRC. Except for the exchange of ambassadors (Ch'en Ch'u for the PRC and Heishiro Ogawa for Japan) and the visit to Japan by a number of Chinese cultural and economic delegations in 1973, as well as the conclusion of an undersea cable accord, development in other areas of Sino-Japanese relations has been rather slower than might have been expected.

Article 9 of the joint statement provided for the conclusion of agreements on trade, navigation, aviation, and fishery. But negotiations for an aviation agreement in early 1973 bogged down because of the Taiwan problem. The PRC contended that since the termination of Japan's peace treaty with Taiwan in September 1972, all intergovernment relations between Japan and Taiwan have ceased to exist, including the air services agreement. Moreover, in the PRC's opinion, it would be "absurd" for a Chinese flag-carrier to use, side by side with another Chinese flag-carrier, the same airport (Haneda) in Tokyo. Such a state of affairs, the PRC maintained, would create the impression of having "two Chinas." Consequently, it insisted that the Japanese government cancel the Japan-Taiwan air route operated by Japan Airlines (JAL) and China Airlines (CAL) or at least reroute CAL's flights to some other Japanese airports, such as Okinawa and Nagoya.[100]

CAL has 21 weekly two-way flights from Taipei to Tokyo and Osaka, and JAL has 37 weekly two-way flights from Tokyo, Nagoya, Osaka, and Fukuoka to Taipei, plus 20 weekly two-way flights to Southeast Asia via Taipei. For CAL this route is a vital link in its regular flights to South Korea and the United States; for JAL it is the second most lucrative route after Honolulu. In 1972 alone more than 580,000 persons used the Japan-Taiwan route, and in the six months from November 1972 to April 1973, 356,397 persons traveled between Japan and Taiwan by the two airlines. Japanese passengers averaged 1,000 a month.

These statistics are highly impressive and the profits involved are certainly substantial. Moreover, from the Japanese point of view, acceptance of the PRC's conditions would create a precedent that might affect future agreements, such as on shipping, and might eventually disrupt the Taiwan trade. In addition, the pro-Taiwan LDP Dietmen led by former Foreign Minister Takeo Fukuda are more influential than the Tanaka faction. They countered the PRC argument by saying that while representatives of the PRC and Taiwan "coexist" in Washington, it is "absurd" that their airplanes cannot sit side by side at Haneda.[101]

At the end of September 1973, a 71-member Japanese Dietmen's delegation led by former Minister of Education Hirokichi Nadao visited Taipei for four days to strengthen Japan's political, economic, and cultural ties with the Nationalist government.[102] The question of Japan's air services with both the Chinese mainland and Taiwan was undoubtedly one of the important items discussed with the Nationalist leaders. No accord, however, seems to have been reached.[103] In Tokyo and Peking, both Prime Minister Tanaka and Vice Premier Teng Hsiao-p'ing expressed the hope that the proposed Sino-Japanese aviation agreement would be concluded at an early date, making it the first major bilateral agreement between the two countries.[104] Since the agreement is an important step in the normalization of Sino-Japanese relations, its realization seems to be only a matter of time.

Related to the question of air services is the prospect of bilateral economic relations. Prior to the rapprochement, Japanese businessmen held out high hopes for a vast increase in trade. After that they even anticipated certain types of Japanese "aid" to the PRC in reciprocation for its renunciation of reparations claims specified in Article 5 of the joint statement.

The fact of the matter is that the PRC operates its economy on a self-reliance basis. Accordingly, it rejects any type of foreign aid except short-term credits, such as the second vinylon plant deal mentioned earlier. In the field of trade, the PRC prefers to maintain an equilibrium to the extent possible. In 1972 its imports from Japan ($609 million) exceeded exports ($490 million) only by $119 million, as compared with Taiwan's $671 million.[105] The total volume of trade registered an increase of about 20 percent over 1971, as compared with Taiwan's 50 percent.

The year 1973, however, has witnessed a rather unusual increase in Sino-Japanese trade. The total value of two-way trade in the period January-August already exceeded the total of 1972, and both Chinese and Japanese trade officials openly predicted that by the end of 1973, the total volume of trade will reach the $2,000 million mark or double the volume for 1972.[106]

Although these figures do not reflect the real growth rate of Sino-Japanese trade in 1973, mainly because of worldwide inflation and the dollar devaluation, they do represent a very substantial increase over the past years. The removal of Japan's restrictions on government-guaranteed credits to China for the importation of complete Japanese plants may be one reason for this sudden trade boom. Another reason obviously is China's desire to accelerate her industrialization, as evidenced by the visit to Japan of a high-powered 33-member Chinese economic delegation headed by a top trade official, Liu Hsi-wen, in September-October 1973. Additional evidence is that preliminary rules for the conclusion of a governmental trade agreement were finally agreed upon after many years of difficult negotiations. By this accord, which was reached on August 30, 1973, each party will grant the other most-favored-nation treatment in tariffs and customs clearance.[107] Thus, although opportunities for large-scale economic cooperation between the two countries will be limited, bilateral trade may further increase after the conclusion of the official trade agreement.

CONCLUSION

Since 1954, when Ichiro Hatoyama became Prime Minister, the question of whether to recognize the PRC as the only legitimate government of China had been the single most explosive issue in Japanese foreign policy. Administrations after Hatoyama were unable to solve the problem partly because of their deference to Washington's China policy and partly because of Japan's self-interest in Taiwan for both economic and political reasons.

In the last two years of the Sato administration, the issue was further complicated by the multipolarization of the world, on the one hand, and by President Nixon's determination to reach a détente with the PRC, on the other. However, Prime Minister Sato was unable to cut the Gordian knot because of his pro-Taiwan stance and the PRC's distrust of his attitude toward a host of bilateral and multilateral issues accumulated during the eight years of his administration, including the "Yoshida Letter" and the 1969 Sato-Nixon communiqué.

Nonetheless, Sato accepted the PRC as the legitimate representative of China on the eve of Dr. Kissinger's second visit to Peking and expressed his willingness to "dispose of" the controversial peace treaty with Taiwan after the PRC's entry into the United Nations. His summit meeting with President Nixon was a disappointment on the China question, and the Shanghai communiqué convinced the Japanese of President Nixon's stand on the China question.

When Prime Minister Tanaka succeeded Sato, the ground was already paved for him to translate Sato's basic policy guidelines into action. In the process of doing this, he made a number of conciliatory gestures to Peking, including a decision to nullify the peace treaty with Taiwan after the establishment of diplomatic relations with the PRC, the abolition of the "Yoshida Letter," the conclusion of a yen-yuan agreement to settle payments, and the removal of travel restrictions on Chinese residents. In addition, he managed to secure an invitation from Premier Chou for a summit conference, a consensus within his own ruling LDP about his China policy, and an understanding with President Nixon. Beyond that he also made a "face-saving" gesture to Taiwan.

On the Chinese side, Premier Chou knew the advantage to be had in striking when the iron was hot. He took a series of initiatives to make the rapprochement possible. These included the dispatch to Japan of two semiofficial envoys at the time when President Nixon's planned visit to China was announced, the waiving of the PRC's reparations claims, and the withdrawal of its demand for the termination of Japan's security arrangements with the United States.

The Chou-Tanaka joint statement restored diplomatic relations between the two countries. However, in their bilateral relations the problem of Taiwan remains a controversial issue. On the basis of the San Francisco peace treaty, to which the PRC is not a party, Japan refused to make a firm commitment on the legal status of that island. Instead, it has replaced its embassy in Taipei with a quasi legation headed by a minister "temporarily on leave" from the Japanese Foreign Office and accepted Taiwan's government-supported organization, the AEAR, as the successor to the Nationalist embassy in Tokyo. An LDP Dietmen's Consultation Committee was formed to promote relations with Taiwan. As a result both trade and tourism between Japan and Taiwan reached a new record high in 1972 and continued to rise in 1973.

Because of Japan's unbroken marriage with Taiwan, the process of normalization of Sino-Japanese relations has been rather slow since the Chou-Tanaka summit. Negotiations for an aviation agreement bogged down in consequence of the PRC's insistence on canceling or rerouting CAL's present flights to Tokyo and Osaka. If Japan accepts Peking's demand in the second round of negotiations, which is scheduled to be held in the near future, it may eventually affect Japan's profitable trade with Taiwan. On the other hand, if Japan rejects the demand, negotiations with the PRC for other agreements important to the normalization of economic and cultural ties will be even more difficult. The Chinese refusal to initial the trade agreement at the end of August 1973 was in part due to the problems associated with the aviation agreement.

In multilateral relations Japan's decision to cooperate with the Soviet Union in the development of Siberia has already become a thorny issue. In this connection the PRC's intention to use Japan as a potential counterweight to the Soviet Union is evidenced by the appointment of a Soviet expert, Ch'en Ch'u, as its first ambassador to Tokyo, its silence on Japan's massive military buildup in conventional weapons, and its tacit approval of Japan's continued military alliance with the United States, which has direct bearing on the defense of Taiwan. However, when the Taiwan issue is solved and the Sino-Soviet tension diminishes, the PRC will eventually like to see a neutral Japan.

On the Japanese side the rapprochement with the PRC means the beginning of the era of "equal-distance diplomacy" not only in terms of its relationship with the Soviet Union and the PRC but also as a demonstration of its independence from Washington. A quotation from Prime Minister Tanaka's speech in October 1972 should suffice to illustrate the point:

> If we look upon the centennial history of Japan since the Meiji Restoration, it appears that there have been two trends of thought on diplomacy: one emphasizing the cooperation with the Western countries and the other attaching greater importance to our relations with the Continent of Asia. I intend to carry out our foreign policy correctly harmonizing these two trends of thought. The normalization of our relations with China has an aspect of

orienting Japan's foreign policy towards the Continent of Asia. This new relationship with China and the maintenance and development of the close ties Japan already has with her friends such as the United States can be and should be made compatible.[108].

Tanaka may have cut the Gordian knot by restoring diplomatic relations with the PRC in less than three months after becoming Prime Minister. But if he intends to use the PRC as a counterbalance to the United States and the Soviet Union, the matter is open to question.[109] It is true that the ground that formed the old partnership with the United States has changed and unless a new arrangement based on equality and mutual benefit is worked out, Japan is likely to drift away from the United States.[110] But Japan is not likely to do it before becoming a full-fledged nuclear power. For the immediate future Japan's "special relationship" with the United States will remain the basis of its foreign policy.[111] In its relationship with the Soviet Union and the PRC, it may be able to play an influential role so long as it remains under the American nuclear umbrella and so long as the Sino-Soviet conflict remains at the verbal level.

In sum, the rapprochement between Japan and the PRC was accelerated by President Nixon's new China policy. It marked the beginning of a long process of normalization. Their present ambivalent relationship is characterized by the coexistence of many conflicting interests, and such coexistence is made possible because of the coincidence of some of their basic national interests in the context of international politics in the Asia-Pacific region.

NOTES

1. Shigeru Yoshida, "Japan and the Crisis in Asia," Foreign Affairs 29, no. 2 (Jan. 1951): 171, 179.
2. For instance, Hisahari Yamada, "The Multipolarization of the Communist World and Japan," in Kajima Institute of International Peace, ed., Japan in Current World Affairs (Tokyo: Japan Times, Ltd., 1971), p. 63.
3. Saiji Hasegawa, "The World Will Revolve Around Peking," ibid., pp. 126, 128.
4. For an American view of the problem, see A. Doak Barnett, "The New Multipolar Balance in East Asia: Implications for United States Policy," Annals 390 (July 1970): 73.
5. Henry Shapiro, "Japan, Russia Ties Improve, Sato Says," St. Louis Post Dispatch, editorial sec., Oct. 2, 1970, pp. 1, 4.
6. See Takashi Oka, "Sato Is Seeking Talks with China," New York Times, Dec. 14, 1969, p. 8. Hereafter cited as NYT.

7. See "Government Policy Seen Badly Shaken by Nixon Move," Japan Times (Tokyo), July 17, 1971, p. 1. Hereafter cited as JT.

8. "No New Approach on China Problem Revealed in Speech," ibid., July 18, 1971, pp. 1, 4.

9. See, for example, "Opposition to Submit Bid on Peking Ties," ibid., p. 1; "China Policy Under Fire," ibid., July 21, 1971, p. 16.

10. The text of the joint statement, dated July 2, 1971, is in Peking Review no. 28 (July 9, 1971): 20-21. Hereafter cited as PR. Also see "Komeito Group Signs Peking Communiqué," JT, July 3, 1971, p. 1.

11. In PR no. 28 (July 9, 1971): 20.

12. See Premier Chou's talks with Professor Ikuo Oyama, Sept. 28, 1953, in Jih-pen wen-t'i wen-chien chi (Collection of documents on the question of Japan; Peking: Shih-chieh chih-shih ch'u-pan-she, 1955), 1: 116; Kuo Mo-jo's talks with Dietman Masanosuke Ikeda, Oct. 29, 1953, ibid., p. 119; Editorial, "On Sino-Japanese Relations," Jen-min jih-pao, Oct. 30, 1953, p. 1.

13. In PR no. 41 (Oct. 8, 1971): 14.

14. During the period from July 1971 to Sato's retirement a year later, the PRC issued five joint statements with the delegations of various Japanese organizations, specifying conditions for the normalization of Sino-Japanese relations. Two of them have been mentioned above. The third was with the Japan-China Friendship Association (Orthodox) on Oct. 16, 1971. In this statement the five principles were repeated. See PR no. 43 (Oct. 22 1971): 16. In the fourth and fifth statements the PRC and its Japanese counterparts upheld the first three principles and dropped the last two. See joint communiqué with the Japan-China Memorandum Trade Office, Dec. 21, 1971, PR no. 53 (Dec. 31, 1971): 4; joint statement with the Democratic Socialist Party of Japan, Apr. 13, 1972, ibid. no. 16 (Apr. 21, 1971): 17.

15. The text of the treaty is in Martin E. Weinstein, Japan's Postwar Defense Policy, 1947-1968 (New York: Columbia University Press, 1969), p. 139. For the text of the communiqué, dated Nov. 21, 1969, see NYT, Nov. 22, 1969, p. 14. For a discussion of the American security structure in the Far East, see Fred Greene, U.S. Policy and the Security of Asia (New York: McGraw-Hill, 1968).

16. See Foreign Trade Quarterly (Taipei) no. 33 (Mar. 1972): 58-59. In trade with the PRC in the same year, Japan registered an export surplus of only $255 million out of a total two-way trade of $900 million. See China Trade Report (Hong Kong) no. 3 (Mar. 1972): 15.

17. See Chung-yang jih-pao (Taipei), Sept. 5, 1972, p. 2; Sept. 19, 1972, p. 1. Hereafter cited as CYJP.

18. See Shen Chun-ju, "On the Prosecution and Punishment of War Criminals (6 September 1951)," in Jih-pen wen-t'i wen-chien chi, 1: 74.

19. See Far Eastern Economic Review (Hong Kong) no. 42 (Oct. 16, 1971): 4. Hereafter cited as FEER.

20. See Shigeru Yoshida, Japan's Decisive Century, 1867-1967 (New York: Praeger Publishers, 1967), p. 73.

21. See the text of Kiichi Aichi's UN speech on the China issue, dated Oct. 19, 1971, JT, Oct. 21, 1971, p. 16.

22. The trip was announced by the White House on Oct. 5, 1971, without a definite date. See NYT, Oct. 6, 1971, pp. 1, 4. Dr. Kissinger left the United States on Oct. 16 and arrived in Peking four days later.

23. "Government Said Trying to Contact Peking," JT, July 29, 1971, p. 1; "Premier Reiterates Peking Visit Desire," ibid., Aug. 18, 1971, p. 5; "At Matsumura's Funeral: Premier Meets Wang," ibid., Aug. 27, 1971, p. 1.

24. In Britannica Book of the Year 1972 (Chicago: Encyclopaedia Britannica, Inc., 1972), p. 397.

25. Richard Halloran, "Japanese to Seek Closer China Ties," NYT, Oct. 20, 1971, pp. 1, 14.

26. "Sato Says Japan-China Ties Would Follow on Albanian Resolution," JT, Oct. 26, 1971, p. 1.

27. Ibid., Nov. 16, 1971, p. 1.

28. Koji Nakamura, "Twice a Loser," FEER no. 47 (Nov. 20, 1971): 12.

29. See "'Bid' to Occupy Taiwan, Statements by Sato and Fukuda Hit by China," JT, Nov. 6, 1971, p. 1.

30. "Government Ready to Make War Crimes Apology," ibid., Dec. 17, 1971, pp. 1, 5.

31, For the text of the communiqué, see Japan Report no. 3 (Feb. 1, 1972): 1.

32. Richard Halloran, "US and Japan: Fears of a Great Unraveling," NYT, "Week in Review," Jan. 16, 1972, p. 4.

33. John M. Lee, "Nixon-Sato Talks Disappoint Japan," NYT, Jan. 16, 1972, p. 8.

34. "Concessions to Japan," St. Louis Post Dispatch, Jan. 8. 1972, p. 1.

35. Richard Halloran, "Japan's Envoy Warns US of Risks in Trip to Peking," NYT, Jan. 11, 1972, p. 1.

36. See joint communiqué, Feb. 28, 1972, PR no. 9 (Mar. 3, 1972): 4-5.

37. See JT, June 18, 1972, p. 1. The full text of the Sato speech is not available. The above quotation is in "Sato Steps Down," PR no. 26 (June 30, 1972): 19.

38. "Tanaka Conference Stresses China Ties," JT, July 6, 1972, p. 1.

39. Kazushige Hirasawa, "Takana-Fukuda 'Cold War,'" ibid., July 14, 1972, p. 1.

40. "Sasaki Arrives in Peking," ibid., July 16, 1972, p. 1; "Chou Offers Japan Talks in Peking," ibid., July 17, 1972, p. 1; "Kozo Sasaki in China," PR no. 30 (July 28, 1972): p. 3.

41. "JSP Ex-Head Has Two-Hour Talks with Chinese Premier," JT, July 18, 1972, p. 1; "Statement by Chou on Tanaka Visit Welcomed," ibid.

42. "Peking Appoints Trade Office Head," ibid., June 20, 1972, p. 11; "Chief of China Trade Office Arrives," ibid., July 4, 1972, p. 13.

43. "Chinese Premier Welcomes Tanaka Policy on China," ibid., July 10, 1972, p. 1; "Tanaka Forms New Cabinet," PR no. 28 (July 14, 1972): 22.

44. "Shanghai Dance-Drama Troupe in Japan," PR no. 29 (July 21, 1972): 21. The troupe arrived in Japan on July 10 and returned to China on August 16.

45. "Premier Chou Welcomes and Invites Prime Minister Tanaka to Visit China," ibid. no. 33 (Aug. 18, 1972): 3.

46. "Tanaka Reported Leaving September 25 on Peking Trip," JT, Sept. 20, 1972, p. 1.

47. "Taiwan Envoy Raps Japan's China Bid," ibid., July 17, 1972, p. 2.

48. "Repayment Terms To Be Decided on 'Quality' Basis," ibid., July 27, 1972, pp. 1, 5. The "Yoshida Letter," named after Prime Minister Hayato Ikeda's special envoy to Taipei, Shigeru Yoshida, was an agreement reached on May 30, 1964, between the Japanese government and Taipei that forbade use of Japanese state funds to finance or guarantee plant exports to the PRC. The full content of the letter has never been disclosed by either Taipei or Tokyo, even after the severance of their diplomatic relations. For a discussion of this matter, see Gene T. Hsiao, "The Role of Trade in China's Diplomacy with Japan," in Jerome A. Cohen, ed., The Dynamics of China's Foreign Relations (Cambridge, Mass.: Harvard University Press, 1970), pp. 41, 47.

49. "Yen-Yuan Settlement Accord Signed in Peking," JT, Aug. 19, 1972, p. 1; "Japan, China Banks Start Yen-Yuan System," ibid., Sept. 13, 1972, p. 3; John Roberts, "Meeting in Peking," in Asia Year Book 1973 (Hong Kong: Far Eastern Economic Review, 1973), p. 182.

50. "Justice Ministry Approves Chinese Reentry in Japan," JT, Sept. 10, 1972, p. 2.

51. "Sun P'ing-hua and Hsiao Hsiang-ch'ien Received by Japanese Prime Minister," PR no. 33 (Aug. 18, 1972): 4.

52. "Komeito Leader Says Peace Pact Also Envisaged," JT, Aug. 29, 1972, p. 1.

53. Koji Nakamura, "Open Door for China," FEER no. 36 (Sept. 2, 1972): 13.

54. For a discussion see Koji Nakamura, "Changing Power Balance," ibid. no. 48 (Nov. 27, 1971): 8; Editorial, "Mr. Chou's Invitation," JT, July 12, 1972, p. 14.

55. "LDP Council Decision: Five Principles Agreed for Ties with China," JT, Aug. 25, 1972, p. 1.

56. "Pro-Taipei Dietmen Hit Speeded up China Ties," ibid., Aug. 30, 1972, p. 1.

57. "LDP Group Modifies Principles on China," ibid., Sept. 6, 1972, p. 1; "LDP Council OK's Five-Point Policy on China Ties," ibid., Sept. 9, 1972, pp. 1, 5. As discussed earlier, all opposition parties except the right wing of the JCP were for restoration of diplomatic ties with Peking. After adoption of the five-point decision by the LDP, the JCP right wing changed its stand on the issue and supported Tanaka's mission. See "JCP Changes Its Stand on Japan-China Ties," ibid., Sept. 10, 1972, pp. 1, 4.

58. The first Japanese advance party, headed by Hiroshi Hashimoto, chief of the China Division in the Ministry of Foreign Affairs, arrived in Peking on Aug. 31 and left Sept. 5. "Japanese Advance Party in Peking," PR no. 36 (Sept. 8, 1972): 4. Also see "First Official LDP Mission Arrives in China Capital," JT, Sept. 15, 1972, p. 1; "LDP Mission Explains Position," ibid., Sept. 17, 1972, p. 1.

59. See "Premier Chou En-lai on Sino-Japanese Relations," PR no. 38 (Sept. 22, 1972): 3; "Mr. Kosaka's Speech," ibid., pp. 3-4.

60. See Minoru Shimuzu, "Big Domestic Issue: China Question Expected to Speed Sato's Exit," JT, Aug. 19, 1971, p. 14.

61. "Ohira Bares Policy on China," ibid., July 9, 1972, p. 4.

62. "Ohira, Kissinger Agree on China in Principle," ibid., Aug. 20, 1972, p. 1.

63. See joint statement of Japan-United States, Sept. 1, 1972, in Japan Report no. 19 (Oct. 1, 1972): 2-3.

64. "Kissinger Says Japan's China Bid Won't Hurt Pact," JT, Sept. 1, 1972, p. 1.

65. The offers were announced in Taiwan hsin-sheng pao (Taipei), Aug. 12, 1972, p. 2; Chung-kuo shih-pao (Taipei), Aug. 18, 1972, p. 1.

66. In CYJP, Sept. 9, 1972, p. 1.

67. These measures were announced on different occasions in August 1972. For a comprehensive report, see CYJP, Sept. 19, 1972, p. 1.

68. In JT, Aug. 29, 1972, p. 5. On Sept. 26, 1972, when Tanaka was visiting Peking, the Nationalist navy detained an "unidentified" Japanese fishing boat for a few hours near the Nansha Islands in the South China Sea. Otherwise, no other incident has occurred. See CYJP, Sept. 27, 1972, p. 1.

69. In CYJP, Sept. 19, 1972, p. 1.

70. In ibid., Sept. 18, 1972, p. 1.

71. "Premier Chiang on Relations with Japan," ibid., Sept. 30, 1972, p. 1.

72. In ibid., Sept. 19, 1972, p. 1.

73. The English text of the joint statement, dated Sept. 29, 1972, is in PR no. 40 (Oct. 6, 1972): 12-13; the Chinese text is in Jen-min jih-pao, Sept. 30, 1972, p. 1.

74. See exchange of notes between Plenipotentiary of Japan Isao Kawada and Plenipotentiary of the Republic of China Yeh Kung-chao, Apr. 28, 1952, in Ministry of Foreign Affairs, ed., Treaties Between the Republic of China and Foreign States, 1927-1957 (Taipei, 1958), pp. 254-55.

75. See "Foreign Minister Ohira Holds Press Conference" (29 September 1972), PR no. 40 (Oct. 6, 1972): 15.

76. "Significance of the Signing of the Sino-Japanese Joint Statement (6 October 1972)," in American Embassy, Summaries of Selected Japanese Magazines (Tokyo), Nov. 1972, pp. 46, 47. (Translated from Toki no ugoki.)

77. See "Liao Cheng-chih on the Conclusion of a Sino-Japanese Peace Treaty," Hua-ch'iao jih-pao (China daily news, New York), May 19, 1973, p. 1.

78. See the joint declaration by Japan and the Soviet Union (Oct. 19, 1956), Art. 9, in The Japanese Annual of International Law no. 1 (1957): 129, 131.

79. See "Tokyo Still Asserts Status of Taiwan Is Not Determined," NYT, Nov. 6, 1972, p. 22.

80. The 1943 Cairo Declaration reads in part: "Japan shall be stripped of all the islands in the Pacific which she has seized or occupied since the beginning of the First World War in 1914, and that all the territories Japan has stolen from the Chinese, such as Manchuria, Formosa (Taiwan), and the Pescadores shall be restored to the Republic of China. . . ." Article 8 of the Potsdam Proclamation reads: "The terms of the Cairo Declaration shall be carried out and Japanese sovereignty shall be limited to the islands of Honshu, Hokkaido, Kyushu, Shikoku, and such minor islands as we [the Allied powers] determine."

81. In "Significance of the Signing of the Sino-Japanese Joint Statement," p. 47.

82. See Treaty of Peace with Japan (Sept. 8, 1951), Art. 2, in U.S. Treaties and Other International Agreements, 3: 3169, 3172.

83. Foreign Minister Chou En-lai's statement, May 5, 1952, in Jih-pen wen-t'i wen-chien chi, 1: 93.

84. For a description of the natural resources in Siberia, see "The Vast New El Dorado in the Arctic," in Time, no. 15 (Apr. 9, 1973): 30, 39. The remark, "unfriendly act," was reported by Richard Halloran, "Japan's Asia Plans Are Merely Ideas," in NYT, March 16, 1973, p. 8.

85. See Koji Nakamura, "China: 'Political' Deal," FEER no. 4 (Jan. 29, 1973): 33; "Sino-US Pincer," ibid. no. 10 (Mar. 12, 1973): 20; "Remember the Foe," ibid. no. 14 (Apr. 9, 1973): 12; "China and Japan: the Wedge-Drivers," ibid. no. 16 (Apr. 23, 1973): 12; "Japan: Statements on Japanese-Soviet Peace Treaty and Northern Territories," PR no. 44 (Nov. 3, 1972): 26; "Japan: Demand for Return of Four Islands," ibid. no. 46 (Nov. 17, 1972): 19; "Demand for Return of Northern Territory," ibid. no. 49 (Dec. 8, 1972): 19. The PRC's offer to develop oil resources is not firm. Latest reports indicate that the PRC has turned down a Japanese government proposal for the joint venture. See "China Said Shunning Japan Aid in Oil Drilling," JT, May 22, 1973, p. 1.

86. "Letter to Brezhnev, Premier Wants Talks on Treaty Resumed," JT, May 8, 1973, p. 1.

87. Koji Nakamura, "The Tanaka Letter," FEER no. 11 (Mar. 19, 1973): 22.

88. In ibid. no. 19 (May 14, 1973): 5; "Talks to Resume Next Year for Japan-Soviet Pact," in JT, Oct. 11, 1973, pp. 1; "Japan-Soviet Bonds Will Improve: Premier," ibid.; "Tanaka, Brezhnev Back Siberia Accord," ibid., p. 10; "Territorial Issue Hangs on Amity, Premier Says," ibid., Oct. 12, 1973, p. 1. For an unofficial translation of the text of the Japan-Soviet Joint Communiqué (Oct. 10, 1973), in ibid., p. 12.

89. See FEER no. 18 (May 7, 1973): 5; "Chou Praises Japanese Bid in Moscow," in JT, Oct. 11, 1973, p. 1.

90. "4,630,000 Million Yen Outlay Nearly Double Last Plan," JT, Oct. 10, 1972, p. 1; Koji Nakamura, "Introducing 'Positive' Defense," FEER no. 43 (Oct. 21, 1972): 15.

91. For an analysis of this subject, see Koji Nakamura, "China and Soviet Relations: Treading the Siberian Tightrope," in Special Report on Japan 1973, FEER no. 19 (May 14, 1973): 6.

92. For trade figures cited above and immediately below, see Japan Economic Review (Tokyo) no. 3 (Mar. 15, 1973): 9.

93. See CYJP Nov. 18, 1972, p. 1.

94. See ibid., Dec. 3, 1972, p. 1.

95. In ibid., Jan. 9, 1973, p. 1.

96. See Huang T'ien-ts'ai, "Readjustment of Sino-Japanese Relations," ibid., Dec. 10, 1972, p. 2. One dollar is equivalent to about 260 yen.

97. See ibid., Dec. 1, 1972, p. 2.

98. See agreement between the Association of East Asia Relations and the Japan Interchange Association, Dec. 26, 1972, ibid., Dec. 27, 1972, p. 1.

99. See ibid., Mar. 14, 1973, p. 1; Mar. 15, 1973, p. 1.

100. See "China-Japan Air Route Meets Difficulty," Economic Salon (Honolulu), Apr. 1973, p. 8; "Government Seen Speeding up Talks on China Air and Fishery Pacts," JT, May 28, 1973, p. 11.

101. See Kazushige Hirasawa, "Sino-Japanese Relations," JT, May 25, 1973, p. 1; "Japan-China Air Pact Opposed by LDP Dietmen," ibid., May 26, 1973, p. 1. For reference to Taiwan's reaction against the proposed Japan-China aviation agreement, see CYJP, May 25, 1973, p. 1; May 27, 1973, p. 1. The above statistics can be found in the sources just cited.

102. See Hirokichi Nadao's press statement at the Taipei airport, in CYJP, Oct. 1, 1973, p. 1.

103. "66 Dietmen Arrive for Taiwan Visit," in JT, Oct. 1, 1973, p. 1; "Pro-Taiwan LDP Group Returns," JT, Oct. 4, 1973, p. 1.

104. "China Desires Aviation Pact," JT, Oct. 15, 1973, p. 12.

105. See Japan Economic Review no. 3 (March 15, 1973): 9.

106. See JT, Oct. 13, 1973, p. 12; "Japan-China Economic Interchange Girding For Steady Gains," Japan Economic Review no. 10 (Oct. 15, 1973): 3.

107. "Japan, China Officials Agree on Trade Rules," JT, Aug. 31, 1973, p. 1.

108. "Prime Minister Tanaka Addresses American-Japan Society (18 October 1972)," Japan Report no. 23 (Dec. 1, 1972): 3, 4.

109. Aside from Tanaka's own statement quoted above, the influential Yumiuri shimbun, for example, once made a strong emotional remark on the issue: "Without the restoration of Japanese-Chinese diplomatic relations, the master-servant relationship between the United States and Japan cannot be changed to a relationship of true equality." In John M. Lee, "Nixon-Sato Talks Disappoint Japan," NYT, Jan. 16, 1972, p. 8.

110. For a discussion of this matter, see Edwin O. Reischauer's testimony in the Committee on Foreign Affairs, House of Representatives, 92nd Congress, 2nd session, The New China Policy: Its Impact on the United States and Asia (Washington, D.C.: U.S. Government Printing Office, 1972), pp. 3-18; James W. Morley's testimony in ibid., pp. 152-59.

111. See "Interview with Japan's Foreign Minister Masayoshi Ohira," in Special Report on Japan 1973, FEER no. 19 (May 14, 1973): 5.

10

THE IMPACT OF
THE SINO-AMERICAN
DÉTENTE ON KOREA
Chong-Sik Lee

The overwhelming impact of the actions of major world powers
upon those of lesser allies has been vividly exemplified by the events
of the last few years. In July 1971, Washington and Peking simultaneously announced President Nixon's acceptance of Premier Chou
En-lai's invitation to visit the People's Republic of China (PRC).
Within a month the South Korean Red Cross Society issued a proposal
to its North Korean counterpart to meet and discuss the problem of
divided families. In February 1972, President Nixon made his historic
journey to China and, beginning in May, high officials of North and
South Korea exchanged unprecedented visits between Pyongyang and
Seoul, and issued the historic joint communiqué of July 4, announcing
basic agreements on a number of important points. In September
Japanese Prime Minister Kakuei Tanaka visited Peking and agreed
on the establishment of diplomatic relations.

Negotiations between China and the United States, as well as
between China and Japan, progressed smoothly; and both the United
States and Japan have exchanged ambassadors (or their equivalents)
with the PRC. There have been frequent exchanges of personnel, and
the trade volume between the PRC and the two new partners is rapidly
rising. Negotiations in Korea, however, have not followed the pace
of progress achieved among the greater powers. Although the Democratic People's Republic of Korea (DPRK) and the Republic of Korea
(ROK) were able to agree on certain basic principles and to agree on
the establishment of mechanisms to facilitate further discussions,
they have not been able to agree on any substantive matters. Even
though it has been nearly two years since the representatives of Red
Cross societies began to negotiate at Panmunjom, not a single private
citizen from either side has crossed the truce line, not a letter has
been exchanged, nor a single dollar's worth of any commodity traded.
In short, while the Sino-American détente created a "structure" that

fostered the initiative of the Koreans to negotiate, the stimulus has
not been powerful enough to coax the Koreans to arrive at the solution
of concrete problems. This paper surveys briefly the events that have
occurred in Korea since July 1971, analyzes the problems involved
in the negotiations and the causes for the delay, and speculates on the
prospect of future negotiations. In the process an attempt will be
made to delineate the impact of the Sino-American détente upon the
Korean peninsula.

THE RED CROSS TALKS AND THE
COORDINATING COMMITTEE

When the ROK leadership perceived that the trend toward a
thaw and a Sino-American détente was irreversible, it caused the
South Korean Red Cross Society to issue, on August 12, 1971, a proposal for a meeting with the North Korean Red Cross Society to discuss the problem of Korea's divided families: how to locate missing
relatives, inform them of each other's condition, and arrange for
reunions. The North Koreans quickly agreed, and on August 20 a
historic four-minute meeting took place at Panmunjom. Millions of
Koreans watched the unfolding of events with great emotion and anticipation that the meeting would, somehow, lead to the eventual reunification of the country. The painful process of "preliminary negotiations"
continued; and finally, on June 16, 1972, 10 months after it all began,
the delegates from both sides agreed on the agenda for future discussions.

By late March 1973, five rounds of talks had been held in Pyongyang and Seoul, but indications are that the delegations are back at
the point where they began, a dispute over the agenda of the talks.

An editorial of March 20, 1973, in Nodong Sinmun (Worker's
News), the organ of the Korean Workers' Party, provides a glimpse
of the arguments. It argued that the conditions and circumstances of
democracy and freedom must be provided as a background to the
effort. If restrictions are imposed by laws and regulations, or any
other obstacles are imposed, the families and relatives will be prevented from freely expressing their wills, finding out what they would
wish, or conducting free activities. It further argued: "As for us, the
northern half of the republic, completely free and democratic circumstances and conditions have been and will be fully guaranteed. . . ."
In the North Korean view, it was only South Korean recalcitrance
that prevented the divided families from reuniting. In the words of
the editorial:

Nevertheless, the South Korean side has failed, up to date,
to advance any practical proposal for solving this question.

It has slung mud at the fair and aboveboard, concrete and realistic proposals put forth by our side and our just stand and efforts for their materialization, describing them as matters of "political character," too vague and broad-ranged arguments, "divergence from humanitarianism" and the like.

They allege that we are creating "difficulties" in the Red Cross work by conducting "political propaganda," but it is none other than the South Korean side who pursues a foul political purpose, crying for "purity" of the Red Cross work, humanitarian work.[1]

The South Korean argument has been that the North Korean delegates have been presenting issues that go beyond the authority of the Red Cross Society. The task of the Red Cross, according to the South Korean view, has been to facilitate humanitarian reunions within the existing legal framework rather than to change the laws. These legal and political questions should be presented to the proper legal authorities rather than burdening the Red Cross talks with political questions. The Red Cross representatives should smooth out the technical problems and proceed to identify, locate, and facilitate re-union of divided families. In any event, nearly two years of talks have yet to produce a major breakthrough.

The surprise announcement in Seoul and Pyongyang on July 4, 1972, that the top leaders of the two regimes had reached an agreement on a number of basic principles concerning Korean unification and that they had agreed to set up a North-South Coordinating Committee to prevent armed clashes, facilitate exchanges, expedite Red Cross talks, and settle the unification problem raised the hopes of the Korean population much higher than the initiation of the Red Cross talks. Virtually no Korean, including the principals involved in the negotiations, thought such an agreement possible even a very short while ago, not only because of the deep animosities between the two sides but also because of the constitutional and legal prohibitions in South Korea against any contacts by citizens of the ROK with any elements of the DPRK. Ever since the ROK was founded in 1948, it has claimed sovereignty over the entire peninsula, and by definition the Communist regime in the North has been considered an antistate and treasonous organization.* The decision of the South Korean leadership officially

---

*While the DPRK also claims sovereignty over the entire peninsula and Premier Kim Il-sung has been acclaimed as the leader of the 40 million people in Korea, the constitution of the DPRK contains no provisions concerning the territory of the DPRK, thus avoiding the

to engage in negotiations with its North Korean counterpart thus reflected the extent of pressure felt by the South Korean leaders from the rapidly changing international situation surrounding the Korean peninsula. The North Korean decision to deal directly with the regime of President Park Chung Hee also attested to a major change in attitude, for the North Korean had long denounced his regime in no uncertain terms. Premier Kim Il-sung's speech of August 6, 1971, in which he expressed his willingness to "come in touch at any time with all political parties including the [ruling] Democratic Republican Party, public organizations and individual personages," for example, had described the South Korean rulers as "the puppet clique . . . clinging as ever to the sleeves of American imperialists." Foreign Minister Ho Tam, who outlined North Korea's eight-point peaceful unification program on April 12, 1971, had expressed his willingness to negotiate on the condition that either "people's power is established in South Korea or patriotic-minded new figures assume power after the withdrawal of the U.S. imperialists and the downfall of traitor Park Chung Hee. . . ."[2]

Now the two regimes that had been virtually at war with each other suddenly halted all hostile acts and proceeded to negotiate. Telephone links were immediately established, propaganda broadcasts and leaflet distribution were terminated, and the North-South Coordinating Committee was officially launched. A secretaries' conference was organized and an agreement was drawn up to establish a Joint Secretariat. A joint statement was issued on November 4, 1972, reaffirming the tasks to be performed by the Coordination Committee.

However, further progress was difficult to attain. The second session of the Coordinating Committee was held in March 1973, but it failed to yield even a joint statement. Once again the basic differences in orientation toward the solution of existing problems on the Korean peninsula became manifest.

As the ROK Foreign Minister had announced in February 1972, the South Korean government had advocated the solution of the "Korean problem" by stages, solving the easiest problems first. According to this plan, the humanitarian problem of divided families should be solved first, followed by nonpolitical talks, and then political talks.[3] Since the gulf separating the two Koreas is deep and wide, only by such stages can trust be built, eventually leading to unification. North Koreans, on the other hand, have been insisting that tension could be eased and trust built only if the state of military confrontation was

---

problem that the ROK President has had to face. The only provision in the 1948 constitution of the DPRK pertaining to this question is Article 103, which designates Seoul as the capital of the republic.

removed, and this could be attained only if the U.S. forces were withdrawn from South Korea and armaments on both sides were reduced.[4]

It might be noted in passing that the Supreme People's Assembly of the DPRK decided to send a letter to the U.S. Congress on April 6 proposing that American troops be withdrawn from South Korea, thus removing "the obstacles lying in the way to Korea's peaceful unification."[5] In a similar letter addressed to "parliaments and governments of all countries of the world," the North Koreans declared: "If the United States forces pull out of South Korea, we are ready to reduce our army strength to 200,000 [half of the present strength] or less, of our own accord."[6] It might be noted also that while the Nodong Sinmun editorial of March 18 mildly reproached the South Koreans for refusing to entertain the question of reducing arms, the chief of the General Staff of the (North) Korean People's Army, General O Chin-u, was less reserved in attacking the South Korean authorities. His remarks of February 7, 1973, on the occasion of the 25th anniversary of the founding of the army, merit attention:

> They refused even our proposal for discontinuing the arms race . . ., reducing munitions production, and curtailing the armed forces as an expression of mutual trust, calling it "premature." This shows that the South Koreans do not want to solve the problems, although they will engage in a dialogue with us, and do not want to put into practice any agreements with which they may concur.
>
> Diametrically opposed to our sincere efforts . . ., the South Korean authorities are taking the dangerous road of aggravating tensions between the north and south and pursuing war by clamoring about "confrontation" and "prevailing over communism."

General O's comments about the United States was even more vehement:

> Today the U.S. imperialists are obdurately hampering the reunification of our country in an attempt to salvage their bankrupt policy of aggression in Asia under the signboard of the so-called "Nixon doctrine" and craftily scheming to attain their aggressive goals more easily by pitting Koreans against Koreans. . . .
>
> The U.S. imperialists should take a straight look at reality and must not recklessly run about. They should leave South Korea at once, taking with them all of their aggressor forces. If despite our repeated warnings the U.S. imperialists continue to obstruct Korean reunification

and dare instigate the bellicose elements in South Korea
to ignite a new war, the entire Korean people and people's
army will crush them in one blow and allow none of them
to return home alive.[7]

THE TWO KOREAS AND THEIR GOALS

Why, then, did the Sino-American détente fail to affect the situation in Korea to a greater degree? Why have the North Koreans been
insisting on the solution of the more basic questions, such as the
reduction of armed forces, while the South Koreans have been insisting
on the prior solution of the more peripheral questions while continuing
their military modernization program?

Answers to these questions require an examination of the nature
of the two regimes in Korea, the geopolitical situation, and the perception of the leadership on both sides concerning the effect of the
Sino-American détente upon their respective positions.

It goes without saying that the natures of the two regimes in
Korea have changed drastically since the end of World War II. It
needs no elaboration that they were the products of the Cold War and
that such words as "puppet" and "tutelage" have had some utility in
describing the relationship between the great powers and the two
political systems in Korea. But these relationships underwent steady
change as the leaders and the people on each side matured, and the
international environment surrounding them has changed. Each side
has developed its own ethos, set of structures, and style of development. Intense nationalism surfaced among the leaders and intellectuals
on each side, and the perspective toward the outside world began to
change. Each side cultivated strong loyalty toward its political system,
identifying loyalty toward the system with loyalty to the nation.

As a result, the great powers no longer possess the kind of
leverage they once had over their "wards" on the Korean peninsula,
although this does not mean that North and South Korea are immune
to external influences. The security and developmental needs of each
system, along with the size and location of the two Koreas, make them
highly susceptible to the changing environment. This fact, however,
should not obscure the point that both Pyongyang and Seoul insist on
the right to make decisions affecting vital interests of their own systems according to their own perspectives.

For this reason the leaders' perceptions of the effect of the
changing environment upon their systems becomes all the more
important. These perceptions are conditioned by the geopolitical
environment of the two Koreas as well as the aims pursued by the
two regimes before the whirlwind of change began to blow around
Korea.

A glance at the map would convince anyone that the DPRK is situated in a highly favorable position vis-à-vis the ROK as far as geopolitical factors are concerned. North Korea's two principal allies are contiguous, while South Korea's only principal military ally is across the Pacific. While Japan is a short distance from South Korea, treaty relationships do not exist between the ROK and Japan as far as military matters are concerned. Prime Minister Sato of Japan did declare in November 1969, in a joint communiqué issued with President Nixon, that the "security of the Republic of Korea is essential to Japan's own security," but such a declaration does not have the effect of a treaty commitment. Assuming that the allies of each side are equally capable and willing to come to their aid in the event of conflict, South Korea is at a disadvantage.

It should also be pointed out that the constitutional frameworks of the respective allies as well as the treaty provisions between the DPRK and her allies, on the one hand, and the ROK and her ally, on the other, are markedly different. The political structures in the Soviet Union and the PRC are such that a relatively few individuals could arrive at major decisions involving the use of the armed forces. In the United States, on the other hand, decisions involving the use of the armed forces requires more elaborate procedures. While Article 1 of the treaty between the DPRK and the Soviet Union and Article 2 of the treaty between the DPRK and the PRC provide for "immediate military and other assistance through all means in the event of military attack from any nation," Article 3 of the treaty between the ROK and the United States provides that in the event of an armed attack, each party "would act to meet the common danger in accordance with its constitutional processes." Even if we assume that all the major powers involved have the determination to abide by the treaty provisions signed with the two Koreas, the ROK faces the possibility of her ally's delaying the decision, which could lead to disastrous consequences.

Space limitations do not permit extensive discussion of the nature of possible warfare on the Korean peninsula or comparison of relative strengths of the military forces. It should be noted, however, that the South Korean authorities frequently have talked of the possibility of a war like the "Six Day War" happening in Korea, of the relative weakness of the South Korean air and naval forces, and of the obsolescence of South Korea's military armaments.

Under these conditions, what goals had the leadership on each side been pursuing before the changes in international environment began? In answering this question one of course encounters the problem of separating the rhetoric from the real goals; but a careful reading of numerous pronouncements by the leaders of both sides, accompanied by scrutinization of policies implemented by the interested governments, leads to the conclusion that the statements of the top leaders are a reasonable approximation of the goals established for each society.

One can, for example, accept Premier Kim Il-sung's address before the Fifth Congress of the Korean Workers' Party (KWP), delivered on November 2, 1970, as an accurate statement of North Korea's goals. In that speech Kim Il-sung talked of the need further to promote socialist economic construction, socialist culture, thought revolution, revolutionization and proletarianization of the entire society, strengthening of defense power, balanced development of people's livelihood, revolution in South Korea and the attainment of unification, consolidation of international solidarity, and the strengthening of Communist Party activities. In short, the internal policy is to accelerate economic development, to bring about ideological consolidation, and to strengthen military power. The policy toward South Korea is to encourage and promote people's revolution that would lead to unification. The policy toward the international Communist camp is to bring about solidarity.

Premier Kim's unification formula as of November 1970 needs to be elaborated further. It called for the overthrow of the regime of President Park Chung Hee, expulsion of the Americans, establishment of a "peace-loving" regime, reduction of the two armies to 100,000 men each or less, conclusion of a nonaggression pact, establishment of economic and cultural intercourse, and the establishment of a "unified democratic government" through "free North-South elections" or establishment of a confederation as a transitional step. In the Premier's words:

> We have made it clear time and again that if democratic personages with a national conscience come to power in South Korea and demand the withdrawal of U.S. troops, release of political prisoners and guarantee of democratic freedom, then we are ready to hold negotiations with them on the question of the peaceful unification of the Fatherland at any time and at any place.8

The South Korean goals can be found in series of Presidential statements.

> Our supereme aim is reunification of our divided national territory. Modernization of our Fatherland is our intermediate goal, while economic development is our immediate task.
> It is an unshaken goal for our advance that we modernize our Fatherland as soon as possible by accelerating

economic development and, on the basis of this accomplishment, stride forward toward the objective of national
reunification."9

> To sum up the key policy [for the year] in one sentence,
> it is to reinforce our national defense and security and also
> to promote economic construction. . . .
> The first task [in foreign policy] is to pursue posi-
> tive diplomacy to guarantee our national security and the
> second mission is to promote "economic diplomacy."10

In short, the South Korean goals have been to guard against in-
vasions and infiltrations from the North while concentrating on economic development. As the President announced in 1968, reunification
was the ultimate goal of South Korea, but this was only a long-range
goal. President Park stated in his new year's message of 1967:

> Unification is not brought closer by wishing or
> deploring. I must caution here that only harm will
> come from those unrealistic unification formulas which are
> are devised to beguile people who are uninformed about
> the cold facts of reality facing us. . . .
> In our present circumstance, the short cut to
> national reunification is economic construction and the
> fostering of democratic capabilities.11

Thus the South Korean leadership, as well as a large segment
of the populace, accepted the status quo and began to concentrate on
economic development while the North Korean leadership was committed to dynamic changes both within North Korea, where revolutionization has been presented as the primary goal, and in the Korean
peninsula as a whole. The South Korean leadership found the North
Korean framework totally unacceptable, not only because it was pred-
icated upon overthrow of the leadership in power but also because it
called for the removal of the American troops, who had served to
counterbalance North Korea's geopolitical advantage. Even if the North
Koreans had not insisted on the overthrow of the ROK regime in power,
the North Korean formula would have placed South Korea in a relatively
disadvantageous position, given the geopolitical factors.

REACTIONS TO THE DÉTENTE

Given these conditions, the reactions of the two regimes toward
the Sino-American détente and the thaw in the international atmosphere

were largely predictable. One of the causes as well as the effects of the improvement in Sino-American relations has been the determination of the United States to reduce her commitment abroad. Another effect has been the marked improvement of the position of the PRC in the world arena. Obviously, American retrenchment would affect the ROK adversely while the improved position of the PRC would affect the DPRK favorably. For the ROK, therefore, the détente was a double loss in its position vis-à-vis the DPRK.

The ROK leader's reaction was sharp and intense. On December 6, 1971, President Park Chung Hee declared a state of national emergency, asserting that the ROK "is at present confronted with a grave situation." He cited the recent seating of the PRC at the United Nations and its implications, the reduction of U.S. support for the ROK's defense and the tenor of debate in the U.S. Senate, and the recent moves of Japan toward the PRC and the DPRK, concluding: "Our national security matters have entered a momentous phase calling for reshaping of our defense posture." He expressed his disagreement with the actions of the allies, stating: "Only we, the Koreans who have had personal experience, can tell how terrible the Asian communist menace is."[12] He dwelt on the aggressive nature of the North Korean regime, the continued infiltration of North Korean agents, and "irresponsible" debate on matters that concern the vital security of the nation, and he imposed total control over the nation. On October 17, 1972, the President proclaimed martial law throughout South Korea, suspended all political activities, and dissolved the National Assembly. A new constitution vesting maximum power in the President, at the same time permitting his indefinite tenure, was promulgated in December to allow him to deal with the "grave situation" without hindrance.

The North Korean reaction was equally predictable. On August 6, 1971, Premier Kim Il-sung declared that "U.S. imperialism had been driven into a blind alley internally and externally." He declared that the "hostile policy toward China . . . has eventually gone to complete bankruptcy, and this denotes that the U.S. imperialists have at least succumbed to the pressure of the mighty anti-imperialist revolutionary forces of the world." Commenting on the impact of the Nixon visit to Peking on the U.S. allies in East Asia, the Premier said:

> In connection with Nixon's plan to visit China, the imperialists camp is now sliding into new confusion and disintegration. Japanese Prime Minister Sato . . . is trying extra hard to veil the bankruptcy of his reactionary policy. . . . Other satellite countries and puppets who had blindly trailed behind U.S. imperialism are at a loss and, especially the Chiang Kai-shek clique and the South

Korean puppet clique, are raising a hue and cry, overcome
with great uneasiness and fear.

The general situation is turning further in favor of
us revolutionary people with each passing day.13

He elaborated further on the plight of the South Korean leadership and offered a remedy:

Taken aback by the situation which is developing in favor
of the revolution as the days go by, the present puppet
clique of South Korea, while clinging as ever to the sleeves
of the U.S. imperialists, are relying all the more on the
Japanese militarists in a foolish attempt to prolong their
remaining days and clamoring more noisily about the so-
called "peaceful unification program" ruse in an attempt
to cover up their treacherous nature and tone down the
tendency towards the peaceful reunification growing with
an irresistible force among the South Korean people.
This stupid deceptive ruse of the South Korean puppet
clique, however, can fool no one, nor can it save their lot
of doom.

What, then, were the remedies suggested?

If the South Korean rulers truly want the peaceful reunification of the country, to begin with, they must not earnestly
beg for the permanent stationing of the U.S. troops but
make them withdraw from South Korea, stop ushering in
South Korea the Japanese militarists in collusion with
them, discontinue the suppression of the political parties
and public organization and democratic personages of
South Korea calling for the peaceful reunification, enable
them to come out for north-south negotiations for the
reunification of the country, and proceed from the stand
that the Korean question should be solved by the Koreans
themselves.14

Except for differences in rhetoric, the leaderships of two Koreas
are essentially in agreement about the impact of the détente on Korea.
They are, however, in sharp disagreement as to the desired solution
of the Korean problem. While the North Koreans would like to have
the U.S. forces withdrawn, armaments reduced, a peace treaty signed,
and then engage in exchanges that would lead to unification, the
South Koreans find such an idea totally unrealistic. These ideas were
unacceptable when President Syngman Rhee was in power. They were

unacceptable in November 1970, when Kim Il-sung proposed them at the Fifth Congress of the KWP. The solution offered on August 6, 1971, was identical with that of November 1970. One should note that the North Korean position has undergone virtually no change since then, even after the negotiations started, except that they are willing to deal with the regime of President Park Chung Hee instead of calling for its overthrow. The North Korean leadership evidently finds the new atmosphere created by the Sino-American détente consonant with the line of argument they have been pursuing, and they do not feel obliged to alter their policies. The South Korean leadership, on the other hand, does not detect any change in the basic goals of its North Korean counterpart and does not wish to jeopardize its position further by acceding to the North Korean demands. Hence the South Korean side insists that the discussions concerning armed forces and other political matters should be postponed and that both sides should concentrate on facilitating exchanges that would contribute to the building of mutual trust.

PROSPECTS FOR THE FUTURE

Since the North Korean demand to deal with the problem of American forces in South Korea as well as the problem of reducing armaments affects the vital security of South Korea, and in view of the fact that the ROK leaders find such talk adversely affecting South Korea's security, no progress is likely to be made in the negotiations as long as the North Korean side adheres to the present position. Does this mean that the two sides are likely to break off the negotiations and return to the previous status of unmitigated hostility? Are the Red Cross talks as well as the hopes of economic, cultural, and other exchanges doomed?

No one outside the small circle of leaders in North and South Korea is, of course, in a position to offer any definitive answers to these questions, but one may hazard an educated guess. One's process of speculation can be aided substantially if he examines the factors that led to the initiation of the negotiations as well as the benefits accruing to each side from them.

The sequence of events discussed at the beginning of this paper leaves little doubt that the dynamic change in the relationship between the PRC and the United States was a prime factor in the initiation of the dialogue between the DPRK and the ROK. Both the PRC and the United States found it to their advantage to terminate the Cold War between them and sought to mitigate tension in East Asia. Continued tension in the Korean peninsula, therefore, would have run counter to the interest of the two powers; and hence it is highly probable that both of them did what they could to persuade their allies to reduce tension on the peninsula. Close resemblence of the wording of the Shanghai communiqué issued by President Nixon and Premier Chou En-lai on February 28, 1972, and the joint communiqué issued on July 4, 1972, in Pyongyang and Seoul further substantiates this interpretation.

As they have been traced in detail, the external influences were not strong enough to overcome the inherent difficulties involved in the Korean situation. Nevertheless, neither the DPRK nor the ROK is in a position to ignore the international environment, and hence neither side is likely to find it in its interest to return to the status quo ante.

Beyond this, of course, are the advantages gained by both sides from the process of negotiation. The DPRK, in particular, found the new atmosphere created by the initiation of North-South negotiations highly favorable in many aspects. The de facto recognition of the DPRK by the ROK government made it possible for the latter to launch an intense offensive that led to the establishment of diplomatic ties with a number of non-Communist countries, including the five Scandanavian nations that decided to recognize and establish official ties with the DPRK in March 1973. Ongoing negotiations in Korea precipitated a rapid change in the attitude of the Japanese leaders toward the DPRK, and the notion of "two Koreas" gained a strong momentum in the Japanese political arena. The changing political climate facilitated rapid increase in the trade volume between the DPRK and Japan, the total rising by 90 percent over the previous year in 1972, followed by another 80 percent increase in 1973. Importation of major industrial plants from Japan on favorable credit terms is expected to contribute significantly to the development of North Korea's economy. While North Korea's overtures toward the United States have not produced any immediate results, an improved relationship between the two Koreas could not fail to affect the attitude of the United States in the future.*

The benefits gained by the ROK are less tangible. The reduction of tension in the peninsula can be said to have benefited the outlook

---

*It should be noted in passing that the DPRK leadership found the new atmosphere created by the Sino-American détente favorable in other respects. As Sino-American relations improved, the rivalry between the Soviet Union and the PRC for the support of the DPRK increased. Thus the DPRK was able to exact an agreement on economic cooperation from the PRC in August 1971, followed by an agreement for military aid in September. In December the Soviet Union agreed to provide additional economic and military assistance to the DPRK between 1971 and 1975.

of the South Korean populace as well as that of foreign investors in South Korea, but the leadership does not seem to feel that the benefits outweighed the losses. The initiation of the negotiations did provide an opportunity—or an excuse, according to President Park's critics, for the South Korean leader to consolidate his power further by a series of fiats, including a constitutional revision that enabled him to succeed himself indefinitely. But whatever benefits the negotiations would bring to the South Korean society as a whole remains to be seen.

If this line of analysis is indeed accurate, the North Korean side is gaining much more from the current negotiations than the South Korean side could hope for. Under such conditions it would be illogical for the DPRK leadership to terminate the negotiations and return to the status quo ante. The South Korean leadership, on the other hand, is not likely to precipitate a breakup in the negotiations, in view of domestic and foreign pressures.

Once both sides arrive at a realistic assessment of the limits to which each side can push the other, both sides will find it relatively easy to agree on less vital matters, such as the reunion of families and economic and cultural exchanges, although even in these areas a great many technical problems remain to be solved. Some discussions have already taken place among top leaders of both sides regarding potential areas of collaboration. Premier Kim Il-sung of the DPRK revealed on April 5, 1973, for example, that his government had proposed the joint utilization of economic potential for the independent development of the national economy in a unified way. His government had "in mind"

> . . . joint exploitation of the abundant underground re-
> sources in the northern half, throwing open the fishing
> grounds of the north and the south to the public, joint
> fishing operations, a joint undertaking on irrigation work
> in the southern half, and the like.[15]

Earlier, the South Korean President Park Chung Hee had publicly speculated on the possibility of jointly developing a tourist park in the Kumgang Mountains in the eastern part of the peninsula.

Assuming that progress will be made in the Red Cross negotiations and that both sides will be able to agree on exchanges and coopera tion in economic and cultural spheres, what will be the effect on the political arena? Is it conceivable that someday the two Koreas will engage in military and diplomatic collaboration, as suggested by Premier Kim Il-sung? If so, under what conditions?

Two propositions can be advanced with respect to the above questions. First, while progress in exchanges and cooperations will certainly be conducive to the escalation of friendly relations, the "spill over effect" from the cultural and economic arena to the political and military arena will not be automatic. Second, collaboration in the political arena will take place only when each side ceases to perceive a threat from the other or feel vulnerable to the other.

The first proposition has already been thoroughly examined by scholars of the European scene, and there will be no need to dwell on it at length. Ernst Haas has conclusively demonstrated that integration in the economic sector does not necessarily lead to political integration; and indeed, as Stanley Hoffmann has argued, political integration is effected independently of economic variables.[16] The lessons obtained in Europe can readily be transferred to the Korean context.

Unlike Western Europe, however, the two Koreas are not divided because of the lack of a sense of national identity. In spite of nearly three decades of division, Koreans in both regions share a strong sense of identity by virtue of common history, race, and language. They are divided by the differences in "ideology, thoughts and systemic structures," the precise factors that Yi Hu-rak and Kim Yong-ju promised (rather nonchalantly) to overcome in their joint communiqué of July 4, 1972. These differences have been reinforced by the catastrophic war between 1950 and 1953 and the prolonged recriminations and intermittent violence since the end of the war. The most crucial question to be answered, then, is how the perception of threat, mutual distrust, and sense of vulnerability can be mitigated.

The North Korean side has argued consistently that the answer lies in removing foreign (American) forces from South Korea, discontinuing the arms race, and in bringing about mutual arms reduction. But for reasons elaborated above, the South Korean leaders do not feel that such a formula would insure the security of South Korea.

This does not mean, of course, that the possibility for arms reduction is totally absent, nor that the perception of threat and vulnerability needs to be perpetuated. If both sides are willing to forego ideological pronouncements, sloganeering, or recriminations for the sake of winning propaganda gains, and if both sides are willing to engage in realistic and complicated discussions of the security needs of the two systems to maintain a balance, military parity at a much reduced armament level could be attained. Before such a process could be initiated, however, the leaders of both sides must agree on the rights of the other side to maintain its sociopolitical system.

The most important factor that has prevented progress in the North-South Korean negotiations and continues to prolong the state of confrontation between the two systems is the inability of the leaders on both sides, as well as the people as a whole, to reconcile their idealism with the reality. In other words, while the reality in Korea calls for the recognition of two separate states with different goals, values and structures of authority, idealism, born out of the history of the ancient and recent past, prevents the Korean people on both sides of the truce line from reconciling themselves to this fact. Thus, while the July 4 pronouncement specified ways to bring about the peaceful coexistence of the two systems, the same document called for the reunification of the country. What is important is that none of the principals or even the critics seem to recognize the internal inconsistency of the document. This is not only because the members of each society have been socialized to reject the legitimacy of the sociopolitical system being consolidated across the truce line but also because neither side recognizes the legitmacy of the division of the country. Indeed, members of each society have been socialized to believe that it is their patriotic and moral duty to destroy the opposing system.

For example, Premier (now President) Kim Il-sung emphatically denounced the idea of peaceful coexistence of two Koreas as early as November 1954 when he said:

> . . . the idea that Korea could be separated into Northern
> and Southern parts and that the parts should coexist with
> each other is very dangerous; it is a view obstructing our
> efforts for unification. Those holding this view would
> relegate the responsibility of revolution in South Korea
> to the South Korean people and relieve the people in
> North Korea of the responsibility of liberating South
> Korea.[17]

The North Korean leadership did not change this line of argument during the next two decades.[18]

Of course, by signing the July 4 communiqué, both sides renounced the use of force to attain unification and the North Korean leaders repeatedly assured the South Koreans that they had no intention of invading the South. Indeed, they denied all charges that the North Koreans had precipitated the war in 1950 by invading the South. The aim of unification, however, has not been abandoned by either side. While the South Korean formula calls for negotiations by stages, the North Korean formula calls for the formation of a united front with all disaffected elements in the South and the eventual establishment of a government that would be more amenable to the North Korean line of policy.

The South Korean leaders and a great majority of the population have too fresh a memory of the war in 1950 to give credence to the North Korean denials of the responsibility for the war; and they fear another Trojan horse in the North Korean proposals, recalling in particular a North Korean proposal, just a week before the outbreak of the war in June 1950, to hold a joint session of both legislatures to discuss the problem of unification. Behind the North Korean "peaceful unification formula," the South Korean leadership perceives a well-developed plan to engage in subversive activities to overthrow the entire structure of authority in the South.

Therefore, mutual perception of threat is likely to continue as long as the two sides persist in presenting unification as one of the major goals to be pursued. It is ironic that the chances for attaining unification through peaceful means would have been enhanced much more substantially had the two sides been able to agree on shelving all talks about unification—both internally and externally—and concentrate on establishing friendly relations on the basis of the Five Principles.* Simple treaties, such as a peace treaty, are not likely to alter anyone's perception. The situation is not likely to improve until the actual policies of each side convince the other that significant changes are indeed occurring and that the other side is not plotting to overthrow one's authority structure.

The Sino-American détente ushered in a new era in the troubled history of modern Korea by bringing the leaders of the two regimes to the negotiating table. But it is likely to require a long period of arduous negotiations before the Korean people experience genuine peace and can afford to shed the siege mentality under which they have labored for too long.†

---

*The Five principles, or Panchi Shila, call for respect for the sovereignty and territorial integrity of all states, nonaggression against other states, noninterference in the internal affairs of other states, equality and mutual benefit, and peaceful coexistence.

†On June 23, 1973, President Park Chung Hee of South Korea declared a major policy swich by announcing his readiness to have the two Koreas simultaneously admitted to the United Nations. Paraphrasing Panchi Shila, he also stated that peace must be maintained in the Korean peninsula, that South and North Korea should not interfere in each other's domestic politics, and that no aggression should take place. Premier Kim Il-sung of North Korea, responding to Park's speech on the same day, on the occasion of welcoming Gustav Husak of Czechoslovakia to Pyongyang, opposed Park's proposal stating that a confederation of the two Korean states should be established first and that the confederation, as a single entity, should become a member of the United Nations.

NOTES

1. Quoted from Nodong Sinmun editorial of Mar. 20, 1973, "Let Us Bring Red Cross Talks to Success to Mitigate Sufferings of Compatriots Caused by Division as Early as Possible and Positively Contribute to Cause of Reunification," by Korean Central News Agency (Pyongyang, KCNA) in English. Foreign Broadcast Information Service (FBIS), Daily Report, Mar. 20, 1973, p. D1.

2. Pyongyang KCNA International Service in English, Apr. 12, 1971, in FBIS, Daily Report, Apr. 12, 1971, p. D11.

3. See Chungang Ilbo, Feb. 12, 1972.

4. From the press conference of Mar. 16 by Vice-Premier Pak Song-ch'ol, as reported by Pyongyang KCNA in English on Mar. 18, in FBIS Daily Report, Mar. 20, 1973, IV, p. 7.

5. Ibid., p. D9.

6. New York Times, Apr. 10, 1973.

7. Pyongyang Domestic Service in Korean, Feb. 7, 1973. FBIS, Daily Report, Feb. 13, 1973, IV, pp. D6-21, see pp. D16, 18).

8. See the English language text in FBIS Daily Report, no. 222, supp. 21, Nov. 16, 1970, p. 34. In Korean, see Nodong Sinmun, Nov. 3, 1970, pp. 1-7.

9. Shun Bum Shik (compiler), Major Speeches by Korea's Park Chung Hee, (Seoul: Hollym Corporation, 1970), p. 122. New Year's message, 1968.

10. Ibid., pp. 207, 211. Press conference, Jan. 10, 1969.

11. Ibid., p. 186.

12. See "Special Statement by the President on the Declaration of a State of National Emergency," issued by the ROK government (Seoul, n.d.).

13. From Premier Kim Il-sung's speech delivered at a mass meeting on Aug. 6, 1971, welcoming Prince Sihanouk, in FBIS, Daily Report, Aug. 6, 1971, IV, p. D8.

14. Ibid., pp D1 and D2.

15. FBIS, Daily Report, no. 79, supp. 15, Apr. 24, 1973, p. 5.

16. See Ernst Haas, Beyond the Nation State (Stanford, Cal.: Stanford University Press, 1964); Stanley Hoffmann, Gulliver's Troubles (New York: McGraw-Hill, 1968), pp. 40-43; and "Obstinate or Obsolete? The Fate of the Nation-State and the Case of Western Europe," Daedalus (Summer, 1966): 862-915.

17. Statement of Nov. 3, 1954, in Kim Il-sung sonjip (Selected works of Kim Il-sung) (Pyongyang: 1960), 4: 189.

18. Selig S. Harrison, reporting from Pyongyang in July 1972, said, "Some North Koreans have cautioned that they are not talking about peaceful coexistence when they forswear the use of force against the South. Peaceful, yes, but coexistence, no, if this means placidly accepting indefinite division of the Korean Peninsula." Washington Post, July 4, 1972, p. A16.

11

THE IMPACT OF
THE SINO-AMERICAN DÉTENTE
ON THE INDOCHINA CONFLICT
Kenneth P. Landon

BACKGROUND

Throughout its history Southeast Asia has been a target of opportunity for powers and influences outside the area. As a consequence
its peoples have acquired a sensitivity to such forces that might affect
their welfare if not their very sovereignty. Symptomatic of this condition was the response of Ho Chi Minh to the Americanizing of the
Indochina war in 1967, when Americans became principally responsible
for search-and-destroy operations while the armed forces of South
Vietnam (ARVN) were being retrained for clear-and-hold operations
in support of the Revolutionary Development Teams that were expected
to win the hearts and minds of the people.

On February 8, 1967, President Lyndon Johnson sent a letter to
Ho Chi Minh suggesting direct talks at which they could reason together
and bring the war to an end. The offer was rejected by Ho Chi Minh
in a letter of February 15 that reaffirmed his familiar precondition:
that the United States end its role in the war and withdraw. In Vietnamese thinking, the one who sues for peace has acknowledged defeat,
the lesser approaching the greater. President Johnson unwittingly
had put himself in the position of confirming Ho's idea that the Americans were losing the war.

The President reaffirmed his role as a supplicant for peace on
November 10, 1967, while speaking on a U.S. carrier in honor of
Veteran's Day. He appealed to Hanoi's leaders to meet him at sea
on a neutral ship.

General William Westmoreland, however, sounded a victory note
on November 21, 1967, at the National Press Club in Washington when
he remarked:

. . . we have reached an important point when the end begins
to come into view. . . . The enemy has many problems: He
is losing control of the scattered population under his influence. . . . He sees the strength of his forces steadily declining. . . . His monsoon offensives have been failures.
He was dealt a mortal blow by the installation of a freely
elected representative government . . . the enemy's hopes
are bankrupt.[1]

Ho Chi Minh's attitude and formula for success were reflected
in a brief article he wrote for Pravda in 1967 to celebrate the 50th
anniversary of the Bolshevik Revolution. He wrote that the Vietnamese
people would defeat the Americans and that "any people, no matter
how small in numbers," could do the same, as it became evident that
"the more new troops the American imperialists send to Vietnam,
the heavier their losses." He acknowledged two vital conditions for
success: that the people be united, determined, and follow the correct
political and military course; and that they receive support from the
socialist community and the revolutionary peoples of the world. Even
while the Sino-Soviet split continued, with China not praising the Soviets
on their 50 years of accomplishment, Ho praised "the great help of
the Soviet Union and the Chinese People's Republic" in the war against
the Americans.

Thus was dramatized the situation of Indochina caught in the
midst of three exploitative powers. The United States was confronting
China and the Soviet Union in an effort to "contain" communism. China
and the Soviet Union were competing for influence over Hanoi and for
leadership among Communist states and the Third World.

President Richard Nixon's announcement on July 15, 1971, that
he would visit Peking before May 1972, followed by his actual visit
February 21, 1972, marked a clear change in U.S. foreign policy and
alerted the Democratic Republic of Vietnam (DRV) that the Ho Chi
Minh formula for success was obsolete. It was a formula that Ho
maintained until his death and was memorialized in his will when he
died on September 4, 1969, at the age of 79.

Ho's will spoke first of the party:

Unity is an extremely precious tradition of our party and
people. All comrades, from the central committee down
to the cell, must preserve the union and unity of mind in
the party as the apple of their eyes.

On the war Ho wrote:

The resistance war against U.S. aggression may drag out.
Our compatriots may have to undergo new sacrifices in

terms of property and human lives. In any case we must
be resolved to fight against the U.S. aggressors till total
victory.

He then turned to the essential factor of Sino-Soviet support to
North Vietnam and stated:

The more I am proud to see the growth of the international
Communist and worker's movement, the more deeply I am
grieved at the dissensions that are dividing the fraternal
parties. I wish that our party will do its best to contribute
effectively to the restoration of unity among the fraternal
parties on the basis of Marxism-Leninism and proletarian
internationalism, in a way consonant to the requirements of
heart and reason.[2]

Ho Chi Minh's death precipitated a lull in the war during which
delegations of mourners arrived from both China and the Soviet Union.
The Chinese arrived first and departed within 24 hours so as to avoid
the Soviet delegation. Premier Aleksei Kosygin apparently was profoundly affected by Ho's expression of his grief at the dissensions
dividing the fraternal parties. After leaving Hanoi by air, Kosygin
backtracked to Peking to meet with Premier Chou En-lai, their first
meeting since February 1965.
    In 1965 the war in Kashmir between India and Pakistan was
brought to an end by joint Soviet and U.S. pressures directly on the
parties and through the United Nations. Premier Aleksei Kosygin
was the good officer, with U.S. blessing, in the Tashkent discussions
of January 1966 between India's Prime Minister Lal Bahadur Shastri
and Pakistan's Prime Minister Ayub Khan. Since China supported
Pakistan's ambitions, the role of the Soviet Premier was displeasing,
especially because he acted with American approval and support. This
led to a coolness that was only briefly interrupted by the plea of Ho
Chi Minh in his will. Soviet and Chinese competitive support of North
Vietnam's war efforts returned to normal coolness toward each other
while they sought advantage in Hanoi.

THE SOVIET ROLE

President Richard Nixon's move to create a détente with China
in 1972, therefore, was a massive stroke to deprive the DRV of one
of the strongest supports of its policy to defeat the Americans. More
was involved in the Nixon move with respect to China than just the
Indochina war. He ended 22 years of major U.S. policy to "contain"

China and by so doing set into motion all major and most minor pieces on the international game board, requiring a search for new foreign policy concepts and attitudes. As for the DRV, it probably seemed to the strategists in Hanoi that time was running out for them to gain control over the rest of Indochina. Their chief remaining supporter, the Soviet Union, disturbed by the implications of a China-U.S. détente, saw an opportunity to enlarge its own influence with Hanoi to the detriment of China.

President Nikolai Podgorny arrived in Hanoi on a state visit on October 3, 1971, the highest-ranking Soviet official since Premier Kosygin attended the memorial rites for President Ho Chi Minh in 1969. His visit had been announced after Peking and Washington had revealed that Nixon would visit Peking. The Podgorny delegation signed agreements with the North Vietnamese covering Soviet military and economic aid for the coming year and setting up a joint committee to work out the details. The Podgorny mission was followed shortly by a high-level Soviet military mission headed by a Marshal of the Soviet Union—and this at a time when the Soviets were cheering on the Indians in their war with Pakistan, a war displeasing to China. The Soviet military mission remained in Hanoi until almost the end of March 1972. During this period substantial Soviet military hardware was brought into North Vietnam, including tanks, long-range artillery and mobile antiaircraft missiles; some 60 of the new SA-2 missiles arrived after Nixon visited Peking in February.

On March 30, 1972, the DRV went for broke, committing 12 of her 13 divisions. Hanoi was confident that the armed forces of South Vietnam would be no match. The possibility of substantial American intervention was apparently discounted in view of the upcoming Presidential election in the United States, the strong antiwar line taken by candidate George McGovern, the war-weary sentiments of the American public, and the planned visit of President Nixon to Moscow, scheduled for May. Surely Nixon would not jeopardize his mission to Moscow. Hanoi may also have hoped that the new American détente with China would be a deterrent to more American military adventures near the China border. For these and perhaps other reasons, Hanoi felt confident that an all-out effort would probably bring a military achievement of her national goals. Once South Vietnam was taken, then Laos and Cambodia would offer only minor problems.

But, to Hanoi's shock, U.S. air and naval forces rapidly escalated their responsive strikes; and by April 16 they attacked Haiphong closely enough to damage four Soviet ships. Moscow issued a stiff protest, but President Nixon did not respond with the apology that might be expected in such a situation. He stated publicly- "Countries which supply offensive equipment to the North Vietnamese to enable them to mount an invasion of South Vietnam share responsibility."

Ordinarily Peking could be counted on to protest such developments. But at this point the American Senators Hugh Scott and Mike
Mansfield were en route to Peking on an official invitation. Even
though the heaviest bombing was going on, Peking did not cancel their
visits and in public statements said the sort of sympathetic thing that
might be expected of witnesses to a disaster in the family of an old
friend to whom little help could be given. The direction of the political
wind from Peking was felt strongly in Hanoi, and it was not favorable.

It was assumed in Washington that Peking would not oppose, and
indeed would favor, moves to frustrate DRV achievements that would
make a more powerful state if that state were made possible by Soviet
support, possibly leading to an enhanced role for the Soviets in Hanoi.
It was further assumed that China would prefer a Balkanized Indochina
with two Vietnams, a weak Laos, and a weak Cambodia. If Hanoi were
to gain control of all of Indochina, it could form one of the most powerful states in Asia—located at the soft belly of China. China had been
hurt twice before by strong alien powers in the Hanoi-Haiphong area:
first the French and then the Japanese.

President Nixon gave both Hanoi and Moscow a mind-blowing
experience on May 8, 1972, when he announced the mining of the harbors
of North Vietnam, stating that the mines would become active on May
11 and warning Moscow that it must remove its shipping before that
date or such shipping would be unable to move without great hazard.
Nixon addressed himself directly and publicly to both Hanoi and
Moscow.

To Moscow he said: "We do not ask you to sacrifice your principles or your friends. But neither should you permit Hanoi's intransigence to blot out the prospects we together have so patiently prepared. We are on the threshold of a new relationship that can serve
not only the interests of our two countries but the cause of world peace.
We are prepared to continue to build this relationship. The responsibility is yours if we fail to do so." He said, in effect, that Moscow's
national interests with the United States were more vital to Moscow
than Moscow's national interests involving North Vietnam—and that
if Moscow wasn't smart enough to understand that, then Moscow wasn't
smart enough, and that if Nixon didn't go to Moscow, it would be
Moscow's own fault.

To Hanoi President Nixon said:

Your people have already suffered too much in your pursuit
of conquest. Do not compound their agony with continued
arrogance. Choose instead the path of a peace that redeems
your sacrifices, guarantees true independence, and ushers
in an era of reconciliation.

To the people of South Vietnam Nixon said:

> You shall continue to have our firm support in your resist-
> ance against aggression. It is your spirit that will deter-
> mine the outcome of the battle. It is your will that will
> shape the future of your country.

It was significant that Nixon did not address the Thieu government but
the people.

The President addressed no words of admonition to China. His
comments to Hanoi and Moscow could not have been spoken if he had
not been confident of the substantial quality of the détente with China.
He apparently felt that he was closing an old and tired era and opening
a new and dynamic period that hinged on détente with China.

The ultimate disappointment to Hanoi with respect to Moscow's
support was administered on May 29, 1972, in Moscow, when the
American and Russian chiefs of state signed a unique document that
was a declaration of principles committing both nations to seek peaceful solutions to disputes. "They will always exercise restraint in
their mutual relations, and will be prepared to negotiate and settle
differences by peaceful means." For Hanoi the time had expired for
possible achievement of her goals by direct military means. The time
had come to turn to other means. And to begin with it would become
necessary to make concessions to the Americans so that the U.S.
involvement in the military aspects of the war could be brought to
an end.

President Nixon's concept of his achievement was reflected in
his address to the Congress on June 1 when he reported on his Moscow
adventures:

> . . . one picture will always remain indelible in our
> memory—the flag of the United States of America flying
> high in the spring breeze above Moscow's ancient Kremlin
> fortress. . . . No one would have believed, even a short
> time ago, that those two apparently irreconcilable symbols
> would be seen together as we saw them. . . .
>   The problem of ending the Vietnam war, which en-
> gages the hopes of all Americans, was one of the most
> extensively discussed subjects of our agenda . . . both the
> United States and the Soviet Union share an overriding
> desire to achieve a more stable peace in the world.

The Soviet message to Hanoi regarding the altered situation
was carried June 15, 1972, by Soviet President Nikolai V. Podgorny.
While Podgorny was en route, the White House announced that Henry

A. Kissinger would go to Peking. The implication was that as Podgorny arrived at a new understanding with Hanoi about short-range necessities and possible long-range planning, Kissinger was going to reassure Peking that the U.S.-China détente was firm and that movement could be expected shortly in the negotiations that would lead to the withdrawal of the American military presence from the Indochina war.

RENEWAL OF NEGOTIATIONS AND THE END
OF THE WAR

On June 17 the United States totally deactivated its last remaining infantry brigade in South Vietnam, officially ending its ground combat role but continuing a 100,000-man air and naval force. And on June 18 in Calcutta, after completing his Hanoi visit, President Podgorny told newsmen that negotiations would be resumed in Paris, after having been broken off by President Nixon on March 13 as fruitless. On June 29 President Nixon announced that the Paris negotiations would be renewed on July 13 "on the assumption that the North Vietnamese are prepared to negotiate in a constructive and serious way."

Henry Kissinger began to move again: August 15 to Paris—then on to Saigon. August 20 to Tokyo, to pick up other threads in the evolving Asian scene, preparing for the September 1 meeting of the new Japanese Prime Minister, Kakuei Tanaka, with President Nixon in Hawaii. Why Japan?

Japan had read the tea leaves and wanted part of the action Japan's Prime Minister went to Peking on September 25-30 and thereby abolished Japan's old China policy by establishing diplomatic relations. The way was cleared for Japan to move in on the shifting Vietnam scene, and on November 29 Prime Minister Tanaka suggested in a news conference that the nations of Asia convene a conference following an Indochina cease-fire to help maintain peace and to assist in the reconstruction of the battle zone. Japan was staking out its claim as an important power in Asia with a national interest in the nature of the peace. It was also a bid to be included in the Paris conference of concerned states to authenticate the peace that was being discussed. If the national interests of such powers as the Soviet Union, the United States, and China were to be represented, then Japan wanted to be at the peace table too.

As the American election drew near, Henry Kissinger escalated his efforts to bring about a negotiated settlement, moving between Washington, Paris, and Saigon in September and October. A four-day session in Paris, October 8-11, probably established the major lines of the final settlement. President Nguyen Van Thieu found some of the proposed language troublesome, which apparently caused Kissinger to attempt some further revisions. Hanoi's leaders attempted to end further discussion or revision on October 26 by revealing a nine-point document that they alleged had been agreed to by Kissinger, demanding that it be signed by October 31, a schedule to which they claimed Kissinger had agreed.

Renewed negotiations in December led to a stalemate, and on December 14 Kissinger returned to Washington while Le Duc Tho returned to Hanoi via Moscow and Peking. Kissinger held a press conference on December 16 at the White House and summed up the situation: "The negotiations have had the character where a settlement was always just within our reach, and was always pulled just beyond our reach when we attempted to grasp it."

Kissinger also said that the President had decided "that we could not engage in a charade with the American people. We are now in this curious position: Great progress has been made, even in the talks. The only thing that is lacking is one decision in Hanoi to settle the remaining issues in terms that two weeks previously they had already agreed to." He concluded: "As Le Duc Tho said yesterday, we will remain in contact."3

The United States resumed a major bombing campaign against all of North Vietnam on December 18 and warned that unrestricted bombing would continue until there was a peace agreement. By December 20 the raids were as heavy as any in the war. Both Moscow and Peking condemned the bombing but did so in humanitarian rather than warlike terms—as though to remark "Too bad, so sorry." The bombing was suspended on Christmas Eve but was renewed on December 27.

That day Mrs. Nguyen Thi Binh, Foreign Minister of the Communist Provisional Revolutionary Government (PRG) made a five-day visit to Peking, which matched in length her official visit to Moscow. She was met by some 4,000 Chinese youths, dancing girls, and hundreds of kindergarten children as well as high officials. The People's Daily stated: "If the U.S. government really wants to have the issue settled, it must stop all its war acts in the whole of Vietnam, conduct negotiations in a serious manner and speedily sign the agreement on ending the war and restoring peace in Vietnam." What was said to the United States was also a reminder to Mrs. Nguyen Thi Binh that the time had come to reach a settlement.

On December 30 President Nixon ordered a halt in the bombing north of the 20th parallel and Kissinger and Tho scheduled a meeting in Paris for January 8, 1973. President Nixon halted all bombing in North Vietnam on January 15 as a peace gesture.

President Nixon was sworn in for a second term on January 20, and three days later Kissinger and Le Duc Tho initialed the final accords, with formal signing scheduled for January 27 by the Foreign Ministers concerned. It was ironic that former President Lyndon

Johnson died January 23, the day the accords were initialed for ending the American involvement in the war. President Nixon made a gracious statement on January 24 regarding President Johnson:

> I remember the last time I talked with him. It was just the day after New Year's. He spoke then of his concern with bringing peace, with making it the right kind of peace, and I was grateful that he once again expressed his support for my efforts to gain such a peace. No one would have welcomed this peace more than he.[4]

The war was officially ended on January 27, 1973, with a cease-fire at 7 p.m. Secretary of State William P. Rogers and the Foreign Minister of North Vietnam, Nguyen Duy Trinh, each affixed his signature 72 times to the peace agreement and protocols dealing with the Armistice Commission, cease-fire, prisoner exchanges, and demining operations of the North Vietnam harbors. Foreign Minister Tran Van Lam for South Vietnam and Mrs. Nguyen Thi Binh for the PRG signed only the peace pact and three of the four protocols—a total of 32 signatures for each. Each document was signed in its English and Vietnamese versions with copies for each of the four parties.

THE JAPANESE ROLE

On January 27, 1973, in Tokyo, Prime Minister Kakuei Tanaka made a major policy address before the opening session of the Diet and said:

> Japan, which has great economic power, should not merely be a recipient of peace but should also participate willingly in the task of creating peace and thereby fulfill its responsibilities. . . the urgent problem facing our nation now is the contribution we can make to the firm establishment of the peace in Vietnam. . . . Japan will make utmost efforts for the rehabilitation of the Indochina peninsula. . . . International politics in Asia are of course far more complicated than those of Europe and it will not be easy to construct the basis for a new stability in this part of the world.
> But if a place for serious discussion is established and if better measures can be found to carry out the postwar reconstruction and to maintain peace on the Indochina peninsula, that peace will eventually lead to the stability of all of Asia.[5]

The Tanaka speech was a strong bid to be included in the Paris conference to be held within 30 days of the signing of the cease-fire agreement. But his comments looked beyond that conference and peace-keeping in the Indochina peninsula and was reminiscent of the proposals of Takeo Miki in 1966 for an Asian-Pacific zone, which at that point in time did not include China. As a result of the U.S. détente with China and the establishment of Japan's diplomatic relations with China, it was now possible to think in more inclusive terms.

This larger concept for Japan's role was implicit in an address, also on January 27 before the Diet, by Foreign Minister Masayoshi Ohira, who referred to the United Nations and, in speaking of the need to strengthen the United Nations in view of new political realities, implied that Japan should take its place as a major power in the Security Council. The national interests of China, Japan, the Soviet Union, and the United States were moving into new configurations as a result of the U.S. détente with China and the formal ending of the Vietnam war. Southeast Asia would form a microcosm within the macrocosm.

Henry Kissinger arrived in Hanoi on February 10, 1973, for further discussions on how to proceed to normalize relations between the two states. The two sides indicated that they welcomed the discussion between the two South Vietnamese parties for the purpose of carrying out the provisions concerning self-determination in South Vietnam. Both sides declared that "the full and scrupulous implementation of the Paris agreement on Vietnam would positively contribute to the cause of peace in Indochina and Southeast Asia on the basis of strict respect for the independence and neutrality of the countries in this region. They also agreed to establish a DRVN-USA Joint Economic Commission charged with the task of developing economic relations."

Dr. Kissinger went on February 15 to Peking, where he was received by Chairman Mao Tse-tung and Premier Chou En-lai. They reaffirmed the Shanghai communiqué of February 1972 to bring about a normalization of relations and agreed on a concrete program of establishing liaison offices in each other's capital. These offices would engage in all normal embassy activities short of formal diplomatic ones and would include programs related to trade, scientific, cultural, and other exchanges. The linkage of the visits to Hanoi and Peking was made by Dr. Kissinger in a news conference on February 22, 1973.

Although the Peking visit was second in time it was first in significance and was so treated by both Kissinger and the press. Kissinger made it clear that the substance of the détente was the two parties' movement "from hostility toward normalization." He acknowledged that he and the Chinese leaders had discussed Indochina and was asked whether the Chinese would cut off the flow of arms to Indochina. He replied:

The problem is whether the major countries now recognize
that the agreement in Vietnam gives everybody an opportunity to return that area for the first time in a generation
to a period of tranquillity and to permit the peoples of Indochina an opportunity to work out their own fate without force
and without outside pressure.

On Hanoi, Kissinger remarked:

> You have to consider that the leaders of the Democratic
> Republic of Vietnam have spent almost all of their lives
> either in prison or conducting guerrilla wars or conducting
> international wars. At no time in their lives have they had
> an opportunity to participate in a normal diplomatic rela-
> tionship with other countries, or to concentrate on the
> peaceful evolution of their country and of their region. . . .
> You should look at the economic aid program not in
> terms of a handout, and not in terms of a program even
> of reconstruction alone, but as an attempt to enable the
> leaders of North Vietnam to work together with other
> countries, and particularly with Western countries, in a
> more constructive relationship . . . the visit was part of
> an attempt to move from hostility towards normalization.
> . . .

It is significant that with respect to Hanoi Kissinger used the
exact phrase, "from hostility towards normalization," that he had used
with respect to Peking. The model was the U.S. détente with China,
which, it was hoped, might be extended with Chinese blessing to North
Vietnam.

Kissinger was asked about Japan's role in Southeast Asia and
he remarked that the United States welcomed a responsible role by
Japan in Southeast Asia: "We have no objection whatever to any
Japanese assistance program to the Democratic Republic of Vietnam
or to any other country of Indochina. Indeed we believe that this would
be a natural exercise of Japan's sense of responsibility for stability
in Asia." When asked why Japan was not invited to participate in the
international guaranteeing conference in Paris, he replied: "The
participants . . . were selected by agreement among the parties that
negotiated the agreement. We had no objection to the participation
of Japan but we could not achieve unanimity about its membership in
the conference." The implication was that the United States had supported the idea of including Japan but that Hanoi had objected.[6]

THE PARIS CONFERENCE: LAOS AND CAMBODIA

As the Paris conference drew near, the United States was reluctant to enter it while continuing to bomb heavily in Laos, a strategy that probably would be the subject of accusatory speeches by Communist delegates. Accordingly, the United States strongly urged the two sides in Laos to reach a cease-fire agreement. With less than a week's leeway the Laotian negotiators initialed a cease-fire on February 20 which was officially signed the next day by Phagna Phoumi Vongvichit for the Pathet Lao (Patriotic Forces) with headquarters at Sam Neua, and by Phagna Pheng Phongsavan for the Vientiane government. Sam Neua was one of the two provinces in northeastern Laos along the border of North Vietnam to which the fighting units of the Pathet Lao withdrew under the arrangements of the 1954 Geneva Agreements, pending general elections and reunification of Laos.

The 1973 agreement contained the following intriguing statement: "The parties concerned in Laos, the United States, Thailand and other foreign countries must strictly respect and implement this agreement." There is not even a hint at any involvement or concern by North Vietnam, nor mention of the some 65,000 North Vietnamese troops generally believed to be in Laos. The agreement went on to describe "the present reality in Laos, which has two zones under the control of two sides" that should solve their problems "on the basis of equality and mutual respect, neither side trying to swallow or oppress the other side."

What was meant by that last phrase was amplified by specifically detailing "the people's various rights and freedoms which must be absolutely respected—for example, privacy, ideology, speech, press, writing, assembly, establishing political organizations and associations, candidacy and elections, traveling, living where one wants and establishing business enterprises and ownership."

Under this agreement the Laotian cease-fire in place began in both zones on February 22, 1973. Two of its provisions were "All armed forces of foreign countries must completely and permanently cease all military movements in Laos" and "The armed forces of all sides must completely cease all military movements encroaching upon one another both on the ground and in the air." In effect the 1973 agreement was a formalizing of the status quo, with the Pathet Lao in control of most of eastern Laos, inhabited chiefly by non-Laotian peoples, while the Vientiane government was in control of the Mekong River side of Laos, containing most of the Laotian speaking people. The two sides were not only geographic and political but also ethnic.

It was further agreed that within 30 days the two sides would set up a national provisional coalition government in which the two sides would be equally represented, plus "two intellectuals who advocate peace, independence, neutrality and democracy, who will be agreed upon by both sides." The role of this provisional coalition government would be "to implement all agreements reached and the political program agreed upon by the two sides." Presumably, if the two sides could not agree on anything, the coalition government would have nothing to do.

The Laotian agreement of February 21, 1973, also provided for a National Political Coalition Council, to be composed in the same fashion as the provisional government, in equal proportions from each side plus some intellectuals satisfactory to both sides. The Council

> . . . has the responsibility to consult with and express views to the National Provisional Coalition Government on major problems relating to domestic and foreign policies and to assist the government in implementing the agreements signed, to scrutinize and endorse the . . . coalition government in holding general elections to establish the national assembly and the permanent national coalition government.

The two sides also agreed to neutralize the royal capital of Luang Prabang, where the King resides, and Vientiane, where the government resides.

Perhaps the most significant statement in the agreement was that pending the establishment of the National Assembly and the permanent national coalition government "in the spirit of Article 6 in Chapter II of the joint Zurich communiqué of 22 June, 1961, the two sides will maintain the territories under their temporary control. . . ." Thus the two sides made it finally clear that the more things seemed to change, the more they remained the same and that Laos would continue to be divided along geographic, political, and ethnic lines running roughly from north to south in a fashion that gave most of the terrain to the Communists and most of the people to the government side. The International Control Commission stemming from the 1954 Geneva Agreements would continue its usual ineffective role.

The 1973 Laotian agreement also included the following optimistic note: "The two sides acknowledge the declaration of the U.S. Government that it will contribute to healing the wounds of the war and the postwar reconstruction in Indochina. The national coalition government will hold discussions with the United States Government in connection with such a contribution regarding Laos."[7]

Most public media commented that the Pathet Lao had their way and got what they wanted. But the text of the agreement does not support that point of view. The agreement consolidated Laos into a pattern familiar since 1954, a pattern that seems satisfactory to China. The agreement should be viewed in the light of the substantial presence

of China in northern Laos along the highway constructed by Chinese
engineers and patrolled by up to 20,000 Chinese troops. The highway
ends at the River U, a small stream that has a matching highway
starting from its eastern side leading through Dien Bien Phu to Hanoi.
The Chinese highway is a political symbol of China's interest in the
nature of the Laos settlement. It would seem that a divided Laos suits
China. It also suits the United States, since Laos would then return
to its traditional role of buffer between Thai and Vietnamese, a convenience to both and a threat to neither.

Phoumi Vongvichit, who signed the Laotian agreement for the
Pathet Lao, left Vientiane a few days later to go to Sam Neua, the
Pathet Lao capital. He did not return until April 26 and accordingly
there was no movement on the various political provisions of the agree-
ment, although the cease-fire was generally observed. Phoumi said he
returned because of pressing demands by Premier Prince Souvanna
Phouma and the Central Committee of the Pathet Lao political front,
Neo Lao Hak Xat.

On February 26 the international conference on Vietnam opened
in Paris "to de-Americanize the peace," as South Vietnamese Foreign
Minister Tran Van Lam remarked. The DRV promptly tried to put
pressure on the United States to be responsible for enforcing the cease-
fire before any more prisoners of war would be released. President
Nixon jarred the conference by ordering Secretary of State Rogers to
demand satisfaction on North Vietnam's suspension of the release of
American POWs before taking up further business at the conference
that was to "guarantee" the January 27 cease-fire accord. But on
March 2 the 12 foreign ministers signed the text of a declaration
"acknowledging the signed agreements guaranteeing the ending of the
war, the maintenance of peace in Vietnam, the respect of the Vietnamese
people's fundamental national rights and the South Vietnamese people's
right to self-determination, and contributing to and guaranteeing peace
in Indochina. . . ."[8]

The Vietnam settlement was specifically extended to include Laos
and Cambodia by noting "the commitment of the parties to the agreement to respect the independence, sovereignty, unity, territorial
integrity and neutrality of Cambodia and Laos as stipulated in the
agreement of January 27, 1973 and agree also to respect them . . . and
call on other countries to do the same."

The 12 foreign ministers represented Canada, the PRC, the
United States, France, the PRG of South Vietnam, Hungary, Indonesia,
Poland, the DRV, the United Kingdom, the Republic of Vietnam and the
Soviet Union; the pact was signed in the presence of the Secretary-
General of the United Nations, who did not sign.

President Nixon held a press conference on March 3 to announce
that President Nguyen Van Thieu would visit him in California on

April 2 and to answer questions on the Paris conference declaration. Concerning Laos, Nixon focused on "the withdrawal of all foreign forces" as the key to the situation, which he felt was simpler than the Cambodian situation, in that in Laos there were clearly two sides to the political equation that could deal with each other.

On Cambodia he remarked:

> Cambodia is more complex because you don't have the governmental forces there that can negotiate with each other . . . the prospects in Cambodia are not as positive as those in Laos, but we do believe that there too, the withdrawal of the North Vietnamese forces which has been agreed to in our agreements with the North Vietnamese, from Cambodia, is the key thing. If those forces are out and if the Cambodians can then determine their own future, we believe the chances for a cease-fire in Cambodia will be very substantial.[9]

In a Telstar interview in Paris after the January 27, 1973, agreements were signed, Ambassador William Sullivan, asked about China's role in achieving the cease-fire agreement, remarked that China wanted a Balkanized Indochina with two Vietnams and independent states of Laos and Cambodia. A united Vietnam with Laos and Cambodia under its control would form one of the strongest states in Asia and might establish a role in Asian affairs inimical to that of China.

North Vietnam has an annual food grain deficit of seldom less than a million tons and a population expanding at the rate of about 600,000 a year. It imports about 15 percent of all its food and has been heavily dependent on China and the Soviet Union to make up the deficit. A united Vietnam with access to Cambodia's rich Battambang rice fields could be self-sufficient. According to Ambassador Sullivan, such a strong, united Indochina would not be to China's liking or advantage.

On the other hand, the Soviet Union encourages and fosters DRV efforts to gain control of Cambodia and South Vietnam. This is a natural extension of Soviet support to Hanoi in its massive 1972 drive south after President Nixon's visit to Peking that established the U.S. détente with China. It is part of the larger pattern of the Soviet design to encompass China and would be an extension of Soviet influence in southern Asia.

In March 1970, when Prince Sihanouk was in Paris, the Acting Prime Minister, Prince Sisowath Sirik Matak, ousted four of Sihanouk's strongest supporters from the cabinet and on March 12 sent letters to the DRV and PRG ambassadors in Phnom Penh demanding that they withdraw their forces from Cambodia by dawn March 15. The

Communist representatives met with Sirik Matak on March 17 to discuss the subject and offered the same deal that they had had with Sihanouk: to become less visible in their use of eastern Cambodia, to permit Cambodian officials to administer or at least to appear to administer the eastern and especially the northeastern provinces without molestation, and to support the principle of Cambodia's neutrality. Cambodia's neutrality had just been reaffirmed by Sihanouk in Paris on March 12, 1970, as he appealed to both Moscow and Peking to restrain and diminish the Communist forces making use of Cambodia in their movements against South Vietnam. Sirik Matak rejected the offer and the same day, March 17, some 30,000 Cambodian youths marched to demand the withdrawal of Communist troops from Cambodia. The DRV and PRG embassies withdrew on March 26 from Phnom Penh.

China also withdrew her embassy and broke diplomatic relations, providing haven for Sihanouk's Government of National Union, which he announced from Peking on May 6, 1970, along with the formation of a National Liberation Army and a Consultative Assembly of peasants, workers, youths, soldiers, and other "anti-imperialist" elements who would form the National United Front of Cambodia.

The Soviet Premier, Aleksei N. Kosygin, on the other hand, declared "Soviet sympathy and support" for Sihanouk's new government and wished it well but, unlike China, did not extend diplomatic recognition to it and continued to maintain the Soviet embassy in Phnom Penh, recognizing the Lon Nol government. On May 18, 1970, Pravda accused the Chinese of blocking a united Communist response on Cambodia and of provoking conflicts between the Vietnamese Communists and the Soviet Union, even attacking Mao Tse-tung by name. China has refused the Soviet Union overflight rights and the use of key air bases in China to carry supplies to Hanoi.

What the DRV and PRG representatives sought to preserve in 1970 in Cambodia is probably what they are seeking to obtain in 1973, taking advantage of the differences between Lon Nol and other Cambodian political elements. The Sihanouk element is playing a difficult role between China's interest to keep Indochina Balkanized and Hanoi's ambition to gain control of Cambodia and South Vietnam. This role is complicated by the original Khmer Rouge, or Communist element, which does not forget that Sihanouk used to hunt it down and execute its members. It is probably the best-led, best-trained, and best-equipped insurgent force and is heavily indebted to Hanoi and Moscow for its training and equipment.

There are also other so-called Khmer Rouge groups, splinter political elements, that help keep the political situation in Cambodia in disarray but are not substantially effective. It is probably the original Khmer Rouge, hard-core Communists, who do most of the fighting, with advisers from Hanoi.

In sum, Hanoi and Moscow are in favor of the "original" Khmer Rouge; China favors Sihanouk because of his past record of stubborn opposition to external forces in his country; the United States would prefer an effective coalition government of non-Communists—currently Lon Nol, Sirik Matak, Cheng Heng, and In Tam, the group that overthrew Sihanouk in 1970 and met together in a High Political Council on April 24, 1973, to unite all political factions.

THE U.S. ROLE

Henry Kissinger set forth a major new policy line with respect to Europe on April 23, 1973, at the annual meeting of the American Newspaper Publishers Association. He was questioned on Indochina and remarked that the cease-fire agreement had been "systematically, not to say cynically, violated by the other side." He insisted that "No one can think we are looking for a pretext to remain involved in Southeast Asia." Asked about the possible role of Prince Norodom Sihanouk, Kissinger suggested that the United States was prepared for him to play a significant role if he was capable of doing so.

Kissinger then said, "The profound problem we face as a nation today is whether we should sign an agreement and when it is totally violated act as if the signature which was then endorsed by an international conference, should simply be treated as irrelevant." He indicated that the administration would not permit transgressions to continue without an American response but asked rhetorically what the United States should do "if we can neither threaten nor offer incentives."[10]

This, however, is not the question. The question is whether the United States should make itself responsible for keeping the peace in a parochial situation in which its national interest is not involved, since the Paris agreements ended the Indochina war as a proxy war in which the United States confronted the Soviet Union and China. The nature of the situation has changed.

The Indochina parties are engaged in a perennial and historic struggle for power among themselves. Indochinese politicians are reverting to patterns familiar to their predecessors before the colonial interlude when Laos and Cambodia were vassal or client areas to Thai and Vietnamese. Parochial politics are complicated now, however, by the differences between Moscow and Peking and their respective efforts to secure additional major sympathy and support. Thus Japan and the United States have become important if not vital factors to be influenced if not manipulated.

China would like to be sure of American support in keeping Indochina Balkanized. The Soviet Union would like to circumvent the

Americans and cheer on Hanoi's adventurers. Both the Soviet Union and China view Japan as an imponderable factor of known economic substance but unknown political weight. Japan's ambivalent political position was reflected in the DRV veto of its desire to be included in the Paris guaranteeing conference.

The White House announced on April 25 that Kissinger and Le Duc Tho would meet again in Paris in mid-May to discuss ways to make the truce effective and that Ambassador William Sullivan, Deputy Assistant Secretary for East Asian Affairs, would meet with Nguyen Co Thach, Deputy Minister for Foreign Affairs of the DRV, in Paris on April 26 for preliminary talks to determine the agenda for Kissinger and Le Duc Tho. North Vietnamese hinted that any progress in the talks would depend on American renewal of discussions on economic aid to North Vietnam and the removal of all mines from her harbors.

On June 13 a 2,500-word communiqué was issued in Paris; it contained 14 points that reflected the areas of concurrence between the United States, the DRV the PRG, and the Republic of Vietnam. The thrust of this supplementary agreement was to achieve a cease-fire throughout Indochina. However, the only reference to Laos and Cambodia was that Article 20 of the earlier agreement should be scrupulously implemented, requiring a cease-fire. Kissinger acknowledged in a press conference that no easy solution was seen for Cambodia and that the United States was not committed to cease bombing there. The United States did commit itself to cease air reconnaissance over North Vietnam and to renew minesweeping and discussions regarding economic assistance. It seemed that the four parties had met to reaffirm the January 27 cease-fire accord.

The problem for the United States is to determine what else, if anything, needs to be done with respect to Indochina in support of China's desires to keep the area Balkanized and to frustrate Hanoi's ambition to unite the area under its control. Perhaps the Brezhnev-Nixon summit meetings in Washington beginning June 16, which by June 21 had resulted in some six agreements, during which Brezhnev declared that he regarded the development of long-term trade relations with the United States to be a major objective. This was a blow to Hanoi, which saw its strongest ally dallying with the United States, its arch foe. At any rate, if it were not for the U.S. détente with China, there would be no further national American interest in an otherwise local Indochina situation.

NOTES

1. Washington Post, Nov. 22, 1967.
2. Ibid., Sept. 10, 1969.

3. Department of State News release, Dec. 16, 1972.
4. Washington <u>Evening Star</u>, Jan. 24, 1973.
5. New York <u>Times</u>, Jan. 28, 1973.
6. Department of State news release, Feb. 27, 1973.
7. New York <u>Times</u>, Feb. 22, 1973.
8. Ibid., Mar. 3, 1973.
9. Ibid., Mar. 4, 1973.
10. Ibid., Apr. 24, 1973.

12

CHINA AND AMERICA:
LIMITED PARTNERS IN
THE INDIAN SUBCONTINENT
William J. Barnds

The July 15, 1971, announcement by the United States and China that Henry Kissinger had spent several days in Peking early that month, and that President Nixon would visit China, eliminated one of the few fixed points on the international scene that had withstood the pressures for change during the 1960s. Bipolarity began to erode after the rise of the Sino-Soviet dispute at the end of the 1950s, but it required more than 10 years for the United States and China to surmount their ideological differences and correct their mutual misperceptions so that the process of accommodation could begin. Now the period of bitter and often unreasoning hostility of these two major powers, one of the key elements in the pattern of world politics for two decades, was drawing to a close. China (soon to take its seat at the United Nations) was no longer the isolated nation it had been in the days of the Cultural Revolution, and President Nixon's earlier assertion that the world was moving from an era of confrontation to one of negotiation was coming to represent reality as well as rhetoric.

Political leaders around the world were stunned by the speed of reconciliation and puzzled about the implications of the Sino-American détente. Preoccupation with their own interests led all of them to be concerned primarily with its meaning for themselves and their own nations. Some went further and interpreted the new turn of events as a move directed against their countries. The Soviet Union and India were in this latter category—Moscow with good reason, New Delhi less so. Moscow could hardly object to a normalization of relations between the United States and China without undermining its claim that it favored reduced tensions and more friendly contacts between nations. Yet the secrecy surrounding the visit and the fears harbored by Soviet leaders regarding American and Chinese motives made them suspicious that their two principal adversaries were motivated more by anti-Soviet considerations than by a desire to improve the outlook for international peace.

The situation called for caution, lest a dangerous mistake be made before the new turn of events could be soberly appraised. At the same time the Soviet leaders were aware that prolonged inaction could be harmful, for it would confirm that the initiative in world affairs lay elsewhere than in Moscow and would give Washington and Peking time for further moves. The obvious place for a riposte was the Indian subcontinent, then caught up in its greatest upheaval since the departure of the British a quarter-century earlier.

The dramatic shift in Sino-American relations would have presented New Delhi with difficult problems in any circumstances, in view of Chinese and Pakistani animosity toward India and their mutual cooperation. The fact that Pakistan had played an important role in fostering Sino-American contacts added an ominous note to the situation and led many Indians to discern the establishment of a Sino-American-Pakistani axis profoundly inimical to Indian interests. And the acuteness of Indian fears was magnified by the dangers and burdens growing out of the civil war in Pakistan. The insistence of the Bengalis of East Pakistan that they could control their own destiny only by winning a degree of provincial autonomy bordering on independence was matched by the determination of the West Pakistanis to preserve the country's territorial integrity by whatever means were necessary. The ensuing conflict had sent millions of refugees (largely Hindu) streaming into eastern India, already one of the most troubled areas in the country. Military action could hardly be ruled out by Indian leaders, but a resort to arms would carry unacceptable risks unless New Delhi secured the support of a major power that could neutralize Chinese and American support—however extensive that might prove to be—of Pakistan.

Thus immediate necessity as well as long-term calculations pushed India toward the Soviet Union. Similarly, Moscow's short-run desire to respond to the new relationship between Washington and Peking and its longer-term goal of sponsoring a collective security system in Asia also argued for a closer tie to India. These overlapping interests led to the signing of a 20-year treaty of peace, friendship, and cooperation on August 9 and to a sharply increased flow of Soviet arms to India.

When war came to the subcontinent in November, Soviet support proved its value to India. Soviet vetoes prevented the UN Security Council from approving any resolution critical of India while the latter quickly brought to bear its superior military power to defeat Pakistan's military forces in East Bengal, thereby bringing independence to Bangladesh and enabling India to send the refugees back to their homes. The large Soviet army on China's northern border clinched Peking's

227

desire to proceed cautiously, and America's ill-considered resort to gunboat diplomacy by sending a carrier task force into the Bay of Bengal infuriated India even while coming too late to prevent the dismemberment of Pakistan. India and Bangladesh were euphoric, Pakistan was shaken and embittered, and the Soviet Union basked in the glow of its greatest victory in the subcontinent since the post-Stalin leaders had discarded his active hostility to bourgeois nationalist governments.

But euphoria is seldom lasting in the affairs of nations. However satisfied Indian leaders were by their ability to counter the immediate challenge posed by the dramatic shift in Sino-American relations, they soon faced the necessity of evaluating and responding to its long-term implications. When the Kissinger visit to Peking was announced, Foreign Minister Sadar Swaran Singh had told Parliament, "While we welcome a rapprochement between Peking and Washington, we cannot look upon it with equanimity if it means domination of the two countries over this region."[1] How real was such a danger in terms of either the plans or the capabilities of Chinese and American leaders? Were the two countries committed to a policy of rebuilding Pakistani strength—and attempting to disrupt India's relations with Bangladesh—so as to check Indian power, or would their unsuccessful attempt to preserve Pakistan give way to acceptance of the "new realities" (as defined by India) in the subcontinent? How much influence could India have on the course that China and America chose? Should New Delhi move closer to Moscow as it only consistent and reliable friend, or would a discreet loosening of Indo-Soviet ties reduce Chinese and American animosity? And—perhaps most important of all—could New Delhi take advantage of its enhanced position vis-à-vis Pakistan to pressure or induce the latter to reach a settlement with India, thereby greatly reducing the scope for involvement by external powers in the affairs of South Asia?

President Zulfikar Ali Bhutto, who had acquired the tattered remnants of power after the debacle brought about by Pakistan's military rulers, had to ask similar questions. Did Pakistan have any choice but to accept a subordinate role to India in the subcontinent? How much support could he count on from the United States and China, and under what circumstances? Was the Soviet Union completely committed to India, or would Moscow respond favorably to Pakistan if it did not rely too heavily on Washington and Peking? And the new and inexperienced rulers of Bangladesh had to ask themselves how much support they could expect from their friends—India and the Soviet Union—as well as how firm and lasting was the opposition they faced from the United States and China.

The leaders of all three countries recognized that their judgments had to be based upon the new constellation of international politics that

was evolving. However, their judgments were inevitably influenced
by their experiences with Washington and Peking during the height of
the Cold War, and especially in the months immediately following the
Sino-American rapprochement. The same was true of American and
Chinese leaders, for it is easy to overlook the fact that they had been
forced by events to become involved in the South Asian crisis before
they had had time to think through the logical implications of their new
relationship for their respective policies in the subcontinent. (Decisions made under the pressure of unexpected events are sometimes
more revealing of official thinking than carefully formulated policy
statements—as with the U.S. decision to intervene in Korea in June
1950—but this is hardly a universal phenomenon.) Thus a short examination of the earlier patterns of Chinese and American relations with
the subcontinent is essential to any appraisal of the impact of the
Sino-American détente on South Asia.

THE COMPLEX LEGACY OF THE COLD WAR

U.S. policy toward the subcontinent has gone through several
distinct phases. These shifts in American policy to a degree grew
out of the changing conditions in the area and the differing perceptions
of particular U.S. administrations. More fundamentally, however,
they reflected the fact that American leaders made decisions affecting
South Asia primarily on the basis of changing ideas of how their policies
toward the subcontinent would affect the central concerns of U.S. foreign policy—balancing Soviet and Chinese power and maintaining close
relations with Western Europe and Japan. The secondary role of
South Asia in American (as well as Soviet and Chinese) calculations
was partially obscured during much of the Cold War, for the stalemates
in Europe and in East Asia after the early 1950s led the major powers
to shift the focus of their competition to the Afro-Asian world in the
hope of besting their adversaries by scoring decisive victories in these
newly independent countries. Such unrealistic hopes were based upon
equally unrealistic fears that the Cold War would be won or lost in the
Third World—then regarded as much more cohesive and homogeneous
than proved to be the case. But the statemen who had witnessed such
unprecedented upheavals as World War II and the end of European
colonialism were conditioned against excluding anything from the
realm of possibility.

Therefore the United States began its policy of seeking military
allies in Asia in order to contain Communist power. Pakistan, in
serious economic trouble and seeking status and security against its
much larger neighbor—as well as control of the disputed state of
Kashmir—responded to the American quest for allies with an alacrity

that surprised and infuriated New Delhi. Unable to prevent the Pakistan-American alliance—which upset what India regarded as the natural order of things in the subcontinent—New Delhi responded by moving closer to both the Soviet Union and China. During this phase of Indo-American hostility it appeared that a relatively clear-cut polarization would result, with Pakistan and the United States lined up against India, the Soviet Union, and China. Yet this never came about, and U.S. policy shifted slowly but perceptibly toward a rapprochement with India. America's desire for political stability and economic progress in Asia gave it a shared interest with India; and however annoying Nehru's nonalignment policy was to the United States, it made India reluctant to move too close to the Communist powers.

The simultaneous development of the Sino-Soviet and Sino-Indian conflicts inaugurated a new and more complex pattern of relationships involving the subcontinent, and brought about the third phase of U.S. policy. Throughout the first half of the 1960s there was growing American apprehension about Chinese "expansionism," which made support for a nonaligned India locked in a bitter dispute with China at least as important as maintaining the alliance with Pakistan. Active U.S. military support of both India and Pakistan, combined with a continuing attempt to persuade them to settle their quarrel with each other so they could jointly attend to the defense of the subcontinent, marked this phase of the American involvement. But just as the United States was unwilling to cut its links with Pakistan in the early 1960s, Indian willingness to cooperate closely with the United States was accompanied by New Delhi's determination to maintain good relations with the Soviet Union—much to American consternation. Nehru saw Soviet rivalry with China as offering India its most lasting hope of being able to deal with both China and Pakistan from a position of strength.

Pakistan's inability to persuade the United States to make its aid to India conditional upon an Indian compromise on Kashmir led first to frustration and then to anger at America. It also led Pakistan and China to draw closer together out of a shared animosity toward India.[2] Fearing that the balance of power in the subcontinent was shifting even more in India's favor, President Muhammad Ayub Khan began his policy of "leaning on India." This hardened rather than softened India's position; and Pakistan attempted to spark a guerilla uprising in Kashmir, which led step by step to the Indo-Pakistan war of 1965. The war brought home to the American government the futility of arming two such hostile countries. Arms aid was quickly halted and economic aid suspended. On September 8 Secretary of State Dean Rusk told Congress:

. . . we cannot be in a position of financing a war in these countries against each other. Nor can we be in a position

230

of using aid under circumstances where the purpose of
the aid is frustrated by the fighting itself. . . .

Our problem has been, and obviously we have not
succeeded, to pursue policies with India and Pakistan
related to matters outside the subcontinent and at the
same time try not to contribute to the clash between the
two within the subcontinent.[3]

Once the war was ended and the two countries—aided by Premier
Aleksei Kosygin at Tashkent—moved down toward their normal level
of hostility, the United States adopted a policy of "evenhandedness."
American frustration with developments in the subcontinent, a growing
recognition that the intense nationalism of such states as India and
Pakistan limited the dangers involved in their links with Communist
countries, and American preoccupation with Vietnam all led to a
partial disengagement. This was to last until 1970. When the policy
of evenhandedness gave way to a new move closer to Pakistan, it did
so far reasons external to the subcontinent. But this was unknown to
India at the time, and the 1970 announcement that the United States
was willing to sell modest quantities of arms to Pakistan was interpreted as a reflection of President Nixon's inexplicable but known
preference for Pakistan rather than as a reward for its services on
a larger issue.

By the last years of the 1960s both Peking and Washington were
coming to realize that their mutual hostility provided the Soviet Union
with an advantage that neither China nor America could afford. Yet
neither could be sure that the faint signals sent out by the other were
to be taken seriously without more extended probing, which initially
required great secrecy. Pakistan, which had managed the remarkable
feat of remaining on good terms with the two hostile powers, now
demonstrated its ability to serve as the go-between for them. This
enhanced its value to both countries, led the United States to move
closer to Pakistan, and was an element behind the American "tilt" in
Pakistan's favor during the upheaval in Bangladesh in 1971. If events
had not moved full circle, they had evolved in a manner that indicated
that Pakistan retained some importance to the United States as well
as to China.

A review of Chinese policy toward the subcontinent reveals far
fewer twists and turns than does American policy. This probably
reflects the necessity China has felt, as a state bordering the area,
to be guided primarily by the direct and fundamental interests it has
there, particularly maintaining its control over the troublesome area
of Tibet and securing Indian acceptance of borders satisfactory to
China.

Peking thought it had secured Indian acquiescence of the Chinese claim of sovereignty over Tibet by the Sino-Indian treaty of 1954, which not only abolished the special rights India inherited from British India but also inaugurated the period of the Five Principles of Peaceful Coexistence (Panch Sheel). The Indian reaction to the Tibetan revolt in 1959—permitting the refugees, especially the Dalai Lama, to enter India—and its unwillingness to accept Chinese proposals for a compromise border settlement not only led, step by step, to the 1962 Sino-Indian border war but also caused Peking to suspect that India did not really accept Chinese control of Tibet. The Soviet position in the dispute—first neutrality and then support of India—turned Chinese suspicions into a firm belief that the Soviet Union (as well as the United States) was working with New Delhi to develop a new and more ominous variant of containment directed against China.

Cooperation with Pakistan was the classic response for a state in China's position, and this was made easier because Peking had never taken umbrage at Pakistan's links with the West. Chinese saber-rattling during the 1965 Indo-Pakistan war probably had little effect on the ultimate stalemate, but it led many Pakistanis to conclude that China was a reliable friend. Peking's uniquely careful treatment of Pakistan during the Cultural Revolution confirmed this Pakistani belief. Thus a rapprochement between China and America, the two major powers most friendly to Pakistan, could only be regarded as great gain by that country's leaders. Conversely, Indian leaders would have been apprehensive about the implications of a Sino-American rapprochement in any circumstances, but their fears were increased by its coming to fruition at a critical juncture for India and by the similar Chinese and American responses to the crisis in the subcontinent.

THE IMPACT OF THE DÉTENTE

Chinese and American leaders were convinced of the value of a less hostile relationship by 1969, but it was not until mid-1971 that they had probed each other's positions sufficiently to warrant the Kissinger trip to Peking. By this time South Asia was in turmoil. President Yahya Khan's troops were ravaging East Bengal "in the name of God and a united Pakistan" but were proving unable to win a quick victory over the determined Bengalis. Indian opinion was inflamed and demanding that New Delhi force Pakistan's military rulers to reach an accommodation with the East Bengalis and permit the return of the refugees, who threatened to become a permanent and unsupportable burden if Pakistani troops crushed or even contained the rebellion.

232

If Pakistan's rulers were in a desperate position, Indian leaders were hardly in an enviable one. When the civil war had broken out in March, the Soviet Union pulled back from its already faltering effort to forge closer relations with Pakistan. President Podgorny sent a letter to Yahya on April 3 (which was promptly published in the Soviet press), calling on Pakistan to end the "bloodshed and repression" and to negotiate a peaceful settlement with the Awami League leaders, who had "received such convincing support by the overwhelming majority" in the December 1970 national elections.[4] But Moscow was not ready to write off Pakistan, and proceeded with considerable caution. Pakistan's attempt to preserve its national integrity won widespread understanding and support in Asia and Africa, especially among Muslim nations. Therefore the Soviet Union continued to call for a settlement acceptable to the "entire people" of Pakistan, which left India uncertain about the extent of Soviet support it could expect.

China's stance added to India's anxiety, for Peking passed up the opportunity to back the Bengalis in an effort to turn an ethnic and cultural struggle into a war of national liberation. Regarding India as the main enemy within the subcontinent, it supported the conservative West Pakistani regime because of its hostility to India. Chou En-lai sent a note to Yahya on April 11 attacking India, the Soviet Union, and the United States for interfering in Pakistani affairs, and China promptly publicized its position in the People's Daily.[5] Perhaps China's conviction that India was in collusion with the United States and the Soviet Union continued, or perhaps Chou En-lai was signaling the United States that its position on the South Asian crisis would be viewed as a test of Washington's earnestness in seeking a new relationship with China. The United States, already at odds with Peking over American ties with Japan and Taiwan, U.S. involvement in Vietnam, and policy toward the Soviet Union, apparently believed it was important that it find some common ground with China.

However, it should be noted that China carefully qualified its support of Pakistan, a policy it continued throughout the crisis. Chou's letter to Yahya stated: "Should the Indian expansionists dare launch aggression against Pakistan, the Chinese government and people will, as always, fully support the Pakistan Government and people in the just struggle to safeguard state sovereignty and national independence."[6] But what would full support involve? Chinese military aid continued, but even when Zulfikar Ali Bhutto went to Peking to seek help as the crisis approached its climax in November, the Chinese remained cautious. China's unwillingness to guarantee Pakistan's territorial integrity was a bitter disappointment to a government trying desperately to hold on to East Pakistan as well as to preserve the independence of West Pakistan if war came. And while Peking did not say so during the civil war in Pakistan, once the issue had been settled, a People's Daily editorial used the tactful device of quoting an unnamed Pakistani as saying that the Pakistani government had made mistakes and very serious mistakes indeed in the past in handling the question of East Pakistan.[7] Peking's choice during 1971 had not been an easy one for a nation that had just emerged from a massive effort by Mao Tse-tung to reestablish the priority of revolutionary ideology over pragmatic considerations.

In any case, it soon became clear that Peking had little need to fear Soviet-American collusion, but that New Delhi had reason to be apprehensive about U.S. policy. The United States had halted most of its arms sales to Pakistan when the civil war began, but it refused to end all of its assistance or to denounce Yahya's resort to force. Even had Washington not been friendly toward Pakistan, a Sino-American rapprochement would have convinced India that it had little hope of active U.S. support if China intervened in a new Indo-Pakistani war. Kissinger had attempted simultaneously to reassure and warn Indian leaders when he stopped in New Delhi just before his secret visit to Peking. He told them that India would have U.S. support in the event of an unprovoked Chinese attack, but he also attempted to restrain New Delhi by cautioning it that India should not expect such support if Chinese military involvement came about as a result of any Indian military move against Pakistan. Once Kissinger's visit to Peking became public, India discounted his reassurance and focused on his warning. Although New Delhi thought its extensive military buildup since the 1962 war gave it the ability to face China, it wanted reliable great-power support to deter Peking rather than risk a two-front war. With Soviet and Indian leaders alike apprehensive of Sino-American collusion, they quickly moved to firm up and formalize their ties by signing a 20-year Indo-Soviet pact.[8]

New Delhi claimed that this pact had been under consideration for two years—perhaps a reference to discussions about Leonid Brezhnev's 1969 collective security proposal for Asia, which New Delhi would not accept but could hardly refuse to discuss.[9] Yet the timing was obviously influenced by the Sino-American rapprochement and the growing crisis in the subcontinent. Although it was not quite a military alliance—neither party was obligated to come to the aid of the other in the event of a war—Article 9 stated that neither party would provide any assistance to a power engaged in armed conflict with either signatory. Moreover, there probably were implicit as well as explicit commitments beyond this. Sharply increased Soviet arms shipments to India in the following months suggest as much, and the two parties may have reached an understanding that the Soviet Union would take some action against China if the latter became involved in a new Indo-Pakistani war. This probably was not clearly spelled out; Soviet caution continued until the outbreak of war, and

Moscow would have been extremely reluctant to lose the power of decision. But India (long the focal point of the Soviet effort in South Asia) needed help, and Pakistan and China needed a warning. Perhaps Soviet leaders also felt they could exert restraint more successfully on New Delhi if they provided it with a sense of security and support.

Surprisingly, both Peking and Washington reacted calmly—indeed, almost with indifference—to the Indo-Soviet pact, perhaps seeing in it nothing more than the formalization of already existing links between Moscow and New Delhi. But apathy was replaced by anxiety in Washington as the autumn wore on and the Indian voices urging military action grew louder. Prime Minister Indira Gandhi parried these for a time, following her own timetable; but with the refugee influx continuing and the approach of winter rendering any Chinese military moves through the Himalayan passes difficult, the danger of war within the subcontinent steadily increased. Mrs. Gandhi visited Washington in November. This was partly a last effort to persuade the United States to put heavy pressure on Yahya to reach an accommodation with the Bengalis but probably was also an attempt to secure U.S. acquiescence, however reluctant, to an Indian military move if this proved necessary.

However, the visit went poorly, as have so many of the meetings between American Presidents and Indian Prime Ministers. The United States did cut off all arms shipments to Pakistan just before Mrs. Gandhi's arrival but insisted that the preservation of international peace must have top priority in South Asia. The United States assured Mrs. Gandhi that it was making progress in convincing Yahya Khan that extensive provincial autonomy for East Pakistan was necessary and said that such an outcome was likely in time. But the leisurely American timetable of a year or two alarmed rather than reassured India, which feared that the refugees would never return if they stayed that long. (Yahya's indications that only the Muslim refugees—a small percentage of the total—could return had heightened Indian concern.) Whereas Pakistan had earlier resisted American efforts to involve the international community in the affair lest its freedom of action be limited, its growing desperation and fear of Indian military action made it more amenable to such measures. Conversely, India's earlier efforts to involve outside powers gave way to an opposition to such proposals as stationing UN border observers between the two countries once New Delhi moved toward a military solution.

Thus when India's stepped-up military pressure along the East Pakistan border sparked Pakistani air strikes against western India in November, India and the United States were once again working at cross purposes. The United States attacked India as bearing the "major responsibility" for the war, cut off its aid to India, and took the lead in the UN to try to halt the war. According to the Anderson papers, the Nixon administration believed that India not only intended to liberate East Pakistan but to destroy West Pakistan as well, which led to the sending of a carrier task force into the Bay of Bengal.[10] Peking did little beyond berating India and the Soviet Union in the UN, but the similarity of American and Chinese policies strengthened Indian and Soviet suspicions that the two were working in collusion. Indo-American relations quickly plummeted to their lowest ebb, and the faint signs of a thaw in Sino-Indian relations gave way to renewed hostility.

THE SUBCONTINENT IN CHINESE AND AMERICAN PERSPECTIVE

Interpreting the past is only slightly less perilous than predicting the future, and much remains unclear about the motivations of Chinese and American policies in the subcontinent—particularly during the fast-moving events of 1971. Yet enough is known to provide some understanding of them and their aftermath. Such an understanding should furnish some notion of the likely impact that the history of recent decades will have on the minds of the peoples and leaders of the nations involved in South Asia as they decide their future course.

The absence of specific and immediate U.S. interests of any great significance in South Asia gives the United States greater freedom than either the Soviet Union or China to formulate its policies toward the subcontinent on the basis of its conception of international order and the needs of the larger balance of power. In the words of a British observer:

> . . . the United States is more or less unrestricted by permanent geographical factors of the kind which have a profound effect upon the attitudes and interests of the "continental" Asian great powers. . . .
> We might, in effect, say that American policy is free to be guided by considerations which need have no relevance to the actual situation in the subcontinent or to the interests of the subcontinental powers as they understand them—much as British policy in Europe at different times in the 19th century enjoyed the same freedom.[11]

This does not mean that only cosmic considerations went into the making of American policy during 1971. President Nixon's preference for (West) Pakistanis and dislike of Indians must be taken into account. This attitude is not untypical of occupants of the White House

(American Presidents and members of the Nehru family had seldom gotten along well) but is particularly strong in the case of President Nixon. Even the most hardheaded advocates of "realism" form their concepts of the national interest on the basis of emotional as well as rational considerations. (It is interesting that the Chinese often express a scorn for the Indians that is more personal than their attacks on other enemies.)

Nonetheless, it would be a mistake to attribute the administration's "tilt" toward Pakistan to nothing more than personal whims; the latter affected the degree rather than the direction of American policy. Nor were concerns involving Pakistan's territorial unity and integrity or the balance of power within the subcontinent primary considerations. The fate of an ally (even a nominal one, as Pakistan had become) is seldom a matter of indifference, for allowing it to go down to defeat carries some political costs even when the alliance (which covered only aggression by a Communist power) is a limited one. But when it became clear that the Pakistani government could not quickly put down the uprising in East Bengal, the administration apparently saw the birth of Bangladesh as inevitable, although it hoped that the birth would be peaceful and gradual—a forlorn hope in the midst of such turmoil. In fact, a concern for the impact of the upheaval upon Indian stability (a matter on which China and the United States saw themselves as having quite different interests) probably led the United States to see some merit in a new political arrangement, although it was obviously concerned about how the new nation ("an international basket case") would manage.

Nor does concern for the balance of power within the subconti-nent—wanting a Pakistan strong enough to be able to counter India— provide more than a partial explanation. The Nixon administration had made no secret of its belief that South Asia occupied a subordinate role in its calculations, and thus the balance of power within such an area is important only insofar as it affects the larger world balance. Therefore, while a strong (West) Pakistan is of considerable direct importance to Peking as a counter to India as long as Sino-Indian enmity persists, the United States has no specific quarrel with India that requires close U.S.-Pakistani ties.

Much of the attention devoted to the Nixon-Kissinger realpolitik approach to world politics has focused upon the method (the manipu-lation of the balance of power) and neglected to give much weight to the goal (the concept of world order). In a revealing essay written shortly before he joined the government, Kissinger stated, "The greatest need of the contemporary international system is an agreed concept of order."[12] President Nixon's Foreign Policy Report for 1971 revealed the administration's concern with both stability and balance:

We will try to keep our activities in the area in balance with those of the other major powers concerned. The policy of the Soviet Union appears to be aimed at creating a compatible area of stability on its southern borders, and at countering Chinese Communist influence. The People's Republic of China, for its part, has made a major effort to build a strong relationship with Pakistan. We will do nothing to harm legitimate Soviet and Chinese interests in the area. We are equally clear, however, that no outside power has a claim to a predominant influence, and that each can serve its own interests and the interests of South Asia best by conducting its activities in the region accordingly.[13]

President Nixon's Foreign Policy Report for 1972 spells out his general approach more fully, claiming that the United States took the position it did during the 1971 Indo-Pakistan war because of an overriding interest in a world order where disputes are settled according to the principles of the UN and of international law. In Nixon's view the larger and more powerful nations must accept a special responsibility in time of crisis to act in a restrained manner—not to attempt to take undue advantage of local opportunities to advance their immediate interests—if the system is to work.

The global implications of this war were clear to the world community. The resort to military solutions, if accepted, would only tempt other nations in other delicately poised regions of tension to try the same. The credibility of international efforts to promote or guarantee regional peace in strife-torn regions would be undermined. The danger of war in the Middle East, in particular, would be measurably increased. . . .
Beyond this, there were implications for great-power relations. . . .
The United States, under the Nixon Doctrine, has struck a new balance between our international commitments and the increasing self-reliance of our friends; the Soviet Union in the 1970s is projecting a political and military presence without precedent into many new regions of the globe. Over the past three years, we have sought to encourage constructive trends in U.S.-Soviet relations. It would be dangerous to world peace if our efforts to promote a détente between the superpowers were interpreted as an opportunity for the strategic expansion of Soviet power. If we had failed

to take a stand, such an interpretation could only have
been encouraged, and the genuine relaxation of tensions
we have been seeking could have been jeopardized.[14]

Statesmen throughout history have, of course, tried to ennoble
their most ignoble deeds by claiming lofty motivations for their actions.
Only the naive could fail to see that the President's words involve
rhetoric designed partly for domestic consumption—and that they are
not consistent with some of the actions of the Nixon administration in
other areas of the world. But it would be a mistake to think these
ideas have no validity in the eyes of U.S. leaders. The administration
feared that India (backed by the Soviet Union) was about to destroy
West Pakistan as well as liberate East Pakistan. At a National Security Council meeting early in December, Kissinger reportedly said,
"We must consider what would be the import of the current situation
in the larger context of world affairs. . . . What we may be witnessing
is a situation wherein a country [India] equipped and supported by the
Soviets, may be turning half of Pakistan into an impotent state and the
other half into a vassal. . . . Can we allow the Indians (and by implication the Soviets) to scare us off?"[15] And the President's 1972 Foreign Policy Report states that on December 6 the U.S. government
received

> . . . convincing evidence that India was seriously con-
> templating the seizure of Pakistani-held portions of
> Kashmir and the destruction of Pakistan's military
> forces in the West. . . . Acquiescence had ominous
> implications for the survival of Pakistan, for the sta-
> bility of many other countries in the world, for the
> integrity of international processes for keeping the
> peace, and for relations among the great powers. . . .[16]

Such concerns led to Kissinger's press background meeting at
the height of the struggle, at which he suggested that the President
might cancel his trip to Moscow if the Soviet did not restrain itself—
and India. This was widely regarded as a bluff, for it seemed unlikely
that Nixon would sacrifice his major interest in visiting Moscow
(especially in an election year) for a secondary matter. Nonetheless,
President Nixon continued to insist that the United States had pursued
the right course. He claimed that U.S. pressure on Moscow had led
the Soviets to insist that India refrain from invading West Pakistan
and that New Delhi had complied— charges that Mrs. Gandhi indignantly
rejected.

New Delhi was tempted to destroy the Pakistani army in the
West, but there were weighty reasons against such a move. Destroying

the Pakistani forces in the West would have necessitated taking considerable territory, which any Indian government would have faced enormous pressure not to return. New Delhi also knew how difficult assimilation of the millions of bitter Muslims would have been. And if West Pakistan had disintegrated, New Delhi would have faced chaos on its west flank at the same time that it acquired the responsibility for setting a war-ravaged Bangladesh on its feet. Soviet leaders may have stressed these dangers, for Moscow wanted to prevent complete chaos and did not want to permanently alienate West Pakistan—an area of greater geopolitical importance to it than Bangladesh. But Mrs. Gandhi's cool-headed handling of the crisis suggests that she recognized these matters on her own.

It was not fear of India's becoming a Soviet pawn that was behind U.S. policy, for in referring to Mrs. Gandhi, Kissinger said, "The lady is cold-blooded and will not turn India into a Soviet satellite out of pique." Rather, it was the old concern with U.S. credibility in a new guise—a psychological domino theory?—and the need to demonstrate that lack of restraint by Moscow would bring a U.S. response that were major factors behind the U.S. moves. That such efforts failed—and thus probably reduced U.S. credibility—is another story. So are questions about the feasibility of a policy that places such a high value on stability in a tumultuous world. Is this a hopeless effort? Or does the existence of so many regional disputes that could lead to war make it imperative to try to contain them, or at least work out an understanding involving mutual restraint by the major powers?

Finally, there is the matter of the importance the administration's attempt to effect a rapprochement with China had on U.S. policy. This breaks down into two separate parts. The first involves the effort to influence China to accept the kind of international order envisaged by the administration. President Nixon said:

> . . . it was our view that the war in South Asia was bound
> to have serious implications for the evolution of the policy
> of the People's Republic of China. That country's attitude
> toward the global system was certain to be profoundly
> influenced by its assessment of the principles by which
> this system was governed—whether force and threat ruled
> or whether restraint was the international standard.17

A more important consideration—but a parallel one—was the administration's attempt to work out a new relationship with China in order to improve the American position vis-à-vis the Soviet Union. One can argue that this was of equal importance to a China that felt threatened by the Soviet Union, and that Peking would have had little choice but to proceed with the rapprochement if the United States had followed a more balanced policy toward India and Pakistan. (An American policy that supported India would have been another matter.) Whatever the force of such an argument, the administration was un-willing to risk the détente with China in order to prevent a sharp deterioration in Indo-American relations. Perhaps the basic reason was its belief that failure to stand by an old friend (Pakistan) under threat by India and the Soviet Union would indicate to a potential new friend (China) that American support was of little value in any conflict with the Soviet Union.

The lack of a Chinese Jack Anderson makes it more difficult to determine the motivations behind Peking's policy during and since the crisis. Yet the nature of Chinese interests in the subcontinent and the statements of Chinese leaders provide the basis for an understanding of the major considerations behind Chinese policy. China's territorial dispute with India would make Peking desirous of good relations with Pakistan in any circumstances. However, the importance of its links with Pakistan are heightened by New Delhi's cooperation with Moscow in what Chinese leaders see as a Soviet scheme to establish a new version of the Dulles containment policy under the guise of Brezhnev's collective security proposal. But if such straightforward considerations are sufficient to explain the basic thrust of Chinese policy toward the subcontinent, it is important to note some of the subtleties involved as well as certain important differences between China and the United States—differences that were obscured by the similarity of their responses to the Bangladesh crisis.

As has already been pointed out, Peking proceeded with considerable caution during 1971. It backed the Pakistani government in important but carefully limited ways. The Soviet military buildup on China's northern border during the late 1960s left Peking with far fewer options than it had enjoyed during earlier crises in the subcontinent. Moreover, Peking was aware that Pakistan's rulers had mishandled the situation in East Pakistan and may have been dubious about the ability of the Pakistani government to suppress the Bengalis by force of arms. Underlying these considerations was the fact that China's interest centered on West Pakistan; thus Peking's major goal was not that Pakistan remain united but that West Pakistan—which borders China and whose people are hostile to India—remain independent of India and friendly to China. China probably wanted to see Pakistan remain a single nation, and its leaders may have been slow to recognize that an independent Bangladesh would end one of their dilemmas by making it possible simultaneously to support a conservative West Pakistani government and radicalism in Bangladesh.

If Peking took a relatively restrained view of the Indo-Soviet treaty when it was signed in August 1971, its concern increased sharply when war broke out in November. The People's Daily compared the

Indian move to set up an independent Bangladesh to the Japanese establishment of Manchukuo in the 1930s.[18] Huang Hua, China's UN representative, revealed one of Peking's fears when he told the Security Council on December 4:

> The Indian Government asserts that the purpose of its
> sending troops to invade East Pakistan is to help the
> refugees of East Pakistan to return to their homeland.
> This is utterly untenable. At present, there are in
> India large numbers of so-called "refugees" from Tibet,
> China; the Indian Government is also grooming Dalai
> Lama, the chieftain of the Tibetan counter-revolutionary
> rebellion. According to the Indian Government's asser-
> tion, are you going to use this also as a basis for aggres-
> sion against China?[19]

But fear of Indian moves against Tibet was clearly a secondary concern to China's leaders, who argued that India was simply a tool of the Soviet Union. On December 6 Huang Hua referred to a Tass statement that explained Soviet concern over the war on the ground that fighting was "occurring in direct proximity to the borders of the U.S.S.R. and, hence, involve its security interests." He charged:

> The "secure boundaries" of the Soviet Union have all of
> a sudden been extended to the Indo-Pakistan Subcontinent
> and the Indian Ocean. The aim of the Soviet leaders is
> to gain control over the Subcontinent, encircle China, and
> strengthen its position in contending with the other super-
> power for world hegemony. What the Soviet leaders of
> today are frantically seeking is the establishment of a
> great empire which the old tsars craved after but were
> unable to realize, a great empire controlling the whole
> Eurasian nation.[20]

Peking's apprehension probably was increased by its awareness that the balance of military forces in Asia left it with no way of countering India or the Soviet Union effectively.

Since the 1971 war China has continued to extend military and economic assistance to Pakistan to help it rebuild its armed forces and its economy—as well as its self-confidence.[21] These moves, together with Peking's veto of Bangladesh's application for membership in the UN, have increased President Bhutto's bargaining power. Yet Peking's fears have remained, as Huang Hua made clear when he opposed Bangladesh's application in August 1972.

It is necessary to point out here that in recent years
Soviet social-imperialism has played and is still playing
a most insidious role in the development of the situation
on the south Asian subcontinent. Last August the Soviet
Government concluded with the Indian Government a so-
called treaty of peace, friendship and co-operation, which
is in essence an aggressive treaty of military alliance,
whereby the Indian Government has finally and openly
stripped off its cloak of "non-alignment." Subsequently,
the Soviet Government directly instigated and supported
India in launching a war of aggression against Pakistan.
. . . The aggressive design of social-imperialism knows
no bounds. . . . Today they push their "secure boundaries"
to the Indian Ocean and the Mediterranean, and the next
day they can press further into the Pacific and the Atlantic. It is known to all what they have done to some of
their "allies," and we will not dwell on it here. . . . Is
there any lack of evidence in this respect? Some of
their schemes have already been revealed, and some are
being revealed. The acts and deeds of social-imperialism
have opened the eyes of the people. If certain people on
the south Asian subcontinent still have some sense of
national confidence, why can't they take the initiative to
unite the south Asian subcontinent first and to facilitate
a reasonable settlement of the relevant issues, and why
should they allow themselves to be led by the nose?[22]

Nonetheless, China has been careful to make clear that it has no
permanent objection to Bangladesh's membership. Huang Hua stated
Peking's position in a speech at the United Nations in November 1972:

We are not fundamentally opposed to the admission of
"Bangladesh" into the United Nations. China has always
cherished profound friendly sentiments for the people of
East Bengal. We hope that the "Bangladesh" authorities
will make their own decisions independently and meet
with the Pakistan leaders at an early date so as to reach
a reasonable settlement of the issues between Pakistan
and "Bangladesh," thus demonstrating that it is a truly
independent state. However, China cannot agree to the
admission of "Bangladesh" under the present circumstances, that is, before the important UN resolutions
are implemented by the parties concerned and a reasonable settlement of the issues between India and Pakistan
and "Bangladesh" is reached.[23]

FUTURE CONSTRAINTS AND OPPORTUNITIES

American support of Bangladesh's application for UN membership is only one of the differences between the policies and interests of China and the United States in South Asia. It is not necessary—or correct—to view the Chinese as wild-eyed revolutionaries intent upon fomenting upheavals and chaos everywhere to be aware that Peking does not share the U.S. interest in stability in the subcontinent. In particular, the two countries' attitudes toward India are noticeably different. The United States has no basic conflict with India such as grows out of the Sino-Indian border dispute, nor does it see Soviet influence in India as being nearly as extensive as China does. During 1972 Peking showed no interest in Indian overtures for a normalization of relations, while the United States and India initiated an effort to work out a more cooperative relationship.

Even with regard to Pakistan there are differences—at least in emphasis—between Chinese and American policies, that reflect Pakistan's greater importance to China than to the United States. The communiqué issued at the end of President Nixon's visit to China illustrates this. The United States said that it

> . . . favours the continuation of the cease-fire between
> India and Pakistan and the withdrawal of all military
> forces to within their own territories and to their own
> sides of the cease-fire line in Jammu and Kashmir;
> the United States supports the right of the peoples of
> South Asia to shape their own future in peace, free of
> military threat, and without having the area become
> the subject of great power rivalry.

China went considerably further in its support of Pakistan, stating that it

> . . . firmly maintains that India and Pakistan should, in
> accordance with the United Nations resolutions on the
> India-Pakistan question, immediately withdraw all their
> forces to their respective territories and to their own
> sides of the cease-fire line in Jammu and Kashmir and
> firmly supports the Pakistan Government and people in
> their struggle to preserve their independence and sover-
> eignty and the people of Jammu and Kashmir in their
> struggle for the right of self-determination.

To point out such differences is not to overlook the fact that both countries are well-disposed toward Pakistan and share a concern for its future, but only to emphasize that the extent of such concern is much greater on the part of China than it is on the part of the United States. Similarly, both countries want to prevent the Soviet Union from exercising a dominant influence in South Asia, but this too is of much greater importance to China than it is to the United States. This is not to play down American concern, for greatly increased Soviet influence in South Asia—and there are many indigenous barriers facing Moscow there—could have an impact on the important oil-producing states of the Persian Gulf. However, the dangers that an expansion of Soviet influence in South Asia would pose for China are more immediate and direct, involving Peking's control of the outlying and troublesome provinces of Sinkiang and Tibet.

It is far from clear at this point whether the similarities or the differences between Chinese and American interests will dominate their future policies toward the subcontinent. This will depend upon many factors, only a few of which can be considered here. Moreover, the legacy of the past will influence how the leaders of all the countries involved in South Asian affairs respond to the challenges and opportunities of the future. For example, Indian resentment of U.S. actions inimicable to the former's interests over the years have led to a growing Indian suspicion that more than a series of differences over particular issues is involved.[24] A growing number of Indians believe that U.S. policy toward the subcontinent has been designed primarily to prevent the emergence of India as a major power. The Indian government is not convinced that such an interpretation of American policy is correct, but Mrs. Gandhi and her colleagues are not confident that it is wrong. Therefore, they are trying to work out a more fruitful and solid relationship with the United States but are not inclined to risk much on the success of this effort.

Similarly, many Indians see China as motivated less by specific disputes over frontiers than as, in Nehru's words, "a country with proudly inimical intentions toward our independence and institutions." Yet Mrs. Gandhi has no desire to be overly dependent on the Soviet Union, especially since she recognizes that Moscow's interest in a Soviet-American détente might work to India's disadvantage if the Soviet Union and United States adopted a "spheres of influence" policy. Nor can New Delhi be sure that there will not be a marked improvement in Sino-Soviet relations at some future point. Mrs. Gandhi has made a number of overtures to Peking for a normalization of relations, but New Delhi will tread cautiously in this effort lest it alienate the Soviet Union, at least until it is confident that China is not implacable in its hostility. China presently appears convinced that New Delhi is so committed to working with Moscow that any effort to improve relations with India would yield no more than marginal benefits. However, the sharp changes in China's policy toward many former enemies

245

suggest that at some point Peking may experiment with a more flexible policy in the subcontinent in an effort to weaken Indo-Soviet ties.

Less prominent but perhaps equally important is the widespread Pakistani resentment over the limited support it has received from China and the United States in times of need. In view of its limited options, the Pakistani government must be somewhat circumspect in voicing this resentment. However, even those officials who realize that the responsibility for the bifurcation of their country rests primarily upon the former rulers cannot help but wonder how much support Pakistan can count on in a future crisis with India. President Bhutto is keeping his own counsel, but he is fully aware that without reliable great power support, continued refusal to reach an accommodation with India would be perilous indeed. And if India and Pakistan ever settle their differences, China's importance to Pakistan will diminish.

However, the most fundamental lesson to be learned from an examination of the past has to do with the entire pattern of relationships involving South Asia rather than with any particular bilateral relationship, for few of these relationships have shown much stability. The Indo-Soviet link is the most conspicuous exception, although even that became frayed when the Soviet Union was courting Pakistan between 1965 and 1971. (Moscow has, it should be noted, moved to reestablish a position in Pakistan since 1971 by renewing its economic assistance program.) Given the many changes that have occurred in the 1950s and 1960s and the unstable nature of some of the present relationships, it is unlikely that the status quo will persist indefinitely. Yet the international political relations in South Asia are so closely intertwined that a change in one nation's policy almost invariably leads to a shift—sometimes subtle, sometimes dramatic—in the policies of the other nations. Realpolitik and the balance of power have operated continuously in this part of the world, and they will continue to do so. Past experiences and present perceptions will influence the policies of all the governments involved in the subcontinent, but the potential for sharp changes in direction over time is considerable.

NOTES

1. Radio Delhi Domestic Service, July 20, 1971, reported in Foreign Broadcast Information Service: Middle East and Africa, July 21, 1971.
2. Pakistan's initial moves were designed to settle any potential differences with China—such as over their disputed border in Pakistani-occupied Kashmir. This done successfully, they moved toward closer cooperation. For an excellent analysis of Sino-Pakistani

relations up to the mid-1960s, see Khalid Bin Sayeed, "Pakistan and China: The Scope and Limitations of Convergent Policies," in A. M. Halpern, ed., Policies Toward China: Views from Six Continents (New York: McGraw-Hill for the Council on Foreign Relations, 1965).

3. U.S. Senate, Committee on Appropriations, Hearings, Foreign Assistance and Related Agencies Appropriations for 1966, 89th Congress, 1st session (Washington, D.C.: U.S. Government Printing Office, 1965), pp. 18-19.

4. Pravda, Apr. 4, 1971, in Current Digest of the Soviet Press 23, no. 14 (May 4, 1971): 35-36.

5. Peking Review, Apr. 16, 1971.

6. Peking Review, Feb. 4, 1972.

7. Karachi Domestic Service, Apr. 12, 1971, reported in Foreign Broadcast Information Service: Middle East and Africa, Apr. 12, 1971.

8. The text of the treaty is in Pravda, Aug. 10, 1971, cited in Current Digest of the Soviet Press 23, no. 32 (Sept. 7, 1971):

9. Ian Clark, "The Indian Subcontinent and Collective Security—Soviet Style," Australian Outlook 26, no. 3 (Dec. 1972):

10. For a more detailed appraisal of American policy, see William J. Barnds, "India, Pakistan and American Realpolitik," Christianity and Crisis 32, no. 10 (June 12, 1972); and Michael J. Brenner, "Great Power Politics and the Indo-Pakistan Crisis," International Spectator 26, no. 20 (Nov. 22, 1972):

11. Robert Jackson, "The Great Powers and the Indian Sub-Continent," International Affairs 49, no. 1 (Jan. 1973):

12. Henry A. Kissinger, "Central Issues of American Foreign Policy," in Kermit Gordon, ed., Agenda for the Nation (Washington, D.C.: The Brookings Institution, 1968).

13. U.S. Foreign Policy for the 1970s: Building for Peace, a report to the Congress by Richard Nixon, Feb. 25, 1971.

14. U.S. Foreign Policy for the 1970s: The Emerging Structure for Peace, a report to the Congress by Richard Nixon, Feb. 9, 1972.

15. New York Times, Jan. 4, 1972.

16. U.S. Foreign Policy for the 1970s: The Emerging Structure for Peace, a report to the Congress by Richard Nixon, Feb. 9, 1972.

17. Ibid.

18. Peking Review, Dec. 10, 1971.

19. Ibid.

20. Peking Review, Dec. 17, 1971. The Tass statement can be found in Current Digest of the Soviet Press 23, no. 49 (Jan. 4, 1972):

21. New York Times, June 3, 1972.

22. Peking Review, Sept. 1, 1972. Huang Hua's Sept. 23, 1972 speech sets forth additional Chinese arguments for refusing Bangladesh's application. New China News Agency, Sept. 24, 1972.

23. *Peking Review*, Dec. 8, 1972.

24. For an examination of Indo-American relations see William J. Barnds, "India and America at Odds," *International Affairs* 49, no. 3 (July 1973).

13

REACTIONS OF THE NATO ALLIES
TO THE SINO-AMERICAN DÉTENTE
Dick Wilson

The first signs of the détente between the United States and China were universally welcomed by the former's allies in the West. That welcome was remarkably widespread, only the extremes of obsessive anti-Communism at the one end of the political spectrum and of blinkered pro-Moscow elements in the Western Communist parties on the other refusing to share in the general relief and applause.

Prime Minister Pierre Trudeau of Canada called the decision of President Nixon to visit Peking "bold and decisive." The French statesman Maurice Couve de Murville also praised Mr. Nixon's courage, commenting that the new American policy should "neither surprise nor shock us."[1] Maurice Schumann, the French Foreign Minister at the time, declared: "If the China-U.S. rapprochement is not directed against anyone, it cannot fail to serve the cause of peace."

Similar approving noises came from most of the other NATO capitals. Western Europe and Canada had, after all, blazed the path now trod by the U.S. President. Typical of press comments on July 17, 1971 (London time), the day after the plans for the Nixon visit were announced, was an editorial in the Times of London, part of which read:

> If all goes well and the visit really takes place it will mean, at the very least, that one of the greatest anomalies in power relations in the world—the lack of proper contact between two of the world's giants—has been removed.
> That in itself would be a gain: the United States and China would be able henceforth to speak to each other as directly as the United States and the Soviet Union now can.
> Such an interchange would not in itself be a guarantee of understanding or friendship: but it would at any rate

provide the possibility of inquiry and explanation between the two sides, and that could be the beginning of progress.

A second and more palpable consequence would be that Washington and Peking would be able to speak more freely about their hopes of peace in Vietnam.

BACKGROUND

Britain had recognized the Communist regime in China as early as January 6, 1950, barely three months after Chairman Mao Tse-tung's proclamation of the People's Republic in Tienanmen Square. The natural British pragmatic instinct for doing business with any government in actual physical control of its territory was reinforced in this case by the desire to protect the status of Hong Kong and to minimize British commercial losses in China.

Denmark followed suit in May (and Sweden and Switzerland in May and September, 1950, respectively), but the outbreak of the Korean War broke the momentum of recognition and caused the remaining NATO allies to harden their attitudes toward Peking. Norway opted for her Scandinavian neighbor's pattern by extending diplomatic recognition in October, 1954, after the Korean armistice, and Holland followed a month later.

There the position froze for a decade, as far as the NATO allies were concerned, with Washington able to use the Taiwan question as a deterrent for any waverers attracted to the British line. The next break in the ranks was led by Charles de Gaulle, whose recognition of Peking in January 1964 was an important breakthrough for China in circumstances that made it a snub for Washington.

French lobbying did not succeed in gaining more converts to the Gaullist view of China among the NATO allies until another head of government of French stock, Pierre Trudeau, came to power on a platform asserting more vigorously Canada's independence from U.S. tutelage, even to the extent of being ready to leave NATO. Mr. Trudeau had visited China privately before he became Prime Minister. Canada's recognition was extended in October 1970, followed closely by Italy's.

When the China representation issue arose in the UN General Assembly at the end of 1970, therefore, the NATO allies were split three ways. Three of them—the United States, Greece, and Turkey—opposed the admission of Peking. A larger and influential group, including Britain, France, Canada, Italy, and the Scandinavians, supported Peking's entry, having already recognized the People's Republic or completed negotiations to do so. A third school of thought (exemplified by Belgium and Holland) preferred to abstain on the issue—largely because they were preparing to change sides.

Turkey recognized Peking in August 1971, Belgium in October 1971, Iceland in December 1971, Greece in June 1972, and West Germany in October 1972—leaving only Portugal and the United States, among the NATO allies, lacking formal diplomatic relations with Peking.

Since the smaller powers in NATO had blazed the trail to Peking, they could hardly protest President Nixon's journey or its professed objectives. Indeed, since the beginning of 1972 almost all the Foreign Ministers of the major NATO powers have been to Peking—beginning with Robert Schumann of France in February 1972 and followed in fairly quick succession by Mitchell Sharp of Canada, Sir Alec Douglas-Home of Britain, Walter Scheel of West Germany (preceded by ex-Foreign Minister Gerhard Schroeder) and Giuseppe Medici of Italy.

It was natural for the French to claim some of the credit for the détente, since in 1969-70 they had provided a channel of communication between Washington and Peking. France has been China's favorite country in the West since the Soviet-U.S. détente of the 1960s brought Mao Tse-tung and Charles de Gaulle into convergence.

The French Planning Minister, M. Bettencourt, and ex-Premier Maurice Couve de Murville both went to China in 1970, well before the general rush; and when Robert Schumann was in Peking in early 1972, he had the signal honor of an audience with the Chairman. Mao Tse-tung does not normally receive visiting Foreign Ministers, but he told his guest on this occasion: "You are not just a Foreign Minister. You are a Minister of France." The Quai d'Orsay was able to observe of the announcement of Nixon's visit to Peking that France had "for a long time" urged that China should not and could not be excluded from world affairs.

Raymond Aron, the veteran commentator on international affairs, spoke for many Frenchmen (and other Europeans) when he spoke of the same event as "a meeting, not between two revolutions, nor even between two imperialisms, but between two great powers which find themselves for the time being in accord, thanks to a mutual return to the traditional practices of diplomacy."[2]

Britain might have found herself in an identical position on this matter. But her insistence (out of loyalty to Washington) on sticking to the letter of the Cairo and Potsdam Declarations in order to maintain the view that the question of Taiwan's status remained unsettled in international law, coupled with the crisis provoked by the overflow of the Cultural Revolution into Hong Kong in the form of the 1967 riots there, prevented Britain from playing a leading role in the détente.

It was nevertheless welcomed, if anything, more heartily in London than in Paris. The British mission in Peking, which had been burned to the ground in 1967, was reopened amid Chinese apologies in February 1971. And one of the first concrete results of the Nixon-Chou communiqué at Shanghai was the removal of the remaining irritant in Sino-British relations, the question of Taiwan's status.

Once President Nixon had acknowledged that the United States "does not challenge" the thesis that Taiwan is a part of China, the British were able to take a similar view. Within days of the Nixon visit, the British reached agreement with China on raising the level of their mutual diplomatic representation to the ambassadorial status, which Peking had denied for more than 20 years. The price that Britain paid for this strategic retreat on the Taiwan question was the withdrawal of her consul accredited to the Taiwan provincial government at Tamsui.

ADVANTAGES TO NATO

Apart from their general preference for the normality of recognition between such large and powerful nations as the United States and China, the European NATO allies saw specific advantages accruing to themselves from the détente. One of the first of these, in the phrase of the Italian analyst Giovanni Bressi, was "the amelioration of their bargaining position with the Soviet Union."[3] NATO was and is, after all, a defense grouping against the threat of Soviet expansionism. The new Sino-American détente could, on one line of argument, leave the United States free to confront any Russian pressures in Europe or the Mediterranean, at the same time leaving China free to bolster up her frontier with the Soviet Union.

The Chinese interest in this is obvious, and there have been reports that Peking has sounded out both the French and the Italian governments about the possibilities of nuclear collaboration. Premier Chou En-lai impressed upon Bettencourt during his visit in 1970 that a powerful and independent Western Europe was "a precious element of world equilibrium"; and few European leaders doubt that their China connection is potentially valuable in their dealings with Moscow, especially in the event of any diminution in the American military presence in Western Europe.

Chancellor Willy Brandt of West Germany is reported to have once remarked: "China is far away, but nevertheless in the political game. West Germany can hold the Chinese card which should not be put aside or ignored."[4]

The most recent example of the connection between events on Russia's western and eastern borders was in March 1969, when the Communist blockade of Berlin was deescalated by the Russian leaders, apparently because of the distraction of frontier skirmishes with Chinese forces on the Ussuri River.

In this particular instance Moscow evidently welcomed the excuse to climb down in Berlin; but in any future crisis in Europe the capacity of Peking to feel free to concentrate its forces on the Sino-Soviet border could prove helpful, even crucial, to the West Europeans. Chairman Mao has already played such a role as between the Kremlin and the small countries of Eastern Europe, notably during the Czechoslovakian crisis of 1968. The East European "rebels"—Yugoslavia, Albania and Rumania—have good reason to value China as a counterweight to the Russian giant.

It has even been argued that a China free from the strains of confronting the United States and enjoying cordial relations with Western Europe could conceivably perform another service to the Europeans: inducing Japan, after her rebuff from the United States, to direct her economic potential toward Asia rather than toward Western Europe.[5] This may sound parochial to American ears, but continental Europe is not yet fully convinced of its place in an open world system of the kind preached by Dr. Henry Kissinger and supported by the offshore British. The suspicion of Japan is deep-seated.

NATO AND THE SOVIET REACTION

However, the effect of the China détente on Europe's relations with the Soviet Union is equivocal. If it were pressed too far and too blatantly as an anti-Soviet move, it could sabotage the patiently constructed détente between Moscow and Western Europe, which remains so fragile but so important. Hence the warning note in Robert Schumann's 1971 comment on the U.S.-China rapprochement, that it was welcome as long as it was not "directed against anyone."

An editorial in Le Monde on July 17, 1971, posed the point succinctly. "Will the USSR," it asked, "see in the Sino-American rapprochement a further reason to discuss with Washington the revitalization of the languishing negotiations on rearmament and on Berlin? Or will it, on the contrary, give way to the anxiety and aggressiveness which could be aroused by any prospect of 'encirclement'?" And André Malraux, one of the surviving confidants of Charles de Gaulle whose views were sought by President Nixon before he departed for Peking, issued warnings about the risk of creating in Moscow and Tokyo apprehension about U.S. leadership.[6]

The possibility of Soviet anger and disillusion was most feared in Bonn, where Chancellor Brandt's Ostpolitik was in the process of implementation. Initial German comments on the China détente were notably more reserved than the others. The 1971 announcement of the Nixon visit to Peking was not actually welcomed. Brandt "hoped" that it would contribute to world peace. A West German government spokesman "believed" that the proposed visit had been previously discussed with the Russians and said that the Soviet reaction was awaited with interest. There was even speculation in Bonn at that time—wishful thinking!—that Nixon might go to Moscow before Peking, to reassure the Kremlin that he was not taking sides in the Sino-Soviet quarrel.

The German priorities were entirely with European affairs—the improvement of relations with Moscow and the East European capitals, the achievement of a Berlin agreement, and ratification of the new treaties with the Soviet Union and Poland. Anything threatening to interfere with this agenda was unwelcome, and for a while the China détente looked like just such a cloud on the horizon.

The distinction was formulated by a European scholar, Vladimir Reisky de Dubnic, in this way: those governments (like the British, French, Rumanian, and Yugoslav) that viewed the Soviet Union as an expanding power welcomed the China-U.S. détente but those, like the West German, that saw the Soviet Union as a satiated power, feared the China détente's adverse effect on Russian goodwill toward the West.[7]

These doubts were eased, of course, by the subsequent speeches of American leaders and by Nixon's successful visit to Moscow in 1972; and West Germany proceeded to establish its own relations with China in 1972 without jeopardy to the Ostpolitik. The very success of the President in maintaining his détente with Moscow even inspired renewed fears in Europe of an American-Soviet understanding behind Europe's back.

China, of course, has an interest in seeing a strong, united Germany emerge on Russia's western flank; and Foreign Minister Chi P'eng-fei told his West German counterpart in October 1972 that the division of Germany was "abnormal" and could not be permanent. Chou En-lai added that reunification was inevitable and reportedly found Scheel wanting in realism in his playing down of the Soviet "threat."

Reisky de Dubnic observes in his analysis of the effect of the China détente on Europe: "A US détente with China cannot be made at the expense of Europe, but a US-Soviet détente could. For this reason Europe instinctively favours the former over the latter."[8] As the Chinese Foreign Minister warned Sir Alec Douglas-Home in Peking at the end of 1972, superpowers can "push expansionism under the facade of 'détente'. . . ."[9]

NATO-CHINA RELATIONS

The British in particular are aware of the historical factors that might make U.S.-China relations, once resumed, extremely close.

As Roderick MacFarquhar, the British politician-sinologist, put it in his analysis of the Nixon visit to Peking: "In the aftermath of the visit, Americans seemed ready to resume, if permitted, their old love affair with China."[10]

Indeed, one of the rarely stated disappointments for the NATO allies is the loss of the artificially boosted importance that their earlier relations with China had acquired. The Guardian (Manchester) had this in mind when it editorialized on July 17, 1971, on U.S. motives for the détente: "The lead which the Canadians, the Japanese and Western Europe already have in dealings with China can now perhaps be won back."

Even Chancellor Brandt, for all his preoccupations with the Soviet Union, East Germany, and Poland, was careful to conclude a trade agreement with China in December 1972, just in time to escape the self-imposed ban by the Common Market on its members' undertaking individual pacts of this kind with foreign partners. By 1971 the NATO allies had acquired almost a quarter of China's total foreign trade: $1,050 million out of an estimated $4,600 million.

Canada was responsible for $225 million, largely because of her wheat sales, and four of the European nations had trade in excess of $100 million—West Germany leading them with $234 million, then France with $184 million, Britain with $146 million, and Italy with $123 million.

The competition to supply China with the equipment and technology she needs for her modernization program is now intense. It is conceded by all that Japan is the most advantageously placed for the overall range of industrial equipment of interest to the Chinese market. But the West Europeans are still contenders for many lucrative contracts at this vital stage when China is in one of her rare moods to buy a great deal of foreign plant and large-scale equipment.

Sales of commercial aircraft (including the controversial Anglo-French Concorde, for which China is one of the few prospective customers still professing interest), rolling stock and locomotives, nuclear energy techniques, oil exploration equipment and know-how, and complete petrochemical, steel, automobile, and electricity-generating plants are among the prizes to be won—and now the United States has muscled in among the ranks of prospective suppliers, thus reducing the amount of trade available to the others. It was only to be expected that this should cause some disappointment in European business circles.

THE SUMMIT TECHNIQUE AND THE RISE
OF MULTIPOLARITY

Two further areas of concern about the China détente can be discovered among America's European allies. One relates to the summit technique. George Kennan put his finger on it in an article on the eve of the Nixon visit to Peking:

> Even in Europe, where the change of policy on United Nations membership was generally felt to be long overdue, the idea of a presidential visit to Peking arouses more uneasiness than it does admiration. It flies, after all, in the face of all professional diplomatic experience, which suggests that meetings at the summit, if they are to have value at all, should take place only after outstanding political questions have been successfully treated, with all the attendant strains and unpleasantness, at the normal diplomatic level, and that the purpose of such meetings should then be only the bestowal of the serene blessing of higher authority on agreements already arrived at.[11]

The drama of the visit by "Marco Polo Nixon," as the Daily Telegraph of London called him, nevertheless made a favorable impact on many sections of public opinion in Canada and Europe. And the diplomatists' fears of summit diplomacy were to a large extent laid to rest by the words of the Shanghai communiqué, which the Economist judged, with evident relief, was "not a sell-out." It "cannot be ruled a defeat or a victory for either side."[12]

The Times of London felt that the communiqué confirmed the anticlimax evident in the earlier stages of the visit, although its editorial stressed that the importance of the meeting lay in its being held at all rather than in its immediate results. "At the very least, the 'accident, miscalculation or misunderstanding' that have brought these two countries to the brink more often and more dangerously than others will not again be possible."[13] There was general relief that Mr. Nixon had not given too much away on Taiwan or other issues and that he had taken care to insist on the U.S. position on the major issues that separated America and China.

Finally, the paeans of praise that President Nixon and his Chinese hosts had for each other in Peking did arouse some deep-seated fears about the inferiority of Western Europe in the new multipolar power system.

The French statesman Edgar Faure was among the first to echo this presentiment in July 1971, after the announcement of the Nixon visit. "It is not possible," he argued, "to envisage an equilibrium limited to three countries of which two are Communist. There is also Japan, perhaps India, and then above all, Europe. It is imperative to organize a genuine European diplomacy. It is not necessary to construct a supranational Europe in order to achieve this. The Nixon-Mao meeting ought to give a crack of the whip to Europe."[14]

256

This is a complex reaction to describe, because it embodies contradictory elements. Europeans want to have their cake and eat it too. They welcome the security and stability that the détente and the concomitant arrival of multipolarity in world affairs assure them, yet they are nostalgic for the past days of European power and regret Europe's loss of status. For China suddenly to loom as the junior member of the "Big Three" in planetary counsels—leapfrogging over Western Europe—is something of a shock. The U.S.-China détente, wrote one European scholar, had "catapulted China into the role of a superpower sooner than the world had expected."[15] MacFarquhar noted: "The leader of the world's most powerful country had arranged to be invited to China, a populous but economically backward and militarily weak country. Chinese prestige was inevitably greatly enhanced by the visit."[16]

CHINA AND THE COMMON MARKET

One could argue that the stimulus to European unity, if such it is, has not been very effective. But the Common Market is currently facing a forced internal digestion problem, and only in the long run will it emerge whether China will have accelerated the European quest for unity. Certainly China is pushing the concept for all it is worth. The summit meeting of the nine heads of government of the Common Market on the eve of enlargement at the end of 1972 was hailed in Peking as a historic event and a "new step forward in the common struggle against the two superpowers." An Italian who accompanied Foreign Minister Medici to Peking in January 1973 remarked of the Chinese counsel on the enlarged Common Market: "I've seldom heard such encouragement."

This was not always so. In the late 1950s a characteristic Chinese judgment of the Common Market was "The formation of a Common Market cannot improve the position of Western Europe, nor can it make West Europe less dependent on the US."[17] But at that time Mao Tse-tung was also developing his concept of a "second intermediate zone" between the socialist (the Soviet Union and China) and the capitalist (the United States) camps to embrace Western Europe, Japan, and Canada. The latter were admittedly followers of the capitalist economic system; but they also suffered from big-power bullying, and to that extent their interests overlapped with the developing countries of Asia, Africa, and Latin America, which constituted the "first intermediate zone." Chinese Communist thought continues to detect important contradictions within the Western alliance that are of use to socialist and Chinese interests. As Alain Peyrefitte— not from the left wing—said in Peking in 1971: "France and China are objective allies."[18]

Now the Chinese are applauding the enlargement of the Common Market with extraordinary warmth and vigor, and they hold out high expectations of both French and British leadership to build a Europe that would no longer depend on American support and would also stand up firmly to any Russian pressure. It is believed that Chou En-lai told Sir Alec Douglas-Home in Peking that he felt disappointed by the equivocal attitudes of both Scheel and Schumann toward the Soviet Union and hoped that Britain would assume a strong lead in the Common Market—a hope doubtless nourished by the skepticism that the British Foreign Secretary evinced in China regarding the West's détente with the Soviets and the European Security Conference in Helsinki.[19]

The Chinese have been as critical of what they term the "European insecurity conference" and the talks on mutual balanced force reductions as they are laudatory of the Common Market. They fear a détente in Europe of this dimension—anxious, in the words of the Swiss scholar and Neuer Zürcher Zeitung commentator Ernst Kux, lest "the projected troop reductions in Europe would permit the Soviet Union to station more troops along its frontier with China." But, Kux adds: "Perhaps from their great distance the Chinese see the situation in Europe more realistically than it appears through some rose-tinted glasses nearer to the scene."[20]

CHINA IN THE MEDITERRANEAN

A highly interesting arena for the interaction of these various currents arising from the Sino-U.S. détente is the Mediterranean and the Middle East. "The Chinese people," according to an article in the Peking Review in 1972, "support resolutely the Mediterranean countries in their just struggle against the rivalry between the U.S. and the Soviet Union for the hegemony in the Mediterranean sea."[21]

Peking has moved remarkably fast in the past year or so in making friends and, it hopes, influencing people in this region, which is so strategic for the Soviet Union. China has always had a pied-à-terre in Albania, but now she has begun to establish a modest presence even in countries like Spain and Greece, which must be ideologically repellent to her.

The Chinese leaders have gone out of their way to befriend the island of Malta, assisting it to maximize its bargaining power for the provision of base facilities to the NATO powers while allowing it to avoid being sucked into the Soviet orbit. Cyprus and Turkey are being courted, as are the North African nations; and it seems clear that the Chinese are actively planning at long last for regular scheduled air service to Europe, probably by way of Pakistan, Iran, and Turkey.

To visiting West Europeans the Chinese leaders dangle the prospect of cooperation in the Middle East (overtly to "protect" that region
from Soviet hegemony, although Peking is well aware of the intensifica-
tion of competition between the United States, the Soviet Union, Western
Europe, and Japan for the security of assured long-term oil supplies
from the chief Arab producers). The neutralization of the Mediterranean is also frequently urged.

It was with unconcealed endorsement that early in 1972 the New
China News Agency quoted the French diplomat Jean Lipkowski as
declaring that the nations of Europe should "unite in a common policy
to keep the Mediterranean from becoming a super-powers' battle-
ground." The U.S.-China détente will allow the Europeans to play
their "Chinese card" more frequently and more effectively in any
game where the object is to alter a local power situation in West
Europe's favor at the expense of either the United States or the Soviet
Union or both.

All of this has rather assumed that the prime object of Canadian
and West European interest has been the change in American policy,
the belated decision by Washington to come to terms with Communist
Chinese reality. But it would be wrong to omit the other side of the
picture. It does, after all, take two to have a détente; and to some
eyes the change in China's policy is the more startling and the more
fraught with consequences. By coming out of her self-imposed isolation, China opens up the possibility of helping to create a regional
balance, a minimal power stability in Eastern Asia that would be the
best guarantee of world peace and order for the rest of this century.

To be sure, it is possible to argue, with the British sinologist
Michael Yahuda, that "the fundamental approach of the Chinese to the
outside world and their understanding of the forces which shape the
currents and tides of international affairs have not basically changed.
What has changed is the international environment affecting China,
the Chinese perception of new dangers as regards Japan, and the
heightening of 'contradictions' in the Capitalist world."[22] But this
surely underestimates the impact of China's perception of the Soviet
threat and overstates the consistency of Peking's policies. Certainly
many in Europe and Canada, having witnessed the tensions of the
1950s and of the Cultural Revolution, view the present affable reason-
ableness and outgoingness of Chinese diplomacy as something different
from, and far preferable to, its preceding phases.

To sum up, America's NATO allies saw in the China détente the
adoption by both sides of the more realistic and pragmatic view that
the former had been wishing and urging on these powers for many
years. While there were initial reservations about the speed and
style (especially the gesture of the Presidential pilgrimage to Peking)

of the American conduct of the détente, its results were applauded, particularly as it became plain that Soviet goodwill was not going to be its victim or its price. This was especially important for West Germany, caught up in delicate and complex negotiations for normalizing her position in Central and Eastern Europe that were highly dependent upon Russian confidence.

Some of the realities of the new multipolar system opened up by the détente are so new that time is needed for Europe to adjust to them: disappointments in the trading field will result, and the disunity of Western Europe becomes more glaring as China takes her regular place in the world system. But these are transient troubles. The big development is Europe's new ability to call in the old world of China to redress the new one of America and Russia. As Giovanni Bressi concludes: "It is in Europe's interest to reinforce China. And it is not fortuitous that China is the only major world power to desire, without reservations, that Europe should become more powerful."[23]

NOTES

1. Figaro (Paris), July 17, 1971.

2. Ibid., July 19, 1971.

3. Giovanni Bressi, "China and Western Europe," Asian Survey 12, no. 10 (Oct. 1972): 834.

4. Izvestiya (Moscow), Mar. 29, 1968.

5. See Bressi, op. cit., p. 835.

6. Daily Telegraph (London), Feb. 21, 1972. This anxiety was well conveyed in a letter to the Economist on Apr. 1, 1972, by Stefan Jedrkiewicz from Rome: "If Russia feels its growing isolation, it will not allow any more independence to its European 'allies' (in order to look more friendly and reliable in respect of Western Europe); possibly Russia's satellites will be even more strictly tied to their leading nation . . . and 'frost' will come back again as the main feature of the Soviet regime." Thaw in Moscow is more important and delectable to West Europeans than thaw in Peking.

7. Vladimir Reisky de Dubnic, "Europe and the New US Policy Towards China," Orbis 16, no. 1 (Spring 1972): 85.

8. Ibid., p. 104.

9. Times (London), Nov. 3, 1972.

10. Roderick MacFarquhar, "Nixon's China Pilgrimage," World Today 28, no. 4 (Apr. 1972): 157.

11. Observer (London), Feb. 20, 1972.

12. Economist, Mar. 4, 1972.

13. Times (London), Feb. 28, 1972.

14. Informations (Paris), July 26, 1971; also reported in Le Monde, July 24, 1971.

15. Reisky de Dubnic, op. cit., p. 85.

16. MacFarquhar, op. cit., p. 157.

17. Ta Kung Pao (Hong Kong), Mar. 28, 1957.

18. Alain Peyrefitte, Sept. 1971.

19. Ernst Kux, "China and Europe," Swiss Review of World Affairs, Jan. 1973; reprinted in Current Scene 11, no. 5 (May 1973).

20. Ibid.

21. Peking Review, Apr. 15, 1972.

22. Michael Yahuda, "China's New Foreign Policy," World Today 28, no. 1 (Jan. 1972): 14.

23. Giovanni Bressi, in Relazioni Internazionali (Milan, 1972); also in European Review (London) (Spring 1973): 4, 10.

14

A FUTURE FOR TAIWAN
Robert W. Barnett

An interplay of power, politics and honor, perceived differently by Peking, Taipei, Tokyo, and Washington, will shape their future modus vivendi for the People's Republic of China and the Republic of China on Taiwan. Because antagonisms in other vocabularies are fixed and deep, economics may be the vocabulary Peking and Taipei will use for a while to discuss possibilities. Despite differences in the achievements, opportunities, and objectives of their two economic systems, Peking and Taiwan may come to see interesting possibilities of complementarity. Whatever vocabulary is used, and whatever the apparent focus of talk, Taipei and Peking, with Washington, Tokyo, and Moscow as deeply interested onlookers, will know that the new general contract for the Taiwan Strait will be of far-reaching importance, not only for China but also for other countries of East and Southeast Asia that are looking for indications of how Peking desires to live with its neighbors.

The Sino-Soviet military confrontation is, of course, the central factor in Peking's power calculations. Replacement of Taipei by Peking as China's voice in the international community, followed by the Shanghai communiqués and the Chou-Tanaka joint statement, is recasting the general setting of international politics within which both Taipei and Peking will be acting. And interpretation of the mutual defense treaty of 1954 between Washington and Taipei will be seen by all of the treaty partners of the United States everywhere in the world as testing U.S. honor.

IMPORTANCE OF THE SHANGHAI COMMUNIQUÉ AND THE CHOU-TANAKA JOINT STATEMENT

With issuance of the Shanghai communiqué and the Chou-Tanaka joint statement, much of the vocabulary previously used in discussing a future for the Chinese on both sides of the Taiwan Strait is obsolete. "Two Chinas" or "one China and one Taiwan" have ceased to describe usefully the practical possibilities for Taipei's future position in East Asia and in the world community. Some may begin to speak of "One China: two Hong Kongs" as Peking and Taipei consider ways to establish a special "provincial status" within China for Taiwan—a status that would envisage a perhaps prolonged period during which Peking would allow Taipei considerable economic, cultural, and administrative separateness. In the United Nations and elsewhere, Peking brushes aside all outside intervention in its relation with colonial Hong Kong. In Peking's eyes Hong Kong is already Chinese, and its separateness persists with Peking's acquiescence; but, we must admit, no Chinese yet speaks of a Hong Kong-type future for Taiwan. Perceived necessity will precede use of such language.

The Shanghai communiqué envisaged conversations among Chinese on both sides of the Taiwan Strait, and today Peking proclaims its readiness and wish to talk and to have contact. In contrast, Taipei, fearing that talk would imply capitulation, denies that it is talking, or wishes to talk, with Peking. Actually, Chinese do not need to talk face to face, nor to have a formal agenda, for talk among them to be real and important. When the Chinese overseas community in Japan, for example, arranges to visit Peking and Taipei simultaneously, then to return to Osaka and Tokyo to compare notes, and to venture forth on additional trips, there is, of course, a kind of conversation involving their recent hosts. We know that radio broadcasts are a form of conversation, as are news stories and editorials in the press, and formal statements, communiqués, and declarations of principle entered into by Taipei and Peking with third countries. Few can doubt that significant Chinese talks are taking place and will continue to take place; their focus will be on the future rather than on the past.

As for the past, Mao Tse-tung and Chou En-lai may not have had Taiwan much on their minds during the Yenan days. They may not have attached much importance, at the time, to the Taiwan references in the Cairo and the Potsdam Declarations. However, when Chiang Kai-shek insisted, obsessively after the summer of 1949, that Taiwan was a province of China, Mao Tse-tung agreed, denying only Chiang's contentions that he was the legitimate sovereign leader of China and that Taipei was China's temporary capital. Events of the Korean war and conclusion of the 1954 mutual defense treaty between Taipei and Washington, though limited to Taiwan and the Pescadores in definition of its area of applicability, did nothing to diminish a common will in Peking and in Taipei to establish a provincial future for Taiwan within one China. Not the United States, nor Japan, nor other countries—nor, indeed, the leadership of the United Nations— suggested, as a practical matter, that the oneness of China be challenged or that the majority Taiwanese population on Taiwan should be allowed an opportunity to approve or to denounce the use of their homeland as a base of operations for continuation of a civil war in which the personalities contesting the legitimacy of China's sovereign authority were Chiang Kai-shek and Mao Tse-tung. Only general acceptance of the concept of one China gave legitimacy to a Republic of China occupancy of the Chinese seat in the General Assembly and in the Security Council from 1945 through 1971, and to coexistence of the structures of national and provincial government on Taiwan. This history, of course, lay behind the Shanghai communiqué and the Chou-Tanaka statement.

These documents have been construed by some as constituting Peking's de facto renunciation of the use of force in the Taiwan Strait; and it is not difficult to discern Peking's motives, if it wishes to be seen as having done so. First, the logic of economics and politics, not the use of weapons, would bring Taipei back under Peking's authority; and the attack capability of a Taiwan unsupported by a major power would never necessitate a preventive strike. Also, the withdrawal of U.S. forces from Vietnam, and Washington's readiness to reduce its military involvements elsewhere in Asia, altered entirely Peking's past fear of an American-supported military encirclement of China. Second, China's perception of danger indicated a need to mobilize its military capability on one, not several, fronts. Peking could foresee no early easing of tensions with its Russian neighbor, for the issues were not solely disputed borders but ideological, cultural, racial, economic, and even personal. Thus motivated to show its readiness to renounce use of force, Peking might even have been prepared to see advantage in some continuation of an American military presence, conscious of a new danger that the Soviet Union could flow into areas vacated by the Americans—even, as a remote possibility, into Taiwan.

THE MUTUAL DEFENSE TREATY OF 1954

In the new setting, interpretation of Washington's obligations under the 1954 treaty with Taipei may be more troubling for Washington than for Peking. For Peking it could appear that the treaty already is becoming a benign curiosity. Not long ago the conventional wisdom was that the United States could not exchange diplomatic missions with the PRC so long as Washington honored a Taipei that claimed to be the sovereign authority of China. That liaison offices have now been exchanged by Washington and Peking, and that U.S.-Chinese relations are moving quite rapidly toward complete normalization, suggest that Peking believes that obstacles to realization of one China are technical and procedural, not strategic.

264

As the process of normalization continues, the White House will find occasions to declare its faithfulness to the 1954 defense treaty with Taipei, knowing that to terminate it would taint the reliability of other American treaty obligations. And Peking will understand that a White House sense of honor must give Taipei some time to practice its diplomatic skills in settling matters with Peking. Moreover, both Peking and the White House know that if Taipei's conduct suggested a wish to provoke war or suggested an intention to use the treaty to impede the full normalization of relations that the United States and China want with each other, the American people and their Congress could cause the White House to give the one-year notice to Taipei, despite the probable destabilizing consequences of such an action. Were a political atmosphere to develop in which such an action became likely, Taipei might begin to hear the voices of more and more American lawyers who would argue that with the "normalization" of relations between Washington and Peking, the validity of Washington's 1954 treaty obligations to Taipei, in light of the premises of the Shanghai communiqué, was already and anyway becoming questionable. Thus, while the 1954 treaty is a strategic asset for Taipei, prudence could suggest that Taipei should seek, in due course, a basis of safety and legitimacy other than reliance solely upon the 1954 treaty. It would seem that this would almost necessarily involve acquiescence by Peking.

The 1971 UN vote, followed by the Shanghai communiqué and the Chou-Tanaka statement, assures Peking increasingly active participation within all international bodies and agencies where China legitimately sits. Fewer and fewer countries will continue to have their representatives in Taipei, however much Taipei's dignified acceptance of its change of status is admired and its economic triumphs are envied by its trading partners everywhere.

TAIWAN'S ECONOMIC SITUATION

Just after the Chou-Tanaka joint statement, there was a period of uncertainty about Taiwan's economic outlook. However, Taiwan's labor force, management skills, and commercial and financial capabilities enabled Taipei's leaders to look without fear at the still unclear implications of the new understandings developing between Peking and Tokyo. The record for 1972 revealed that Taiwan, accepting a $671 million bilateral trade deficit with Japan, still accumulated net reserves at a rate of $1 million a day as a result of its powerful competitive capabilities in over 50 markets, including some in Eastern Europe. A possible intimation of a Peking attitude toward Taiwan came as some Japanese businessmen observed that they could carry on their operations both in Taiwan and on the mainland, disregarding the Chou En-lai "Four Principles" that previously had obliged Japanese companies to choose between doing business with one part of China or the other. And in some Japanese business circles, it was even thought that Peking encouraged Japan to make some kinds of investment in Taiwan. Still, Taipei knows that under certain circumstances Peking could ask all countries with which it traded to make an absolute choice between Peking and Taipei, thus turning the "Four Principles" into a global strategy. Peking's fussiness during the Japan Air Lines quest for landing rights in Peking, without giving up the lucrative Taipei route, may have been intended to remind Taipei and Tokyo of that capability. Were Peking to try to make its trading partners choose absolutely between Peking and Taipei, Taiwan's trade might shrink quite radically and its economy could confront dangerous uncertainties and difficulties for which durable solutions might become impossible without Peking's acquiescence or support.

Thus, the challenge to Taiwan's diplomats—and few diplomats in the world are more skilled—will be to find a scheme of arrangements in which Taiwan's ideological and administrative differences from the other provinces of China and its physical separateness would be perceived in Peking as offering advantages to all Chinese on both sides of the Taiwan Strait. If such arrangements would enable Taiwan to pursue with confidence the trade and investment policies that have made possible the past growth of its economy, but on terms that served the economic well-being of all Chinese, Peking might consider the economic gain in exchange for some political compromise a good bargain. To cease worrying about military tension in the Taiwan Strait would be the rest of the bargain.

Resumption of travel, trade, and other contact between the two sides, as happened in Germany and as, indeed, slowly comes in sight in Korea, would seem to be a logical concomitant of edging toward this goal. But so far Taiwan has sternly declared that it desires no economic relations with China and sees no gain in having them.

For 20-odd years, Taiwan followed Washington's lead in practicing comprehensive economic warfare, and a generation of achievement in pursuance of its growth nad trade policies gives Taipei reason to claim the absence of economic complementarity as a justification for rejecting possibilities for useful contact and cooperation. Hong Kong's economic links with China, when cited, are brushed aside in Taipei as irrelevant. Hong Kong, unlike Taiwan, is dependent on Kwangtung for food and water, and Hong Kong has generally been a richly remunerative market for Chinese exports. But government denials of any possibility for economic interdependence may not represent what others in Taiwan—now silent—may be thinking. To trade at all means to create complementarity. The real question is not possible economic complementarity; it is political. Before making irreversible economic commitments, how should Taipei assess the political life expectancy of China's present leadership? That leadership may now be rational and outward-looking, but hitherto it has been conspicuously inconsistent in defining national strategies and tactics. Self-reliance and egalitarianism have been the guiding principles for the economy of the PRC: the principles persisted, differently applied, through all phases of China's development, the Great Leap Forward and the Cultural Revolution being excessive expressions of them.

TAIWAN'S DIPLOMATIC SITUATION

If it could confirm a Peking intention to pursue "pragmatic" domestic and foreign policies, Taiwan, though it has embraced other principles upon which to base its doctrines for growth and welfare, might wish to explore with Chou En-lai his hints as to Taiwan's place in China's scheme of things. Given expectation of a stable political outlook for China, a modus operandi between Peking and Taipei would present negotiable difficulties for both sides. Negotiators might agree that Taiwan should look like Hong Kong, or like a Kaohsiung free port area, or should become a member of a kind of Chinese Zollverein. Indeed, during talks Taipei might find that it was tempting Peking, at its present stage of foreign exchange deficiency, to consider creating its own export-oriented and foreign investment-accommodating sector somewhere along the coast, possibly based on Shanghai and the lower Yangtze delta and potentially a great competitive threat to Hong Kong and Taiwan, particularly if it began to attract Japanese capital into joint ventures. However, Peking's fear that dependency upon foreign credits and involvement in joint ventures would undermine China's self-reliance and jeopardize the egalitarianism of its system could cause it to ask Taiwan to play that "export-oriented, foreign investment accommodating" role for China and to share some of its profits with Peking.

If Taiwan does not choose to accept the dangerous consequences of perpetual hostility toward China, Taiwan's diplomats, referring to the spectacular achievements of China's somewhat separate community of nuclear scientists and engineers, could undertake to persuade Peking to tolerate different "Chinese" systems in Taiwan, in Hong Kong, and possibly in a regime for China's shelf resources, which, being offshore, would be quarantined from the rest of China's "continental system" and still produce advantage for China.

In 1958 a quarrel in the Taiwan Strait over Quemoy presented the possibility of escalating major-power military engagement. Through the midsummer and early autumn uproar Taipei was

supported firmly, even recklessly, by Washington, while Peking found
Moscow's backing of its cause to be significantly, and unforgettably,
deficient. At Quemoy monolithic Communism was stared down by the
Free World—or at least that was the rhetoric. The experience became
for Peking a sour milepost in Sino-Soviet relations. For Taipei it
was a breathtaking chapter in Taiwan's history of siege, and to this
day the cream of Taipei's military forces is regularly stationed in
Quemoy, impressively alert and well supplied. Still, few analysts
could imagine Peking wanting to seize or to starve out Quemoy—almost
none sees Taipei and Washington as able or willing to pay the costs
required to rescue it were Peking to make such an attempt. But Peking
will not take these islands, except as part of a "Taiwan package deal":
Quemoy was in 1958, and remains, a linchpin that connects Taiwan
with the mainland. Notwithstanding its accommodation of about one-
third of Taiwan's military establishment, Quemoy's strategic weight
lies somewhere between impotence and irrelevance; Quemoy is, like
Hong Kong and Macao, already Chinese.

Cannot we suppose that the very large military forces on Taiwan
could become, strategically, similarly impotent and irrelevant? Cannot we imagine that Peking, with its major strategic concerns related
to the Soviet Union, Japan, and the United States, would wait as long
as or longer than another 15 years before seeing any necessity for
what the world might regard as a Taiwan showdown? Meanwhile, the
opportunity—if not the necessity—exists for Chinese diplomats in
Taipei and in Peking to recognize the still unexplored economic com-
plementarities of their social systems, to bargain with factors of
power and politics external to China itself at this stage, and to work
toward a modus operandi for creating the one China that both sides
cherish. China's neighbors will watch particularly for how Chinese
arrangements, shaped by power, politics, and honor, take account of
the traditions, the welfare, and the aspirations of its Taiwan-born
citizens.

FUTUROLOGY

Any attempt to assess the implications of the Sino-American détente must be considered an exercise in social forecasting—an exercise, if you will, in the ephemeral art of futurology.

Of all the modes of forecasting, political forecasting must be considered the most indeterminate. Key political issues invariably involve conflict situations in which the protagonists must make rather uncertain calculations about one another, usually on the basis of rather sketchy and often unreliable information. While a student of game theory might structure the matrix of choices available to each participant, only specific information about the motives of each will permit one to say which choice will be made.

In the article "Asia After Vietnam," in the October 1967 issue of <u>Foreign Affairs</u>, President Nixon said:

> Military security has to rest, ultimately, on economic and political stability. One of the effects of the rapidity of change in the world today is that there can no longer be static stability; there can only be dynamic stability. A nation or a society that fails to keep pace with change is in danger of flying apart. It is important that we recognize this, but equally important that in trying to maintain a dynamic stability we remember that stability is as important as dynamism.

'A generation of peace" is the slogan of the day, yet whatever importance is attached to international peace or to international stability as an objective, it is useful to remember that a nation-state or a system of nation-states can have no primary objective other than its own survival. Balance of power, or, if you will, balance of interests, is nothing more than the "right" degree of tension between the survival and aggrandizement of any particular nation-state and the interests of the system as a whole—with each nation-state attempting to maximize its freedom of action.

President Nixon has called the United States a Pacific power, yet, despite the balance-of-power rhetoric that comes out in foreign policy speeches made by U.S. officials, one wonders if there is a "great plan" for the structure the President is trying to build in the Pacific. Does he still believe, as he did in 1967, ". . . that the world cannot be safe until China changes. Thus our aim, to the extent that we can influence events, should be to induce change. . . ."? Does China consider itself just another great power, ready to take its position in a balance-of-power balance-of-interest arrangement, or does it have a Middle Kingdom syndrome, moving in a messianic way to restructure the world into its own emerging image?

Though it may not be possible for any group of scholars to predict the future, it is possible to identify an "agenda of questions" that will confront the protagonists in the Asian drama—and this is what the participants in the conference "Sino-American Détente and Its Implications" have accomplished.

THE END AND THE BEGINNING

Whether they were playing out the last act of a public relations charade for the benefit of the American public, or were fighting a last-ditch battle in defense of an outmoded policy in which they believed, the U.S. delegation to the UN knew at 4:30 P.M. on October 25, 1971, as debate in the General Assembly was proceeding on the resolution asking the Assembly to decide that any proposal that would result in depriving the Republic of China of representation in the UN was an important question under Article 18 of the Charter requiring a two-thirds majority vote, that the U.S. "two China" policy was in trouble.

The historic debate on the seating of the delegation from the PRC in the UN opened on October 18, 1971; and U.S. representatives, though rumors were rampant that the United States was willing to see its "two China" resolution defeated, did everything they could to line up votes for their position. While U.S. representatives, with the assistance of the Japanese, who had been persuaded to cosponsor the resolution, were actively pressuring delegates as early as 9 A.M., the facts that Dr. Henry Kissinger was in Peking during the time of the debate and that President Nixon was scheduled to visit Peking were not overlooked by the delegates.

270

After the permanent representative of Tunisia spoke on Monday, October 25, the permanent representative of the United States sensed that the vote, if taken that night, would be very close. He decided that he would try for an adjournment of debate until the next morning and, in the meantime, attempt to line up additional votes for the United States position.

The American Ambassador is reputed to have asked a friend, an Ambassador from a Middle East country, to speak briefly to the resolution and then move for adjournment. This Ambassador, not noted for his brevity, took the rostrum—and after an hour and a half was still there. By that time many Ambassadors were quite incensed, and some had made up their minds that whatever he proposed, they would vote against it. When he finally moved for adjournment, many who would have voted for adjournment voted against and the adjournment resolution was defeated: 56 for, 53 against, and 19 abstentions.

The General Assembly continued in session; and when the vote was taken, "the important question" resolution failed to pass—the vote was 55 for, 59 against, and 15 abstentions. The U.S. motion for a separate vote on the clause calling for the expulsion of the representative of Chiang Kai-shek was rejected by a vote of 51 for, 61 against, and 16 abstentions. The resolution to recognize the representatives of the PRC as the only legitimate representatives of China to the UN, which required only a simple majority, was adopted by a vote of 76 for, 35 against, and 17 abstentions.

On October 26, U.S. representatives noted, with some bitterness, that the fight to keep the Republic of China in the UN was lost because seven countries had reneged on their commitment to the United States. Secretary of State William P. Rogers stated, "We will make it clear to the nations that told us one thing and did another—that we don't particularly like it."

Thus, in an atmosphere of frustration, the 22-year parliamentary struggle by the United States to keep the PRC out of the United Nations came to an end. The struggle started when the representation question was raised by the Foreign Minister of the PRC in 1949, then came before the Security Council in January 1950 and the General Assembly later in 1950. There was a King Canute-like quality to the actions of the United States, which in effect commanded the tide of world public opinion favoring the PRC to cease its advance toward the UN. Support for the U.S. position eroded as country after country recognized Peking. When action to seat the PRC finally succeeded, it came as a result of actions by Third World countries and defections by NATO allies of the United States. By October 1971, 10 of the 15 NATO countries had already recognized Peking.

The PRC made its first appearance in the General Assembly on November 15, and the event was marked by statements of welcome.

Almost as a group of sinners publicly renouncing their transgressions, representative after representative took the rostrum to wish the Chinese delegation success and to assure their cooperation. The representative of India recalled that his country was the first to propose that the Chinese seat in the UN be occupied by the PRC after its establishment in 1949. The representative of France said that injustice and absurdity had ended now that China was finally seated. The representative of Burundi, speaking on behalf of the majority of African countries, said that China had become one of the main actors on the international scene. The Minister for Foreign Affairs of Denmark, on behalf of Denmark, Finland, Iceland, Norway, and Sweden, said that this was a day of great satisfaction for those who never failed to support the right of the PRC to take its seat.

On the completion of the welcoming statements, the representative of the PRC addressed the General Assembly with what appears to be a summary of the nation's position. He pointed out that there were only 51 member states when the UN was founded; and of the 80 states that joined later, the overwhelming majority had achieved independence after World War II. He reminded the representatives that the PRC had been deprived of its lawful rights in the UN because of obstructist tactics by the United States. He noted that the General Assembly vote on October 25 was a defeat of the plans of the United States, with the support of Japan, to create two Chinas in the UN, and he reminded the representatives that the United States had stated in the past that the Taiwan question was an internal affair for China in which the United States had no intention of interfering. He concluded by saying that one or two superpowers had utilized the UN and had done many things in contravention of the UN Charter, and that the situation could not continue.

With the entrance of the PRC into the UN, the wide and apparently unbridgeable chasm that separates the PRC and the Soviet Union has been brought into full view. One serious student of UN affairs has remarked that there is not a single subject or point in the UN on which the PRC and the Soviet Union have agreed. Even when they vote the same way on any issue, the PRC representatives go to great pains to point out why the two nations had different reasons for voting as they did.

As they become knowledgable about the workings of the UN, the Chinese are beginning to face the question of staff, both for the specialized agencies and for the Secretariat. While they do have a shortage of trained talent and prefer to keep their good men in the delegation, they are beginning to recognize the importance of staffing key positions within the international civil service of the UN. By their actions the Chinese have shown that they want to be where the Soviets are—even if it takes a reorganization of the UN Secretariat to achieve their purpose.

There are some 150 citizens of the Republic of China on Taiwan who are members of the UN international civil service, but the PRC has taken no action for their dismissal. Some have visited mainland China while on home leave and have returned as ardent supporters of the PRC.

On matters of substance the major powers have been dealing directly with each other, openly circumventing the UN. It will be interesting to see if the PRC will follow the big-power pattern or will act to strengthen the UN by bringing its own problems to the UN for resolution.

The PRC may well try to be the Third World's spokesman in the UN and may bring the latter's problems to the Security Council and General Assembly, but its major-power status may deprive it of the opportunity to lead the revolutionary disaffected of the world. The Third World has already found out that when the security of the PRC is affected, Machiavelli takes precedence over Mao.

NEW POLICY INITIATIVES

The New York Times fixes 1966 as the date of President Nixon's conversion to the conviction that ". . . any American policy toward Asia must come urgently to grips with the reality of China." In 1967 he made an extended tour through Asia and became convinced that a new effort should be made to normalize relations with the PRC, and his thinking on the subject was summarized in his article "Asia After Vietnam." After he became President, he initiated a series of studies to prepare for negotations with the PRC if and when the time for negotiations became propitious. The studies were prepared by a special group chaired by the Secretary of State, working directly with the National Security Council staff.

The lesson of overriding importance to students of foreign policy formulation is that without significant political leadership, dramatic changes in policy or changes in the assumptions that underlie policy formation are impossible. It is worth noting here that in his successful negotiations with the Chinese, President Nixon used the unilateral gesture approach, not the classic quid pro quo approach.

When the Communists came into power in October 1949, the United States left its diplomatic and consular personnel on the mainland of China to see what kind of relationship could be established. However, the new government of China announced its pro-Soviet policy and did not appear interested in having mutually beneficial relationships with the United States. Nevertheless, early in 1950 the possibility of extending diplomatic recognition to the new regime was under active consideration in the United States.

The Korean war then broke out; and the developing hostility between the United States and the PRC became fixed. The entry of the Chinese into the Korean war confirmed the U.S. view that the Chinese were aggressive and expansionist; the U.S. race to the Yalu River confirmed the Chinese belief that the United States was a threat to China's security. The Cold War was then at its height. Conversations between the two countries ceased, and each side saw the other as some kind of monster: that state of affairs between the two countries became accepted by many as inevitable and irreversible.

Nothing much happened to bridge the chasm between the United States and the PRC until talks commenced in 1955 at the Ambassadorial level, first at Geneva and then at Warsaw. A total of 134 talks were held; and the 135th, originally scheduled for February 20, 1969, a month after President Nixon's inauguration, was abruptly canceled by the Chinese.

On December 3, 1969, Ambassador Walter J. Stoessel, Jr., met Lei Yang, the PRC Chargé d' Affaires, at a Yugoslav cultural exhibit—and told him that the United States was ready to resume the Ambassadorial discussions. A meeting followed on December 11, and the 135th talk at the Ambassadorial level took place in Warsaw on January 20, 1970.

Throughout 1969, 1970, and 1971, President Nixon carried out a sequence of unilateral actions designed to improve relations with the PRC. Trade and travel restrictions were eased on July 21, 1969; some existing controls on U.S. trade, under embargo since 1950, were raised December 19, 1969; controls on U.S. oil companies were lifted in August 1970, permitting them to supply fuel oil to Free World ships carrying nonstrategic cargoes to China; restrictions on travel by U.S. citizens to China were lifted in March 1971; restriction for visits to the United States by citizens of the PRC were relaxed April 1971; the embargo on trade of nonstrategic goods with China was lifted in August 1971; and direct telephone communication with mainland China was restored in September 1971. These unilateral actions were accompanied by speeches made by high public officials, beginning with the speech made by Secretary of State William P. Rogers in Australia in August 1969. The tone of all these speeches was conciliatory, and China was now called by its proper name—the People's Republic of China.

The fall of 1970 brought a favorable response from the Chinese, through the private and reliable communication channels available to them. The spring of 1971 saw a sequence of private and public actions that culminated in Henry Kissinger's trip in July 1971.

The question that apparently recurred in the Geneva and Warsaw Ambassadorial discussions was how to move the Chinese on to other questions if no understanding was reached on the subject of Taiwan.

Whether the most difficult negotiations as to the form and substance of the agreements with China took place in Washington or in Peking is of no consequence. Nixon's trip to China was a success, and the Shanghai communiqué was a tangible result. The final form of the communiqué included statements to which both parties agreed and parallel statements that covered the differences. The key, of course, was the Taiwan question, on which the United States said ". . . the United States acknowledges that all Chinese on either side of the Taiwan Strait maintain there is but one China and that Taiwan is a part of China. The United States does not challenge that position. . . ."

The Shanghai communiqué has raised all sorts of constructive policy questions. If China is seriously interested, as it obviously is, in better relations with the United States, what does this really do for the United States in Southeast Asia? What are the U.S. interests, and what does it really want in Southeast Asia? What are the purpose of its deployments? Does deployment of troops in Asia have any value in the absence of a direct threat? Must the United States think in terms of protecting a country against Communism and Communist aggression, whether the aggression be direct or indirect?

There is general acceptance now that negotiation and even co-operation with the Chinese is possible. More important, there is also the recognition that in any consideration of what the United States wants in the area and what its interests require, it must keep in mind what the Chinese interests are and what the Chinese want, and seek to develop positions which will accommodate both.

THE JAPAN FACTOR

The announcement in July 1971 of President Nixon's plan to visit China, the announcement in August of a series of new economic policies, and the subsequent ultimatum on textile negotiations that almost threatened Japan with the application of the Trading with the Enemy Act shocked Japan. The greatest shock, though, was the President's decision to go to China, over Japan's head so to speak, without prior consultation with Prime Minister Eisaku Sato. This one action by the United States helped rock Sato out of office.

Was the Japan factor taken into consideration in planning the President's trip to China, or was there a myopia on this subject so far as the political leadership of the United States was concerned?

One cannot help but feel that the Japan factor was discussed within the U.S. government and that the decision was consciously taken not to inform the Japanese that the President's envoy was going to Peking. Personal pique may have been a factor in this decision because of the failure of Prime Minister Sato to live up to what the United States claimed was his agreement to deliver the Japanese textile people's agreement to voluntary export controls. Another factor in the decision may have been the porous nature of the Japanese government. The Japanese press is noted for its ability to ferret out almost any kind of secret; the Japanese government is noted, almost equally, for its inability to keep a secret.

The general feeling is that if the Japanese government had been consulted before the trip, the subject would most likely have appeared in the Taiwan press the next day and the trip would have been a failure. However, there were many ways open to the United States to handle the situation other than not informing the Japanese. One option was to inform them 24 hours before the event—or, for that matter, an hour before.

Her long, close ties with the United States have denied Japan the freedom to follow its own interests in foreign policy. Because it was a pensioner of the international system after World War II, Japan was encouraged to devote its immense energies and talents to the task of raising its gross national product and increasing its world trade.

It may well be that the Nixon shocks finally liberated the Japanese from their dependence on the United States. In any event, they moved the government of Prime Minister Kakuei Tanaka, which took office in the summer of 1972, toward normalizing Japan's diplomatic relations with the PRC.

By his trip to Peking, President Nixon brought into focus the strategic-diplomatic relationships between the PRC, the United States, and the Soviet Union, all of which are nuclear powers and members of the UN Security Council. Japan, the other element in the four-country balance-of-power system, is an economic power, not a strategic power in the military sense, and this makes for an interesting contradiction.

Japan cannot really be considered an independent power politically, nor can it have an equal say in any future Asian settlement so long as it is a nuclear ward of the United States. If a four-country balance-of-power system in Asia is to be realized in the traditional sense, Japan will have to arm itself to reduce its dependence on the United States nuclear umbrella. President Nixon, in his article "Asia After Vietnam," said:

> . . . Not to trust Japan today with its own armed forces and with responsibility for its own defense would be to place its people and its government under a disability which, whatever its roots in painful recent history, ill accords with the role Japan must play in helping secure the common safety of non-communist Asia.

Yet no matter how it arms itself, Japan is small in area and densely populated, with 20 percent of its population in three great metropolitan clusters, all vulnerable to attack. Her economy is tied to oil and her supply routes to the Middle East, the long line of huge tankers 50 miles apart, is truly vulnerable to economic as well as military enemies.

Some observers sense a hostility in Japan toward picking up the burdens laid down by the United States as a result of the Nixon Doctrine, a hostility that has its roots in the sensitivities of Japan's neighbors, in the psychological reaction in Japan to military matters, and in the concentration on economic and social matters. But despite all this, Prime Minister Sato, while he was in office, repeatedly made it clear that Japan would have to play a role in the defense of Asia.

While there is an almost insurmountable body of opinion on the Japanese domestic scene against nuclear weapons for Japan, there is also a concern by the three major powers in Asia that Japan may be driven toward nuclear weapons development. The price the three nuclear powers in the four-country balance-of-power system may have to pay for Japan's continued nonnuclear status is the inclusion of Japan as a permanent member of the UN Security Council, complete with veto power.

But even if Japan were willing to pay the high price for nuclear parity with China, the United States, and the Soviet Union, some observers feel that Japan can never play a major role in Asia. Despite its dramatic economic achievement, becoming the world's third-ranking economic power, not a single country in Asia looks to Japan for political partnership or protection. The image Japan projects, as a result of its trade policies and its foreign aid policies, where much of its aid is tied to the purchase of Japanese goods, is that of an "economic animal" concerned only with economic exploitation of its neighbors for its own benefit. Further, Japan has to live with its past image as one of the most brutal aggressors in modern history.

While Japan's limitations as a member of the four-country balance-of-power system have been noted, there is also a real question as to how much power the PRC can really exercise strategically, politically, and economically. China is the weakest member of the nuclear weapons club, and its ability to project its conventional military strength beyond its borders is very limited. Economically, China's gross national product is roughly equal to that of Italy, and China's foreign trade will remain only a mere fraction of its growing internal trade.

THE ASIAN DILEMMA

The authors of the articles in this book have done a masterful job of analyzing the political implications of the Sino-American détente. The political and balance-of-power problems are great, but the economic and social problems the countries of Asia face stagger the imagination.

In today's world, where even the national airlines of the poorer countries have jet aircraft, only a few hours of travel separate the United States from the underdeveloped countries of Asia. In terms of economic distance, the gap is like that between the Dark Ages from the present. Over the past century the rich countries have grown steadily richer; with very few exceptions the poor have remained poor. In the ten year period 1961-1970, the United Nations estimates that the investments by the developing countries totaled $432 billion (in 1960 prices)—and poverty is still the common lot.

With a gross world product in 1971 of about U.S. $3,900 billion and a population of about 3.6 billion, the average income in the world was about $1,075 per person. The United States, with its trillion-dollar gross national product had an average per capita income of $5,000. The poor countries, with a population totaling about 2.3 billion persons, had a combined gross national product of $500 billion and an average per capita income of $212.50.

Poverty is an ancient, not a modern, condition; but in today's world the poor have become aware of being poor and are resolved that something must be done about their poverty. An awareness of the living standards of advanced countries has not escaped the poor and has lead to increasing demands for economic development, no matter what the cost.

India and China, which together contain roughly a third of this planet's population, represent two dramatically different approaches to economic and social development. Both countries have instituted government planning to achieve their ends: economic planning in India is undertaken by a democratically elected state in the context of mixed private and public enterprise; China, a socialist state, has moved to direct and control every aspect of development, social as well as economic.

Whatever time will record as the final lesson of the Chinese experience, both countries have demonstrated that starting the development process in an undeveloped country is an agonizing undertaking. China plunged into the task and incurred, in terms of human suffering, what many fear are unsupportable costs. India, on the other hand, has taken a more humanistic approach than the Chinese and has achieved only limited gains—and even these gains required that a substantial portion of its investment needs come from abroad.

Asia, as prospected so far, does not appear to be well-endowed with economic minerals. Yet most of the mineral output of Asia and the other continents is consumed in the richer countries, and demand for mineral resources has risen far faster than the rise in population.

Between 1960 and 1969, while population worldwide increased about 19 percent, the production of oil increased 97 percent, that of natural gas 97 percent, and that of bauxite 86 percent. The United States, Japan, West Germany, the United Kingdom, France, and Italy together have about 22 percent of the world's population, yet in 1968 they consumed 85 percent of the copper, 82 percent of the aluminum, 87 percent of the nickel, 86 percent of the crude steel, and 69 percent of the petroleum.

Today 56 percent of the world's population lives in Asia: more than 60 percent of the babies born are Asian. By the turn of the century more than 60 percent of this planet's population will be concentrated in Asia. At the present rates of growth, roughly 50 million people will be added to Asia's population this year. Every two years a population the size of Japan's is added; in two and a half years a population the size of Indonesia's; in almost a dozen years a population the size of India's. With an expected planetary population at the end of the century of about 6.5 billion persons, the agricultural yield of every square inch of cultivable land must be doubled just to maintain the present standard of living.

Another aspect of the population problem is the massive drift to cities; the specter of dismal, poverty-stricken urbanization already hangs over Calcutta, Bombay, and Manila. Even in Japan people are moving into the heavily industrialized Inland Sea area, where a "strip city" runs almost without interruption from Tokyo to Hiroshima. For every farming family that settles on new land, hundreds of families are moving to the cities, begging or stealing for a living. Many Asian countries have come to the point where half the total population is under 15 years of age.

The poor countries of the world encircle the rich, giving rise to what some writers have called an "external proletariat." With patterns of economic development as they exist today, the class struggles during the closing decades of this century may well be between nations rather than within nations. This is a very ominous prospect, and one that was raised in September 1965 by Mao Tse-tung's former number-two man, Lin Piao, in his paper "Long Live the Victory of People's War."

PREMIER CHOU EN-LAI'S TOAST,
FEBRUARY 21, 1972

Mr. President and Mrs. Nixon,
Ladies and Gentlemen,
Comrades and Friends,

First of all, I have the pleasure on behalf of Chairman Mao Tse-tung and the Chinese Government to extend our welcome to Mr. President and Mrs. Nixon and to our other American guests.

I also wish to take this opportunity to extend on behalf of the Chinese people cordial greetings to the American people on the other side of the great ocean.

President Nixon's visit to our country at the invitation of the Chinese Government provides the leaders of the two countries with an opportunity of meeting in person to seek the normalization of relations between the two countries and also to exchange views on questions of concern to the two sides. This is a positive move in conformity with the desire of the Chinese and American peoples and an event unprecedented in the history of the relations between China and the United States.

The American people are a great people. The Chinese people are a great people. The peoples of our two countries have always been friendly to each other. But owing to reasons known to all, contacts between the two peoples were suspended for over twenty years. Now, through the common efforts of China and the United States, the gate to friendly contacts has finally been opened. At the present time it has become a strong desire of the Chinese and American peoples to promote the normalization of relations between the two countries and work for the relaxation of tension. The people, and the people alone, are the motive force in the making of world history. We are confident that the day will surely come when this common desire of our two peoples will be realized.

The social systems of China and the United States are fundamentally different, and there exist great differences between the Chinese Government and the United States Government. However, these

---

Source: Peking Review 15, nos. 7-8 (Feb. 25, 1972): 8.

differences should not hinder China and the United States from establishing normal state relations on the basis of the Five Principles of mutual respect for sovereignty and territorial integrity, mutual non-agression, non-interference in each other's internal affairs, equality and mutual benefit, and peaceful coexistence; still less should they lead to war. As early as 1955 the Chinese Government publicly stated that the Chinese people do not want to have a war with the United States and that the Chinese Government is willing to sit down and enter into negotiations with the United States government. This is a policy which we have pursued consistently. We have taken note of the fact that in his speech before setting out for China, President Nixon on his part said, . . . "What we must do is to find a way to see that we can have differences without being enemies in war." We hope that, through a frank exchange of views between our two sides to gain a clearer notion of our differences and make efforts to find common ground, a new start can be made in the relations between our two countries.

In conclusion, I propose a toast
to the health of Mr. President and Mrs. Nixon,
to the health of our other American guests,
to the health of all our friends and comrades present, and
to the friendship between the Chinese and American peoples !

PRESIDENT NIXON'S TOAST, FEBRUARY 21, 1972

Mr. Prime Minister and all of your distinguished guests this evening:

On behalf of all of your American guests, I wish to thank you for the incomparable hospitality for which the Chinese people are justly famous throughout the world. I particularly want to pay tribute, not only to those who prepared the magnificent dinner, but also to those who have provided the splendid music. Never have I heard American music played better in a foreign land.

Mr. Prime Minister, I wish to thank you for your very gracious and eloquent remarks. At this very moment, through the wonder of telecommunications, more people are seeing and hearing what we say than on any other such occasion in the whole history of the world. Yet, what we say here will not be long remembered. What we do here can change the world.

As you said in your toast, the Chinese people are a great people, the American people are a great people. If our two peoples are enemies, the future of this world we share together is dark indeed. But if we can find common ground to work together, the chance for world peace is immeasurably increased.

In the spirit of frankness which I hope will characterize our talks this week, let us recognize at the outset these points: We have at times in the past been enemies. We have great differences today. What brings us together is that we have common interests which transcend those differences. As we discuss our differences, neither of us will compromise our principles. But while we cannot close the gulf between us, we can try to bridge it so that we may be able to talk across it.

So, let us, in these next five days, start a long march together, not in lockstep, but on different roads leading to the same goal, the goal of building a world structure of peace and justice in which all may stand together with equal dignity and in which each nation, large or small, has a right to determine its own form of government, free of outside interference or domination. The world watches. The world listens. The world waits to see what we will do. What is the world?

Source: Peking Review 15, nos. 7-8 (Feb. 25, 1972): 9.

In a personal sense, I think of my eldest daughter, whose birthday is today. As I think of her, I think of all the children in the world, in Asia, in Africa, in Europe, in the Americas, most of whom were born since the date of the foundation of the People's Republic of China.

What legacy shall we leave our children? Are they destined to die for the hatreds which have plagued the old world, or are they destined to live because we had the vision to build a new world?

There is no reason for us to be enemies. Neither of us seeks the territory of the other; neither of us seeks domination over the other; neither of us seeks to stretch out our hands and rule the world.

Chairman Mao has written:

So many deeds cry out to be done,
and always urgently;
The world rolls on,
Time presses.
Ten thousand years are too long,
Seize the day, seize the hour!
[See Appendix C.]

This is the hour. This is the day for our two peoples to rise to the heights of greatness which can build a new and a better world.

In that spirit, I ask all of you present to join me in raising your glasses to Chairman Mao, to Prime Minister Chou, and to the friendship of the Chinese and American people which can lead to friendship and peace for all people in the world.

REPLY TO COMRADE KUO MO-JO
to the melody of
"Man Chiang Hung"
[any edition]

On this tiny globe
A few flies dash themselves against the wall,
Humming without cease,
Sometimes shrilling,
Sometimes moaning.
Ants on the locust tree assume a great nation swagger*
And mayflies lightly plot to topple the giant tree.†
The west wind scatters leaves over Changan,‡
And the arrows are flying, twanging.

So many deeds cry out to be done,
And always urgently;
The world rolls on,
Time presses.
Ten thousand years are too long,
Seize the day, seize the hour!

The Four Seas are rising, clouds and waters raging,
The Five Continents are rocking, wind and thunder roaring.

———————————

*In the short story "Prefect of the Southern Branch" by Li Kung-tso, a writer of the Tang dynasty, a man dozing under a locust tree dreamed that he married the princess of the Great Locust Kingdom and was made prefect of the Southern Branch. When he awoke, he found that the kingdom was an ants' hole under the tree.

† In one of his poems Han Yu (768-824), a distinguished writer of the Tang dynasty, sarcastically compared people overreaching themselves to "mayflies which attempt to shake the giant tree."

‡ An allusion to the famous lines of Chia Tao (779?-843), a Tang poet:

The west wind sweeps over the waters of Wei
And everywhere leaves are falling in Changan.

Away with all pests !
Our force is irresistible.

Mao Tse-tung
January 9, 1963

PRESIDENT NIXON'S TOAST FEBRUARY 25, 1972

It's a great privilege that while we are guests in your country to be able to welcome you and the Chinese who are present here as our guests this evening, and on behalf of Mrs. Nixon and all of the members of our official party, I want to express my deep appreciation for the boundless and gracious hospitality which you have extended to us.

As you know, it is the custom in our country that the members of the press have the right to speak for themselves and that no one in Government can speak for them. But I am sure that all those from the American press who are here tonight will grant me the rare privilege of speaking for the press in extending their appreciation to you and your Government for the many courtesies you have extended to them.

You have made it possible for the story of this historic visit to be read, seen and heard by more people all over the world than on any previous occasion in history. Yesterday, along with hundreds of millions of viewers on television we saw what is truly one of the wonders of the world—the Great Wall.

As I walked along the wall, I thought of the sacrifices that went into building it. I thought of what it showed about the determination of the Chinese people to retain their independence throughout their long history. I thought about the fact that the wall tells us that China has a great history and that the people who built this wonder of the world also have a great future.

The Great Wall is no longer a wall dividing China from the rest of the world. But it is a reminder of the fact that there are many walls still existing in the world which divided nations and people. The Great Wall is also a reminder that for almost a generation there has been a wall between the People's Republic of China and the United States of America. In these past four days, we have begun the long process of removing that wall between us.

We began our talks recognizing that we have great differences. But we are determined that those differences not prevent us from living together in peace.

Source: New York Times, Feb. 28, 1972, p. 10

It is not our common beliefs that have brought us together here, but our common interests and our common hopes. The interests each of us has to maintain our independence and the security of our people and the hope that each of us has to build a new world order in which nations of people with different systems and different values can live together in peace, respecting one another while disagreeing with one another, letting history rather than the battlefield be the judge of their different ideas.

Mr. Prime Minister, you have noted that the plane which brought us here is named the Spirit of '76. Just this week we have celebrated in America the birth of George Washington, the father of our country, who led America to independence in our revolution and served as our first President. He bade farewell at the close of his term with these words to his country: "Observe good faith and justice toward all nations. Cultivate peace and harmony with all."

It is in that spirit, the spirit of '76, that I ask you to rise and join me in a toast to Chairman Mao, to Premier Chou, the people of our two countries and to the hope of our children that peace and harmony can be the legacy of our generation to them.

PREMIER CHOU EN-LAI'S TOAST
FEBRUARY 25, 1972

Mr. President and Mrs. Nixon, ladies and gentlemen, comrades and friends. First of all, on behalf of all my Chinese colleagues here, and in my own name, I would like to express my appreciation to Mr. President and Mrs. Nixon for inviting us to this banquet.

The President and his party are leaving Peking tomorrow to visit southern parts of China. In the past few days President Nixon met with Chairman Mao Tse-tung and our two sides held a number of further talks in which we exchanged views on the normalization of relations between China and the United States and on other questions of concern to the two sides.

There exists great difference of principle between our two sides. Through earnest and frank discussion, a clearer knowledge of each other's positions and stands has been gained. This has been beneficial to both sides.

The times are advancing and the world changes. We are deeply convinced that the strength of the people is powerful and that whatever zigzags and reverses there will be in the development of history, the general trend of the world is definitely toward light and not darkness.

It is the common desire of the Chinese and American peoples to enhance their mutual understanding and friendship and promote the normalization of relations between China and the United States. The Chinese Government and people will work unswervingly toward this goal.

I now propose a toast: To the great American people, to the great Chinese people, to the friendship of the Chinese and American peoples, to the health of President Nixon and Mrs. Nixon, and to the health of all the other American guests present.

Source: New York Times, Feb. 28, 1972, p. 10.

TRANSCRIPT OF SESSION
HELD WITH HENRY KISSINGER

News conference at Shanghai, February 27, 1972, of Dr. Henry Kissinger and Assistant Secretary of State Marshall Green.

Mr. Ziegler: You have had a chance to read over the communiqué. Dr. Kissinger is here to discuss it with you and take your questions. What Dr. Kissinger says is on the record. Together with Dr. Kissinger is Assistant Secretary of State Marshall Green, who, as you know, participated in all the meetings with Secretary of State Rogers when he met with the Foreign Minister, and he is here also to discuss the communiqué with you and to take your questions. . . .

We will begin with Dr. Kissinger.

Dr. Kissinger: Let me make a few preliminary observations before we go to your questions. Let me do it in two parts: the process, and there is obviously the communiqué produced; and secondly, what does it mean in general terms? Then I believe that I will be prepared to answer questions.

First, how was the communiqué produced? From the beginning of our contacts with the People's Republic of China, there were some obvious general considerations of what the outcome of a meeting between the President and the leaders of the People's Republic might be.

During the interim visit there were some exploratory conversations of an outcome in the conventional sense, in which both sides tend to state general positions which they afterwards choose to interpret, each in their own way.

It was therefore decided early in the meetings on this occasion between the President and Prime Minister that such an approach would make no sense. It would not be worthy of the purposes that were attempted to be served.

Source: Originally published by the New York Times, reproduced in Committee on Foreign Affairs, House of Representatives, 92nd Cong., 2nd Sess., The New China Policy: Its Impact on the United States and Asia (Washington, D.C.: U.S. Government Printing Office, 1972), Appendix 7, pp. 279-83.

It was therefore decided that each side would state its position on issues in a section which it would produce more or less independent of the other. It would not pretend to an agreement which did not exist and which would have to be interpreted away in the subsequent implementations. Therefore, the beginning part of the communiqué represents in effect a statement by each side of some of its general principles.

On our side, they were deliberately not phrased in a contentious way. While in discussions some of the arguments made by the Chinese side were, of course, rebutted, we did not feel that this was the appropriate vehicle to do so, but rather to state what our positive view was.

For that matter, the Chinese side did not rebut arguments which we made in our section that they did not particularly agree with.

In order to present these two views on an equal basis, it had been decided that in the text issued by the American Government, the United States position would be stated first; and in the text to be issued by the Chinese Government, the Chinese version would be stated first.

I mention this only so that you will not be surprised if the Chinese version follows a different sequence from the American version. This is by agreement. Both versions are official and are being put out on the basis of this agreement.

The procedure that was followed here was that issues of general principle were first discussed in the meetings between the President and the Prime Minister. They were then, after they had been explored for some time, transferred to the meetings chaired by the Secretary of State and the Foreign Minister of the People's Republic of China. Then, if any additional issues arose, they might be referred back to the meeting of the President and the Prime Minister.

In drafting the communiqué, various sections were produced by various elements of the American side. I played the role of go-between on our side, and the Vice Foreign Minister, whose name I despair of ever learning to pronounce, on the Chinese side.

In this manner, as we put together the various paragraphs that were supplied to us on our side by various individuals, if we reached a point at which agreement seemed near or possible, we would then go back to our principals and to the Secretary of State. Through this process, the communiqué was finally achieved.

For example, some of the sessions were quite prolonged. The last few nights the sessions went on until the early hours of the morning with the President. In Peking, the Chinese delegation had a house in the guest complex, and most of the sessions took place in that house. As a paragraph was finished, it would typically go back then to the President, who was in the next house, and this went on Friday night until about 5 in the morning.

So much for the process. Let me say something about the content. Obviously neither side would have written this communiqué this way if it had been able to draft it entirely by itself. Therefore, it represented an attempt by two countries that had been out of contact for a long time to find a basis to convey first some immediate understandings, but beyond that, to start a process by which they could bring about a closer relationship over a period of time and by which they could, where interests converged, act in a more nearly parallel fashion and where interests differed, to mitigate the consequences of those disagreements.

So the communiqué ought to be seen in two aspects: first, in terms of the specific principles and conclusions it states; and second, in terms of the direction to which it seeks to point. It is on that basis that we are presenting it to the American people and on which the People's Republic is presenting it as well.

Now, this is all that I want to say by way of introduction. I wonder whether Marshall Green would like to add a few words, and then we will be glad to answer questions.

Mr. Green: I have just a few words. First of all, with regard to the People's Republic of China authority with whom Dr. Kissinger was maintaining the discussions, it was Chiao Kuan-hua—just to clarify that point.

I don't think I really have much to add. Our talks under Secretary Rogers on our side, and Foreign Minister Chi Peng-fei for the People's Republic of China, extended over, I believe, 10 hours altogether.

But it was not just the talks themselves. We had frequent occasion, as you could imagine with all the fine food you have eaten—occasionally waiting to have that fine food to have extensive talks also, and a number of matters could be discussed in that context.

Also, it was not just that, but the Secretary did have a chance to meet on a number of occasions with the Prime Minister. Most recently, coming down on the plane, he had an hour and a half from Peking to Hangchow. And then today the Prime Minister called on him in his hotel room for about 40 minutes.

I would say that the talks and the counterpart meetings were characterized by candor, friendliness, and courtesy and hospitality, as I am sure you have all seen, on the part of our Chinese hosts. There was no pulling of punches—not physically, of course. They were outspoken, no effort to cover up or paper over differences, but to have it out. It is good for the system. I think in so doing one has a much better appreciation of the other person's point of view.

As far as the specifics are concerned in the talks, I really can't say much more than what already appears in the communiqué itself, although some of the points there may raise questions.

Question: On Page 4, in stating that the United States will progressively reduce its forces in military installations on Taiwan, was that decision a result of the discussions here in China?

Dr. Kissinger: No; this is a general statement of our policy which we have enunciated on innumerable occasions in innumerable forms. It says that we maintain the amount of forces that is required by the general situation and not by any abstract determination. It is a statement of our general policy, but not a mutual decision.

Question: Is there any sign now that the conditions would lead to a reduction of the American military force in Taiwan shortly?

Dr. Kissinger: I don't want to speculate on what will be done over a period of time, but if you speak about "shortly," I would not expect that.

Question: Why did not the United States Government reaffirm its treaty commitment [sic] to Taiwan, as the President and you have done on numerous occasions?

Dr. Kissinger: Let me take this occasion to deal with that particular aspect, and let me deal with it once and not answer it in innumerable elliptical forms in which, no doubt, it will be presented.
    The particular issue which Mr. Kraslow [David J. Kraslow, Los Angeles Times] raised is, of course, an extraordinarily difficult one to discuss on the territory of a country with which we do not maintain formal diplomatic relations and for which this particular issue is a matter of profound principle.
    Let me, therefore, state in response to this and any related question—and let me do it once and not repeat it: We stated our basic position with respect to this issue in the President's world report, in which we say that this treaty will be maintained. Nothing has changed on that position.
    But I would appreciate it if that would be all that I would be asked to say about it in these circumstances. But the position of the world report stands and has been unaltered.

Question: Dr. Kissinger, the possibility is mentioned of the United States sending a representative to Peking from time to time. Is there any likelihood that this process might be reversed and Peking might send a representative to Washington?

Dr. Kissinger: The situation of the two sides is not exactly equal in this respect, because in Washington there is a Chinese representation different from that that would be sent under the hypothesis which you mention. However, what we envisage is the establishment of a contact point, to begin with, in which the discussions about the exchanges and trade that are mentioned in the preceding paragraphs will be formally conducted and as soon as this contact point has been established, it will be announced and the visit of a U.S. representative to Peking would take place as the need arises, and as particular issues of great importance need to be discussed. This, however, is not to the exclusion of any other possibility.

Question: What do you mean by "a contact point"?

Dr. Kissinger: For example, there existed for a while, and formally still exists, a forum in Warsaw where United States and Chinese officials met—something of this kind. As soon as that is established, which we expect will be in the reasonably near future, we will announce it.

Question: Will that be established in the United States or Canada or some other country?

Dr. Kissinger: I don't expect it to be in the United States, but I don't want to speculate beyond that.

Question: Can we assume that the President and Prime Minister discussed all these differences face-to-face, specifically their differences over Vietnam and the reduction of troops on Taiwan? Were these positions stated openly?

Dr. Kissinger: All differences were discussed by the President and the Prime Minister face to face, candidly and seriously, including those which you mentioned.

Question: Can you point to anything in this document in which the People's Republic of China goes any significant step beyond its position at the time of the first ping-pong exchanges?

Dr. Kissinger: Let me say two things: We are not approaching this from the point of view of a scoreboard of seeing who scored how many points on which issue. At the time of the first ping-pong exchange, if I understand the position of the People's Republic of China, it was that some very low-level people-to-people exchanges would occur.
The formalization of exchanges encouraged by the two governments, the opening of trade encouraged by the two governments, the

establishment of diplomatic mechanisms for continued contact, the joint statement of some general principles of international relations, the joint statement of some basic approaches to the view of the world with respect to, for example, the section which includes the reference to hegemony—these, I believe, are matters that most of us would have considered unthinkable at the time of the invitation to the ping-pong team.

But I would put them on the basis of mutuality rather than of any unilateral movement on the part of the People's Republic of China.

Question: Henry, is this the first time that a President of the United States has formally picked up the language of the five principles of peaceful coexistence?

Dr. Kissinger: I have to say I am simply not sure. All I would reply, again, would be an answer in the same terms as I did to Mr. Frankel [Max Frankel, New York Times]. The question is not who put forward the proposals. The question is: Does it contain principles that we can live by, and since we have said we are prepared to apply these principles during the next one on the nonuse of force, and since both sides have stated this, it does not really make a crucial difference who put it forward first.

Question: How much progress was there made in advancing the ball, in response to the question asked by George Ball on the trips, "Is this necessary?" How much further did we go than in your original discussions with Premier Chou?

Dr. Kissinger: The character of the discussions inevitably is entirely different when the President of the United States talks than when an assistant talks who cannot make any definite statement. The basic objective of this trip was to set in motion a train of events and evolution in the policy of our two countries which both sides recognized would be slow at first and present many difficulties and in which a great deal depended on the assessment by each side of the understanding by the other of what was involved in this process and of the assessment by each side of the reliability of the other in being able to pursue this for the amount of time necessary to see it prevail.

In this sense it almost had to be conducted by the heads of the two governments, and in this sense I would say that in the depth and seriousness of the discussions it went, obviously, beyond what had been discussed in my visits and beyond our expectations.

Question: Did Chairman Mao participate? Did his participation go to the detailed substance of this matter, or was it largely philosophical and general?

Dr. Kissinger: I don't believe that it would be appropriate for me to go into detail about the content of the conversation with Chairman Mao. I may say, however, that Chairman Mao and the President discussed each of the essential categories in a general way and we have every reason to believe that the Prime Minister checked with the Chairman at every step along the way. But it was not just a vague philosophical discussion.

Question: The assertion of respect for sovereignty and territorial integrity, combined with the statement of respect for one China, could that be construed as meaning that the United States notes the claim of the Government of the People's Republic of China, its claim to sovereignty over Taiwan?

Dr. Kissinger: Our view with respect to Taiwan has been exhaustively stated in that paragraph you refer to, and we add nothing to it.

Question: Dr. Kissinger, can you tell us whether there is any timetable under which you are going to undertake to facilitate the contacts and exchanges in cultural, sports, and journalistic areas?

Dr. Kissinger: There is no precise timetable, Walter, but I think it is correct to say that both sides understand that this will be pursued with some dispatch.

Question: Dr. Kissinger, in the light of the statement by the Government of China that the Chinese side said that the Taiwan question is the crucial question obstructing the normalization of relations, does this timetable depend on further progress in the solution of the Taiwan question?

Dr. Kissinger: No. This is independent of the other, though at what point the two would become interdependent again, I cannot judge. But as this is written now, my answer to Walter Cronkite stands on its own feet.

Question: Dr. Kissinger, where the communiqué states, "Both sides are of the view that it would be against the interests of the people of the world for any major country to collude with another against other countries, or for major countries to divide up the world into spheres of interest," was that a result of your talks about Sino-Soviet tensions or was the Soviet Union involved in the talks? Does this refer to how the United States views the relationship between China and the United States and the Soviet Union?

Dr. Kissinger: We have said on many occasions, and I will say it again here, that as far as the United States is concerned, our relationship with the People's Republic of China is not directed against the Soviet Union, and while the People's Republic is well able to speak for itself—and my megalomania has not reached the point where I believe that I can speak for it—I believe that it is clear to us that neither is the policy of the People's Republic of China in its relations with us directed against the Soviet Union.

We are pursuing our policy with the People's Republic of China on the ground that a stable peace in the world is difficult to envisage if 800 million people are excluded from a dialogue with the most powerful nation in the world, and we are conducting our discussions with the People's Republic entirely on the merits of that relationship.

The paragraph on hegemony will arise only if any country should seek it, but we had no particular country in mind when it was being drafted.

Question: In the paragraph referring to the reduction of forces and military installations on Taiwan as the tension in the area diminishes, is this an exclusive reference to Indochina as the area?

Dr. Kissinger: No. It is a reference to the general area. It is not a reference to any particular part of Asia.

Question: What conditions in that area would keep American troops in Taiwan? What tensions in the area of Taiwan now require the presence of American troops there?

Dr. Kissinger: We are talking about the general state of relationships in Asia and in the world. It is in reference to that that our general decisions on deployments will be made.

Question: Dr. Kissinger, the President said in a television interview the beginning of January that he would bring up the question of American prisoners of war in Vietnam when he came to China. Can you tell us if it came up and what the reaction was?

Dr. Kissinger: Obviously, as the communiqué makes clear, the issue of Vietnam was discussed, and it is also clear that we would not discuss it without mentioning our concern with respect to the prisoners. The position of the People's Republic is, as stated in the communiqué, that it supports the seven-point proposal made by the Provisional government—by the People's Government, and I think it is a fair characterization of the basic positions.

Question: Dr. Kissinger, there is a paragraph that says "International disputes should be settled on this basis, without resorting to the use or threat of force." Since the People's Republic says the difficulty with us on Taiwan is an international issue, does this mean that they have agreed not to use force or the threat of force in settling or solving that?

Dr. Kissinger: The formal position of the People's Republic of China with respect to Taiwan is a matter, of course, of extreme delicacy for us to discuss here at all. Clearly, they do not, as they have stated in their part of the section on Taiwan, consider it an international problem in any normal sense. Clearly, the formal statements with respect to this issue have to be drafted with the various perspectives in mind.

Reporter: Thank you, gentlemen.

JOINT COMMUNIQUÉ FEBRUARY 28, 1972

President Richard Nixon of the United States of America visited the People's Republic of China at the invitation of Premier Chou En-lai of the People's Republic of China from February 21 to February 28, 1972. Accompanying the President were Mrs. Nixon, U.S. Secretary of State William Rogers, Assistant to the President Dr. Henry Kissinger, and other American officials.

President Nixon met with Chairman Mao Tse-tung of the Communist Party of China on February 21. The two leaders had a serious and frank exchange of views on Sino-U.S. relations and world affairs.

During the visit, extensive, earnest and frank discussions were held between President Nixon and Premier Chou En-lai on the normalization of relations between the United States of America and the People's Republic of China, as well as on other matters of interest to both sides. In addition, Secretary of State William Rogers and Foreign Minister Chi Peng-fei held talks in the same spirit.

President Nixon and his party visited Peking and viewed cultural, industrial and agricultural sites, and they also toured Hangchow and Shanghai where, continuing discussions with Chinese leaders, they viewed similar places of interest.

The leaders of the People's Republic of China and the United States of America found it beneficial to have this opportunity, after so many years without contact, to present candidly to one another their views on a variety of issues. They reviewed the international situation in which important changes and great upheavals are taking place and expounded their respective positions and attitudes.

The Chinese side stated: Wherever there is oppression, there is resistance. Countries want independence, nations want liberation and the people want revolution—this has become the irresistible trend of history. All nations, big or small, should be equal; big nations should not bully the small and strong nations should not bully the weak. China will never be a superpower and it opposes hegemony and power politics of any kind. The Chinese side stated that it firmly supports the struggles of all the oppressed people and nations for freedom and liberation and that the people of all countries have the right to choose

Source: Peking Review 15, no. 9 (Mar. 3, 1972): 4-5.

their social systems according to their own wishes and the right to safeguard the independence, sovereignty and territorial integrity of their own countries and oppose foreign aggression, interference, control and subversion. All foreign troops should be withdrawn to their own countries.

The Chinese side expressed its firm support to the peoples of Viet Nam, Laos and Cambodia in their efforts for the attainment of their goal and its firm support to the seven-point proposal of the Provisional Revolutionary Government of the Republic of South Viet Nam and the elaboration of February this year on the two key problems in the proposal, and to the Joint Declaration of the Summit Conference of the Indochinese Peoples. It firmly supports the eight-point program for the peaceful unification of Korea put forward by the Government of the Democratic People's Republic of Korea on April 12, 1971, and the stand for the abolition of the "U.N. Commission for the Unification and Rehabilitation of Korea." It firmly opposes the revival and outward expansion of Japanese militarism and firmly supports the Japanese people's desire to build an independent, democratic, peaceful and neutral Japan. It firmly maintains that India and Pakistan should, in accordance with the United Nations resolutions on the India-Pakistan question, immediately withdraw all their forces to their respective territories and to their own sides of the ceasefire line in Jammu and Kashmir and firmly supports the Pakistan Government and people in their struggle to preserve their independence and sovereignty and the people of Jammu and Kashmir in their struggle for the right of self-determination.

The U.S. side stated: Peace in Asia and peace in the world requires efforts both to reduce immediate tensions and to eliminate the basic causes of conflict. The United States will work for a just and secure peace: just, because it fulfills the aspirations of peoples and nations for freedom and progress; secure, because it removes the danger of foreign aggression. The United States supports individual freedom and social progress for all the peoples of the world, free of outside pressure or intervention. The United States believes that the effort to reduce tensions is served by improving communication between countries that have different ideologies so as to lessen the risks of confrontation through accident, miscalculation or misunderstanding. Countries should treat each other with mutual respect and be willing to compete peacefully, letting performance be the ultimate judge. No country should claim infallibility and each country should be prepared to re-examine its own attitudes for the common good.

The United States stressed that the peoples of Indochina should be allowed to determine their destiny without outside intervention; its constant primary objective has been a negotiated solution; the eight-point proposal put forward by the Republic of Viet Nam and the United

States on January 27, 1972, represents a basis for the attainment of that objective; in the absence of a negotiated settlement the United States envisages the ultimate withdrawal of all U.S. forces from the region consistent with the aim of self-determination for each country of Indochina. The United States will maintain its close ties with and support for the Republic of Korea; the United States will support efforts of the Republic of Korea to seek a relaxation of tension and increased communication in the Korean peninsula. The United States places the highest value on its friendly relations with Japan; it will continue to develop the existing close bonds. Consistent with the United Nations Security Council Resolution of December 21, 1971, the United States favors the continuation of the ceasefire between India and Pakistan and the withdrawal of all military forces to within their own territories and to their own sides of the ceasefire line in Jammu and Kashmir; the United States supports the right of the peoples of South Asia to shape their own future in peace, free of military threat, and without having the area become the subject of great power rivalry.

There are essential differences between China and the United States in their social systems and foreign policies. However, the two sides agreed that countries, regardless of their social systems, should conduct their relations on the principles of respect for the sovereignty and territorial integrity of all states, non-aggression against other states, non-interference in the internal affairs of other states, equality and mutual benefit, and peaceful coexistence. International disputes should be settled on this basis, without resorting to the use or threat of force. The United States and the People's Republic of China are prepared to apply these principles to their mutual relations.

With these principles of international relations in mind the two sides stated that:

● progress toward the normalization of relations between China and the United States is in the interests of all countries;

● both wish to reduce the danger of international military conflict;

● neither should seek hegemony in the Asia-Pacific region and each is opposed to efforts by any other country or group of countries to establish such hegemony; and

● neither is prepared to negotiate on behalf of any third party or to enter into agreements or understandings with the other directed at other states.

Both sides are of the view that it would be against the interests of the peoples of the world for any major country to collude with another against other countries, or for major countries to divide up the world into spheres of interest.

The two sides reviewed the long-standing serious disputes between China and the United States. The Chinese side reaffirmed its position:

The Taiwan question is the crucial question obstructing the normalization of relations between China and the United States; the Government of the People's Republic of China is the sole legal government of China; Taiwan is a province of China which has long been returned to the motherland; the liberation of Taiwan is China's internal affair in which no other country has the right to interfere; and all U.S. forces and military installations must be withdrawn from Taiwan. The Chinese Government firmly opposes any activities which aim at the creation of "one China, one Taiwan," "one China, two governments," "two Chinas," an "independent Taiwan" or advocate that "the status of Taiwan remains to be determined."

The U.S. side declared: The United States acknowledges that all Chinese on either side of the Taiwan Strait maintain there is but one China and that Taiwan is a part of China. The United States Government does not challenge that position. It reaffirms its interest in a peaceful settlement of the Taiwan question by the Chinese themselves. With this prospect in mind, it affirms the ultimate objective of the withdrawal of all U.S. forces and military installations from Taiwan. In the meantime, it will progressively reduce its forces and military installations on Taiwan as the tension in the area diminishes.

The two sides agreed that it is desirable to broaden the understanding between the two peoples. To this end, they discussed specific areas in such fields as science, technology, culture, sports and journalism, in which people-to-people contacts and exchanges would be mutually beneficial. Each side undertakes to facilitate the further development of such contacts and exchanges.

Both sides view bilateral trade as another area from which mutual benefit can be derived, and agreed that economic relations based on equality and mutual benefit are in the interest of the peoples of the two countries. They agree to facilitate the progressive development of trade between their two countries.

The two sides agreed that they will stay in contact through various channels, including the sending of a senior U.S. representative to Peking from time to time for concrete consultations to further the normalization of relations between the two countries and continue to exchange views on issues of common interest.

The two sides expressed the hope that the gains achieved during this visit would open up new prospects for the relations between the two countries. They believe that the normalization of relations between the two countries is not only in the interest of the Chinese and American peoples but also contributes to the relaxation of tension in Asia and the world.

President Nixon, Mrs. Nixon and the American party expressed their appreciation for the gracious hospitality shown them by the Government and people of the People's Republic of China.

COMMUNIQUÉ, FEBRUARY 23, 1973

Dr. Henry A. Kissinger, Assistant to the U.S. President for National Security Affairs, visited the People's Republic of China from February 15 to February 19, 1973. He was accompanied by Herbert G. Klein, Alfred Le S. Jenkins, Richard T. Kennedy, John H. Holdridge, Winston Lord, Jonathan T. Howe, Richard Solomon, and Peter W. Rodman.

Chairman Mao Tse-tung received Dr. Kissinger. Dr. Kissinger and members of his party held wideranging conversations with Premier Chou En-lai, Foreign Minister Chi Peng-fei, Vice-Foreign Minister Chiao Kuan-hua, and other Chinese officials. Mr. Jenkins held parallel talks on technical subjects with Assistant Foreign Minister Chang Wen-chin. All these talks were conducted in an unconstrained atmosphere and were earnest, frank and constructive.

The two sides reviewed the development of relations between the two countries in the year that has passed since President Nixon's visit to the People's Republic of China and other issues of mutual concern. They reaffirmed the principles of the Joint Communiqué issued at Shanghai in February 1972 and their joint commitment to bring about a normalization of relations. They held that the progress that has been made during this period is beneficial to the people of their two countries.

The two sides agreed that the time was appropriate for accelerating the normalization of relations. To this end, they undertook to broaden their contacts in all fields. They agreed on a concrete program of expanding trade as well as scientific, cultural and other exchanges.

To facilitate this process and to improve communications it was agreed that in the near future each side will establish a liaison office in the capital of the other. Details will be worked out through existing channels.

The two sides agreed that normalization of relations between the United States and the People's Republic of China will contribute to the relaxation of tension in Asia and in the world.

Source: Peking Review 16, no. 8 (Feb. 23, 1973): 4.

Dr. Kissinger and his party expressed their deep appreciation for the warm hospitality extended to them.

CHOU EN-LAI's POLITICAL REPORT TO THE
TENTH NATIONAL CONGRESS OF THE CHINESE
COMMUNIST PARTY (AUGUST 24, 1973)

Comrades!

The Tenth National Congress of the Communist Party of China is convened at a time when the Lin Piao anti-Party clique has been smashed, the line of the Party's Ninth National Congress has won great victories and the situation both at home and abroad is excellent.

On behalf of the Central Committee, I am making this report to the Tenth National Congress. The main subjects are: On the line of the Ninth National Congress, on the victory of smashing the Lin Piao anti-Party clique and on the situation and our tasks.

On the Line of the Ninth National Congress

The Party's Ninth Congress was held when great victories had been won in the Great Proletarian Cultural Revolution personally initiated and led by Chairman Mao.

In accordance with the theory of Marxism-Leninism-Mao Tsetung Thought on continuing the revolution under the dictatorship of the proletariat, the Ninth Congress summed up the experience of history as well as the new experience of the Great Proletarian Cultural Revolution, criticized Liu Shao-chi's revisionist line and re-affirmed the basic line and policies of the Party for the entire historical period of socialism. As comrades may recall, when the Ninth Congress opened on April 1, 1969, Chairman Mao issued the great call, "Unite to win still greater victories." At the First Plenary Session of the Ninth Central Committee on April 28 of the same year, Chairman Mao once again clearly stated: "Unite for one purpose, that is, the consolidation of the dictatorship of the proletariat." "We must ensure that the people throughout the country are united to win victory under the leadership of the proletariat." In addition he

---

Source: Peking Review, 16, nos. 35-36 (Sept. 7, 1973): 17-25.

predicted: "Probably another revolution will have to be carried out after several years." Chairman Mao's speeches and the political report of the Central Committee adopted at the congress formulated a Marxist-Leninist line for our Party.

As we all know, the political report to the Ninth Congress was drawn up under Chairman Mao's personal guidance. Prior to the congress, Lin Piao had produced a draft political report in collaboration with Chen Po-ta. They were opposed to continuing the revolution under the dictatorship of the proletariat, contending that the main task after the Ninth Congress was to develop production. This was a refurbished version under new conditions of the same revisionist trash that Liu Shao-chi and Chen Po-ta had smuggled into the resolution of the Eighth Congress, which alleged that the major contradiction in our country was not the contradiction between the proletariat and the bourgeoisie, but that "between the advanced socialist system and the backward productive forces of society." Naturally, this draft by Lin Piao and Chen Po-ta was rejected by the Central Committee. Lin Piao secretly supported Chen Po-ta in the latter's open opposition to the political report drawn up under Chairman Mao's guidance, and it was only after his attempts were frustrated that Lin Piao grudgingly accepted the political line of the Central Committee and read its political report to the congress. However, during and after the Ninth Congress, Lin Piao continued with his conspiracy and sabotage in spite of the admonishments, rebuffs and efforts to save him by Chairman Mao and the Party's Central Committee. He went further to start a counter-revolutionary coup d'etat, which was aborted, at the Second Plenary Session of the Ninth Central Committee in August 1970, then in March 1971 he drew up the plan for an armed counter-revolutionary coup d'etat entitled <u>Outline of Project "571"</u>, and on September 8, he launched the coup in a wild attempt to assassinate our great leader Chairman Mao and set up a rival central committee. On September 13, after his conspiracy had collapsed, Lin Piao surreptitiously boarded a plane, fled as a defector to the Soviet revisionists in betrayal of the Party and country and died in a crash at Undur Khan in the People's Republic of Mongolia.

The shattering of the Lin Piao anti-Party clique is our Party's greatest victory since the Ninth Congress and a heavy blow dealt to enemies at home and abroad. After the September 13th incident, the whole Party, the whole Army and the hundreds of millions of people of all nationalities in our country seriously discussed the matter and expressed their intense proletarian indignation at the bourgeois careerist, conspirator, double-dealer, renegade and traitor Lin Piao and his sworn followers, and pledged resolute support for our great leader Chairman Mao and the Party's Central Committee which he headed. A movement to criticize Lin Piao and rectify style of work has been launched throughout the country. The whole Party, Army and people have been conscientiously studying Marxism-Leninism-Mao Tsetung Thought, conducting revolutionary mass criticism of Lin Piao and other swindlers like him and settling accounts with the counter-revolutionary crimes of these swindlers ideologically, politically and organizationally, and have raised their own ability to distinguish genuine from sham Marxism. As facts showed, the Lin Piao anti-Party clique was only a tiny group which was extremely isolated in the midst of the whole Party, Army and people and could not affect the situation as a whole. The Lin Piao anti-Party clique has not stemmed, nor could it possibly have stemmed the rolling torrent of the Chinese people's revolution. On the contrary, what it did further aroused the whole Party, Army and people to "unite to win still greater victories."

Thanks to the movement to criticize Lin Piao and rectify style of work, the line of the Ninth Congress is more deeply rooted among the people. The line of the Ninth Congress and the proletarian policies of the Party have been implemented better than before. New achievements have been made in struggle-criticism-transformation in all realms of the superstructure. The working style of seeking truth from facts and following the mass line and the glorious tradition of modesty, prudence and hard work, which were for a time impaired by Lin Piao, have been further developed. The Chinese People's Liberation Army, which won fresh merit in the Great Proletarian Cultural Revolution, has made new contributions in strengthening the preparations against war and in taking part in revolution and construction together with the people. The great revolutionary unity of the people of all nationalities led by the proletariat and based on the worker-peasant alliance is stronger than ever. Having rid itself of the stale and taken in the fresh, our Party, with a membership of twenty-eight million, is now an even more vigorous vanguard of the proletariat.

Spurred by the movement to criticize Lin Piao and rectify style of work, the people of our country overcame the sabotage by the Lin Piao anti-Party clique, surmounted serious natural disasters and scored new victories in socialist construction. Our country's industry, agriculture, transportation, finance and trade are doing well. We have neither external nor internal debts. Prices are stable and the market is flourishing. There are many new achievements in culture, education, public health, science and technology.

In the international sphere, our Party and Government have firmly implemented the foreign policy laid down by the Ninth Congress. Our revolutionary friendship with fraternal socialist countries and with the genuine Marxist-Leninist Parties and organizations of various countries and our cooperation with friendly countries have been further

strengthened. Our country has established diplomatic relations with
an increasing number of countries on the basis of the Five Principles
of Peaceful Coexistence. The legitimate status of our country in the
United Nations has been restored. The policy of isolating China has
gone bankrupt; Sino-U.S. relations have been improved to some extent.
China and Japan have normalized their relations. Friendly contacts
between our people and the people of other countries are more extensive
than ever; we assist and support each other, impelling the world
situation to continue to develop in the direction favourable to the people
of all countries.

Revolutionary practice since the Ninth Congress and chiefly
the practice of the struggle against the Lin Piao anti-Party clique
have proved that the political and organizational lines of the Ninth
Congress are both correct and that the leadership given by the Party's
Central Committee headed by Chairman Mao is correct.

On the Victory of Smashing the
Lin Piao Anti-Party Clique

The course of the struggle to smash the Lin Piao anti-Party
clique and the crimes of the clique are already known to the whole
Party, Army and people. So, there is no need to dwell on it here.

Marxism-Leninism holds that inner-Party struggle is the reflection within the Party of class struggle in society. The Liu Shao-chi
renegade clique collapsed and the Lin Piao anti-Party clique sprang
out to continue the trial of strength with the proletariat. This was
an acute expression of the intense domestic and international class
struggles.

As early as January 13, 1967, when the Great Proletarian
Cultural Revolution was at high tide, Brezhnev, the chief of the Soviet
revisionist renegade clique, frantically attacked China's Great Proletarian Cultural Revolution in his speech at a mass rally in Gorky
Region and openly declared that they stood on the side of the Liu
Shao-chi renegade clique, saying that the downfall of this clique was
"a big tragedy for all real communists in China, and we express our
deep sympathy to them." At the same time, Brezhnev publicly announced continuation of the policy of subverting the leadership of the
Chinese Communist Party, and ranted about "struggling . . . for
bringing it back to the road of internationalism." (Pravda, January
14, 1967). In March 1967 another chief of the Soviet revisionists
said even more brazenly at mass rallies in Moscow that "sooner or
later the healthy forces expressing the true interests of China will
have their decisive say," "and achieve the victory of Marxist-Leninist
ideas in their great country." (Pravda, March 4 and 10, 1967). What

307

they called "healthy forces" are nothing but the decadent forces representing the interests of social-imperialism and all the exploiting classes;
what they meant by "their decisive say" is the usurpation of the supreme
power of the Party and the state; what they meant by "victory of ideas"
is the reign of sham Marxism-Leninism and real revisionism over
China; and what they meant by the "road of internationalism" is the
road of reducing China to a colony of Soviet revisionist social-
imperialism. The Brezhnev renegade clique has impetuously voiced
the common wish of the reactionaries and blurted out the ultra-Rightist
nature of the Lin Piao anti-Party clique.

Lin Piao and his handful of sworn followers were a counter-
revolutionary conspiratorial clique "who never showed up without
a copy of Quotations in hand and never opened their mouths without
shouting 'Long Live' and who spoke nice things to your face but stabbed
you in the back." The essence of the counter-revolutionary revisionist
line they pursued and the criminal aim of the counter-revolutionary
armed coup d'etat they launched were to usurp the supreme power
of the Party and the state, thoroughly betray the line of the Ninth
Congress, radically change the Party's basic line and policies for
the entire historical period of socialism, turn the Marxist-Leninist
Chinese Communist Party into a revisionist, fascist party, subvert
the dictatorship of the proletariat and restore capitalism. Inside
China, they wanted to reinstate the landlord and bourgeois classes,
which our Party, Army and people had overthrown with their own hands
under the leadership of Chairman Mao, and to institute a feudal-
comprador-fascist dictatorship. Internationally, they wanted to capitu-
late to Soviet revisionist social-imperialism and ally themselves with
imperialism, revisionism and reaction to oppose China, communism
and revolution.

Lin Piao, this bourgeois careerist, conspirator and double-dealer,
engaged in machinations within our Party not just for one decade but
for several decades. On his part there was a process of development
and self-exposure, and on our part there was also a process of getting
to know him. Marx and Engels said in the Manifesto of the Communist
Party that "all previous historical movements were movements of
minorities, or in the interest of minorities. The proletarian movement
is the self-conscious, independent movement of the immense majority,
in the interest of the immense majority." Chairman Mao has made
"working for the interests of the vast majority of people of China
and the world" one of the principal requirements for successors to
the cause of the proletarian revolution, and it has been written into
our Party Constitution. To build a party for the interests of the vast
majority or for the interests of the minority? This is the watershed
between proletarian and bourgeois political parties and the touchstone
for distinguishing true Communists from false. Lin Piao joined the

Communist Party in the early days of China's new-democratic revolution. Even at that time he was pessimistic about the future of the Chinese revolution. Right after the Kutien Meeting [December 1929—Tr.], Chairman Mao wrote a long letter "A Single Spark Can Start a Prairie Fire" to Lin Piao, trying seriously and patiently to educate him. But, as the facts later proved, Lin Piao's bourgeois idealist world outlook was not at all remoulded. At important junctures of the revolution he invariably committed Right opportunist errors and invariably played double-faced tricks, putting up a false front to deceive the Party and the people. However, as the Chinese revolution developed further and especially when it turned socialist in nature and became more and more thoroughgoing, aiming at the complete overthrow of the bourgeoisie and all other exploiting classes, the establishment of the dictatorship of the proletariat in place of the dictatorship of the bourgeoisie and the triumph of socialism over capitalism, Lin Piao and his like, who were capitalist-roaders in power working only for the interests of the minority and whose ambition grew with the rise of their positions, overestimating their own strength and underestimating the strength of the people, could no longer remain under cover and therefore sprang out for a trial of strength with the proletariat. When under the baton of Soviet revisionism he attempted to have his "decisive say" in order to serve the needs of domestic and foreign class enemies, his exposure and bankruptcy became complete.

Engels rightly said, "The development of the proletariat proceeds everywhere amidst internal struggles. . . . And when, like Marx and myself, one has fought harder all one's life long against the alleged socialists than against anyone else (for we only regarded the bourgeoisie as a class and hardly ever involved ourselves in conflicts with individual bourgeois), one cannot greatly grieve that the inevitable struggle has broken out. . . ." (Frederick Engels' letter to August Bebel, October 28, 1882)

Comrades!

In the last fifty years our Party has gone through ten major struggles between the two lines. The collapse of the Lin Piao anti-Party clique does not mean the end of the two-line struggle within the Party. Enemies at home and abroad all understand that the easiest way to capture a fortress is from within. It is much more convenient to have the capitalist-roaders in power who have sneaked into the Party do the job of subverting the dictatorship of the proletariat than for the landlords and capitalists to come to the fore themselves; this is especially true when the landlords and capitalists are already quite odious in society. In the future, even after classes have disappeared, there will still be contradictions between the superstructure and the economic base and between the relations of production and the productive forces. And there will still be two-line struggles reflecting these contradictions, i.e., struggles between the advanced and the backward and between the correct and the erroneous. Moreover, socialist society covers a considerably long historical period. Throughout this historical period, there are classes, class contradictions and class struggle, there is the struggle between the socialist road and the capitalist road, there is the danger of capitalist restoration and there is the threat of subversion and aggression by imperialism and social-imperialism. For a long time to come, there will still be two-line struggles within the Party, reflecting these contradictions, and such struggles will occur ten, twenty or thirty times. Lin Piaos will appear again and so will persons like Wang Ming, Liu Shao-chi, Peng Teh-huai and Kao Kang. This is something independent of man's will. Therefore, all comrades in our Party must be fully prepared mentally for the struggles in the long years to come and be able to make the best use of the situation and guide the struggle to victory for the proletariat, no matter how the class enemy may change his tactics.

Chairman Mao teaches us that "the correctness or incorrectness of the ideological and political line decides everything." If one's line is incorrect, one's downfall is inevitable, even with the control of the central, local and army leadership. If one's line is correct, even if one has not a single soldier at first, there will be soldiers, and even if there is no political power, political power will be gained. This is borne out by the historical experience of our Party and by that of the international communist movement since the time of Marx. Lin Piao wanted to "have everything under his command and everything at his disposal," but he ended up in having nothing under his command and nothing at his disposal. The crux of the matter is line. This is an irrefutable truth.

Chairman Mao has laid down for our Party the basic line and policies for the entire historical period of socialism and also specific lines and policies for specific work. We should attach importance not only to the Party's lines and policies for specific work but, in particular, to its basic line and policies. This is the fundamental guarantee of greater victories for our Party.

Having summed up the experience gained in the ten struggles between the two lines within the Party and particularly the experience acquired in the struggle to smash the Lin Piao anti-Party clique, Chairman Mao calls on the whole Party: "Practise Marxism, and not revisionism; unite, and don't split; be open and aboveboard, and don't intrigue and conspire." He thus puts forward the criterion for distinguishing the correct line from the erroneous line, and gives the three basic principles every Party member must observe. Every one of our comrades must keep these three principles firmly in mind, uphold them and energetically and correctly carry on the two-line struggle within the Party.

Chairman Mao has constantly taught us: It is imperative to note that one tendency covers another. The opposition to Chen Tu-hsiu's Right opportunism which advocated "all alliance, no struggle" covered Wang Ming's "Left" opportunism which advocated "all struggle, no alliance." The rectification of Wang Ming's "Left" deviation covered Wang Ming's Right deviation. The struggle against Liu Shao-chi's revisionism covered Lin Piao's revisionism. There were many instances in the past where one tendency covered another and when a tide came, the majority went along with it, while only a few withstood it. Today, in both international and domestic struggles, tendencies may still occur similar to those of the past, namely, when there was an alliance with the bourgeoisie, necessary struggles were forgotten and when there was a split with the bourgeoisie, the possibility of an alliance under given conditions was forgotten. It is required of us to do our best to discern and rectify such tendencies in time. And when a wrong tendency surges towards us like a rising tide, we must not fear isolation and must dare to go against the tide and brave it through. Chairman Mao states, "Going against the tide is a Marxist-Leninist principle." In daring to go against the tide and adhere to the correct line in the ten struggles between the two lines within the Party, Chairman Mao is our example and teacher. Every one of our comrades should learn well from Chairman Mao and hold to this principle.

Under the guidance of the correct line represented by Chairman Mao, the great, glorious and correct Communist Party of China has had prolonged trials of strength with the class enemies both inside and outside the Party, at home and abroad, armed and unarmed, overt and covert. Our Party has not been divided or crushed. On the contrary, Chairman Mao's Marxist-Leninist line has further developed and our Party grown ever stronger. Historical experience convinces us that "this Party of ours has a bright future." Just as Chairman Mao predicted in 1966, "If the Right stage an anti-Communist coup d'etat in China, I am sure they will know no peace either and their rule will most probably be short-lived, because it will not be tolerated by the revolutionaries, who represent the interests of the people making up more than 90 percent of the population." So long as our whole Party bears in mind historical experience, and upholds Chairman Mao's correct line, all the schemes of the bourgeoisie for restoration are bound to fail. No matter how many more major struggles between the two lines may occur, the laws of history will not change, and the revolution in China and the world will eventually triumph.

On the Situation and Our Tasks

Chairman Mao has often taught us: We are still in the era of imperialism and the proletarian revolution. On the basis of fundamental Marxist principle, Lenin made a scientific analysis of imperialism as the highest stage of capitalism." Lenin pointed out that imperialism is monopolistic capitalism, parasitic or decaying capitalism, moribund capitalism. He also said that imperialism intensifies all the contradictions of capitalism to the extreme. He therefore concluded that "imperialism is the eve of the social revolution of the proletariat," and put forward the theories and tactics of the proletarian revolution in the era of imperialism. Stalin said, "Leninism is Marxism of the era of imperialism and the proletarian revolution." This is entirely correct. Since Lenin's death, the world situation has undergone great changes. But the era has not changed. The fundamental principles of Leninism are not outdated; they remain the theoretical basis guiding our thinking today.

The present international situation is one characterized by great disorder on the earth. "The wind sweeping through the tower heralds a rising storm in the mountains." This aptly depicts how the basic world contradictions as analysed by Lenin show themselves today. Relaxation is a temporary and superficial phenomenon, and great disorder will continue. Such great disorder is a good thing for the people, not a bad thing. It throws the enemies into confusion and causes division among them, while it arouses and tempers the people, thus helping the international situation develop further in the direction favourable to the people and unfavourable to imperialism, modern revisionism and all reaction.

The awakening and growth of the Third World is a major event in contemporary international relations. The Third World has strengthened its unity in the struggle against hegemonism and power politics of the superpowers and is playing an ever more significant role in international affairs. The great victories won by the people of Viet Nam, Laos and Cambodia in their war against U.S. aggression and for national salvation have strongly encouraged the people of the world in their revolutionary struggles against imperialism and colonialism. A new situation has emerged in the Korean people's struggle for the independent and peaceful reunification of their fatherland. The struggles of the Palestinian and other Arab peoples against aggression by Israeli Zionism, the African peoples' struggles against colonialism and racial discrimination and the Latin American peoples' struggles for maintaining 200-nautical-mile territorial waters or economic zones all continue to forge ahead. The struggles of the Asian, African and Latin American peoples to win and defend national independence and safeguard state sovereignty and national resources

312

have further deepened and broadened. The just struggles of the Third World as well as of the people of Europe, North America and Oceania support and encourage each other. Countries want independence, nations want liberation, and the people want revolution—this has become an irresistible historical trend.

Lenin said that "an essential feature of imperialism is the rivalry between several Great Powers in the striving for hegemony." Today, it is mainly the two nuclear superpowers—the U.S. and the U.S.S.R.—that are contending for hegemony. While hawking disarmament, they are actually expanding their armaments every day. Their purpose is to contend for world hegemony. They contend as well as collude with each other. Their collusion serves the purpose of more intensified contention. Contention is absolute and protracted, whereas collusion is relative and temporary. The declaration of this year as the "year of Europe" and the convocation of the European Security Conference indicate that strategically the key point of their contention is Europe. The West always wants to urge the Soviet revisionists eastward to divert the peril towards China, and it would be fine so long as all is quiet in the West. China is an attractive piece of meat coveted by all. But this piece of meat is very tough, and for years no one has been able to bite into it. It is even more difficult now that Lin Piao the "super-spy" has fallen. At present, the Soviet revisionists are "making a feint to the east while attacking in the west," and stepping up their contention in Europe and their expansion in the Mediterranean, the Indian Ocean and every place their hands can reach. The U.S.-Soviet contention for hegemony is the cause of world intranquillity. It cannot be covered up by any false appearances they create and is already perceived by an increasing number of people and countries. It has met with strong resistance from the Third World and has caused resentment on the part of Japan and West European countries. Beset with troubles internally and externally, the two hegemonic powers—the U.S. and the U.S.S.R.—find the going tougher and tougher. As the verse goes, "Flowers fall off, do what one may," they are in a sorry plight indeed. This has been further proved by the U.S.-Soviet talks last June and the subsequent course of events.

"The people, and the people alone, are the motive force in the making of world history." The ambitions of the two hegemonic powers—the U.S. and the U.S.S.R.—are one thing, but whether they can achieve them is quite another. They want to devour China, but find it too tough even to bite. Europe and Japan are also hard to bite, not to speak of the vast Third World. U.S. imperialism started to go downhill after its defeat in the war of aggression against Korea. It has openly admitted that it is increasingly on the decline; it could not but pull out of Viet Nam. Over the last two decades, the Soviet revisionist ruling clique, from Khrushchov to Brezhnev, has made a socialist country degenerate into a social-imperialist country. Internally, it has restored capitalism, enforced a fascist dictatorship and enslaved the people of all nationalities, thus deepening the political and economic contradictions as well as contradictions among nationalities. Externally, it has invaded and occupied Czechoslovakia, massed its troops along the Chinese border, sent troops into the People's Republic of Mongolia, supported the traitorous Lon Nol clique, suppressed the Polish workers' rebellion, intervened in Egypt, causing the expulsion of the Soviet experts, dismembered Pakistan and carried out subversive activities in many Asian and African countries. This series of facts has profoundly exposed its ugly features as the new Czar and its reactionary nature, namely, "socialism in words, imperialism in deeds." The more evil and foul things it does, the sooner the time when Soviet revisionism will be relegated to the historical museum by the people of the Soviet Union and the rest of the world.

Recently, the Brezhnev renegade clique has talked a lot of nonsense on Sino-Soviet relations. It alleges that China is against relaxation of world tension and unwilling to improve Sino-Soviet relations, etc. These words are directed to the Soviet people and the people of other countries in a vain attempt to alienate their friendly feelings for the Chinese people and disguise the true features of the new Czar. These words are above all meant for the monopoly capitalists in the hope of getting more money in reward for services in opposing China and communism. This was an old trick of Hitler's, only Brezhnev is playing it more clumsily. If you are so anxious to relax world tension, why don't you show your good faith by doing a thing or two—for instance, withdraw your armed forces from Czechoslovakia or the People's Republic of Mongolia and return the four northern islands to Japan? China has not occupied any foreign countries' territory. Must China give away all the territory north of the Great Wall to the Soviet revisionists in order to show that we favour relaxation of world tension and are willing to improve Sino-Soviet relations? The Chinese people are not to be deceived or cowed. The Sino-Soviet controversy on matters of principle should not hinder the normalization of relations between the two states on the basis of the Five Principles of Peaceful Coexistence. The Sino-Soviet boundary question should be settled peacefully through negotiations free from any threat. "We will not attack unless we are attacked; if we are attacked, we will certainly counter-attack"—this is our consistent principle. And we mean what we say.

We should point out here that necessary compromises between revolutionary countries and imperialist countries must be distinguished from collusion and compromise between Soviet revisionism and U.S. imperialism. Lenin put it well: "There are compromises and compromises. One must be able to analyse the situation and the concrete conditions of each compromise, or of each variety of compromise. One must learn to distinguish between a man who gave the bandits money and firearms in order to lessen the damage they can do and facilitate their capture and execution, and a man who gives bandits money and firearms in order to share in the loot." ("Left-Wing" Communism, an Infantile Disorder) The Brest-Litovsk Treaty concluded by Lenin with German imperialism comes under the former category; and the doings of Khrushchov and Brezhnev, both betrayers of Lenin, fall under the latter.

Lenin pointed out repeatedly that imperialism means aggression and war. Chairman Mao pointed out in his statement of May 20, 1970: "The danger of a new world war still exists, and the people of all countries must get prepared. But revolution is the main trend in the world today." It will be possible to prevent such a war, so long as the peoples, who are becoming more and more awakened, keep the orientation clearly in sight, heighten their vigilance, strengthen unity and persevere in struggle. Should the imperialists be bent on unleashing such a war, it will inevitably give rise to greater revolutions on a worldwide scale and hasten their doom.

In the excellent situation now prevailing at home and abroad, it is most important for us to run China's affairs well. Therefore, on the international front, our Party must uphold proletarian internationalism, uphold the Party's consistent policies, strengthen our unity with the proletariat and the oppressed people and nations of the whole world and with all countries subjected to imperialist aggression, subversion, interference, control or bullying and form the broadest united front against imperialism, colonialism and neo-colonialism, and in particular, against the hegemonism of the two super-powers—the U.S. and the U.S.S.R. We must unite with all genuine Marxist-Leninist Parties and organizations the world over, and carry the struggle against modern revisionism through to the end. On the domestic front, we must pursue our Party's basic line and policies for the entire historical period of socialism, persevere in continuing the revolution under the dictatorship of the proletariat, unite with all the forces that can be united and work hard to build our country into a powerful socialist state, so as to make a greater contribution to mankind.

We must uphold Chairman Mao's teachings that we should "be prepared against war, be prepared against natural disasters, and do everything for the people" and should "dig tunnels deep, store grain everywhere, and never seek hegemony," maintain high vigilance and be fully prepared against any war of aggression that imperialism may launch and particularly against surprise attack on our country by Soviet revisionist social-imperialism. Our heroic People's Liberation Army and our vast militia must be prepared at all times to wipe out any enemy that may invade.

Taiwan Province is our motherland's sacred territory, and the people in Taiwan are our kith and kin. We have infinite concern for our compatriots in Taiwan, who love and long for the motherland. Our compatriots in Taiwan can have a bright future only by returning to the embrace of the motherland. Taiwan must be liberated. Our great motherland must be unified. This is the common aspiration and sacred duty of the people of all nationalities of the country, including our compatriots in Taiwan. Let us strive together to attain this goal.

Comrades!

We must be aware that although we have achieved great successes in socialist revolution and socialist construction, we are always lagging behind the needs of the objective situation. We still face very heavy tasks in our socialist revolution. The tasks of struggle-criticism-transformation in the Great Proletarian Cultural Revolution need to be carried on in a thoroughgoing way on all fronts. More efforts are required to overcome the shortcomings, mistakes and certain unhealthy tendencies in our work. Our whole Party must make good use of the present opportune time to consolidate and carry forward the achievements of the Great Proletarian Cultural Revolution and work well in all fields.

First of all, we should continue to do a good job of criticizing Lin Piao and rectifying style of work. We should make full use of that teacher by negative example, the Lin Piao anti-Party clique, to educate the whole Party, Army and the people of all nationalities of our country in class struggle and two-line struggle, and criticize revisionism and the bourgeois world outlook so that the masses will be able to draw on the historical experience of the ten struggles between the two lines in our Party, acquire a deeper understanding of the characteristics and laws of class struggle and two-line struggle in the period of socialist revolution in our country and raise their ability to distinguish genuine from sham Marxism.

All Party members should conscientiously study works by Marx, Engels, Lenin and Stalin and by Chairman Mao, adhere to dialectical materialism and historical materialism, combat idealism and metaphysics and remould their world outlook. Senior cadres, in particular, should make greater efforts to "read and study conscientiously and have a good grasp of Marxism," try their best to master the basic theories of Marxism, learn the history of the struggles of Marxism against old and new revisionism and opportunism of all descriptions, and understand how Chairman Mao has inherited, defended and developed Marxism-Leninism in the course of integrating the universal truth of Marxism-Leninism with the concrete practice of revolution. We hope that through sustained efforts "the vast numbers of our cadres

316

and the people will be able to arm themselves with the basic theories of Marxism."

We should attach importance to the class struggle in the super-structure, including all spheres of culture, transform all parts of the superstructure which do not conform to the economic base. We should handle correctly the two types of contradictions of different nature. We should continue to carry out in earnest all of Chairman Mao's proletarian policies. We should continue to carry out well the revolution in literature and art, the revolution in education and the revolution in public health, and the work with regard to the educated youth who go to mountainous and other rural areas, run the May 7 cadres schools well and support all the newly emerging things of socialism.

Economically ours is still a poor and developing country. We should thoroughly carry out the general line of going all out, aiming high and achieving greater, faster, better and more economical results in building socialism, grasp revolution and promote production. We should continue to implement the principle of "taking agriculture as the foundation and industry as the leading factor" and the series of policies of walking on two legs, and build our country independently and with the initiative in our own hands, through self-reliance, hard struggle, diligence and frugality. Marx pointed out that "the greatest productive power is the revolutionary class itself." One basic ex-perience from our socialist construction over more than two decades is to rely on the masses. In order to learn from Taching in industry and to learn from Tachai in agriculture, we must persist in putting proletarian politics in command, vigorously launch mass movements and give full scope to the enthusiasm, wisdom and creativeness of the masses. On this basis, planning and co-ordination must be strengthened, rational rules and regulations improved and both central and local initiative further brought into full play. Party organizations should pay close attention to questions of economic policy, concern themselves with the well-being of the masses, do a good job of in-vestigation and study, and strive effectively to fulfil or overfulfil the state plans for developing the national economy so that our socialist economy will make still greater progress.

We should further strengthen the centralized leadership of the Party. Of the seven sectors—industry, agriculture, commerce, culture and education, the Army, the government and the Party—it is the Party that exercises overall leadership. Party committees at all levels should study "On Strengthening the Party Committee System," "Methods of Work of Party Committees" and other writings by Chair-man Mao, sum up their experience and further strengthen the central-ized leadership of the Party ideologically, organizationally as well as through rules and regulations. At the same time the role of revolutionary committees and mass organizations should be brought into full play. We should strengthen the leadership given to primary organizations in order to ensure that leadership there is truly in the hands of Marxists and in the hands of workers, poor and lower-middle peasants and other working people, and that the task of consolidating the dictatorship of the proletariat is fulfilled in every primary organization. Party committees at all levels should apply democratic centralism better and improve their art of leadership. It should be emphatically pointed out that quite a few Party committees are engrossed in daily routines and minor matters, paying no attention to major issues. This is very dangerous. If they do not change, they will inevitably step on to the road of revisionism. It is hoped that comrades throughout the Party, leading comrades in particular, will guard against such a tendency and earnestly change such a style of work.

The experience with regard to combining the old, the middle-aged and the young in the leadership, which the masses created during the Great Proletarian Cultural Revolution, has provided us with favourable conditions for training millions of successors to the revolutionary cause of the proletariat in accordance with the five requirements put forward by Chairman Mao. Party organizations at all levels should keep on the agenda this fundamental task which is crucial for generations to come. Chairman Mao says: "Revolutionary successors of the proletariat are invariably brought up in great storms." They must be tempered in class struggle and two-line struggle and educated by both positive and negative experience. Therefore, a genuine Communist must be ready to accept a higher or lower post and be able to stand the test of going up or stepping down many times. All cadres, veteran and new alike, must maintain close ties with the masses, be modest and prudent, guard against arrogance and impetuosity, go to any post as required by the Party and the people and firmly carry out Chairman Mao's revolutionary line and policies under every circumstance.

Comrades! The Tenth National Congress of the Party will have a far-reaching influence on the course of our Party's development. We will soon convene the Fourth National People's Congress. Our people and the revolutionary people of all countries place great hopes on our Party and our country. We are confident that our Party, under the leadership of Chairman Mao, will uphold his proletarian revolutionary line, do our work well and live up to the expectations of our people and the people throughout the world

The future is bright, the road is tortuous. Let our whole Party unite, let our people of all nationalities unite, be resolute, fear no sacrifice and surmount every difficulty to win victory!

Long live the great, glorious and correct Communist Party of China!

Long live Marxism-Leninism-Mao Tsetung Thought!

Long live Chairman Mao! A long, long life to Chairman Mao!

CHINA AND THE GREAT POWERS: Relations with the
United States, the Soviet Union, and Japan
edited by Francis O. Wilcox

CHINA AND SOUTHEAST ASIA: Peking's Relations
with Revolutionary Movements
Jay Taylor

DOING BUSINESS WITH CHINA: American Trade
Opportunities in the 1970s
edited by William W. Whitson

LAND REFORM IN THE PEOPLE'S REPUBLIC OF CHINA:
Institutional Transformation in Agriculture
John Wong

THE NEUTRALIZATION OF SOUTHEAST ASIA
Dick Wilson
foreword by Gene T. Hsiao

SOUTHEAST ASIA UNDER THE NEW BALANCE OF POWER*
edited by Sudershan Chawla,
Melvin Gurtov, and
Alain-Gerard Marsot

TRADE WITH CHINA: Assessments by Leading Businessmen
and Scholars
Patrick M. Boarman
with the assistance of
Jayson Mugar

*Also available in paperback as a PSS Student Edition.